Seventh graders of Evanston, Illinois, guided by Elinor Rice, dramatize a scene from Mark Twain's story of THE PRINCE AND THE PAUPER.

# STORIES TO DRAMATIZE

Selected and Edited by

WINIFRED WARD

Introduction by

AGNES HAAGA

Copyright 1952; renewed 1980 and 1981

anchorage press

PO Box 8067
New Orleans, Louisiana 70182

iii

By the same author:

CREATIVE DRAMATICS

THEATRE FOR CHILDREN

PLAYMAKING WITH CHILDREN

irst Printing 1952
ond Printing 1955
ird Printing 1959
irth Printing 1969
fth Printing 1981
xth Printing 1986

TO HAZEL EASTON

# FOREWORD

This collection of stories has been made in response to many requests from students in my university classes, and from teachers, recreation leaders, and children's theatre directors in the institutes and workshops I have been conducting over the country.

They are offered here for improvised drama only. Special permission of publishers must be obtained if a playwright wishes to base written plays on any of them which are not in the public domain.

Though the stories are intended primarily for use in creative dramatics, they are equally good for reading and telling. A great many stories which are interesting to read are ineffective for dramatization, but all stories which are good for dramatizing are also entertaining for reading and telling.

Out of all the fine stories that children enjoy, I have tried to choose the best from classic and modern literature which are particularly suitable for dramatization. The list is necessarily far from exhaustive, and every teacher is sure to miss some of her favorites.

A number which I very much wanted were not available for one reason or another. *The Little Rabbit That Wanted Red Wings*, for instance, cannot now be used because of having been made into a complete book. The same is true of James Daugherty's delightful *Andy and the Lion* and others.

Some stories have been listed rather than included because of their length and their accessibility. "Aladdin" is one of these. Chapters from books have in some cases been included, though I hope that whenever possible the book will be read at least by the teacher, and told to the children. Introductions are given, however, so that they can be used if the entire story is not available.

In limiting my stories to literature, I am fully aware that there are other kinds of material for dramatization. I believe that every teacher who is experienced in creative dramatics, however, will agree that the best of all stories for dramatization are found in good literature.

This book is intended to be used with my text on creative dramatics, *Playmaking With Children*, but it does contain material on the philosophy and techniques of creative dramatics, on the basis of choosing stories to dramatize, and on the correlation of various subjects with a creative play at the center. The suggestions given for dramatizing some of the stories are for the use of teachers inexperienced in guiding children in this work. Experienced teachers will have plenty of ideas of their own.

I am grateful to many people for their suggestions of stories to include, and to James Popovich, of the University of Georgia, who first suggested that I edit such a book. Geraldine Brain Siks, of the University of Washington, has been wonderfully helpful with advice concerning the inclusion of certain types of stories, and has written the versions of "The Peddler and His Caps" and "The Legend of Spring" especially for this book. Agnes Haaga and Margaret Woods, also of the University of Washington, have suggested several of the stories I have included.

Rita Criste and her staff in the dramatic department of the Evanston elementary schools, Mildred Harter Wirt and her auditorium teachers in the public schools of Gary, Eleanor Chase of Michigan State College, Jean Mills of Allegheny College, Dorothy Kester and Esther Simonetti of the Akron schools, and Barbara McIntyre of the University of Pittsburgh, have all made excellent suggestions.

Harriett Crummer and the other children's librarians of the Evanston Public Library have been especially kind in looking up material and information which I needed, and Berne Thune of the Oakland, California, Public Library, has suggested a list of stories. Hazel Easton and George Anne Feldt have given valuable help with my manuscript.

It is to save many hours at the library that I offer these stories—some easy and simple for inexperienced teachers and children, others difficult, for the experienced. I hope that it will be a welcome contribution to the field of creative drama, and serve to bring to many children the happiness of playing fine stories.

WINIFRED WARD

viii

# INTRODUCTION

I never fully appreciated the width of Winifred Ward's influence nor the depth of the on-going creative energy she personified and released in others until I became chief fundraiser for the national scholarship program established in her memory by the Children's Theatre Association of America. Gifts and letters pour in, testifying to the timelessness of that influence.

"I was in Winifred's first children's theatre play — **Snow White and the Seven Dwarfs** (1925). I was also the guinea pig, the first cadet teacher teaching creative drama in the Evanston schools (1924)." — Grace Gilson Macduff

"Enclosed is a check — the proceeds from another benefit performance for the Winifred Ward Scholarship Fund — our tenth. The students call it Grandmother Ward's Fund."

—Milton Hamlin

(Neither Hamlin nor his students at Seattle's Shoreline High School knew personally the one they continually honor.)

"Am pleased you have started a fund in memory of Winifred Ward for I too trained under her and loved her dearly."

— Ann Liberman Marks

I trust you will understand why I share a large portion of my response to Ann Marks:

"Dear Ann,

**You** were the one who "introduced" me to Winifred Ward and to creative dramatics and my first formal children's theatre experience. I shall always remember the afternoon in the autumn of my 10th grade in high school when a group of us students came to audition for **The Emperor's New Clothes** at Memphis' James Lee Academy of Arts. I and my dear friend, Norman Shapiro, were scared stiff. To our surprise, instead of putting us through the agony of reading for parts you picked up on our conversation which focused on the sideshows at the Mid-South Fair. Quickly and easily we were all on our feet — simultaneously performing in pairs, one being a side show entertainer, the other a barker. I was a snake charmer, Norman a barker. In the midst of all the sound and action I thought — "Look at me, look at **us**; we're acting, we're acting, and we're **enjoying** it!"

It was quite a revelation — the difference in us high school students in this spontaneous improvisational type of drama and what most of us did in our speech/drama class at school. The difference made a great impression on me, and after that first session I went up to you and asked: "What do you call this way of doing drama?"
"Creative dramatics," was your reply.
"Where did you learn to do drama this way?"
"At Northwestern University," was your answer.
"Who was your teacher?"
"Winifred Ward."
"Well," said I, I'm going to Northwestern University and she's going to be my teacher."

"And I went and she was. By the way, Ann, I never remember any formal tryouts for **The Emperor's New Clothes.** We went on doing drama creatively. We were told stories — simple stories like "The Old Woman and the Tramp." With more experience in creating our own characters, action and dialogue came longer stories — "Beauty and the Beast," the artisan scene from **A Midsummer Night's Dream,** "The Emperor's New Clothes." One day you announced who was going to play what roles in **The Emperor . . . ,** and we moved naturally and happily into working with Charlotte Chorpenning's play script based on the story. And for once in my life I was not assigned to play someone's mother. I was the fiery weaver, Fah . . .''

It is now over fifty years later, and the influence of Winifred Ward — artist teacher, writer, administrator, leader — is as strong as ever as her students teach students who teach students ad infinitum.

Endless, too, is Winifred Ward's influence through the written word as represented in this new edition of her **Stories to Dramatize.** The quality of this book lies partially in the timelessness of the literature she collected and edited with impeccable taste and judgment, a keen sense of what is playable and a knowledge of what is of natural interest to young players and playmakers. The great law of human action that Tom Sawyer discovered is as applicable today as on that Saturday morning when inspiration burst upon him in a dark and hopeless moment.

Winifred Ward believed that in our literary and historical roots lies the substance to give wings to the child's innate dramatic impulse and imagination. "Indeed," she wrote, "literature is the perfect fabric for creative dramatics, for it is closest to drama and to life itself." She discovered long ago what the Rockefeller Foundation panelists reported in a recent paper on "The Humanities in American Life," e. g. that "for learning about values few strategies can rival the time-honored practice of identifying with characters in literature and history who, caught in ethical dilemmas, have to make a choice."

But while Winifred Ward could wonder with Joseph Campbell that "the efficacy to touch and inspire deep creative centers dwells in the smallest nursery fairy tale — as the flavor of the ocean is contained in a droplet . . ." and would agree with poet Francis Thompson that children possess the potential "to turn pumpkins into coaches, and mice into horses . . . nothing into everything," she knew from experience that the magic is more certain to be present when the dramatic process is guided by an imaginative adult.

She believed, "You, as teacher or leader, are indispensable as a guide in creative education." The experienced and the inexperienced in being such a guide will discover anew or for the first time how valuable in that guidance is this new edition of Winifred Ward's **Stories to Dramatize.**

Agnes Haaga, Professor Emeritus
University of Washington, Seattle

March, 1981

# CONTENTS

xiii

# CHAPTER I

# Creative Drama and Its Objectives

Once upon a time, a thousand years ago or more, some children may have acted out an exciting hero tale which they had heard the night before from the ancient storyteller of the tribe. All their lives, make-believe had been one of their natural kinds of play; but now they gave it form in story dramatization.

Creative dramatics, of which story dramatization is a part, is no modern innovation. It doubtless began before recorded time. Only in education's use of it is it recent. Formal plays, designed for the entertainment of audiences, have for a number of years had a small and not at all distinguished part in the elementary school program. But creative drama, though still comparatively new in most schools, is destined to be used more and more widely, since it is approved by leading educators as having something significant to contribute to a child's development.

The unique thing about this kind of dramatics is that it is always improvised. When a story is put into dramatic form, the play is planned by the group, and then played with spontaneous action and dialogue. It is never fixed by being written and memorized, but is different at each playing. For a group to write a play is a profitable experience, but it is not an experience in creative dramatics.

The objectives of this informal playmaking are different in certain respects from those of formal drama. Instead of being a series of rehearsals for a performance to be presented for a future audience, it is an immediate experience; and its values are for the *players* rather than for any audience.

Briefly, these are the values which should come to children from participation in creative dramatics:

1. Experience in thinking creatively and independently—sorely needed by future citizens of a democracy;

2. Practice in strongly-motivated social cooperation. Few activities have such strong incentives for social adjustments;

3. Opportunities to grow in understanding people who have a different viewpoint from themselves; (This from the study and enactment of characters in history, literature, or contemporary life.)

4. Controlled emotional release, which every child needs;

5. Experience in thinking on one's feet, and expressing ideas clearly and fearlessly—another need for every citizen of a democracy;

6. Fun—just plain fun! Is there any schoolroom which would not be better off with more of it?

One might very well add other values: the poise and initiative which come from assurance in expressing oneself effectively; the unforgettable impression made by factual information when it is brought alive; and the beginning of an appreciation for a great art—an appreciation which always makes life more interesting and enjoyable.

A scientific use of creative dramatics, in psychodrama, is being made by psychiatrists in their treatment of the mentally disturbed. This therapeutic aspect of creative dramatics, for the adjustment of personal problems, uses as material the experiences of the patients themselves rather than stories from literature.

To a certain extent, the teacher of creative dramatics can make good use of problems of everyday life as content for normal children. But it would be cheating the children to use only such material, and deprive them of the great stories that extend their horizons and introduce them to characters who are both fascinating and ennobling.

Children who are handicapped physically or mentally can get much from story dramatization. They have fewer ways of enjoying themselves than do other children, and for this reason should be allowed the fun of dramatizing. Stories with less physical action can be chosen for the physically handicapped, and very simple stories for the children with low intelligence. As for the speech-handicapped, many correctionists use the dramatic method constantly. Children rarely stutter in a story dramatization, and those with speech substitutions find dramatics a strong incentive for speech improvement.

Because emphasis is not placed upon finished performances, talent is not necessary in creative dramatics. Whereas, for formal plays only children with some dramatic ability can ever hope to be chosen for the desired roles, in creative dramatics, where there is constant changing of parts, any child may have the joy of being the Sleeping Beauty, or Robin Hood, or Scrooge.

When children do give their play for other groups of boys and girls, it should always be done informally. If it is costumed at all—and that is not necessary—the costumes are often merely suggested. To produce a creative play with complete scenery and costumes is to implant in the minds of the audience the idea that it is supposed to be a polished production. Then the sometimes halting speeches of the players seem the more crude because the audience has been led to expect something different from what it gets.

One school supervisor said that the top ten percent of his classroom teachers regularly used a dramatic approach in their teaching. The others? Just here and there was one who had caught the gleam! Whether or not this is generally true, the reaction of most teachers who give their children a chance to dramatize is surprise at the response it brings, and the discovery that she has established a rapport with the children that she never had before.

One such teacher made her first use of dramatic play in her fourth grade during a big snowstorm. At the recess period she asked them if they would like to pantomime "some of the things people will be doing today because of the storm." The results were more than she had hoped: automobiles stuck in the snow, a child looking for his snow suit, a woman hanging out clothes with cold fingers and getting snow in her face, Jack Frost painting windows, and as many other activities as there were children in the room. As each child gave his pantomime, the others guessed who he was and what he was doing. It was a delightful recess!

The morning after their dramatization, the teacher found under her desk-blotter a little paper rainbow painted by one of the children. On the back it said, "May you always have as much happiness as you gave me yesterday." The teacher's comment on the incident: "It has paid me dividends already!"

3

# CHAPTER II

# The Choice of Material

What children do with a story when they dramatize it is of greater significance than the story itself. With a skillful, imaginative teacher who has a fine understanding of children and their needs, a group of boys and girls often get from the dramatizing of a commonplace story values that are inestimable; while a tale of great distinction may be cheapened by a leader who is satisfied if her children have only a superficial understanding of it.

There is no doubt, however, that a well-chosen story goes far toward insuring a successful play experience. Many excellent pieces of children's literature are entirely unsuitable for dramatizing because (a) they do not present good conflict situations; (b) they have not enough action—or, at least, the kind of action which can be done satisfactorily; (c) their characters are not individualized enough to play well; (d) they depend too much for their effectiveness on beauty of description or cleverness of dialogue; and (e) they have not a strong appeal to the interests of the particular group with whom they are to be used.

What, then, are the essential qualities of stories which *are* good to use?

1. The idea should be of some worth, and the writing carefully done. This is much more important in a story to be dramatized than merely read because dramatization requires more time and makes a deeper impression. It need not have an abstract theme such as contentment with one's lot or racial tolerance. It need not (and should not often) teach any lesson. But it should show us some aspect of life with fresh significance. *The Boy Knight of Reims,* for example, gives a wonderful insight into medieval life and the guilds. *The Bishop's Candlesticks* introduces us to a character whom no one can know without being lifted up.

4

Perhaps a story is pure fun, even nonsense. This, too, has its place, if well written, for there is nothing so refreshing as laughter, so therapeutic for the release of tensions, for balance in our emotions. From "The Tar Baby" to "Hungry Hans," children experience a delightful relaxation in playing stories that are just for fun.

2. The central situation should involve conflict of some sort. There must be something we want very much to have happen. Suspense, carrying the children from one episode to the next, with real interest in the fortunes of the central characters, is one of the aspects of a story which children most enjoy. But there must be economy in the number of incidents which lead to the climax or the boys and girls will lose interest. For the process of dramatization is slow if the play is carefully developed, and when the story is long, it is often advisable to dramatize only the most interesting episodes. Then, if the children play it for another group, a narrator can easily weave it together. "The Moor's Legacy" is a good illustration of this point.

3. There should be essential action in the development of the plot, and it should be action which can be carried out satisfactorily. A story which takes place on the back of a camel, or jumps from one spot to another in many short episodes, is seldom a wise choice. Action such as that in "The Peddler and His Caps" heightens the enjoyment immensely, but the kind of action in "Paul Bunyan" and "Pecos Bill" can seldom be played with any degree of satisfaction.

4. The characters should seem real, whether they are human, or animals with human characteristics. Even a strange creature in a fairy tale can be believable, once we have accepted the fantasy. Not all the people need to be strongly individualized. But even though some will always be types, and others merely background for the main characters, children's imaginations, working on them in the playing, can always give them at least one definite characteristic.

The more unlike the character is to the child playing it, the less self-conscious he will probably be. A child can project himself into the character of an old man, a troll, or a witch, far more easily than he can play a child of his own age and background. Most children will choose to be the troll in "The Three Billy Goats," the mean sisters in "Cinderella," and the witches in *Macbeth* rather than the straight characters.

5. The situations should call for interesting dialogue. Some stories, as "Ask Mr. Bear," for instance, supply most of the necessary conversation. For very little children, whose vocabularies are small, it is good to have dialogue ready to use. But it is a greater

challenge to the imaginations of the older children if a good deal of it has to be improvised. When they play "Doorbells," they have to make up all the dialogue, the poem giving plenty of opportunity but providing no ready-made conversation.

6. Poetic, or ideal, justice almost invariably characterizes the outcomes of stories for little children. It does not give them an entirely realistic view of life as it is. But it is life as it *should* be, and while their standards are forming, it would be utterly confusing to them to hear stories in which evil triumphs over good.

As children grow older, it is better if they do not always read and play stories with happy endings—endings that bring *material* rewards, at least. Gradually they should come to understand that spiritual rewards are even more to be desired. It is impossible for young children to understand that one's own self-respect and peace of mind are worth more than any material reward which could come to them. Indeed, many adults never grow up enough to realize that true goodness is even worth failing for. But, at least, *sympathy should always be rightly placed*. No clever rascal should ever be so attractive that he wins sympathy. No fine person should be made to seem ridiculous. No story should be used if it is likely to lower moral standards.

Many children are constantly exposed to questionable standards in their everyday life. This is no reason for accepting such standards as normal. Without making children feel ashamed of their home life, it is possible through stories to help them to see truer values. And though poetic justice alone does not make a story worth using (note the number of cheap comics with poetic justice), in a really good story the ethical standards will always be sound.

7. The story chosen for dramatization should suit the interests and tastes of the children who are to use it. No matter how well written it is, no matter how dramatic, if it does not have a strong appeal to the boys and girls, the dramatization will be at best half-hearted. (This is not to say that the teacher's presentation of the material does not make a tremendous difference in the children's attitude toward it.)

Some stories are liked by an occasional group, though not generally successful. But there are others which can be counted on to be favorites of *every* group in the age level they fit. Such a one is "Goldilocks and the Three Bears" for little folks. And almost as popular is "The Three Billy Goats Gruff." "Cinderella" is a universal favorite with girls a little older; and at ten and eleven, both boys and girls delight in "The Emperor's New Clothes," "The

6

Wise People of Gotham," "The Voyage of the Wee Red Cap," and several of the Robin Hood stories.

So universal is the interest in Dickens' "A Christmas Carol," that a dramatization of it is absorbing to every seventh grader in school. The old ballad "Get Up and Bar the Door," and Irving's fascinating story of "The Moor's Legacy" are other "sure-fire" stories for dramatization. Eighth graders with considerable experience in creative dramatics almost invariably like to play the stories of "The Taming of the Shrew," "A Midsummer Night's Dream," and the witches' scenes from "Macbeth."

Often the choice of material will come from the children themselves. If they see good possibilities for a play in a story in one of their readers, their initiative will go far toward making it a success. If it turns out to be a poor choice, a teacher can help them finish their dramatization in short order; and it may help them to judge better next time. But in the future, it is well to see to it that they make no more mistakes or it will spoil their interest in creating plays. As in every other activity, the teacher's or leader's guidance can help children to evaluate material wisely; and by reading to them various stories in this collection, any one of which has excellent possibilities for a good play, she can, if she wishes, give them the opportunity to choose for themselves the ones they will most enjoy developing into plays.

# CHAPTER III

# How To Dramatize A Story

"If she had a broomstraw
Stuck into her hat,
We'd think it was a feather—
She's like that."[1]

Children with the imagination of "the little girl next door" will do surprising and beautiful things with the stories in this book. The printed page leaps into life when touched by their fancy; and the creative drama that they plan and play will turn broomstraws into feathers and bare rooms into enchanted forests.

Magic such as this comes about, however, only when they are guided by an imaginative adult. For if their play is to be anything more than a bare synopsis, they need a teacher with wider experience than their own to help them read between the lines of a story and appreciate its possibilities. Then they will not be content, if they are dramatizing "Rumpelstiltskin," for instance, to begin with the miller boasting to the king that his daughter can spin straw into gold. For they are telling a story in action, and in order to make it clear, they must begin their play at an earlier point. Perhaps they will decide to open it in the middle of an argument which takes place at the mill. The miller and several of his cronies may be inordinately proud of their daughters' accomplishments, and their voices get louder and louder as they boast of how skillful they are at baking and spinning and making butter.

"Why, it's like magic the way my daughter can spin!" exclaims the miller. "Give her straw and I'll wager she could spin it into gold!"

[1] "The Little Girl Next Door." By permission of the author, Mildred Bowers Armstrong.

8

At this moment it may happen that the king is driving past the mill. Hearing the argument, he may send a servant to see what is going on; and the man may come back with the news that the miller says his daughter can spin straw into gold. Then the king himself can question the miller, who scarcely knows what he is saying, so excited is he at the king's attention. Doubtless, then, the children will end the scene with the summons to the palace; and succeeding scenes will build up and up to a climax, affording variety and suspense rather than a mere repetition of the dwarf's visits.

You, as teacher or leader, are indispensable as a guide in creative education. It is not enough that children are given freedom to create pictures or poems or songs or plays. You must be by to recognize their best attempts; to encourage; to give them incentives to do the best work of which they are capable. Otherwise, their work will remain always at a low level.

So, before introducing a story, you will study all its possibilities. You will do research if it has aspects about which you are not informed; you may find pictures which will stir the children's imaginations; arrange for excursions or bring in an author or someone who grew up in the country which forms the setting for the story.

Folk and fairy tales, as well as stories of contemporary life may require little if any research. But they will need much reading between the lines if one is to see all the dramatic possibilities. "Get Up and Bar the Door," for example, gives a complete plan of action; yet it is far more delightful and valuable to the children if amplified by their imagination.

All the time you are thinking it through, however, you need to remind yourself that the children's ideas may be far different from yours. This is to be *their* play, and you must not influence them to do it your way or they will lose faith in their own ability to create. It may not be so good as yours might have been, but that is not what counts. Yet you need to have many ideas so that if theirs do not come freely, you can ask leading questions which will stir up their thinking.

### SETTING THE MOOD FOR MAKE-BELIEVE

Creativity needs a free, relaxed, friendly feeling on the part of both teacher and children. When pupils feel that you have confidence that they are perfectly capable of creating the play, they will come forth eagerly with ideas. There must be a feeling of happiness, however, if the children are to give their best.

After they have found out that you enjoy making-believe with

9

them, they respond immediately in dramatizing a story. With younger children, magic spectacles, in order to see feathers where others see only broomstraws; velvet shoes in which to walk noiselessly down the hall to the drinking fountain; a magic wand which changes boys and girls into rabbits or brownies or lumbering bears; perhaps even a pixie who comes to see you now and then—occasional dramatic play such as this establishes a delightful relationship between you and the children which makes them feel free in using their imaginations to develop a play.

The season is a strong factor in setting a special mood for a story. October means Hallowe'en; November, Thanksgiving; December, Christmas. The weather, too, gives a certain feeling to the group: cold, blustery winds, a fairylike snowfall, a dark, rainy day. Take advantage of a mood already set for a certain type of story.

A really interesting tale, however, is such a fascinating thing to boys and girls that a good storyteller can set any kind of mood she chooses. Pictures help; properties and bits of costume, too.

### PRESENTING THE STORY

When you tell or read a story for dramatization (and it is much better to tell it when little children are to dramatize it) be very sure that the presentation is very clear and direct. Complications in plot confuse children, so that unless you believe your group is entirely capable of thinking them through and profiting by the extra effort of cutting away complications, it is advisable to make minor adaptations before presenting the story. It may be that some rearrangement will make it more dramatic, and at the same time less baffling to the children.

Be alive and strongly interested in your telling; visualize every scene, know each character, and make all distinct. Avoid a rapid rate in telling any story which requires children's careful thinking. Use direct discourse whenever possible. Build up and up to the climax, and then stop almost immediately.

If there is humor in the tale, be very sure to let the children see your appreciation of the fun. Keep all the values of mystery, wonder, suspense, beauty. And tell it with zest!

What you are will determine the kind of emphasis you will give to life values in the story you tell. Sometimes the lightest touch will lift the standards of a story into something fine. Romance, when encountered in a tale, will always be kept on a high level. Heroes and heroines will be worthy of admiration.

## THE DISCUSSION

If, before telling the story, you have asked the children to look for some particular thing, this will naturally be the starting-point for the discussion. "See how plainly you can picture the five characters as I say the poem 'Doorbells'." "What is Tyll Ulenspiegel's purpose in playing this prank?"

Often during the discussion of what the characters are like, the children "try them on"—project themselves into the character of "Rumpelstiltskin," for example, in some specific situation such as dancing about in glee when the queen cannot guess his name. Many can do this in pantomime at the same time, thus getting the feel of the people in the story. This trying on of characters is definitely worth-while both for sensing what they are like and for allowing general participation.

Older children can discuss the author's meaning in the story. What is the point made in "The Emperor's New Clothes"? In "The Old Woman and the Tramp"? The question of whether a character was justified in a particular deed comes up in some "Robin Hood" stories and in "The Moor's Legacy." Some child may have perception enough to question whether a king so greedy for gold as the one in "Rumpelstiltskin" would make a desirable husband! (In such a case, the class may decide to marry the miller's daughter to the king's *son* as in the Chorpenning play.[1])

### PLANNING THE DRAMATIZATION

During the discussion, plans will be made for the play. At what point shall it begin? Where will the scene take place? Just what will be happening at the start? We must remember to make it very clear, for we are telling a story. How much of the story will be told in this scene? How will it end? What shall the other scenes be? (Discussion on these will be very general at first.)

If we are playing all over the room rather than on a stage—and the younger the children, the more desirable it is just to have space rather than a stage—where shall we place the mill? The palace? The woods?

In planning both the play and the characters, you as leader will guide the children wisely enough so that they will not drastically change them. For we do have an obligation both to traditional stories and to authors of modern ones, and good judgment and

[1] *Rumpelstiltskin*, by Charlotte Chorpenning. Published by The Children's Theatre Press.

taste tell us that there are limits to the amount of change we should make.

Now we are ready to begin playing. What characters will come into the first scene? If a good deal is going to happen in this scene, let us play only a bit of it at a time. We shall make better progress that way, for we can all easily remember what is to happen. Furthermore, many of the group will have a chance to play during the period, for we shall be changing roles oftener.

We find that it is better to choose our casts by letting the children volunteer for parts, because in that way they have a choice as to what they will play. It usually works out most satisfactorily to choose the popular characters first. Then, if the children do not get their first choice, they will volunteer for less desirable roles. We are very careful in choosing this first cast because (1) it is very important that the scene be done reasonably well to arouse interest in the story's possibilities; yet (2) we must avoid using all the most imaginative or talented children in one cast, thus risking a poorer playing the second time.

We shall do well, then, to choose one or two of the most talented children in each casting, along with several of less ability who will be carried along by the leaders. For it is important for their own self-respect that each one of the children feel in some measure successful in what he does.

It is a good thing to tell the children that it is a rule of the game to stay in character once they have assumed it. Then, from the time the scene is begun, they are not interrupted nor corrected. They can thus keep their full attention on the content of the scene—and they have plenty to think about: the characters they are "being," with their reactions to the other characters; the dialogue, which must always be in character, and in which they must respond to others; and their responsibility in making the story progress.

### FIRST PLAYING OF THE SCENE

If the children have tried on most of the characters in pantomime, they are ready to use dialogue at once in the playing of the scene. If not, it is of great value to play it first without words. In this way they can concentrate all of their attention on interpreting story and character through action, without having to think about dialogue. It is an interesting game to see how much meaning they can express through pantomime, and it has the effect of freeing their bodies and making them more expressive.

The first playing is often disappointing, especially if the children are inexperienced in creative dramatics. Hughes Mearns has said that first efforts in any kind of creative education are like stirring up mud at the bottom of a pool. The best does not come forth at once, and many a child with good ideas discovers that it is harder to express what he has in his mind than he had any idea it would be.

It is nothing to be discouraged about, however, if the scene goes off with the speed of a rocket, and the players forget most of what they had intended to do and say. It is only a beginning, and they can develop it by evaluating their efforts and gradually building it into a real scene.

### EVALUATION

Certain aspects of the dramatization are important in the evaluation which follows each playing. Others are secondary and should not be stressed. (Very little evaluation is done for the youngest children. Keep the playing a delightful game and merely commend aspects which show thought and imagination.) The following are significant for the older children:

1. The story. Was the part of it which was to be played in this scene made clear? Would anyone not acquainted with the story understand the situation and know who the characters were?

2. The characters. Were they interpreted according to the story? Were they believable as real people? Did the players stay in character throughout the scene? Did they use their imaginations to add something of their own?

3. The action. Was it true to the story and the characters? Was there enough action to make the play move? Too much?

4. The dialogue. Was it true to the characters? Did it carry the story ahead or ramble off into matters which were of no consequence? Was there enough dialogue? If not, what might the people talk about?

5. The timing. Did the scene move along at a natural pace?

6. The teamwork. Did they react to one another, listen to what others were saying, and respond in character? If they were a family, did they *seem* like one?

7. Enunciation and projection. Could we all hear and understand what was said? (Mistakes of grammar and pronunciation are noted by the teacher, and drill later given on common faults.)

In addition, older children with experience become cognizant of grouping, movement, finer shades of interpretation. While their playing should remain just as sincere as with younger children, they grow steadily in the feeling that they should play effectively for an audience. This is especially true when they have occasional opportunities to play in a children's theatre.

Unimportant aspects to criticize in story dramatization, such as slips of the tongue, walking through an imaginary wall, and forgetting that one was holding an imaginary property, may be considered after due attention has been given to more important points.

### PRAISE AND ENCOURAGEMENT FIRST

It is so much easier to tell what is wrong with a dramatization than what to do to make it better that you as teacher have to insist that the "good comments," as the children usually call them, are given first. "They kept in character." "The scene moved right along." "They thought of some funny new things!" "The miller was excited when the king asked him about his daughter." "And," you may add, "didn't you like the fact that the miller never actually said that his daughter could spin straw into gold? I can't imagine any father making such an exaggerated claim, can you?"

"Now, how can we make it better?" (Not what was wrong with it!)

"The miller's cronies should boast more." "The miller's daughter should come into the scene sooner. She could come on an errand." "Oh, yes, and that could start the boasting about their daughters."

Criticisms are kept impersonal by using the names of the characters rather than the names of the players. The teacher can see to it that no child is hurt by unkind or personal criticism. And before a second playing, it is a good idea to sum up about three of the more pertinent suggestions for the benefit of the next cast.

### WHEN THE TEACHER ENTERS THE PLAY

The second playing should show considerable improvement, for the children who play it have the assurance of having seen it done once, and the benefit of suggestions to improve it. It is surprising, however, how many good suggestions are forgotten or ignored, not only in the second but in subsequent playings. Instead of reaching out for new and interesting interpretations, many children are content to copy what was done the first time.

This is when you, as the leader, may decide to stir up new ideas by entering the play yourself. If the story happened to be the good

14

old standby "The Stone in the Road," for example, and every character was following more or less the same pattern: surprise at the appearance of a stone in the middle of the road, complaint that someone has not moved it, elaborate care in going around it, you may, without any warning, become a poet, perhaps, walking down the road, note-book in hand, enthralled by an idea for a poem. With head in air, and eyes on the thrush in yonder tree, you stumble over the stone, look at it vaguely, sit on it, and complete your poem before going on down the road!

The next child who comes along is very likely to bestir his imagination and be a politician, perhaps, practicing a speech standing on the stone, or a lazy man who thinks of moving it, hoping to be paid by the duke; but, after giving it a slight shove, decides that it requires too much effort.

### MAKE IT REAL

In developing a creative play, keep it real, genuine, sincere. Always it must come from the inside. The children are *being* characters, not acting them. That is one reason why it is better not to use a stage for young children. And constantly encourage them to use their imaginations.

Do not make little children aware of playing for an audience. If you need to suggest that they are all crowding around a character, you can say, "We'd like to see." (Not "the audience must see.") If they play their dramatization for another group of children, let it be their natural way of doing it, never a formal play.

Keep before you constantly the objectives of creative dramatics. What should the children be getting out of this experience? If they are doing some independent thinking, growing in their insight into people, playing together happily, and having a healthy emotional outlet, you should be able to throw your desire for perfection to the winds and be glad that they are getting the things which matter most.

# *The Stories*

The divisions in which these stories have been arranged according to age levels is purely tentative. Groups of children differ so widely in maturity, in background, and in experience, that the teacher must be the judge of what her children are capable of dramatizing.

Some very simple stories have been placed in the older lists. They are for beginners in creative dramatics. These can also be used for younger children, but their content is such that older children do not think them childish.

Remember that until children have had a good deal of experience in dramatizing stories, they should not be given difficult material. They need to have confidence that they can make a good play from the story or they will be held back by a feeling of inadequacy. Children can enjoy reading stories much too difficult to dramatize with any degree of success. But after they have some skill in planning and playing stories, there is nothing they will not attempt!

It is not easy to generalize about children's story interests, but some things seem to be common to most children at certain age levels. It is on the basis of experience with many children that these divisions have been made.

# CHAPTER IV

# *The World is Young*

## TALES FOR CHILDREN OF FIVE, SIX, AND SEVEN YEARS

Dramatic play is the natural expression of the kindergarten child, and so we use it more than story dramatization for the five-year-old. Dr. Arnold Gesell's comment, "There are endless opportunities for dramatic assimilation of experiences,"[1] is illustrated by children who see a safety film and then come back and play it, laying out streets and sidewalks with blocks, being patrol boys, pedestrians, etc. The movie without the play would not teach its lesson half so effectively.

Playing out various activities and problems is another way of assimilating experiences which is being used more and more in primary grades. What would you do if—

1.—You met a big dog on your way to school?
2.—You were the only child at home and your mother was busy?
3.—Your little brother tore your book?

These are examples of possible problems which to some extent can be solved by dramatic play. For the children play first one role, then the opposite one, and so get both sides of the problem.

It would be a great pity, however, if dramatic play were not very often used for pure fun. Our children live in a hurried, tense world. They need to know how to relax, to have fun. "Laughter dissolves tensions. If we can laugh together, we can live together."[2] And so let us not forget the importance of cultivating a sense of humor.

One kindergarten teacher says that she and the children sometimes spend an entire day being somebody else. She may be an Indian chief while they are braves and squaws; or perhaps she is a queen with all her subjects. With such impromptu dramatic ex-

---

[1] *Children from Five to Ten*, Harper and Sons.
[2] May Hill Arbuthnot, *Children and Books*, Scott Foresman & Co.

pression, a teacher can establish a delightful rapport between herself and her pupils.

Another teacher tells of a boat which the children built of blocks, on which she went with them for a sail, with a picnic lunch of cookies. The rug was an island—their destination. After they arrived and were having a wonderful time telling stories and eating their lunch, the door opened and the principal came in. The children looked at the teacher with wide eyes, and were *so* relieved when she called out to the principal,

"Look out! You are getting all wet in our lake!"

The principal hurriedly backed out and closed the door. (The teacher apologized to him later!) "My partnership with the children," she adds, "was strengthened considerably by just that single act."

Stories used are of the simplest for kindergartners, and a step more difficult for first and second graders who have dramatized stories before. Short stories with much repetition are good, telling of things they know about. But though they concern familiar people and things, surprising adventures often befall the characters. Think of Goldilocks walking into the house of three bears! Or of a rabbit getting all stuck up by a tar baby!

We must begin where the children are, but see to it that they do not remain there! Horizons are pushed out by stories, and gradually new meanings are absorbed and acquaintance with people is broadened.

Animals are good as characters if they are humanized. And there must be plenty of action, for little children like people who *do* things. The ending must be completely satisfying, with everything coming out all right.

Many children in the second grade who have dramatized stories for a year or two can easily play some of the stories in the third grade group. But one should always remember that if children are to enjoy dramatizing stories, the material should be well within their power to do so successfully.

## MOTHER GOOSE

*The rollicking Mother Goose rhymes are the best of all material for little children's dramatizations. Full of action, fun, and delightful characters, these classics of childhood should be played by every generation of kindergartners. Here are a few of them.*

## LITTLE MISS MUFFET

*What fun to be Miss Muffet trying not to watch the big spider crawling toward her, his face all screwed up to look as fearsome as possible! Then, at that crucial moment when he comes upon her, the big scream and the dash to safety! When all the girls are Miss Muffet and all the boys the spider, it's exciting and jolly. Sometimes this is all there is to the dramatization; again it may be developed into a complete play.*

Little Miss Muffet
Sat on a tuffet
Eating some curds and whey;
Along came a spider,
And sat down beside her,
And frightened Miss Muffet away.

## THREE LITTLE MICE

*Dainty, lively music may accompany the mice as they go out to find something for tea. As Pussy comes stealthily up they are unaware of danger until suddenly the music warns them. Seeing Pussy's bright eyes, they scurry away to safety—or at least most of them do. Pussy sometimes catches one of them! It isn't necessary to limit the number who play.*

Three little mice went out to see
What they could find to eat for tea,
For they were dainty, saucy mice,
And liked to nibble something nice;
But Pussy's eyes, so big and bright
Soon sent them scampering out of sight.

## OLD KING COLE

*Sometimes the dramatization of this rhyme may grow out of being an orchestra or hearing one play. Older children would weave it into a story, but younger ones will usually be satisfied with it as it is.*

Old King Cole
Was a merry old soul,
And a merry old soul was he;
He called for his pipe,
And he called for his bowl,
And he called for his fiddlers three!

## SING A SONG OF SIXPENCE

*This rhyme has so many possibilities that one has to be careful not to let it become too complex. Children often like to have the live birds hidden in the pie (as was sometimes really done) as a surprise for the king's birthday. A unified story can be developed from the two stanzas, or the first one may be used alone.*

Sing a song of sixpence, a pocket full of rye;
Four and twenty blackbirds baked in a pie;
When the pie was opened, the birds began to sing;
Wasn't that a dainty dish to set before the king?

The king was in the counting-house, counting out his money;
The queen was in the parlor, eating bread and honey;
The maid was in the garden, hanging out the clothes;
Along came a blackbird and pecked off her nose.

## HICKORY DICKORY DOCK

*Some Mother Goose rhymes may be used as springboards for the imagination rather than as stories to be dramatized. The mood for this one is sometimes set by the toy clocks by which the children learn to tell time. Then there may be some conversation about various kinds of clocks they have seen, and their characteristic way of ticking or striking. Perhaps each child will play he is some kind of a clock or watch, and when the teacher winds him the other children will guess what he is from the sound he makes. This may lead to the playing of a clock shop, with timepieces, a shopkeeper, and customers.*

*Only then do they arrive at the rhyme itself. A grandfather clock which is bought stands now in a house where there is not only a human family, but also a little family wearing fur coats and living in the basement. From here on, the playing may follow the rhyme.*

Hickory, dickory, dock,
The mouse ran up the clock;
The clock struck one,
The mouse ran down,
Hickory, dickory, dock.

## THE QUEEN OF HEARTS

*A perfect story to play. Six-year-olds will elaborate on the plot if they have had any previous experience in dramatization. Perhaps it is the king's birthday and the tarts are to be a special treat. Shall*

20

*anyone help the Queen? How does she make them? And who is this knave? What happens at the end?*

> The Queen of Hearts she made some tarts,
> All on a summer's day;
> The Knave of Hearts he stole those tarts,
> And took them clean away.

> The King of Hearts called for the tarts,
> And beat the Knave full sore;
> The Knave of Hearts brought back the tarts,
> And vowed he'd steal no more.

### MY LADY WIND

*A delicate little poem which is charming for pantomime with music.*

> My lady Wind, my lady Wind,
> Went round about the house to find
> A chink to get her foot in;
> She tried the keyhole in the door,
> She tried the crevice in the floor,
> And drove the chimney soot in.

## THREE BILLY GOATS GRUFF[1]

### George Webbe Dasent

*A favorite story with a very real idea. The goats need to cross the bridge to get food. The troll is the obstacle, successfully over-come by the three billy goats.*

Once upon a time there were three Billy Goats who were to go up the hillside to make themselves fat, and the name of the three was "Gruff."

On the way up was a bridge over a burn they had to cross; and under the bridge lived a great ugly Troll, with eyes as big as saucers and a nose as long as a poker.

So first of all came the youngest Billy Goat Gruff to cross the bridge.

"Trip, Trap! Trip, Trap!" went the bridge.

"WHO'S THAT tripping over my bridge?" roared the Troll.

[1] From *Popular Tales from the Norse.*

"Oh! it is only I, the tiniest Billy Goat Gruff; and I'm going up the hillside to make myself fat," said the Billy Goat, with such a small voice.

"Now, I'm coming to gobble you up," said the Troll.

"Oh, no! pray don't take me. I'm too little, that I am," said the Billy Goat. "Wait a bit till the second Billy Goat Gruff comes; he's much bigger."

"Well! be off with you," said the Troll.

A little while after, came the second Billy Goat Gruff to cross the bridge.

"Trip, Trap! Trip, Trap! Trip, Trap!" went the bridge.

"WHO'S THAT tripping over my bridge?" roared the Troll.

"Oh! it's the second Billy Goat Gruff, and I'm going up the hillside to make myself fat," said the Billy Goat, who hadn't such a small voice.

"Now, I'm coming to gobble you up," said the Troll.

"Oh, no! don't take me. Wait a little till the big Billy Goat Gruff comes; he's much bigger."

"Very well! Be off with you," said the Troll.

But just then up came the big Billy Goat Gruff.

"TRIP, TRAP! TRIP, TRAP! TRIP, TRAP! TRIP, TRAP!" went the bridge, for the Billy Goat was so heavy that the bridge creaked and groaned under him.

"WHO'S THAT tramping over my bridge?" roared the Troll.

"It's I! THE BIG BILLY GOAT GRUFF," said the Billy Goat, who had an ugly hoarse voice of his own.

"Now, I'm coming to gobble you up," roared the Troll.

"Well, come along! I've got two spears,
And I'll poke your eyeballs out at your ears;
I've got besides two curling-stones,
And I'll crush you to bits, body and bones."

That was what the Big Billy Goat said; and so he flew at the Troll and thrust him with his horns, and crushed him to bits, body and bones, and tossed him out into the burn, and after that he went up the hillside. There the Billy Goats got so fat they were scarce able to walk home again; and if the fat hasn't fallen off them, why they're still fat; and so—

"Snip, snap, snout,
This tale's told out."

# A RIDDLE[1]

*Children guess fairies, snowflakes, dandelion fluff—all kinds of fluffy white things—before they arrive at clothes on a line! They delight in playing they are shirts, blue jeans, dresses, sheets, and the rest of the articles, especially if the teacher is the laundress. One child is the wind, and sometimes a garment blows off the line. When there are no human beings around, the clothes talk among themselves.*

> Hand in hand they dance in a row,
> Hither and thither, to and fro;
> Flip, flap, flop, and away they go,
> Fluttering creatures as white as snow.

## GOLDILOCKS AND THE THREE BEARS

### Adapted from Robert Southey

*Here is one of the most popular of all stories for dramatization. A perfect plot, fascinating action, suspense, quick climax and ending. The characters are the kind that all children can take to their heart—and there is no one to hate! The youngest children often play it as it is written; but six and seven-year-olds may begin before the bears get up in the morning, and add such details as an alarm clock, the morning paper (perhaps "The Bear Facts"!), Papa Bear's spectacles, stoutness exercises and the like. And they may decide to have the Bears admire the sleeping child and call to her to come back and play with Baby Bear!*

Once upon a time there were three bears: a big Papa Bear, a middle-sized Mama Bear, and a wee little Baby Bear. And they lived in a neat little cottage in the middle of the woods.

One morning Mama Bear made a batch of porridge for breakfast. She filled a big bowl for Papa Bear, a middle-sized bowl for her middle-sized self, and a wee little bowl for Baby Bear. Then they all went out in the woods to get berries while the porridge was cooling.

While they were gone a little girl came along. She was called Goldilocks because her hair was like gold. She had walked far into

---

[1] Author untraced.

the woods to pick flowers, and now she found herself in a part of the woods where she had never been before.

As she was wondering which path led toward home, she saw through the trees a neat little cottage.

"I wonder who lives there," she said to herself. "I'll just ask them the way out of the woods."

She knocked on the door but no one came, and without stopping to think that perhaps she should not go where she wasn't invited, she opened the door and peeped in.

No one was in the room, but there on the table she saw three bowls of porridge.

"I'm very hungry," said Goldilocks to herself. "Maybe they wouldn't care if I took just a taste of the porridge." So first she tasted the porridge in the big Papa Bear bowl.

"This is too hot," she said.

Then she tasted the porridge in the middle-sized Mama Bear bowl.

"This is too cold," she said.

Then she tasted the porridge in the wee Baby Bear bowl.

"This is just right," she said. So she ate it all up!

Then Goldilocks decided to sit down and rest.

First she tried the big Papa Bear chair.

"This is much too hard for me," she said.

Then she sat in the middle-sized Mama Bear chair.

"This is much too soft for me," she said.

Then she tried the wee Baby Bear chair.

"This is just right," she said.

But no sooner had she sat down in it than there was a crash and a bang. The wee Baby Bear chair broke all to pieces.

Then Goldilocks went into the bedroom. The beds looked very inviting, and as she was tired, she decided to take a nap.

First she tried the big Papa Bear bed.

"This is too hard," she said.

Then she tried the middle-sized Mama Bear bed.

"This is too soft," she said.

Then she tried the wee Baby Bear bed.

"This is just right," she said.

So she curled up and fell fast asleep.

After a while the three bears came home from their walk. They could see that someone had been in their house.

"SOMEONE'S BEEN TASTING MY PORRIDGE!" roared Papa Bear in his great big voice.

"SOMEONE'S BEEN TASTING MY PORRIDGE!" cried Mama Bear in her middle-sized voice.

"Someone's been tasting my porridge," squealed Baby Bear in his wee little voice, "and has eaten it all up!"

Then Papa Bear saw his chair with the cushion all flattened down.

"SOMEONE'S BEEN SITTING IN MY CHAIR!" he roared in his great big voice.

"SOMEONE'S BEEN SITTING IN MY CHAIR!" cried Mama Bear in her middle-sized voice.

"Someone's been sitting in my chair," squealed Baby Bear in his wee little voice, "and broken it all to pieces!"

Then they all went into the bedroom and saw the beds with the covers all crumpled up.

"SOMEONE'S BEEN LYING ON MY BED!" roared Papa Bear in his great big voice.

"SOMEONE'S BEEN LYING ON MY BED!" cried Mama Bear in her middle-sized voice.

"Someone's been lying on my bed!" squealed Baby Bear in his wee little voice, "and here she is!"

Just then Goldilocks woke up. When she saw great big Papa Bear and middle-sized Mama Bear and wee little Baby Bear all standing there looking at her, she jumped up, rushed to the window, climbed out, and ran and ran home as fast as her legs could carry her.

And never again did she wander off into the woods alone, and never again did she see the neat little cottage of the three bears.


## THE ADVENTURE OF THREE LITTLE RABBITS

### Author Untraced

*An exceptionally good situation for a tiny play, especially if the humor, as well as the suspense, is built up in the dramatization. It is equally suitable for six-, seven-, and eight-year-olds.*

"Deary me," said the Little Old Woman as she peered into the cupboard. "Not a thing in the house to eat except treacle!"

Then she looked into the bread crock. "Oh, here is enough bread for the Goodman and me. I declare, it will taste right good with the treacle. But I do wish we had a bit of meat!"

She reached up for the jar of treacle. It was heavier than she expected, and when she pulled it toward her, it suddenly slipped off the shelf and smashed on the floor.

"Oh! Oh!" she exclaimed in dismay. "Dinner gone, and this sticky treacle spreading all over the floor like a lake!"

She carefully picked her way around to the corner for the mop. It wasn't there. She looked for it behind the door, by the fire-place, everywhere.

"Oh, now I remember," she said to herself. "Dame Hodge borrowed it yesterday. I'll have to go and borrow it back or this treacle will get so thick that I'll not be *able* to mop it up!"

She hurried out the door just as a little head with two long ears popped up in the open window.

"Sniff! Sniff!" went the little nose. "There's something sweet in here. But do I dare go in?"

The rabbit looked about timidly, and then hopped over the sill— and right down into the treacle! His feet stuck a little, but he didn't mind that. This treacle was really delicious!

In a moment a second head appeared in the window. And soon, not only a second but a third little rabbit was enjoying the treacle.

Right in the midst of a wonderfully sweet meal, they were startled by the sound of someone coming. They tried to hop away, but they *could not* pull their feet out of the thick treacle!

Just then the door opened and they saw the Goodman coming in!

"What's this?" he cried. "Rabbits! Three of them! Wife!" he called to the Little Old Woman, returning with the mop. "Look here!"

"They're caught in the treacle!" she exclaimed in delight. "Now we can have rabbits for dinner! Catch them while I make a fire!"

"What's the use?" chuckled the Goodman. "They can't get free. We've got them all right. I'll go out to the garden and dig some potatoes to eat with them; and by the time you get the fire made, I'll be back to catch them." And he hurried off.

Meanwhile, the three little rabbits pulled and pulled to get loose. But no sooner did they free one foot than another stuck more tightly. The littlest one even got an ear stuck in the thick treacle. The future looked dark indeed for those three little rabbits!

Then something happened! As the fire grew hotter, the treacle began to get thin! And by the time the Little Old Woman went to the door to call the Goodman, the rabbits had discovered that it was much easier to move about.

"I'm ready for the rabbits!" she called out. "Bring what potatoes you've dug and come along."

In a moment the Goodman came up to the door. And as the Little Old Woman turned to come in, do you know what she saw? Just the little white powder-puff tail of the last rabbit disappearing over the window sill!

## THE THREE LITTLE KITTENS

### Eliza Lee Follen

*What will happen before the kittens lose their mittens? Perhaps they are new and pretty gifts, and undoubtedly the mother will warn her children to be careful. How do the kitten happen to lose their mittens? Is the cat cross or is she kind and motherly?*

Three little kittens lost their mittens;
  And they began to cry,
    "Oh, mother dear,
    We have much fear
  That we have lost our mittens."
    "Lost your mittens!
    You naughty kittens!
  Then you shall have no pie!"
      "Mee-ow, mee-ow, mee-ow."

The three little kittens found their mittens;
  And they began to cry,
    "Oh, mother dear,
    See here, see here!
  See, we have found our mittens!"
    "Put on your mittens,
    You silly kittens,
  And you may have some pie."
      "Purr-r, purr-r, purr-r,
  Oh, let us have the pie!
    Purr-r, purr-r, purr-r."

The three little kittens put on their mittens,
  And soon ate up the pie;
    "Oh, mother dear,
    We greatly fear
  That we have soiled our mittens!"

"Soiled your mittens!
You naughty kittens!"
Then they began to sigh,
    "Mee-ow, mee-ow, mee-ow."
Then they began to sigh,
    "Mee-ow, mee-ow, mee-ow."

The three little kittens they washed their mittens,
And hung them out to dry;
    "Oh, mother dear,
    Do not you hear
That we have washed our mittens?"
"Washed your mittens!
    Oh, you're good kittens!
But I smell a rat close by,
    Hush, hush!  Mee-ow, mee-ow."
"We smell a rat close by,
    Mee-ow, mee-ow, mee-ow."

## TEENY TINY

### English Folk Tale

*Tiny folk enjoy playing this version of the old tale, which is not gruesome like the churchyard version.*

Once upon a time there was a teeny-tiny woman who lived in a teeny-tiny house in a teeny-tiny village.

Now, one day, this teeny-tiny woman put on her teeny-tiny bonnet, and went out of her teeny-tiny house to take a teeny-tiny walk.

And when this teeny-tiny woman had gone a teeny-tiny way, she came to a teeny-tiny gate; so the teeny-tiny woman opened the teeny-tiny gate, and went into a teeny-tiny garden.

And when this teeny-tiny woman had got into the teeny-tiny garden, she saw a teeny-tiny scarecrow, and the teeny-tiny scarecrow wore a teeny-tiny bonnet and a teeny-tiny dress.  And the teeny-tiny woman said:  "That teeny-tiny bonnet and that teeny-tiny dress will fit my teeny-tiny self."

So the teeny-tiny woman hung the teeny-tiny dress and the teeny-tiny bonnet over her teeny-tiny arm, and then she went home to her teeny-tiny house.

Now when the teeny-tiny woman got home to her teeny-tiny house, she was a teeny-tiny bit tired; so she went up her teeny-tiny stairs to her teeny-tiny bed, and put the teeny-tiny dress and the teeny-tiny bonnet into a teeny-tiny closet. And when this teeny-tiny woman had been asleep a teeny-tiny time, she was awakened by a teeny-tiny voice from the teeny-tiny closet which said:

"Give me my clothes."

At this the teeny-tiny woman was a teeny-tiny bit flustered; so she hid her teeny-tiny head under the teeny-tiny bed clothes and went to sleep again.

And when she had been asleep again a teeny-tiny time, the teeny-tiny voice cried out from the teeny-tiny closet a teeny-tiny bit louder:

"Give me my clothes."

This made the teeny-tiny woman a teeny-tiny bit more flustered; so she hid her teeny-tiny head a teeny-tiny bit farther under the teeny-tiny bed clothes. And when the teeny-tiny woman had been asleep again a teeny-tiny time, the teeny-tiny voice from the teeny-tiny closet said again a teeny-tiny bit louder:

"*Give me my clothes.*"

Then this teeny-tiny woman put her teeny-tiny head out of the teeny-tiny bed clothes and said in her loudest teeny-tiny voice:

"TAKE 'EM!"


## THE TALE OF PETER RABBIT[1]

### Beatrix Potter

*After* Mother Goose, *this is the first childhood favorite. Less simple than some of the others, it can be played most successfully by a small group which has had some experience in dramatizing.*

Once upon a time there were four little Rabbits, and their names were Flopsy, Mopsy, Cotton-tail, and Peter.

They lived with their mother in a sand bank, underneath the root of a very big fir tree.

"Now, my dears," said old Mrs. Rabbit one morning, "you may go into the fields or down the lane, but don't go into Mr. McGregor's garden. Your father had an accident there; he was put in a pie by Mrs. McGregor. Now run along, and don't get into mischief. I am going out."

[1] Published by Frederick Warne.

Then old Mrs. Rabbit took a basket and her umbrella, and went through the wood to the baker's. She bought a loaf of brown bread and five currant buns.

Flopsy, Mopsy, and Cotton-tail, who were good little bunnies, went down the lane to gather blackberries; but Peter, who was very naughty, ran straight to Mr. McGregor's garden, and squeezed under the gate.

First he ate some lettuces and some French beans; and then he ate some radishes; and then, feeling rather sick, he went to look for some parsley.

But round the end of a cucumber frame, whom should he meet but Mr. McGregor!

Mr. McGregor was on his hands and knees planting out young cabbages, but he jumped up and ran after Peter, waving a rake and calling out, "Stop, thief!"

Peter was most dreadfully frightened; he rushed all over the garden, for he had forgotten the way back to the gate.

He lost one of his shoes amongst the cabbages, and the other shoe amongst the potatoes.

After losing them, he ran on four legs and went faster, so that I think he might have got away altogether if he had not unfortunately run into a gooseberry net, and got caught by the large buttons on his jacket. It was a blue jacket with brass buttons, quite new.

Peter gave himself up for lost, and shed big tears; but his sobs were overheard by some friendly sparrows, who flew to him in great excitement, and implored him to exert himself.

Mr. McGregor came up with a sieve, which he intended to pop upon the top of Peter; but Peter wriggled out just in time, leaving his jacket behind him, and rushed into the tool shed, and jumped into a can. It would have been a beautiful thing to hide in, if it had not had so much water in it.

Mr. McGregor was quite sure that Peter was somewhere in the tool shed, perhaps hidden underneath a flower pot. He began to turn them over carefully, looking under each.

Presently Peter sneezed—"Kerty-schoo!" Mr. McGregor was after him in no time, and tried to put his foot upon Peter, who jumped out of a window, upsetting three plants. The window was too small for Mr. McGregor, and he was tired of running after Peter. He went back to his work.

Peter sat down to rest; he was out of breath and trembling with fright, and he had not the least idea which way to go. Also he was very damp with sitting in that can.

After a time he began to wander about, going lippity—lippity—not very fast, and looking all around.

He found a door in a wall; but it was locked, and there was no room for a fat little rabbit to squeeze underneath.

An old mouse was running in and out over the stone doorstep, carrying peas and beans to her family in the wood. Peter asked her the way to the gate, but she had such a large pea in her mouth that she could not answer. She only shook her head at him. Peter began to cry.

Then he tried to find his way straight across the garden, but he became more and more puzzled. Presently, he came to a pond where Mr. McGregor filled his water cans. A white cat was staring at some goldfish; she sat very, very still, but now and then the tip of her tail twitched as if it were alive. Peter thought it best to go away without speaking to her; he had heard about cats from his cousin, little Benjamin Bunny.

He went back towards the tool shed, but suddenly, quite close to him, he heard the noise of a hoe—scr-r-ritch, scratch, scratch, scritch. Peter scuttered underneath the bushes. But presently, as nothing happened, he came out, and climbed upon a wheelbarrow and peeped over. The first thing he saw was Mr. McGregor hoeing onions. His back was turned towards Peter, and beyond him was the gate!

Peter got down very quietly off the wheelbarrow, and started running as fast as he could go, along a straight walk behind some black-currant bushes.

Mr. McGregor caught sight of him at the corner, but Peter did not care. He slipped underneath the gate, and was safe at last in the wood outside the garden.

Mr. McGregor hung up the little jacket and shoes for a scarecrow to frighten the blackbirds.

Peter never stopped running or looked behind him till he got home to the big fir tree.

He was so tired that he flopped down upon the nice soft sand on the floor of the rabbit-hole and shut his eyes. His mother was busy cooking; she wondered what he had done with his clothes. It was the second little jacket and pair of shoes that Peter had lost in a fortnight!

I am sorry to say that Peter was not very well during the evening.
His mother put him to bed, and made some camomile tea; and she gave a dose of it to Peter!

"One tablespoonful to be taken at bedtime."

But Flopsy, Mopsy, and Cotton-tail had bread and milk and blackberries for supper.

## ASK MR. BEAR[1]

### Marjorie Flack

*This story is practically in dramatic form as it is written. For beginning groups, and especially for shy children it is a good choice. And it has a charming idea!*

Once there was a boy named Danny. One day Danny's mother had a birthday.

Danny said to himself, "What shall I give my mother for her birthday?"

So Danny started out to see what he could find.

He walked along, and he met a Hen.

"Good morning, Mrs. Hen," said Danny. "Can you give me something for my mother's birthday?"

"Cluck, cluck," said the Hen. "I can give you a nice fresh egg for your mother's birthday."

"Thank you," said Danny, "but she has an egg."

"Let's see what we can find then," said the Hen.

So Danny and the Hen skipped along until they met a Goose.

"Good morning, Mrs. Goose," said Danny. "Can you give me something for my mother's birthday?"

"Honk, honk," said the Goose. "I can give you some nice feathers to make a fine pillow for your mother's birthday."

"Thank you," said Danny, "but she has a pillow."

"Let's see what we can find then," said the Goose.

So Danny and the Hen and the Goose all hopped along until they met a Goat.

"Good morning, Mrs. Goat," said Danny. "Can you give me something for my mother's birthday?"

"Maa, maa," said the Goat. "I can give you milk for making cheese."

[1] Copyright, 1932, by The Macmillan Co., and used with their permission.

"Thank you," said Danny, "but she has some cheese."

"Let's see what we can find then," said the Goat.

So Danny and the Hen and the Goose and the Goat all galloped along until they met a Sheep.

"Good morning, Mrs. Sheep," said Danny. "Can you give me something for my mother's birthday?"

"Baa, baa," said the Sheep. "I can give you some wool to make a warm blanket for your mother's birthday."

"Thank you," said Danny, "but she has a blanket."

"Let's see what we can find then," said the Sheep.

So Danny and the Hen and the Goose and the Goat and the Sheep all trotted along until they met a Cow.

"Good morning, Mrs. Cow," said Danny. "Can you give me something for my mother's birthday?"

"Moo, Moo," said the Cow, "I can give you some milk and cream."

"Thany you," said Danny," but she has some milk and cream."

"Then ask Mr. Bear," said the Cow. "He lives in the woods over the hill."

"All right," said Danny, "let's go and ask Mr. Bear."

"No," said the Hen.

"No," said the Goose.

"No," said the Goat.

"No," said the Sheep.

"No—no," said the Cow.

So Danny went alone to find Mr. Bear. He ran and he ran until he came to the hill, and he walked and he walked until he came to the woods and there he met—Mr. Bear.

"Good morning, Mr. Bear," said Danny. "Can you give me some-thing for my mother's birthday?"

"Hum, hum," said the Bear. "I have nothing to give you for your mother's birthday, but I can tell you something you can give her."

So Mr. Bear whispered a secret in Danny's ear.

"Oh," said Danny. "Thank you, Mr. Bear!"

Then he ran through the woods and he skipped down the hill and he came to his house.

"Guess what I have for your birthday!" Danny said to his mother.

So his mother tried to guess.

"Is it an egg?"

"No, it isn't an egg," said Danny.

"Is it a pillow?"

"No, it isn't a pillow," said Danny

"Is it a cheese?"

"No, it isn't a cheese," said Danny.

"Is it a blanket?"

"No, it isn't a blanket," said Danny.

"Is it milk or cream?"

"No, it isn't milk or cream," said Danny.

His mother could not guess at all. So—Danny gave his mother a Big Birthday Bear Hug!


## WHY THE EVERGREEN TREES KEEP THEIR LEAVES IN WINTER[1]

### Florence Holbrook

*A nature myth with a fine idea, good opportunity for characterization, and some interesting action. Even the trees have a chance for characteristic movement.*

Winter was coming, and the birds had flown far to the south, where the air was warm and they could find berries to eat. One little bird had broken its wing and could not fly with the others. It was alone in the cold world of frost and snow. The forest looked warm, and it made its way to the trees as well as it could, to ask for help.

First it came to a birch-tree. "Beautiful birch-tree," it said, "my wing is broken, and my friends have flown away. May I live among your branches till they come back to me?"

"No, indeed," answered the birch-tree, drawing her fair green leaves away. "We of the great forest have our own birds to help. I can do nothing for you."

"The birch is not very strong," said the little bird to itself, "and it might be that she could not hold me easily. I will ask the oak." So the bird said, "Great oak-tree, you are so strong, will you not let me live on your boughs till my friends come back in the springtime?"

"In the springtime!" cried the oak. "That is a long way off. How do I know what you might do in all that time? Birds are always

[1] From *The Book of Nature Myths*. Reprinted by permission of and arrangement with Houghton Mifflin Company, the authorized publishers.

looking for something to eat, and you might even eat up some of my acorns."

"It may be that the willow will be kind to me," thought the bird, and it said, "Gentle willow, my wing is broken, and I could not fly to the south with the other birds. May I live on your branches till the springtime?"

The willow did not look gentle then, for she drew herself up proudly and said, "Indeed, I do not know you, and we willows never talk to people whom we do not know. Very likely there are trees somewhere that will take in strange birds. Leave me at once."

The poor little bird did not know what to do. Its wing was not strong, but it began to fly away as well as it could. Before it had gone far, a voice was heard. "Little bird," it said, "where are you going?"

"Indeed, I do not know," answered the bird sadly. "I am very cold."

"Come right here, then," said the friendly spruce-tree, for it was her voice that had called. "You shall live on my warmest branch all winter if you choose."

"Will you really let me?" asked the little bird eagerly.

"Indeed, I will," answered the kind-hearted spruce-tree. "If your friends have flown away, it is time for the trees to help you. Here is the branch where my leaves are thickest and softest."

"My branches are not very thick," said the friendly pine-tree, but I am big and strong, and I can keep the north wind from you and the spruce."

"I can help too," said a little juniper-tree. "I can give you berries all winter long, and every bird knows that juniper berries are good."

So the spruce gave the lonely little bird a home, the pine kept the cold north wind away from it, and the juniper gave it berries to eat.

The other trees looked on and talked together wisely.

"I would not have strange birds on my boughs," said the birch.

"I shall not give my acorns away for any one," said the oak.

"I never have anything to do with strangers," said the willow, and the three trees drew their leaves closely about them.

In the morning all those shining green leaves lay on the ground, for a cold north wind had come in the night, and every leaf that it touched fell from the tree.

"May I touch every leaf in the forest?" asked the wind in its frolic.

"No," said the frost king. "The trees that have been kind to the little bird with the broken wing may keep their leaves."

This is why the leaves of the spruce, the pine, and the juniper are always green.

## THE SNOW MAN

### Author Untraced

*All the incentive needed for the playing of this little poem is snowy weather. If the children have been making snow men so much the better. Action may start with just what happens in the verse, or with snowflakes and the making of a snow man. However they play it, all the children may have a part in it. It is suggested that before playing the whole poem, children play it in parts, everybody being snowflakes or children making a snow man; or half being the north wind and half the snow man. After they have had fun in this way, one child may be the snow man, another the north wind, and still others may be snowflakes or children in the house, surprised to see the snow man come lumbering in and finally melting. It may be played with or without music.*

> Once there was a Snow Man
> Stood outside the door.
> Thought he'd like to come inside
> And run around the floor;
> Thought he'd like to warm himself
> By the firelight red,
> Thought he'd like to climb
> Upon the big white bed;
> So he called the North Wind,
> "Help me now I pray,
> I'm completely frozen
> Standing here all day."
> So the North Wind came along
> And blew him in the door—
> Now there's nothing left of him
> But a puddle on the floor.

# THE LITTLE BLUE DISHES

## Author Untraced

*A Christmas story which can be played very simply by little children, though it has much scope for creativity.*

Once upon a time there was a poor woodcutter who lived with his wife and three children in a forest in Germany. There was a big boy called Hans and a little boy named Peterkin and a dear little sister named Gretchen, just five years old. Christmas came and the children went to the toy shop to look at all of the toys. (*Enumerate toys.*)

"Gretchen," said Peterkin, "what do you like best?"

"Oh! That little box of blue dishes," said Gretchen. "That is the very best of all."

On Christmas Eve the children hung up their stockings, although their mother had said they were so poor they could not have much this Christmas. Hans ran out after supper to play with the big boys. Gretchen and Peterkin sat talking before the fire about the Christmas toys and especially about the box of blue dishes. By and by Gretchen went off to bed and was soon asleep. Peterkin hurried to look in his bank. Only one penny, but he took it and ran quickly to the toy shop.

"What have you for a penny?" said he to the toy man.

"Only a small heart with a picture on it," said the man.

"But I want that set of blue dishes," said Peterkin.

"Oh, they cost ten cents," said the man.

So Peterkin bought the candy heart and put it in Gretchen's stocking and then Peterkin ran off to bed.

Pretty soon Hans came home. He was cold and hungry. When he saw Gretchen's stocking he peeked in, and then put his hand in and drew out the candy heart. "Oh," said Hans, "how good this smells," and before you could say a word he had eaten the candy heart. "Oh, dear," he said, "that was for Gretchen's Christmas. I'll run and buy something else for her," so he went to his bank and he had ten pennies. (*Count pennies.*) Quickly he ran to the toy store.

"What have you for ten pennies?" he asked the store-keeper.

"Well, I'm almost sold out," said the toy man, "but here in this little box is a set of blue dishes."

"I will take them," said Hans and home he ran and dropped them in Gretchen's stocking. Then he went to bed.

Early in the morning the children came running downstairs.

"Oh!" said Gretchen, "look at my stocking," and when she saw the blue dishes she was as happy as could be, but Peterkin could never understand how his candy heart changed into a box of blue dishes. Can you?

## LITTLE BLACK SAMBO[1]

### Helen Bannerman

*May Hill Arbuthnot says, "This story has about it an effortless perfection which baffles analysis." Certain it is that it is a captivating story to play.*

Once upon a time there was a little boy and his name was Little Black Sambo. His mother was called Black Mumbo. His father was called Black Jumbo.

Black Mumbo made him a beautiful little red coat, and beautiful blue trousers, and a beautiful little green umbrella and a lovely pair of purple shoes with crimson soles and crimson linings.

And then wasn't Little Black Sambo grand?

He put on his fine clothes and went for a walk in the jungle. By and by he met a Tiger.

The Tiger growled at him and said, "Little Black Sambo, I'm going to eat you up!"

Little Black Sambo said, "Oh, please, Mr. Tiger, don't eat me up, and I'll give you my beautiful little red coat."

So the Tiger said, "Very well, I won't eat you this time, but you must give me your beautiful red coat."

Little Black Sambo took off his beautiful red coat and the Tiger put it on, and off he went with his head in the air, saying, "Now I'm the grandest Tiger in the jungle."

Little Black Sambo went still farther and he met another Tiger.

The Tiger growled at him and said, "Little Black Sambo, I'm going to eat you up!"

Little Black Sambo said, "Oh, please, Mr. Tiger, don't eat me up, and I'll give you my beautiful blue trousers."

Then the Tiger said, "Very well, I won't eat you up this time, but you must give me your beautiful blue trousers."

[1] Used by permission of the publishers, J. B. Lippincott Company.

Little Black Sambo took off his beautiful blue trousers, and the Tiger put them on, and off he went with his head in the air, saying, "Now I'm the grandest Tiger in the jungle."

Little Black Sambo went farther and he met another Tiger.

The Tiger growled at him and said, "Little Black Sambo, I'm going to eat you up!"

Little Black Sambo said, "Oh, please, Mr. Tiger, don't eat me up, and I'll give you my lovely purple shoes with the crimson soles and crimson lining."

But the Tiger said, "Oh no; your shoes wouldn't do me any good. I have four feet and you have only two. I'm going to eat you up."

Then Little Black Sambo said, "You could put them on your ears."

"So I could," said the Tiger, "that's a very good idea. Very well, I won't eat you up this time."

Little Black Sambo took off his lovely purple shoes with the crimson soles and crimson lining and the Tiger put one on each ear, and off he went with his head in the air, saying, "Now I'm the grandest Tiger in the jungle."

Little Black Sambo went still farther and he met another Tiger.

The Tiger growled at him and said, "Little Black Sambo, I'm going to eat you up!"

Little Black Sambo said, "Oh, please, Mr. Tiger, don't eat me up, and I'll give you my beautiful green umbrella."

The Tiger said, "Oh, no; your umbrella wouldn't do me any good, and I couldn't carry it. You see I have to use my four feet to walk on. I'm going to eat you up."

"Oh," said Little Black Sambo, "I know what you could do. You could tie a knot in your tail and carry it that way."

"So I could," said the Tiger. "Very well, I won't eat you up this time."

So he tied a knot in his tail and slipped the beautiful green umbrella through it, and off he went with his head in the air, saying, "Now I'm the grandest Tiger in the jungle."

Poor Little Black Sambo had lost all his fine clothes and he started home, crying.

By and by he heard a terrible noise that sounded like:

"Gr-r-r-r-r-rrrrrrrrrrrr!"

It grew louder and louder.

"Oh, dear," said Little Black Sambo, "what shall I do? Here come the Tigers to eat me up!"

He ran and hid behind a palm tree. After a while he peeped round it to see what the Tigers were doing.

There were all the Tigers fighting. Each said that he was the grandest Tiger in the jungle. At last they grew so angry that they took off their fine clothes and began to fight still harder.

They came rolling and tumbling right to the foot of the tree where Little Black Sambo was hiding. Little Black Sambo jumped quickly and hid behind his little green umbrella. The Tigers went round and round the tree, one Tiger with another Tiger's tail in his mouth.

Little Black Sambo called out, "Tigers, don't you want your fine clothes any more? If you don't want them, say so, and I'll take them back."

But the Tigers wouldn't let go of each other's tails. All that they said was:

"Gr-r-r-r-r-r-rrrrrrrrrrr!"

Then Little Black Sambo put on all his fine clothes again and walked off.

When the Tigers saw this, they were very, very angry, but they wouldn't let go of each other's tails. They ran round and round the tree, faster and faster, trying to eat each other up. Finally they ran so fast that they just melted away, and there was nothing left of them but melted butter round the foot of the tree.

That evening Black Jumbo was coming home from work with a big brass pot in his arms. When he saw what was left of the Tigers, he said:

"Oh, what nice melted butter! I'll take some home for Black Mumbo to cook with."

So he filled up the big brass pot and carried it home to Black Mumbo.

When Black Mumbo saw the melted butter, wasn't she pleased!

"Now," she said, "we will have pancakes for supper!"

So she mixed up some flour and eggs and milk and sugar and the butter, and made a huge platter of lovely pancakes.

Then they all sat down to supper. Black Mumbo ate twenty-seven pancakes because she made them.

Black Jumbo ate fifty-five because he brought the butter home.

But Little Black Sambo ate one hundred and sixty-nine pancakes because he was so hungry.

# THE LITTLE RED HEN AND THE GRAIN OF WHEAT

## An English Folk Tale

Once upon a time a Little Red Hen was in the farm yard with her chicks, looking for something to eat, when she came upon a grain of wheat. That gave her an idea.

"Now who will help me plant this wheat?" she called.

"Not I," said the Duck.

"Not I," said the Mouse.

"Not I," said the Pig.

"Then I'll plant it myself," said the Little Red Hen. And she did.

The grain of wheat sprouted, and it grew until it was tall and golden and ripe.

"Now who will help me cut the wheat?" called the Little Red Hen.

"Not I," said the Duck.

"Not I," said the Mouse.

"Not I," said the Pig.

"Then I'll cut it myself," said the Little Red Hen. And she did.

When the wheat was cut, she called, "Now who will help me thresh the wheat?"

"Not I," said the Duck.

"Not I," said the Mouse.

"Not I," said the Pig.

"Then I'll thresh it myself," said the Little Red Hen. And she did.

When the wheat was ready to be ground into flour, the Little Red Hen called, "Now who will help me take the wheat to the mill?"

"Not I," said the Duck.

"Not I," said the Mouse.

"Not I," said the Pig.

"Very well, I'll take it myself," said the Little Red Hen. And she did.

When the wheat was ground, the Little Red Hen called, "Who will help me bake the bread?"

"Not I," said the Duck.

"Not I," said the Mouse.

"Not I," said the Pig.

"Then I'll bake it myself," said the Little Red Hen. And she did.

When the bread was baked, the Little Red Hen called, "Now who will help me eat the bread?"

"I will!" quacked the Duck.

"I will!" squeaked the Mouse.

"I will!" grunted the Pig.

"No, you won't!" said the Little Red Hen. "I'll do it myself. Cluck! Cluck! My chicks! I earned this bread for you. Eat it up! Eat it up!" And they did.

## THE ELF AND THE DORMOUSE[1]

### Oliver Herford

*A dramatization of this poem, such as is described in PLAY-MAKING WITH CHILDREN, gives every child in the group a chance to be the Elf, the Dormouse, or the Toadstool, all at the same time! There is a whole field of toadstools over the room, and as many elves and dormice. It is usually a bright, sunny day at first, and the Elf is frolicking about in his new suit of clothes. But clouds come up and then a clap of thunder. Where shall he run for shelter? Home? No, that is too far. In the Mole's tunnel? That won't do. And after discarding half a dozen ideas, he sees a toadstool. The very thing!*

*This is a delightful poem to play with music, the piano telling the story.*

> Under a toadstool
>   Crept a wee Elf,
> Out of the rain,
>   To shelter himself.
>
> Under the toadstool
>   Sound asleep,
> Sat a big Dormouse
>   All in a heap.
>
> Trembled the wee Elf,
>   Frightened, and yet
> Fearing to fly away
>   Lest he get wet.

[1] From *Artful Anticks*, by Oliver Herford. By permission of Appleton-Century-Crofts, Inc.

To the next shelter—
Maybe a mile!
Sudden the wee Elf
Smiled a wee smile,

Tugged till the toadstool
Toppled in two.
Holding it over him,
Gayly he flew.

Soon he was safe home,
Dry as could be.
Soon woke the Dormouse—
"Good gracious me!

Where is my toadstool?"
Loud he lamented.
—And that's how umbrellas
First were invented.


## THE MUSICIANS OF BREMEN[1]

### The Brothers Grimm

*An old favorite which is easy to develop into a creative play. By playing all over the room children can do it in one continuous scene.*

An honest farmer had once an ass that had been a faithful servant to him a great many years, but was now growing old and every day more and more unfit for work. His master therefore was tired of keeping him and began to think of putting an end to him; but the ass, who saw that some mischief was in the wind, took himself slyly off and began his journey toward the great city, "For there," thought he, "I may turn musician."

After he had traveled a little way, he spied a dog lying by the road-side and panting as if he were very tired. "What makes you pant so, my friend?" said the ass.

"Alas!" said the dog, "my master was going to knock me on the head because I am old and weak and can no longer make myself

[1] From Edgar Taylor, *Grimm's Popular Stories.*

useful to him in hunting; so I ran away; but what can I do to earn my livelihood?"

"Hark ye!" said the ass. "I am going to the great city to turn musician; suppose you go with me and try what you can do in the same way?" The dog said he was willing, and they jogged on together.

Before they had gone far, they saw a cat sitting in the middle of the road with a face as long as a wet week. "Pray, my good lady," said the ass, "what's the matter with you? You look quite out of spirits!"

"Ah, me!" said the cat, "how can one be in good spirits when one's life is in danger? Because I am beginning to grow old and had rather lie at my ease by the fire than run about the house after the mice, my mistress laid hold of me and was going to drown me; and though I have been lucky enough to get away from her, I do not know what I am to live upon."

"Oh!" said the ass, "by all means go with us to the great city. You are a good night-singer and may make your fortune as a musician." The cat was pleased with the thought and joined the party.

Soon afterwards, as they were passing by a farmyard, they saw a cock perched upon a gate, crowing with all his might and main. "Bravo!" said the ass; "upon my word you make a famous noise; pray what is all this about?"

"Why," said the cock, "I was just now saying that we should have fine weather for our washing-day, and yet my mistress and the cook don't thank me for my pains, but threaten to cut off my head tomorrow and make broth of me for the guests that are coming on Sunday."

"Heaven forbid!" said the ass; "come with us, Master Chanticleer; it will be better, at any rate, than staying here to have your head cut off! Besides, who knows? If we take care to sing in tune, we may get up some kind of concert; so come along with us."

"With all my heart," said the cock; so they all four went on jollily together.

They could not, however, reach the great city the first day: so when night came on they went into a wood to sleep. The ass and the dog laid themselves down under a great tree, and the cat climbed up into the branches while the cock, thinking that the higher he sat the safer he should be, flew up to the very top of the tree, and then, according to his coustom, before he went to sleep, looked out on all sides of him to see that everything was well. In doing this, he saw afar off something bright and shining; and calling to his companions said, "There must be a house no great way off, for I see a light."

"If that be the case," said the ass, "we had better change our quarters, for our lodging is not the best in the world!"

"Besides," added the dog, "I should not be the worse for a bone or two, or a bit of meat." So they walked off together towards the spot where Chanticleer had seen the light; and as they drew near, it became larger and brighter, till they came close to a house in which a gang of robbers lived.

The ass, being the tallest of the company, marched up to the window and peeped in. "Well, Donkey," said Chanticleer, "what do you see?"

"What do I see?" replied the ass. "Why I see a table spread with all kinds of good things, and robbers sitting round it making merry."

"That would be a noble lodging for us," said the cock.

"Yes," said the ass, "if we could only get in"; so they consulted together how they should contrive to get the robbers out; and at last they hit upon a plan. The ass placed himself upright on his hind-legs, with his fore-feet resting against the window; the dog got upon his back; the cat scrambled up to the dog's shoulders, and the cock flew up and sat upon the cat's head. When all was ready, a signal was given, and they began their music. The ass brayed, the dog barked, the cat mewed, and the cock screamed; and then they all broke through the window at once and came tumbling into the room, amongst the broken glass, with a most hideous clatter! The robbers, who had been not a little frightened by the opening concert, had now no doubt that some frightful hobgoblin had broken in upon them, and scampered away as fast as they could.

The coast once clear, our travelers soon sat down and dispatched what the robbers had left, with as much eagerness as if they had not expected to eat again for a month. As soon as they had satisfied themselves, they put out the lights and each one once more sought out a resting-place to his own liking. The donkey laid himself upon a heap of straw in the yard; the dog stretched himself upon a mat behind the door; the cat rolled herself up on the hearth before the warm ashes; and the cock perched upon a beam on the top of the house; and, as they were all rather tired with their journey, they soon fell asleep.

But about midnight, when the robbers saw from afar that the lights were out and that all seemed quiet, they began to think that they had been in too great a hurry to run away; and one of them, who was bolder than the rest, went to see what was going on. Finding everything still, he marched into the kitchen and groped about till he found a match in order to light a candle; and then, espying the glittering fiery eyes of the cat, he mistook them for live coals and held the match to them to light it. But the cat, not understanding this joke, sprang at his face, and spit, and scratched at him. This frightened him dreadfully, and away he ran to the back door; but there the dog jumped up and bit him in the leg; and as he was crossing over the yard the ass kicked him; and the cock, who had been awakened by the noise, crowed with all his might.

At this the robber ran back as fast as he could to his comrades and told the captain "how a horrid witch had got into the house, and had spit at him and scratched his face with her long bony fingers; how a man with a knife in his hand had hidden himself behind the door and stabbed him in the leg; how a black monster stood in the yard and struck him with a club, and how the devil sat upon the top of the house and cried out, 'Throw the rascal up here!' "

After this the robbers never dared to go back to the house; but the musicians were so pleased with their quarters that they took up their abode there; and there they are, I dare say, at this very day.

## THE LITTLE PINK ROSE[1]

### Sara Cone Bryant

*A tiny, delicate story which is easy for little children to play.*

Once there was a little pink Rosebud and she lived in a little dark house under the ground. One day she was sitting there, all by herself, and it was very still. Suddenly, she heard a little *tap, tap, tap,* at the door.

"Who is that?" she said.

"It's the Rain, and I want to come in," said a soft, sad, little voice.

[1] From *Stories to Tell to Children*. Reprinted by permission of and arrangement with Houghton Mifflin Company, the authorized publishers.

"No, you can't come in," the little Rosebud said.

By and by she heard another little *tap, tap, tap* on the window pane.

"Who is there?" she said.

The same soft little voice answered, "It's the Rain, and I want to come in!"

"No, you can't come in," said the little Rosebud.

Then it was very still for a long time. At last, there came a little rustling, whispering sound, all round the window: *rustle, whisper, whisper.*

"Who is there?" said the little Rosebud.

"It's the Sunshine," said a little, soft, cheery voice, "and I want to come in!"

"N — no," said the little pink rose, "you can't come in." And she sat still again.

Pretty soon she heard the sweet little rustling noise at the key-hole.

"Who is there?" she said.

"It's the Sunshine," said the cheery little voice, "and I want to come in, I want to come in!"

"No, no," said the little pink rose, "you cannot come in."

By and by, as she sat so still, she heard *tap, tap, tap* and *rustle, whisper, rustle,* all up and down at the window pane, and on the door, and at the key-hole.

*"Who is there?"* she said.

"It's the Rain and the Sun, the Rain and the Sun," said two little voices together, "and we want to come in! We want to come in! We want to come in!"

"Dear, dear!" said the little Rosebud, "if there are two of you, I s'pose I shall have to let you in."

So she opened the door a little wee crack, and in they came. And one took one of her little hands, and the other took her other little hand, and they ran, ran, ran with her, right up to the top of the ground. Then they said,—

"Poke your head through!"

So she poked her head through; and she was in the midst of a beautiful garden. It was springtime, and all the other flowers had their heads poked through; and she was the prettiest little pink rose in the whole garden!

# FANCY DRESS[1]

## Marion St. John Webb

*In blossom time the mood is set for the playing of this pleasing
little poem. Be sure the children know what a gnome is before
presenting it to them. Some groups decide to have a bumble bee
bring the invitation to the fairies; others like a grasshopper or a
bird. All the fairies may beg the gnome for blossoms or only one;
but every group will want to add other creatures or elves. Music
enhances the delight in playing this little story.*

> "You're a very naughty fairy"
> Cried the angry little gnome,
> Who lived up in the apple tree,
> "You come and spoil my home!
> Why will you shake the apple tree
> And make the blossoms fall?
> You really don't deserve to be
> A fairy girl at all!"

> "Well, I'm sorry to annoy you,"
> Laughed the fairy, "but I've planned
> To make myself a fancy dress
> Of flowers, you understand—
> A dress of apple-blossom frills,
> To dance in at the ball.
> So let me shake the bough again,
> Just once again—that's all!"

> "No, indeed, you naughty fairy!"
> Cried the gnome, so angry now
> That in a rage he stamped his foot
> Upon the loaded bough,
> Which shook a dozen blossoms off!
> "Ah, twelve more frills of stuff,
> I thank you, sir," the fairy laughed,
> "That will be quite enough."

[1] From *Orchard Fairies* by Marion St. John Webb. By permission of The
Medici Society Ltd.

# THE ELVES AND THE SHOEMAKER[1]

## The Brothers Grimm

*The cheerful, kindly shoemaker and his wife, along with the gay little elves, make a charming set of characters in a story which many children enjoy playing.*

There was once a shoemaker who worked very hard and was very honest; but still he could not earn enough to live upon, and at last all he had in the world was gone, except just leather enough to make one pair of shoes. Then he cut them all ready to make up the next day, meaning to get up early in the morning to work. His conscience was clear and his heart light amidst all his troubles; so he went peaceably to bed, left all his cares to heaven, and fell asleep. In the morning, after he had said his prayers, he set himself down to his work, but to his great wonder, there stood the shoes, all ready made, upon the table. The good man knew not what to say or think of this strange event. He looked at the workmanship; there was not one false stitch in the whole job, and all was so neat and true that it was a complete masterpiece.

That same day a customer came in, and the shoes pleased him so well that he willingly paid a price higher than usual for them; and the poor shoemaker with the money bought leather enough to make two pairs more. In the evening he cut out the work and went to bed early that he might get up and begin betimes next day; but he was saved all the trouble, for when he got up in the morning the work was finished ready to his hand. Presently in came buyers, who paid him handsomely for his goods, so that he bought leather enough for four pairs more. He cut out the work again over night, and found it finished in the morning as before; and so it went on for some time; what was got ready in the evening was always done by daybreak, and the good man soon became thriving and prosperous again.

One evening about Christmas time, as he and his wife were sitting togther, he said to her, "I would like to sit up and watch to-night, that we may see who it is that comes and does my work for me." The wife liked the thought; so they left a light burning and hid themselves in the corner of the room behind a curtain that was hung up there, and watched what would happen.

[1] From Edgar Taylor, *Grimm's Popular Stories.*

As soon as it was midnight, there came two little naked dwarfs; and they sat themselves upon the shoemaker's bench, took up all the work that was cut out, and began to ply with their little fingers, stitching and rapping and tapping away at such a rate that the shoemaker was all amazement and could not take his eyes off for a moment. And on they went till the job was quite finished, and the shoes stood ready for use upon the table. This was long before daybreak; and then they bustled away as quick as lightning.

The next day the wife said to the shoemaker, "These little wights have made us rich, and we ought to be thankful to them and do them a good office in return. I am quite vexed to see them run about as they do; they have nothing upon their backs to keep off the cold. I'll tell you what, I will make each of them a shirt, and a coat and a waistcoat, and a pair of pantaloons into the bargain; do you make each of them a little pair of shoes."

The thought pleased the good shoemaker very much; and one evening, when all the things were ready, they laid them on the table instead of the work that they used to cut out, and then went and hid themselves to watch what the little elves would do. About midnight they came in and were going to sit down to their work as usual; but when they saw the clothes lying for them, they laughed and were greatly delighted. Then they dressed themselves in the twinkling of an eye, and danced and capered and sprang about as merry as could be, till at last they danced out at the door and over the green, and the shoemaker saw them no more; but everything went well with him from that time forward, as long as he lived.


## THE WONDERFUL TAR-BABY STORY[1]

### Joel Chandler Harris

*Only one of the inimitable* Uncle Remus *stories is included in this collection because of the dialect. Though it should be read or told as it is written, many children will drop the dialect in playing it. The important thing is to keep the fun in full measure!*

"Brer Rabbit he fool Brer Fox so many times dat Brer Fox say to hisse'f dat he'd put up a game on Brer Rabbit. So one day he went ter wuk en got 'im some tar en mix it wid some turkentime, en fix

[1] From *Uncle Remus, His Songs and Sayings*, by Joel Chandler Harris. Published by Appleton-Century-Crofts, Inc. Used by permission of Lucien Harris.

up a contrapshun wat he call a Tar-Baby, en he tuck dish yer Tar-Baby en he sot'er in de big road, en den he lay off in de bushes fer to see what de news wuz gwineter be. En he didn't hatter wait long, nudder, kaze bimeby here come Brer Rabbit pacin' down de road—lippity-clippity, clippity-lippity—dez ez sassy ez a jay-bird. Brer Fox, he lay low. Brer Rabbit came prancin' 'long twel he spy de Tar-Baby, en den he fotch up on his behime legs like he wuz 'stonished. De Tar-Baby, she sot dar, she did, en Brer Fox, he lay low.

" 'Mawnin'!' sez Brer Rabbit, sezee—'nice wedder dis mawnin',' sezee.

"Tar-Baby ain't sayin' nothin', en Brer Fox, he lay low.

" 'How duz yo' sym'tums seem ter segashuate?' sez Brer Rabbit, sezee.

"Brer Fox, he wink his eye slow, en lay low, en de Tar-Baby, she ain't sayin' nothin'.

" 'How you come on, den? Is you deaf?' sez Brer Rabbit, sezee. 'Kaze if you is, I kin holler louder,' sezee.

"Tar-Baby stay still, en Brer Fox, he lay low.

" 'Youer stuck up, dat's w'at you is,' says Brer Rabbit, sezee, 'en I'm gwineter kyore you, dat's w'at I'm a gwineter do,' sezee.

"Brer Fox, he sorter chuckle in his stummuck, he did, but Tar-Baby ain't sayin' nothin'.

" 'I'm gwineter larn you howter talk ter 'specttubble fokes ef hit's de las' ack,' sez Brer Rabbit, sezee. 'Ef you don't take off dat hat en tell me howdy, I'm gwineter bus' you wide open,' sezee.

"Tar-Baby stay still, en Brer Fox, he lay low.

"Brer Rabbit keep on axin' 'im, en de Tar-Baby, she keep on sayin' nothin', twel present'y Brer Rabbit draw back wid his fis', he did, en blip he tuck 'er side er de head. Right dar's whar he broke his merlasses jug. His fis' stuck, en he can't pull loose. De tar hilt 'im. But Tar-Baby, she stay still, en Brer Fox, he lay low.

" 'Ef you don't lemme loose, I'll knock you agin,' sez Brer Rabbit, sezee, en wid dat he fotch 'er a wipe wid de udder han', en dat stuck. Tar-Baby she ain't sayin' nothin', and Brer Fox, he lay low.

" 'Tu'n me loose, fo' I kick de natal stuffin' outen you,' sez Brer Rabbit, sezee, but de Tar-Baby, she ain't sayin' nothin'. She des hilt on, en den Brer Rabbit lose de use er his feet in de same way. Brer Fox, he lay low. Den Brer Rabbit squall out dat ef de Tar-Baby don't tu'n 'im loose he butter'er cranksided. En den he butted, en his head got stuck. Den Brer Fox, he sa'ntered fort', lookin' dez ez innercent ez one er yo' mammy's mockin'-birds.

"'Howdy, Brer Rabbit,' sez Brer Fox, sezee. 'You look sorter stuck up dis mawnin',' sezee, en den he rolled on de groun', en laughed en laughed twel he couldn't laugh no mo'.

"'Well, I speck I got you dis time, Brer Rabbit, sezee'; 'maybe I ain't, but I speck I is. You been runnin' roun' here sassin' atter me a mighty long time, but I speck you done come ter de end er de row. You bin cuttin' up yo' capers en bouncin' 'roun' in dis neighborhood ontwel you come ter b'leeve yo'se'f de boss er de whole gang. En den youer allers some'rs whar you got no bizness,' sez Brer Fox, sezee. 'Who ax you fer ter come en strike up a'quaintance wid dish yer Tar-Baby? En stuck you up dar whar you iz? Nobody in de roun' worril. You des tuck en jam yo's'f on dat Tar-Baby widout waitin' fer enny invite,' sez Brer Fox, sezee, 'en dar you is, en dar you'll stay twel I fixes up a bresh-pile and fires her up, kaze I'm gwineter bobby-cue you dis day, sho,' sez Brer Fox, sezee.

'Den Brer Rabbit talk mighty 'umble.

"'I don't keer w'at you do wid me, Brer Fox,' sezee, 'so you don't fling me in dat brier-patch. Roas' me, Brer Fox,' sezee, 'but don't fling me in dat brier-patch,' sezee.

"'Hit's so much trouble fer ter kindle a fier,' sez Brer Fox, sezee, 'dat I speck I'll hatter hang you,' sezee.

"'Hang me des ez high as you please, Brer Fox,' sez Brer Rabbit, sezee, 'but fer de Lord's sake don't fling me in dat brier-patch,' sezee.

"'I ain't got no string,' sez Brer Fox, sezee, 'en now I speck I'll hatter drown you,' sezee.

"'Drown me des ez deep ez you please, Brer Fox,' sez Brer Rabbit, sezee, 'but don't fling me in dat brier-patch,' sezee.

"'Dey ain't no water nigh,' sez Brer Fox, sezee, 'en now I speck I'll hatter skin you,' sezee.

"'Skin me, Brer Fox,' sez Brer Rabbit, sezee, 'snatch out my eyeballs, t'ar out my years by de roots, en cut off my legs,' sezee, 'but do please, Brer Fox, don't fling me in dat brier-patch,' sezee.

"Co'se Brer Fox wanter hurt Brer Rabbit bad ez he kin, so he cotch 'im by de behime legs en slung 'im right in de middle er de brier-patch. Dar wuz a con-siderbul flutter whar Brer Rabbit struck de bushes, en Brer Fox sorter hang 'roun' fer ter see w'at wuz gwineter happen. Bimeby he hear somebody call 'im, en way up

52

de hill he see Brer Rabbit settin' cross-legged on a chinkapin log koamin' de pitch outen his har wid a chip. Den Brer Fox know dat he bin swop off mighty bad. Brer Rabbit wuz bleedzed fer ter fling back some er his sass, en he holler out:

" 'Bred en bawn in a brier-patch, Brer Fox—bred en bawn in a brier-patch!' en wid dat he skip out des ez lively ez a cricket in de embers."

# CHAPTER V

# *Where Wonders Are*

STORIES FOR CHILDREN OF EIGHT AND NINE YEARS

This is an especially delightful age for story dramatization. Interest in fantasy is at its height at eight, and all the old and modern fairy tales are welcomed, along with the realistic stories which are also enjoyed. The world about them is no longer novel to eight-year-olds, and most of them thrill to "once upon a time."

Dramatic play, which has no plot, is still a part of their make-believe, and they especially like to do pantomimes and have the others guess them. Perhaps someone has a birthday and a magic box is passed, out of which not only the birthday child but everyone else may take and use anything he chooses. The most surprising things will come out of the box! Activities on a picnic, funny things that happen on a windy day, all kinds of people and actions suggested by music—these and many other bits of dramatic play may be done either in one's own character or as someone quite different.

Dramatizations of situations involving manners are valuable. When one notes how few adults know the correct procedures in introductions—especially which is the person to be presented to the other—and how many children are uncouth because they simply do not know what is correct, he realizes that either parents and teachers have been remiss, or they have merely *told* their children what is correct. If, instead, the children had played all kinds of situations involving manners, they would not forget the proper things to do.

Real problems of the children themselves arouse a great deal of interest when put into dramatic scenes. A fourth grade group of city children, for instance, most of whom had no place to play except at a club run by a community chest agency, dramatized a situation which had made them very angry the day before. A ball with which some of them had been playing was accidentally thrown into a neighbor's garden, and that irate lady ended the ball game by keeping the ball. In vain the children begged, gave excuses and promises. Finally one child said to another, "Go get Miss Davis" (the real head of the club). The boy marched off and returned with a little girl as Miss Davis, who talked most calmly and sensibly to the neighbor, saying among other things, "I don't think the children know their own strength!"

Needless to say, the neighbor gave back the ball, and the children, with Miss Davis, planned how they could avoid a repetition of this thing which so frequently had happened. By this time the children were completely over their indignation, and there were no more plans to get even with the neighbor!

Stories for children of this period can be a bit longer and more complex than for the younger children, especially if they have had some experience in dramatizing. Suspense and climax become stronger than before, humor may be a little finer, and though action is still very important, a good deal can depend on dialogue. Characters are far more varied and interesting in stories for children of this age, for there are people with magic powers: fairy godmothers, changeling children, and queer little leprechauns. They are still definitely good or bad, however, and poetic justice always triumphs in the end.


## THE PEDDLER AND HIS CAPS

### An Old Tale Retold by Geraldine Brain Siks

*Here is a big joke that a peddler played on some monkeys who thought they were playing a joke on him!*

There was once a little old man who lived all alone in a cottage on the edge of a forest. He was a good man, a wise man, and almost always he was jolly and friendly.

Of all the ways there were in the world to earn one's living the little old man decided to be a peddler. And, of all the things there were in the world to peddle, he decided to peddle caps.

He made the caps all by himself. Day after day he would sit crosslegged on his doorstep, and he would sew caps of every kind and caps of every color. He made caps with bells, caps with tassels, caps with feathers, caps with fringe. And he made red caps, blue caps, purple, lavender, yellow, orange, and emerald caps. Whenever he finished making a cap he would place it very carefully in a big, brown pack, and whenever the big pack was full, the peddler knew that the time had come for him to go out into the world to earn his living.

One summer morning, bright and early, the little old man put a geranium red cap upon his head, and he lifted his big, brown pack up and over his shoulder. Then he started down the forest path, for he was on his way to sell caps. He had not gone far when he saw a beautiful patch of golden dandelions. He stopped and picked a long stemmed one and stuck it in the top of his cap. Then he took a long look at the sky. There was something about the clouds that told the little old man that it would be wise for him to go to the south for the day. And with his mind made up he was soon on his way again.

As he walked along he thought about all the pretty caps he had made, and before he knew it, he had made up a gay little song to help him sell his wares. He sang his song aloud to see how it sounded:

"Caps for sale, caps for sale!
Red and pink and white and green,
The finest caps you've ever seen,
Caps for sale, caps for sale!"

The peddler liked his song, and he sang it again and again until he made up just the kind of tune he wanted. He was so busy with singing while he walked along that he didn't know that he had come to the edge of a little village. Many of the villagers had heard his singing and they had stopped their work to listen. It was not often that a peddler came through their town, and whenever one did happen by, all of the village folk came out to see what it was that he had to sell. As the little old peddler walked down the dusty road all of the villagers hurried to the village square to see him. Merchants and bakers, and cobblers and weavers left their shops. Farmers came in from nearby fields, and women and children joined the others along the main street of the town.

"My," said the peddler to himself, "with so many people I will sell all my caps in a hurry."

He sang his song gayly, and everyone watched him as he stopped in the village square and opened his pack right in the middle of the street. He handed caps to everyone so that all might try them on and see how pretty they were. The peddler was pleased when he saw the mayor and many of the villagers wearing his caps and admiring each other.

The mayor, who was very well liked by all the townspeople, took off the yellow-fringed cap he was wearing, and he looked at it very closely. He looked at all the caps the villagers were wearing. Then he shook his head and he walked over to the peddler.

"This cap is much too pretty for me," he laughed, and with a friendly nod he handed it back to the peddler.

All of the villagers watched the mayor. They looked closely at the caps they had been wearing as they tried to make up their minds whether they should buy.

"What would I do with a cap like this?" the farmer asked as he took off a blue and yellow striped cap, and placed it on top of the peddler's pack.

"It's far too warm for a cap today," said the butcher as he gave a rainbow cap back to the little old man.

"Yes, sir, it's much too warm to wear a cap today," said a friendly little grandmother as she took a soft pink cap from the head of her little granddaughter. She handed the cap to the peddler and said in a friendly way, "Come back again when the weather is cool. Then we will buy your caps."

"Yes, yes, come back another day," called several villagers as they returned the caps to the peddler.

The peddler could see that no one wanted to buy a cap so he put them carefully back into his pack. "Thank you for looking at my caps," he called to the villagers, "I will come back on a day before winter." Then he put the pack over his back and started on down the road again.

When he had walked quite a distance from the village he came into a grove of tall palm trees. "What a cool, shady place," he said as he stopped. "I think I'll rest here for a while."

The peddler put his pack beside him, and sat down and leaned against the trunk of a palm tree. Before he knew it he was sound asleep.

Now in this forest there lived a family of monkeys. They were hiding in the branches at the top of the tall trees. The peddler was so tired that he didn't see them. When the monkeys saw the peddler sleeping in their forest they became so curious about him that they climbed down the trees and gathered around him. A bold little monkey began to chatter to the others.

"Tchee, tchee, tchee," he said as he pointed his monkey paw toward the big brown pack.

"Tchee, tchee, tchee," chattered all of the others.

The bold little monkey tiptoed up to the peddler's pack without making a sound. All of the other monkeys were quiet as they watched him. The bold monkey reached his little monkey paw inside the pack, and he brought out a bright red cap just like the one the peddler was wearing. At once he put it on his head, leaped into the air, and danced in the clearing.

"Tchee, tchee, tchee," he chattered for he felt so happy with a new cap.

The other monkeys did just what the brave monkey had done. Each one tiptoed up to the pack and got a cap for himself.

"Tchee, tchee, tchee," they all chattered as they danced around the tree where the peddler was sleeping. The monkeys felt so good that they chattered louder and louder.

Soon the peddler began to wake up. The bold little monkey saw the peddler stretch his arms and legs. "Tchee, Tchee," the monkey shouted to the others. All the monkeys scampered up into the tree tops. They were very quiet.

The peddler yawned and stretched. "What a good rest I've had! I'll be on my way and see if I can sell some caps today," he said. He picked up his pack slowly.

"What!" he shouted, "Where are my caps?" The peddler had suddenly discovered that his pack was empty. He looked all around the tree. He looked into the forest. He looked in the direction of the village.

"I wonder what has become of them," he said as he scratched his left ear. The monkeys were watching from the tree tops. They had played a good joke on the peddler, and they had a hard time to keep from laughing. Finally the bold little monkey laughed aloud. "Tchee, tchee, tchee," he chuckled.

"Tchee, tchee, tchee," chuckled all the monkeys.

"My caps!" cried the peddler as he looked up into the trees and saw the monkeys wearing them.

He was so surprised that he shook his fist at the monkeys, and he called loudly to them, "Monkeys! Bring me my caps!"

The monkeys shook their little monkey paws at him, and they chattered just as he had done, "Tchee! Tchee, tchee, tchee, tchee!"

This made the peddler very cross. He stamped his foot and said, "Monkeys!"

The monkeys stamped their monkey feet and they chattered, "Tchee!"

The peddler clapped his hands together and said in a quiet, friendly way, "Please, monkeys, I want my caps."

Up in the trees the monkeys clapped their paws together and said in much the same way, "Tchee, tchee, tchee tchee tchee tchee."

The little old peddler folded his arms and shook his head for he didn't know what to do. The monkeys folded their paws and shook their heads just as the peddler had done. The peddler sat down on the ground and stroked his chin as he tried to think of what he might do to get his caps back again.

The monkeys sat down on the branches of the trees and stroked their chins as they watched the peddler.

The peddler thought and thought. Suddenly he had an idea. "The monkeys do as I do," he whispered to himself.

He stood up quickly. The monkeys stood up too. The peddler reached for his cap. He took the bright red cap off his head and with a friendly bow to the monkeys he tossed his cap to the ground. At the same time he called, "Thank you, monkeys! Thank you!"

"Tchee tchee, tchee! Tchee tchee!" the monkeys called and they did just what the peddler had done.

Caps came falling down from the trees. The peddler was very much excited. He picked up his caps, and put them into his pack as fast as he could. When he had the last cap he put his pack on his back, and as he waved goodbye he shook his finger and called out, "You little monkeys!"

The little monkeys, high in the tree-tops, called, "Tchee, tchee, tchee!" And they chuckled all afternoon about the good joke they had played on the peddler.

# A GOBLINADE[1]

## Florence Page Jaques

*Can you introduce more than three characters into a dramatiza-
tion of this charming story?*

A green hobgoblin,
  Small but quick,
Went out walking
  With a black thorn stick.

He was full of mischief,
  Full of glee.
He frightened all
  That he could see.

He saw a little maiden
  In a wood.
He looked as fierce as
  A goblin should.

He crept by the hedge row,
  He said, "Boo!"
"Boo!" laughed the little girl,
  "How are you?"

"What!" said the goblin,
  "Aren't you afraid?"
"I think you're funny,"
  Said the maid.

"Ha!" said the goblin,
  Sitting down flat.
"You think I'm funny?
  I don't like that.

[1] Used by permission of the author.

"I'm very frightening.
  You should flee!"
"You're cunning," she said
  "As you can be!"


Then she laughed again, and
  Went away.
But the goblin stood there
  All that day.


A beetle came by, and
  "Well?" it said.
But the goblin only
  Shook his head.


"For I am funny,"
  He said to it.
"I thought I was alarming,
  And I'm not a bit.


"If I'm amusing,"
  He said to himself,
"I won't be a goblin,
  I'll be an elf!


"For a goblin must be goblin
  All the day,
But an elf need only
  Dance and play."


So the little green goblin
  Became an elf.
And he dances all day, and
  He likes himself.

# MRS. MALLABY'S BIRTHDAY[1]

## Helen Earle Gilbert

*Each of the seven characters in this charming little story is a definite individual, and though it is written practically in dramatic form, it is a good study in characterization.*

There was once an old lady who was very, very old. She was so old that she didn't even know herself how old she really was. Her name was Mrs. Mallaby, and she lived all alone in a little brick house with a green door, seven windows, and a pretty bright garden growing all around it.

One morning as Mrs. Mallaby was finishing her breakfast she heard a knock. "That's the postman," said Mrs. Mallaby. "There must be a letter!" So she hurried to the door.

There was the postman, in his blue coat. "Good morning, Mrs. Mallaby," he said. "I believe I have something for you this morning." And he began to hunt through his bag.

"Good morning, Mr. Walker," said Mrs. Mallaby. "Oh, what will it be?"

"Here it is," said the postman.

Sure enough. There was a little blue envelope with a stamp, and it said: *Mrs. Mallaby.*

Mrs. Mallaby was much excited. She did not often have any mail. She thanked Mr. Walker, took the letter into the house, and opened it. Inside there was a pretty card with flowers and a ribbon on it and a message that said: *Happy Birthday, Mrs. Mallaby! Many Happy Returns of the Day!*

"It must be my birthday!" Mrs. Mallaby said.

She put the card up on the mantel and sat down to count. She counted for nearly an hour. Then she said, "I do believe I'm a hundred years old today. My goodness, how time flies! Well, I rather wish I had a kitten."

Just then there was another knock at the door. Mrs. Mallaby hurried to open it.

There stood the neighbor who lived next door—Mrs. Bowe. She was holding a large package carefully in both hands.

"Many happy returns of the day, Mrs. Mallaby!" said Mrs. Bowe. "I've brought you a little remembrance for your birthday."

[1] Used by permission of Charles Coleman Sellers.

"How very sweet of you," said Mrs. Mallaby. *"I hope it's a kitten."*

She said the last words very low, to herself, so that Mrs. Bowe wouldn't know she was disappointed if it wasn't a kitten.

Mrs. Bowe set the package on the table and took off the wrappings. Inside was an enormous birthday cake, with one hundred candles on it.

"Oh, thank you, Mrs. Bowe!" cried Mrs. Mallaby. "How very nice of you!"

Mrs. Bowe was pleased. "We'll light the candles," she said, "and then it'll look quite pretty."

So Mrs. Mallaby got the matchbox and she and Mrs. Bowe lighted the one hundred candles.

"You must have the first piece," she said to Mrs. Bowe.

She cut Mrs. Bowe quite a large piece of the birthday cake. Then she took a piece herself.

"It's just lovely!" she said. "I've never had such a beautiful cake before."

They sat down and ate their pieces of cake to the last crumb. It was delicious. Then Mrs. Bowe said "Good-by" and "Happy Birthday" and went home.

Then Mrs. Mallaby went around her house as she did every day to see that everything was clean and in order.

She washed the dishes and put them away. Then she heard another knock on the door.

She hurried to the door, and who should it be but Dr. Blight, another neighbor who lived down the street. Dr. Blight was holding a very large, interesting-looking package tightly under one arm.

"How do you do?" he said. "Well, well, well!" (He always said that, even when people were sick.) "I hear you're a hundred! Well, well, well! Many happy returns, Mrs. Mallaby, and here's a little birthday present for you!"

Mrs. Mallaby ran to get her glasses.

*"Perhaps it will be the kitten this time,"* she said to herself.

Inside the wrappings was a handsome green silk umbrella, with a bird for a handle.

"Why, how pretty!" cried Mrs. Mallaby. "How did you know just what I wanted to take to church on rainy Sundays! Thank you very much, Doctor. Really, I wanted an umbrella more than anything else *except a kitten.*"

Mrs. Mallaby said the last words to herself, very low. She didn't want to hurt the kind doctor's feelings or let him see that she was disappointed.

"You must have a piece of my birthday cake," she said.

So Mrs. Mallaby gave the doctor quite a large piece of her birthday cake. And he said "Well, well, well!" again and "Thank you!" and went away.

"Well, well, well!" said Mrs. Mallaby to herself. "If I couldn't have a kitten, of course I would rather have a birthday cake with a hundred candles and a green silk umbrella with a bird for a handle than anything else there is in the world."

She had no sooner said this than there came another rap at the door. There stood Peter, the little boy who lived across the street.

"Happy birthday, Mrs. Mallaby!" shouted Peter. He was holding his hands behind him.

"Why, hello, Peter," said Mrs. Mallaby. She was greatly pleased. "How in the world did you know it was my birthday?"

"I have a present for you!" cried Peter. He drew it out from behind him. It was a large bundle wrapped in paper.

Mrs. Mallaby's heart began to beat very fast. *Perhaps it would be a kitten.*

"Bring it right in," she cried, "and we'll open it."

They put the bundle on the floor. Peter danced about while Mrs. Mallaby untied the string. Inside was a big pasteboard box. Mrs. Mallaby lifted the cover. There was a beautiful big wooden boat.

"Why, *Peter!*" said Mrs. Mallaby. She was so astonished that she could not say another word.

"I made it myself," said Peter. "I made it in school and painted it, too. It's for your birthday."

He took it out of the box and held it up for Mrs. Mallaby to see.

"It's made of two blocks of wood. You put one on top of the other and pound them together with nails," he explained. "There are two smokestacks—look! And a string to pull it by. I'll come and sail it for you sometimes if you want me to."

"How beautiful it is!" said Mrs. Mallaby. "And to think that you made it all yourself."

"It wasn't very hard," said Peter.

"I never thought I should have a boat like this," said Mrs. Mallaby. "Would you like a piece of my birthday cake, Peter?"

64

"Yes, thank you," said Peter. "What a lot of candles! On my birthday I had six."

Peter ate a large piece of cake and then said good-by.

"You don't know where I could get a kitten, do you, Peter?" asked Mrs. Mallaby.

"No," said Peter. "I wish I had one myself. Good-by."

Then there was quite a long while when nobody came.

But just as Mrs. Mallaby was watering her geraniums, she heard another rap at the door. She hurried to open it. There on the step stood the postman's wife, looking very smiling. She was holding a package.

"Happy Birthday!" she said. "I've been planning a little present for your birthday, Mrs. Mallaby, and here it is. Many happy returns of the day."

"Why, Mrs. Walker," Mrs. Mallaby said, "how very nice of you!" She looked at the box her neighbor was holding and her eyes grew bright. She felt very happy.

"*I do believe it's a ---*" And Mrs. Mallaby stopped just in time, for while she was talking she had untied the ribbon and out of the box tumbled a beautiful handmade apron.

"Why, dear me!" cried Mrs. Mallaby. "What a beautiful apron it is! Blue, with red squares. I am so fond of blue. And I do believe there is a pocket!"

She bent over it hastily to look at the stitches, for she didn't want her good friend Mrs. Walker to see the tears in her eyes. But she really did want a kitten more and more. The more she thought about it the more she felt she just *must* have a kitten.

"Won't you have a piece of my birthday cake, Mrs. Walker?" she asked. "Mrs. Bowe made it for me."

"Oh, thank you," replied Mrs. Walker, looking admiringly at the beautiful cake with roses and hills of sugar and green leaves around the edge and what were left of the one hundred candles.

So Mrs. Mallaby cut a piece of cake for Mrs. Walker, and she went away saying, "Thank you very much," and that she thought it was going to rain later on in the day.

And now it was time for Mrs. Mallaby to get her lunch. She decided to have crisp bacon, two fried eggs, corn bread, gingerbread, and tea—and a little blackberry jam. Just as she was about to sit down, what should she hear but another knock at the door! She was quite excited!

And there stood Mr. Cobb, the grocer! He had taken off his white coat and put on his Sunday one, which was black and had tails going down behind. And he had on a shiny derby hat. And he was carrying in his hand a little basket, a covered basket, which he was holding high and carefully.

Mrs. Mallaby tried hard not to look at the basket, but her heart began to beat very fast and something in her mind kept saying, *"It's a kitten basket. If ever I saw a kitten basket in my life that's a kitten basket!"*

Her fingers trembled and she could hardly hear what the grocer was saying.

"Mrs. Mallaby," he was saying, "you've been a good customer to me for many years than I can remember. Mrs. Bowe told me it is your birthday and that you are a hundred years old. When I told that to my wife, she said we must certainly make you a little present." And he lifted the basket and held it out to Mrs. Mallaby.

Mrs. Mallaby could hardly wait to peer under the cover. When she saw what was there she almost cried. Inside the basket was a neat little package wrapped in white tissue paper and tied with a big silver bow. It couldn't possibly be a kitten!

She turned away so Mr. Cobb couldn't see how much she had hoped it would be a kitten.

But Mrs. Mallaby was very brave, and she was also very polite (which was why she had so many friends, really) and so she said, "Thank you, Mr. Cobb," and, "Won't you have a piece of my birthday cake?"

Then at last she opened the package, and what was inside? Why, a handsome sugar bowl with silver handles and a silver top!

Mrs. Mallaby was tremendously surprised. She stared at it and lifted the cover. It was full of lumps of sugar. "It's lovely!" she said. "It was so nice of you and Mrs. Cobb to remember me. A sugar bowl—think of it!"

About two o'clock that afternoon, after Mrs. Mallaby had finished her lunch and done the dishes and put them away and the kitchen was as clean as a new pin, she sat down by the fire and looked at her presents.

She laid them all out on the table and looked at each one.

There was the pretty birthday card with flowers and a ribbon on it.

There was all that was left of the enormous birthday cake with

66

the one hundred candles, the roses and hills of sugar, and green leaves around the edge.

There was the handsome green silk umbrella with the bird for a handle.

There was the beautiful big wooden boat with two smokestacks.

And there was the lovely glass sugar bowl with silver handles and a silver top, and full of lumps of sugar.

"They are very, very nice," said Mrs. Mallaby. And because she was such a polite little old lady she would not even let herself think, "*I did want a kitten!*"

Then, because she was really a hundred years old and very sleepy, Mrs. Mallaby began to nod a little. She leaned forward in her chair and dozed off into a nap.

It began to rain. The rain beat down steadily against the windows.

And as Mrs. Mallaby was dreaming, she heard a little sound:

"M-iaow! M-iaow! M-iaow!"

Mrs. Mallaby awoke with a jerk. "What's that?" she said. "Was I dreaming? Have I been asleep?"

She looked all around. There was nothing to be seen and nothing to be heard but the sound of the rain against the windows. Her eyes began to close once more.

Then suddenly she heard it again.

"Mi-a-o-w! Mi-a-o-o-o-w!" very faint and wet and lonesome.

Mrs. Mallaby ran to the door and threw it open. There on the doorstep in the rain stood a little black and white kitten. He looked right up at Mrs. Mallaby and said, "*Mi-a-o-o-w! Mi-a-o-o-w! Mi-a-o-o-w!*"

"Well, bless your heart," cried Mrs. Mallaby. "Did you come on my birthday to live with me?"

And the kitten said, "Mi-a-ow, Mi-a-o-o-w, Mi-a-o-o-w!" which meant that he had.

So Mrs. Mallaby took him into the house and dried him with a clean towel. She ran into the pantry and got a white bowl with roses on it and filled it with milk. The kitten drank all the milk. Then Mrs. Mallaby fixed a basket for him to sleep in.

The kitten said, "Mi-a-o-o-w!" and Mrs. Mallaby said, "What a beautiful birthday!"

And from that day to this, Mrs. Mallaby and the kitten have

**67**

lived happily together in the little brick house with the green door, seven windows, and a garden all around.


## THE MISER AND HIS MONKEY[1]

### Adapted from a fable of La Fontaine

*In developing the three or four incidents in this story, there is much scope for imagination.*

There was once a rich miser who had a large chest in an upstairs room. The chest was almost filled with money. The miser hoped that some day it might be filled to the very top. He, therefore, put into the chest every bit of gold he could save. He never thought of using the money for himself nor of giving any of it to his friends or to those who were in need.

One day the rich miser bought a monkey for a low price, hoping to sell it again at a very high price. In this way he hoped to make more money to hide away in his money chest.

One afternoon the rich miser went for a walk. While he was gone the monkey saw a kind neighbor throw a piece of money out of a window to a poor begger on the street below. Now a monkey likes to do what he sees others do, so he went to his master's money chest, opened it, and began to take out one piece of money after another and throw it out of the window.

When the people saw the gold coming out of the rich miser's window they came in crowds to pick it up. More and more people came. All were shouting and laughing as they scrambled for the money. When the chest was almost empty the rich miser came up the street. When he saw what was going on, he became very angry. "Oh, you wicked, foolish animal!" he cried, shaking his fist at the monkey.

"Don't do that," said one of his neighbors, "because while it is foolish to throw money away, it is no more foolish than to put it in a chest and never make use of it. Money is of value only when it is put to use."

# TIGGER HAS BREAKFAST[1]

## A. A. Milne

*It would never do to leave out Winnie-the-Pooh, and so here he is with Piglet, Eeyore, Kanga, Roo, Christopher Robin, and the newcomer, Tigger. There are Pooh stories just as delightful as this one, but probably none which is such fun to dramatize.*

Winnie-the-Pooh woke up suddenly in the middle of the night and listened. Then he got out of bed, and lit his candle, and stumped across the room to see if anybody was trying to get into his honey-cupboard, and they weren't, so he stumped back again, blew out his candle, and got into bed. Then he heard the noise again.

"Is that you, Piglet?" he said.

But it wasn't.

"Come in, Christopher Robin," he said.

But Christopher Robin didn't.

"Tell me about it to-morrow, Eeyore," said Pooh sleepily.

But the noise went on.

"*Worraworraworraworraworra,*" said Whatever-it-was, and Pooh found that he wasn't asleep after all.

"What can it be?" he thought. "There are lots of noises in the Forest, but this is a different one. It isn't a growl, and it isn't a purr, and it isn't a bark, and it isn't the noise-you-make-before-be-ginning-a-piece-of-poetry, but it's a noise of some kind, made by a strange animal. And he's making it outside my door. So I shall get up and ask him not to do it."

He got out of bed and opened his front door.

"Hallo!" said Pooh, in case there was anything outside.

"Hallo!" said Whatever-it-was.

"Oh!" said Pooh. "Hallo!"

"Hallo!"

"Oh, *there* you are!" said Pooh. "Hallo!"

"Hallo!" said the Strange Animal, wondering how long this was going on.

Pooh was just going to say "Hallo!" for the fourth time when he thought that he wouldn't, so he said: "Who is it?" instead.

---

[1] From *The House at Pooh Corner* by A. A. Milne. Published and copyright, 1928, E. P. Dutton & Co., Inc., New York.

"Me," said a voice.

"Oh!" said Pooh. "Well, come here."

So Whatever-it-was came here, and in the light of the candle he and Pooh looked at each other.

"I'm Pooh," said Pooh.

"I'm Tigger," said Tigger.

"Oh!" said Pooh, for he had never seen an animal like this before. "Does Christopher Robin know about you?"

"Of course he does," said Tigger.

"Well," said Pooh, "it's the middle of the night, which is a good time for going to sleep. And to-morrow morning we'll have some honey for breakfast. Do Tiggers like honey?"

"They like everything," said Tigger cheerfully.

"Then if they like going to sleep on the floor, I'll go back to bed," said Pooh, "and we'll do things in the morning. Good night." And he got back into bed and went fast asleep.

When he awoke in the morning, the first thing he saw was Tigger, sitting in front of the glass and looking at himself.

"Hallo!" said Pooh.

"Hallo!" said Tigger. "I've found somebody just like me. I thought I was the only one of them."

Pooh got out of bed, and began to explain what a lookingglass was, but just as he was getting to the interesting part, Tigger said:

"Excuse me a moment, but there's something climbing up your table," and with one loud *Worraworraworraworraworra* he jumped at the end of the tablecloth, pulled it to the ground, wrapped himself up in it three times, rolled to the other end of the room, and, after a terrible struggle, got his head into the daylight again, and said cheerfully: "Have I won?"

"That's my tablecloth," said Pooh, as he began to unwind Tigger.

"I wondered what it was," said Tigger.

"It goes on the table and you put things on it."

"Then why did it try to bite me when I wasn't looking?"

"I don't *think* it did," said Pooh.

"It tried," said Tigger, "but I was too quick for it."

Pooh put the cloth back on the table, and he put a large honeypot on the cloth, and they sat down to breakfast. And as soon as they sat down, Tigger took a large mouthful of honey . . . and he looked up at the ceiling with his head on one side, and made exploring noises with his tongue and considering noises, and what-have-we-got-*here* noises . . . and then he said in a very decided voice:

"Tiggers don't like honey."

"Oh!" said Pooh, and tried to make it sound Sad and Regretful. "I thought they liked everything."

"Everything except honey," said Tigger.

Pooh felt rather pleased about this, and said that, as soon as he had finished his own breakfast, he would take Tigger round to Piglet's house, and Tigger could try some of Piglet's haycorns.

"Thank you, Pooh," said Tigger, "because haycorns is really what Tiggers like best."

So after breakfast they went round to see Piglet, and Pooh explained as they went that Piglet was a Very Small Animal who didn't like bouncing, and asked Tigger not to be too Bouncy just at first. And Tigger, who had been hiding behind trees and jumping out on Pooh's shadow when it wasn't looking, said that Tiggers were only bouncy before breakfast, and that as soon as they had had a few haycorns they became Quiet and Refined. So by and by they knocked at the door of Piglet's house.

"Hallo, Pooh," said Piglet.

"Hallo, Piglet. This is Tigger."

"Oh, is it?" said Piglet, and he edged round to the other side of the table. "I thought Tiggers were smaller than that."

"Not the big ones," said Tigger.

"They like haycorns," said Pooh, "so that's what we've come for, because poor Tigger hasn't had any breakfast yet."

Piglet pushed the bowl of haycorns towards Tigger, and said: "Help yourself," and then he got close up to Pooh and felt much braver, and said, "So you're Tigger? Well, well!" in a careless sort of voice. But Tigger said nothing because his mouth was full of haycorns. . . .

After a long munching noise he said:

"Ee-ers o i a-ors."

And when Pooh and Piglet said "What?" he said "Skoos ee," and went outside for a moment.

When he came back he said firmly:

"Tiggers don't like haycorns."

"But you said they liked everything except honey," said Pooh.

"Everything except honey and haycorns," explained Tigger.

When he heard this, Pooh said, "Oh, I see!" and Piglet, who was rather glad that Tiggers didn't like haycorns, said, "What about thistles?"

"Thistles" said Tigger, "is what Tiggers like best."

"Then let's go along and see Eeyore," said Piglet.

So the three of them went; and after they had walked and walked and walked, they came to the part of the Forest where Eeyore was.

"Hallo, Eeyore!" said Pooh. "This is Tigger."

"What is?" said Eeyore.

"This," explained Pooh and Piglet together, and Tigger smiled his happiest smile and said nothing.

Eeyore walked all round Tigger one way, and then turned and walked all round him the other way.

"What did you say it was?" he asked.

"Tigger."

"Ah!" said Eeyore.

"He's just come," explained Piglet.

"Ah!" said Eeyore again.

He thought for a long time and then said:

"When is he going?"

Pooh explained to Eeyore that Tigger was a great friend of Christopher Robin's, who had come to stay in the Forest, and Piglet explained to Tigger that he mustn't mind what Eeyore said because he was *always* gloomy; and Eeyore explained to Piglet that, on the contrary, he was feeling particularly cheerful this morning; and Tigger explained to anybody who was listening that he hadn't had any breakfast yet.

"I knew there was something," said Pooh. "Tiggers always eat thistles, so that was why we came to see you, Eeyore."

"Don't mention it, Pooh."

"Eeyore, I didn't mean that I didn't *want* to see you—"

"Quite—quite. But your new stripy friend—naturally, he wants his breakfast. What did you say his name was?"

"Tigger."

"Then come this way, Tigger."

Eeyore led the way to the most thistly-looking patch of thistles that ever was, and waved a hoof at it.

"A little patch I was keeping for my birthday," he said; "but, after all, what *are* birthdays? Here to-day and gone to-morrow. Help yourself, Tigger."

Tigger thanked him and looked a little anxiously at Pooh.

"Are these really thistles?" he whispered.

"Yes," said Pooh.

"What Tiggers like best?"

"That's right," said Pooh.

"I see," said Tigger.

So he took a large mouthful, and he gave a large crunch.

"Ow!" said Tigger.

He sat down and put his paw in his mouth.

"What's the matter?" asked Pooh.

"*Hot!*" mumbled Tigger.

"Your friend," said Eeyore, "appears to have bitten on a bee."

Pooh's friend stopped shaking his head to get the prickles out, and explained that Tiggers didn't like thistles.

"Then why bend a perfectly good one?" asked Eeyore.

"But you said," began Pooh—"you *said* that Tiggers liked everything except honey and haycorns."

"*And* thistles," said Tigger, who was now running round in circles with his tongue hanging out.

Pooh looked at him sadly.

"What are we going to do?" he asked Piglet.

Piglet knew the answer to that, and said at once that they must go and see Christopher Robin.

"You'll find him with Kanga," said Eeyore. He came close to Pooh, and said in a loud whisper:

"*Could* you ask your friend to do his exercise somewhere else? I shall be having lunch directly, and don't want it bounced on just before I begin. A trifling matter, and fussy of me, but we all have our little ways."

Pooh nodded solemnly and called to Tigger.

"Come along and we'll go and see Kanga. She's sure to have lots of breakfast for you."

Tigger finished his last circle and came up to Pooh and Piglet.

"Hot!" he explained with a large and friendly smile. "Come on!" and he rushed off.

Pooh and Piglet walked slowly after him. And as they walked Piglet said nothing, because he couldn't think of anything, and Pooh said nothing, because he was thinking of a poem. And when he had thought of it he began:

What shall we do about poor little Tigger?
If he never eats nothing he'll never get bigger.
He doesn't like honey and haycorns and thistles
Because of the taste and because of the bristles.
And all the good things which an animal likes
Have the wrong sort of swallow or too many spikes.

"He's quite big enough anyhow," said Piglet.

"He isn't *really* very big."

"Well, he *seems* so."

Pooh was thoughful when he heard this, and then he murmured to himself:

But whatever his weight in pounds, shillings, and ounces,
He always seems bigger because of his bounces.

"And that's the whole poem," he said. "Do you like it, Piglet?"

"All except the shillings," said Piglet. "I don't think they ought to be there."

"They wanted to come in after the pounds," explained Pooh, "so I let them. It is the best way to write poetry, letting things come."

"Oh, I didn't know," said Piglet.

. . . . .

Tigger had been bouncing in front of them all this time, turning round every now and then to ask, "Is this the way?"—and now at last they came in sight of Kanga's house, and there was Christopher Robin. Tigger rushed up to him.

"Oh, there you are, Tigger!" said Christopher Robin. "I knew you'd be somewhere."

"I've been finding things in the Forest," said Tigger importantly. "I've found a pooh and a piglet and an eeyore, but I can't find any breakfast."

Pooh and Piglet came up and hugged Christopher Robin, and explained what had been happening.

"Don't *you* know what Tiggers like?" asked Pooh.

"I expect if I thought very hard I should," said Christopher Robin, "But I *thought* Tigger knew."

"I do," said Tigger. "Everything there is in the world except honey and haycorns and—what were those hot things called?"

"Thistles."

"Yes, and those."

"Oh, well then, Kanga can give you some breakfast."

So they went into Kanga's house, and when Roo had said, "Hallo, Pooh," and "Hallo, Piglet" once, and "Hallo, Tigger" twice, because he had never said it before and it sounded funny, they told Kanga what they wanted, and Kanga said very kindly, "Well, look in my cupboard, Tigger dear, and see what you'd like." Because she knew at once that, however big Tigger seemed to be, he wanted as much kindness as Roo.

"Shall I look, too?" said Pooh, who was beginning to feel a little eleven o'clockish. And he found a small tin of condensed milk, and something seemed to tell him that Tiggers didn't like this, so he took it into a corner by itself, and went with it to see that nobody interrupted it.

But the more Tigger put his nose into this and his paw into that, the more things he found which Tiggers didn't like. And when he had found everything in the cupboard, and couldn't eat any of it, he said to Kanga, "What happens now?"

But Kanga and Christopher Robin and Piglet were all standing round Roo, watching him have his Extract of Malt. And Roo was saying, "Must I?" and Kanga was saying "Now, Roo, dear, you remember what you promised."

"What is it?" whispered Tigger to Piglet.

"His Strengthening Medicine," said Piglet. "He hates it."

So Tigger came closer, and he leant over the back of Roo's chair, and suddenly he put out his tongue, and took one large golollop, and, with a sudden jump of surprise, Kanga said, "Oh!" and then clutched at the spoon again just as it was disappearing, and pulled it safely back out of Tigger's mouth. But the Extract of Malt had gone.

"Tigger *dear!*" said Kanga.

"He's taken my medicine, he's taken my medicine, he's taken my medicine!" sang Roo happily, thinking it was a tremendous joke.

Then Tigger looked up at the ceiling, and closed his eyes, and his tongue went round and round his chops, in case he had left any outside, and a peaceful smile came over his face as he said, "So *that's* what Tiggers like!"

·   ·   ·   ·   ·

Which explains why he always lived at Kanga's house afterwards, and had Extract of Malt for breakfast, dinner, and tea.

And sometimes, when Kanga thought he wanted strengthening, he had a spoonful or two of Roo's breakfast after meals as medicine.

"But I think," said Piglet to Pooh, "that he's been strengthened quite enough."

## HIDING[1]

### Dorothy Aldis

*Children so universally love hide-and-seek that they enjoy playing this little poem and thinking of many other unusual places to hide.*

I'm hiding, I'm hiding,
And no one knows where;
For all they can see is my
Toes and my hair.

And I just heard my father
Say to my mother—
"But, darling, he must be
Somewhere or other;

"Have you looked in the ink well?"
And Mother said, "Where?"
"In the INK WELL," said Father.  But
I was not there.

Then, "Wait!" cried my mother—
"I think that I see
Him under the carpet."  But
It was not me.

"Inside the mirror's
A pretty good place,"
Said Father and looked, but saw
Only his face.

[1] From *Everything and Anything* by Dorothy Aldis.  Copyright 1925, 1926, 1927, by Dorothy Aldis.  Courtesy of G. P. Putnam's Sons.

"We've hunted," sighed Mother
"As hard as we could
And I AM so afraid that we've
Lost him for good."

Then I laughed out aloud
And wiggled my toes
And Father said—"Look, dear,
I wonder if those

Toes could be Benny's.
There are ten of them. See?"
And they WERE so surprised to find
Out it was me!


## HOW THE ROBIN'S BREAST BECAME RED[1]

### Flora J. Cooke

*Here is an Indian myth worth pantomiming with music.*

Long ago in the far North, where it is very cold, there was only one fire. A hunter and his little son took care of this fire and kept it burning day and night. They knew that if the fire went out the people would freeze and the white bear would have the Northland all to himself.

One day the hunter became ill and his son had all the work to do. For many days and nights he bravely took care of his father and kept the fire burning.

The great white bear was always hiding near, watching the fire. He longed to put it out, but he did not dare, for he feared the hunter's arrows. When he saw how tired and sleepy the little boy was, he came closer to the fire and laughed wickedly to himself.

One night the poor boy grew so tired that he could keep awake no longer and fell asleep. Then the white bear ran as fast as he could and jumped upon the fire with his wet feet, and rolled upon it until he thought it was all out. Then he trotted happily away to his cave among the icebergs.

[1] From *Nature Myths and Stories*, by Flora J. Cooke. Published by A. Flanagan. Permission from author.

But a little gray robin had been flying near, and had seen what the white bear was doing.

She was greatly worried when she thought that the fire might be out, but she was so little that she could do nothing but wait until the bear was out of sight.

Then she darted down swiftly and searched with her sharp little eyes until she found a tiny live coal. This she fanned patiently with her wings for a long time.

Her little breast was scorched red, but she did not stop until a fine red flame blazed up from the ashes.

Then she flew away to every hut in the Northland. Wherever she touched the ground a fire began to burn.

Soon, instead of one little fire, the whole north country was lighted up, so that people far to the south wondered at the beautiful flames of red and yellow light in the northern sky.

But when the white bear saw the fires, he went farther back into his cave among the icebergs and growled terribly. He knew that now there was no hope that he would ever have the Northland all to himself.

This is the reason that the people in the north country love the robin, and never tire of telling their children how its breast became red.


# THE CLOWN WHO FORGOT HOW TO LAUGH[1]

## Retold from a play by Eleanore Leuser

*This story will require little from the children in originating dialogue, but it will give them good experience in characterization. They should not memorize any lines, and they will probably enlarge on the conversations.*

The gay notes of a circus band drifted faintly through the warm June air from the big tent on the distant countryside. The afternoon performance was well under way, and about now the clowns were burlesquing the daring feats of the tightrope walkers.

But there was one clown missing from that light-hearted troupe— the littlest clown of all. Instead of tripping the big clowns, or innocently joggling the wire so that they would lose their balance,

[1] From PLAYS magazine, February, 1949. By permission of the editor, A. S. Burack.

he was sitting sadly on a log at the side of the road, his head in his hands.

Three little girls came running along just then, bouncing a ball to one another, laughing and talking, and sometimes squealing when they missed the ball.

"Look!" cried one of them as she caught sight of the Little Clown.

"Why, he must be a clown from the circus," said another. They all stopped to look at him.

"But he's not laughing and funny like other clowns," added the third girl. "What in the world is the matter with him?"

The first girl came up to the little fellow. "What's the matter, Little Clown?" she asked. "Why aren't you laughing like other clowns?"

The Little Clown stood up slowly. "I can't. I've forgotten how," he replied.

"Forgotten how!" they all exclaimed incredulously.

"Yes," he answered. "Suddenly, out of a clear sky, I forgot how to laugh. Now the circus doesn't want me any more. I haven't a job."

"Oh, you'll learn how again," said one sympathetically. "It's so easy just to laugh."

"Why don't you try reading comic books? They make me laugh," added another.

"I've read practically all the comic books in the world," answered the Little Clown, "and no laughter comes with them."

"You are stupid, Little Clown! Come on, girls," exclaimed one. "We can't help him."

"I'm glad *we* can still laugh!" said another. And, as the three ran down the road arm in arm, one of them giggled, "We even think it's funny that a clown has forgotten how to laugh!"

The Little Clown looked after them. "They don't appreciate how hard it is to be a clown," he thought. "And a clown without a job is tragic!"

Soon a fat man came along, carrying a long loaf of bread under one arm and a huge sausage under the other. He seemed to find a great deal of pleasure in taking a bite first from the bread, then the sausage. Seeing how sad the Little Clown looked, he asked what the trouble was.

"Why don't you try eating?" he asked when he had heard the Little Clown's story. "Look at me—I eat and eat and I'm perfectly happy. Try eating a thumping good meal and I'll guarantee you'll be so full of satisfaction that you can't help smiling." And he held out the sausage to the Little Clown.

The sad-faced clown thanked him but shook his head, and the fat man went off laughing. "Sorry, Little Clown, sorry! It's good sausage, too.—Well, all the more for me."

"I'm afraid nobody can show me how to laugh," said the Little Clown sadly, leaning against a tree. "I wish—I wonder what those boys are laughing at."

As the two boys came closer, all the time looking back and laughing, the Little Clown touched one of them on the shoulder and asked what he was laughing at. The boy pointed to someone who had fallen in a mud puddle; and then, surprised to see a clown here, and a sad one, at that, he said, "You're a queer sort of clown. Aren't you supposed to laugh at everything?"

"I used to," said the Little Clown wearily, "but now I can't find anything to laugh at."

"There must be something wrong with him," he said to the other boy. "Come on, let's go over and try to peek in the circus tent."

"Let's," was the reply. "Maybe we'll see some *real* clowns." And they hurried off toward the circus.

As the Little Clown stood there looking disconsolately after the boys, a tall, wise-looking man, coming from the opposite direction, almost bumped into him.

"Oh, I beg your pardon," he said solemnly. "I was so busy reading that I didn't notice you."

"Aren't you afraid you'll have an accident some day if you go along the road reading like that?" asked the Little Clown.

"That is the chief trouble with being a Wise Man," sighed the man. I have to read so much."

The Little Clown was delighted to hear that he was actually talking to a Wise Man, and he lost no time asking for his help. The man adjusted his spectacles, looked through his big book for information about laughing, and put his finger on the place.

"Here it is," he said. "Anyone may be taught to laugh. Simply practice steadily for fifteen minutes a day. There are many different kinds of laughs—hearty laughter—giggles—laughs of scorn—laughs of—' "

"I don t think I understand," said the Little Clown doubtfully. "How can you laugh without feeling like it?"

"It's very simple," replied the Wise Man. "Just go ahead and do it like this." He suddenly started to laugh and as suddenly turned it off.

"No, no!" cried the Little Clown. "When I was a clown I laughed only when I felt like it. But I felt like it most of the time. Then I could make other people laugh. Now I no longer laugh and I cannot be a clown."

"Why don't you stop thinking about yourself so much? That might help," said the Wise Man as he buried his nose in his book again and walked off down the road.

The Little Clown sank down on his log again, gloomily, as a sour-faced woman, meeting the Wise Man, turned aside just in time to avoid a collision. So her look was even more sour as she stopped to look at the sad little clown.

"Hmp! A clown without a smile on his face!" she said. "So you have your troubles, too, like the rest of us. Seems like a clown wouldn't have any—"

"When a clown can't laugh, he's in lots of trouble," said the Little Clown.

"Don't do much laughing myself—never could see it was worth while really," commented the woman still more sourly. "I say it's all foolishness. If you feel bad, you might as well let the world know about it."

"I don't know," replied the Little Clown doubtfully. "It seems as if the world is a nicer place when people smile. I know I've felt miserable since I've stopped laughing."

"Well, the world's a poor place to live in. That's my idea," said the woman, and she walked off, as sour-faced as she had come.

If the Little Clown had wanted to laugh before, he was now determined that he *must* find a way. How terrible it would be, he thought, if everybody went around with a face as long as hers!— What was it the Wise Man said? I wonder—

As he sat there thinking, a little girl came running down the road, crying. He jumped up and asked her why she was feeling badly.

"I've lost my money! I've looked everywhere!" she sobbed.

"Now that's too bad," said the Little Clown. "But it could be worse, couldn't it? Maybe you can get some more. How much did you lose?"

"You don't understand!" and she sobbed harder than ever. "It's too late to get any more. It was my money for the circus. I've looked so long that now the circus is most over and I won't get to see the clowns or anything."

"I see," answered the Little Clown slowly. Then, of a sudden, he said, "Listen: I'm a clown. I used to be in the circus. I can show you what clowns do if you'll only stop crying."

The child looked up at him doubtfully. "You aren't a very funny clown. What can you do?"

"I can stand on my head." And he did so. "I can turn hand-springs." And he did his best handsprings for her.

"That's not very funny," said the little girl, beginning to cry again.

"Please don't cry! See, I'll balance this stick on the end of my nose." And he tried so hard to be funny that gradually the child stopped crying and began to smile.

"I like that! Do it some more!" And she clapped her hands de-lightedly.

The Little Clown went through his whole repertoire of tricks. The more she laughed, the harder he tried, until finally he sat down on the ground all out of breath, and laughed himself.

"You're better than a whole circus, Mr. Clown! You're *so* funny!"

The Little Clown got up quickly. "You mean that?"

" 'Course. I don't even mind losing my money any more."

"Do you know something?" he said, excited. "You've taught me the whole secret of feeling like laughing." And then he told her how, when he was trying to stop her crying, the first thing he knew he was feeling good, and chuckling all over.

"Come on, let's go," he said, taking her hand.

"Where?"

"To the circus, of course. Even if it is almost over, we can get in the back entrance and I can introduce you to all the clowns."

"You mean I'll meet other clowns like you?"

"Sure, because now I can get my job back. I'll never forget how to laugh and be funny any more—all you have to do is just try to make the other fellow forget his troubles. Come on, let's go!"

And taking her hand, he hurried her off, still trying to balance the stick on the end of his nose.

82

# PADDY'S CHRISTMAS[1]

## Helen A. Monsell

*A story that charms children from the first grade to the fifth. The older the children, the more they develop the scenes with the human beings. The illustrations in the book of that name add much to their enjoyment.*

Once upon a time, in a blue-black cave in the heart of the woods, there lived a brown, bouncing bear cub named Paddy. His father and his mother and his uncle and his aunt lived there, too. All through the winter, though, these grownups just dozed and slept in the blue-black cave in the heart of the woods, leaving Paddy to tumble and frolic in front of the cave all by his lonesome self.

That is why—one clear, frosty morning in the winter, when the snow was on the treetops and the sun was making warm splotches on the ground where it shone through the woods—Paddy, with no one to watch him, slipped and tumbled and tumbled and slipped down the mountainside, until he almost rolled into a log cabin standing where the valley ended and the mountain began.

Now Paddy was a wise youngster. He knew he shouldn't let the human beings in that cabin see him—human beings do strange things to bouncing bear cubs when they get a chance. He stopped his slipping and tumbling in a hurry and hid in the bushes.

He had a suspicion he ought to turn around and go back home; but his father and his mother and his uncle and his aunt had told him so many things about human beings, and he was feeling so very gay and frolicsome and adventuresome. . . .

He decided to listen for a while. He did more—he saw and he felt and he smelled. When the sun began to go down and he was forced to climb and crawl back to the blue-black cave in the heart of the woods, he was so excited, he didn't know what to do.

He hurried into the blue-black cave and called his mother and his father and his uncle and his aunt. He bounced against them and tickled them and pulled their ears until they were really awake enough to know what he was talking about.

"What is Christmas?" he asked them excitedly. "It's pretty, it's lots of fun, and it makes you feel good from the inside out."

"I don't know," said Father, and rumbled back to sleep.

"I don't know," said Mother, and tumbled back to sleep.

"I don't know," said Uncle, and rumbled back to sleep.

"I don't know," said Aunt, and tumbled back to sleep.

Then Paddy waked them all up again, and he looked very determined as he did it.

"I've got to find out," he told them, "because I want one so bad. If you don't tell me, I'll go back down and ask the human beings themselves, and you ought to know what they do when they catch bouncing bear cubs. They'll take me, and keep me, and teach me how to dance."

This frightened the grown-up bears so that Uncle lumbered to his feet, and said he would go find out what Christmas was, and bring one back to Paddy. He lumbered down the mountainside to the little log cabin where the valley ended and the mountain began, and he listened and he watched, and he smelled and he felt. Then he came back to Paddy.

"Christmas," he told Paddy, "is holly and mistletoe, and running cedar, and things like that. You get them, and decorate, and sing songs about it, and that is Christmas."

Then all the grownups went back to sleep.

But Paddy went back in the woods, and he gathered holly and mistletoe and running cedar, and things like that, and hung them all around the walls of the blue-black cave. Then he sang songs such as he had heard the children sing in the cabin where the mountain ended and the valley began. For a time, he was very happy, but finally, he began to feel that something was wrong. He thought it all over, and at last he went back and wakened his father and his mother and his uncle and his aunt.

"Uncle Bear was wrong," he told them. "This isn't Christmas. There is something more, because when human beings have it, it's pretty, and it's loads of fun, and it makes you feel good from the inside out. The mistletoe and holly and things like that are pretty, but that's all. What is Christmas?"

This time it was Aunt Bear who said she would go find out. She rambled down the mountainside to the little log cabin where the mountain ended and the valley began, and she listened and she watched and she smelled and she felt. Then she came back to Paddy.

84

"Christmas," she told Paddy, "is getting presents. You get toys and good things to eat, and play and have a good time, and that is Christmas. Here, I brought you some presents on my way back."

She gave him a log full of honey, some big crinkly pine cones to play ball with, and a big blue ribbon to tie 'round his fur collar. Then all the grownups went back to sleep.

Paddy went back into the woods, and he dressed up in his ribbon and ate honey, and played with his pine cones. For a while, he was happy as the day was long, but he finally felt something was wrong. He thought and he thought about it, and at last he went back into the blue-black cave and waked them all up again.

"Aunt Bear was wrong," he told them. "This isn't Christmas. There is something more, because when human beings have it, it's pretty, and it's loads of fun, and it makes you feel good from the inside out. These presents are pretty, and they are loads of fun, but that is all. What is Christmas?"

Then Mother, who understood Paddy better than the others, said she would go find out. She scrunched off down the mountain-side to the little log cabin where the mountain ended and the valley began, and she listened and she watched and she smelled and she felt. Then she came back to Paddy.

"Christmas," she said, "is more than mistletoe and holly; it is more than presents, too. It is giving something to somebody else, and making them happy as well as yourself."

Then all the grownups went back to sleep.

Paddy went back to the woods, and he found a stick for his father to use when he climbed around the mountains. He hunted until he found a whole pawful of nuts for Uncle Bear, and some bright red feathers the cardinal had dropped for Aunt Bear. For his mother, he picked a bunch of stiff grasses and tied them into a broom with which she could sweep out the blue-black cave. Laden down with all these things, he went back to the cave and, for the last time, he waked his father and his mother and his uncle and his aunt. He gave them all his presents and then just lay back and rolled with delight when he saw how surprised and pleased they were.

"Merry Christmas!" cried Paddy, and he knew that it was, for it was pretty, and it was loads of fun, and it made him feel good from the inside out.

AND A MERRY CHRISTMAS TO ALL OF YOU, TOO.

# THE WONDERFUL WEAVER

## George Cooper

*A poem for which the mood can best be set by music.  One group especially enjoyed pantomiming it with the record of* Clair de Lune, *by Debussy.*

There's a wonderful weaver
    High up in the air,
And he weaves a white mantle
    For cold earth to wear,
With the wind for his shuttle,
    The cloud for his loom,
How he weaves!   How he weaves!
    In the light, in the gloom.


Oh! with finest of laces
    He decks bush and tree,
On the bare flinty meadows
    A cover lays he.
Then a quaint cap he places
    On pillar and post,
And he changes the pump
    To a grim, silent ghost.


But this wonderful weaver
    Grows weary at last,
And the shuttle lies idle
    That once flew so fast;
Then the sun peeps abroad
    On the work that is done;
And he smiles: "I'll unravel
    It all just for fun!"

# THE DWARF AND THE COBBLER'S SONS[1]

## Adapted from a Christmas Story by Mary Brecht Pulver

*If you can't stand on your head, it is quite possible that the rivers of goodies will pour out of your pockets while you are standing on your feet!*

A long, long time ago there lived a poor cobbler and his three sons, Franz, Friedrich, and Fritz. The cobbler had a hard time indeed, for people were poor. Few were the shoes to be mended, and fewer still were the people who could pay for the mending. With the winter's snows lying deep on the ground and the winter's winds howling, the cobbler was finding it hard to keep three boys a tiny bit warm. As for filling the stomachs of three hungry boys, the best that the cobbler could offer were chunks of boiled corn meal.

Now, as anyone can see, there seemed little chance for a gay and warm Christmas that year, and Franz, Fritz, and Friedrich could not help being sad. And so was the cobbler. But on Christmas Eve word came that a fine princess had damaged one of her best shoes while dancing—quite clumsily—and the cobbler was asked to come and repair it.

"My sons," said the cobbler in a great whirl of delight, "with the money I'll make from this night's work, we'll have a good Christmas dinner—at least, something much better than corn meal that's just boiled. So, though it's a long walk and a cold one, I'll go to the palace.

"I'll not be able to get home before morning, but you lie quiet and still in the bed and try to keep warm until I return. And let no one in while I am gone. Sometimes the wolves prowl on cold winter nights. Anyway, even to open the door will make you that much the colder."

And the three little boys promised to follow the cobbler's instructions.

The cobbler tucked them into bed as well as he could with one thin, ragged blanket, which was all that he owned, and gave each

[1] From *Tales That Nimko Told* by Mary Brecht Pulver. Copyright, 1925, Century Company. Reprinted by permission of the publishers, Appleton-Century-Crofts, Inc. Adaptation from *The Golden Christmas Book*, by permission of Simon & Schuster—Artists and Writers Guild.

of them a lump of corn meal, which was the last food he had to his name. Then away he went to the palace.

The three boys stayed in bed as they had promised, and they kept little Fritz in the middle, for he was the youngest and should be the warmest. Suddenly there was a loud knock on the door.

"Who is there?" cried Friedrich bravely.

"Dear me! Dear me!" cried a voice. "I am COLD! I am HUNGRY! Let me IN!"

"It is the wind," decided little Fritz.

"It is the wolf," decided Franz.

"Peek out the window and see," suggested Friedrich.

So Franz stole out of bed and peeked out the window. And all he could see through the frosty glass was a small peaked cap.

"Not the wolf," said Franz. "Not the wind. Neither of those wears a small peaked cap."

"It is someone who needs help," said Friedrich. "We must let him in. I am sure that Father would never want us to refuse help to some traveler."

So he hopped out of bed and opened the door.

Into the room came a dwarf—a tiny old man dressed from head to toe in bright, bright red. And almost to his toes hung a gray beard.

"Well!" he said. "So at last you got around to opening the door for me." And his eyes snapped angrily.

"Father told us not to open the door while he was gone," said Friedrich. "I am very sorry." The dwarf said nothing to this, but his eyes sparkled more angrily than ever.

"Well," he cried. "A fine warm bed and three big good-for-nothings in it. Out of my way, you loafers, I am cold and tired."

The little dwarf jumped into the middle of the bed and wrapped the only blanket snugly around him. Fritz, being only a baby, began to cry, but Friedrich said to him in a whisper, "Do not cry, little Fritz. He is old and much colder than we are. We must give our best to a tired traveler."

Just then the dwarf saw the chunks of corn meal. "See here," he said angrily, "will you lie in bed and fill your stomachs with fine, rich food while I have nothing at all to eat?" And the cross little dwarf snatched at Fritz's chunk of corn meal. But Fritz, being only a baby, began to cry.

"Excuse him, sir," said Franz. "Fritz is so very small! Won't you take mine instead?"

"And mine," offered Friedrich.

So the dwarf ate both chunks of corn meal and then tried to go to sleep. Suddenly he sat up. "There is not room in this bed for so many," he said. "You are crowding me. One of you will have to get out. Friedrich, you are the oldest. You shall go first. The others can take turns with you. Go to the corner and stand on your head."

Friedrich thought this a strange thing to ask. It was bad enough to be forced out of his own bed by an ill-natured stranger. But to be expected to stand on his head! However, the cobbler had taught him to obey older people. So Friedrich went to the corner. Down went his head and up went his heels. And when he got his heels up into the air, out of his pockets there rolled with thumps and bangs and pops and taps a river of nuts and apples and oranges. Hickory nuts, walnuts, chestnuts, butternuts, peanuts, apples by the dozens and apples by the hundreds, oranges big as balloons for eating, oranges small and juicy for squeezing.

"Well!" shouted the dwarf, and the angry snapping of his eyes didn't seem nearly so angry, "So you've been hiding treasures from me, have you? And the rest of you have treasures, too, I've no doubt. We'll see about this. Franz, you stand on your head."

Down went Franz's head and up went his heels. His pockets, too, seemed to be filled, for down on the floor, with thumps and bangs and pops and taps fell a river of bright candies—every kind you ever heard about in all this world. Chocolates by dozens, marshmallows by the cloudful, lemon-drops and gum-drops by hundreds.

The brothers laughed and shouted as they gathered up these treasures, and the little dwarf's eyes did not seem to snap angrily at all. "Little Fritz is next," he said.

Friedrich and Franz had to help Fritz, for he was much too small to be able to get his heels up in the air. So down went his head and up went his heels, with the help of Franz and Friedrich. And out of his pockets there rolled with thumps and bangs and pops and taps a river of money—gold pieces and silver pieces aplenty, enough for new warm blankets and new warm beds, new warm coats and new warm mittens. Enough for a fine turkey for Christmas and enough for good meat the whole year around.

Friedrich remembered his manners and stopped staring at the money. He knew that the dwarf had come to test them. He knew the dwarf had come to learn whether they would give what they had to a stranger who needed it—even a very cross and unpleasant stranger.

"Oh, thank you," began Friedrich, and then he stopped. For the little dwarf was gone. Not a sign could they see of his long gray beard or his red, red clothes. All that was left of the dwarf was his merry voice drifting in through the window.

"A merry, merry Christmas to the cobbler and his three fine sons!"

## THE PRINCESS WHO COULD NOT CRY[1]

### Rose Fyleman

*If you keep the climax a surprise by not showing the action that leads to tears, the play will be much more fun. Build suspense by having the court wait anxiously outside the nursery door while Marigold tries to make the Princess cry.*

There was once a little princess who could not cry.

That wouldn't have mattered so very much, but the trouble was that she laughed at everything, often on the most unsuitable occasions, and this was an extremely vexing and awkward habit, especially for a princess.

Her parents were very troubled about it, and they called in a wise old fairy in order to get her advice. She went into the matter thoroughly, and finally told them that if the princess could only once be made to cry, the spell would be broken for ever and she would thenceforward be just like other people.

This wasn't particularly helpful, but it gave them some hope, and they immediately set about the task of making the princess weep. Of course it was a rather difficult matter, because naturally they didn't want her to be really miserable, and they hardly knew how to begin. Finally they offered a reward of five hundred crowns to anybody who should succeed in making their daughter cry without doing her any harm.

Wise men came from all over the kingdom to see what they could do, and many things were tried, but all to no purpose.

One of them suggested that she should be shut up in a room by herself and fed on bread and water for a whole week. The queen

[1] From *The Rainbow Cat*, by Rose Fyleman. Copyright 1923 by Doubleday & Company, Inc.

thought this very cruel, but the king persuaded her to try it. She insisted, however, that at any rate it should be bread and *milk*. But every time they came to bring the princess her basin of bread and milk they found her laughing, and at the end of the week she was still as cheerful as ever.

"Look," she said, "my feet have grown so thin that I can't keep my slippers on." And she kicked her foot into the air and sent her slipper flying across the room, and laughed to see the scandalized face of the butler.

But her mother burst into tears. "My poor starved lamb," she said, "they shall not treat you so any longer." And she rushed into the kitchen and ordered soup and chicken and pink jelly to be sent up to the princess for her next meal.

Another wise man came who said that for six months he had been practicing pulling the most awful faces and making the most terrible noises imaginable, in order to be able to cure the princess. Children, he said, were so frightened by him that they had to be carried shrieking and howling from the room, and even grown-up people were so terrified that they wept aloud. He requested that he might be left alone with the princess; but the queen waited outside the door and listened.

She trembled with anxiety as she stood there, for the noises the wise man made were so bloodcurdling that she could hardly bear to hear them herself, and it seemed dreadful that her child should be left alone to endure such a trial. But in a few minutes she heard peals of laughter coming from inside the room, and presently the wise man opened the door. He was quite done up, and blue in the face, with the efforts he had been making. "It's no use," he said rather crossly. "No use at all," and went away looking much annoyed.

The princess came running out to her mother. "Oh, he *was* a funny man," she said. "Can't he come and do it again?"

Another wise man suggested that all her favourite toys should be broken up. But when he went into the nursery and began smashing her beautiful dolls and playthings, the princess clapped her hands and jumped about and laughed more heartily than ever.

"What fun, what fun," she said, and she too began throwing the things about. So that plan had to be given up also.

Other wise men came, but as many of their suggestions were cruel and unkind ones, naturally the king and queen would not hear of them, and at last they began to fear that nothing could be done.

Now in a small village on the borders of the king's great park, there lived a widow with her little daughter Marigold.

They were very poor, and the mother earned what she could by doing odd jobs of washing, sewing, or cleaning for her neighbors. But she fell ill, and poor Marigold was in great trouble, for she had no money to buy comforts for her mother.

Their little savings had to go for food to keep them alive, and every day these grew less and less.

Marigold knew all about the little princess of the castle. She had often heard of her, and had even seen her sometimes riding about the roads on her white pony. And one day as she was cooking the midday meal an idea came into her head.

As soon as dinner was over, she put on her hat and cloak and told her mother that she was going up to the king's palace to see if she could make the princess cry and so earn the five hundred crowns.

Her mother did her best to persuade her not to go.

"How can you hope to succeed," she said, "when so many clever people have tried and failed? You are my own dear little Marigold, but it is useless for you to attempt such a task. Give it up, my child."

But Marigold was determined, and when her mother saw this she said no more, but lay and watched her rather sadly as she set bravely off for the castle with her little basket over her arm.

When Marigold came to the castle gates she felt frightened. The gates were so big and she was so small. But she thought of her mother and of the five hundred crowns which would buy her everything she needed, and she stood on tiptoe on the top step and pulled the bell handle so hard that she was quite frightened at the noise it made.

A very grand footman opened the door, and when he saw Marigold standing there in her woolen frock and cloak with her little basket, he said, "Back entrance!" in a loud, cross voice, and shut the door in her face.

So she went round to the back entrance. This time the door was opened by a red-faced kitchen-maid. "We've no dripping to give away to-day," she said, and she too was about to shut the door.

But the queen happened to be in the kitchen giving her orders for the day, and she saw Marigold through the window and called to her.

"What is it, my child?" she asked, for Marigold stood there looking the picture of unhappiness.

"I've come to make the princess cry, please your Majesty," she said, and made a curtsey, for the queen looked very magnificent with her crown on her head and her lovely ermine train held up over her arm to keep it off the kitchen floor.

When the queen heard what Marigold had come for, she smiled and shook her head, for how could a little country girl hope to do what so many wise men had been unable to accomplish? But Marigold was so earnest and so sure that she could make the princess cry that at last the queen promised to let her attempt it.

"You won't hurt her?" she said. But she smiled as she said it. Marigold had such a kind little face she did not look as if she could hurt any one.

She was taken to the princess's apartments, and the queen went with her into the nursery and introduced her to the princess and explained why she had come.

The princess was delighted to see a nice little rosy-cheeked girl instead of the dull old men who so often came to visit her. The queen shut the door and left them alone together.

By this time the news of the little village girl who had come to make the princess cry, had spread all over the palace; and presently a whole crowd of people were standing anxiously waiting outside the nursery door.

"It's such nonsense," said the Chamberlain to the Prime Minister. "A village child. I don't suppose she's ever been outside the village."

"Quite ridiculous," whispered the ladies-in-waiting to the court pages. "Do you think she knows how to make a correct curtsey?"

At last the king and queen could stand the suspense no longer. They quietly opened the door and peeped in. And what do you think they saw? The princess, standing at the table in the middle of the room with Marigold's basket in front of her, busily peeling onions as hard as she could go, while the tears streamed down her face all the while. She was crying at last!

The king and queen rushed in and clasped her in their arms, onions and all. The ladies-in-waiting stood with their perfumed handkerchiefs pressed to their noses, the pages tittered, and the cook, who was standing at the bottom of the stairs, muttered to himself when he heard the news, "Well, *I* could have done that," while the Prime Minister rushed about the room with his wig on one side and shook everybody violently by the hand, exclaiming, "Wonderful, wonderful! And so simple! We must get out a proclamation at once. Where are my spectacles? Where is my pen?"

And so the Princess was cured, and from that time she became like everybody else and cried when she was unhappy and laughed when she was glad, though I am pleased to say that she always laughed a great deal more than she cried.

As for Marigold, she got her five hundred crowns, of course, and was able to give her mother everything she needed, so that she was soon quite well. The king and queen were most grateful, and often invited her up to the palace to play with their little daughter, and loaded her with presents.

Because she was sweet and modest she didn't get spoiled, but grew up charming, kind and beautiful. I did hear that in the end she married a king's son and that they had an onion for their crest, but I'm not at all sure about that.


## DOORBELLS[1]

### Rachel Field

*Few poems have such opportunity for character study as does this one. Children enjoy "trying on" each of the five characters by making up situations involving two or three of them. Often they create a complete story using all of the characters and perhaps several others.*

You never know with a doorbell
　　Who may be ringing it—
It may be Great-Aunt Cynthia
　　To spend the day and knit;
It may be a peddler with things to sell
　　(I'll buy some when I'm older),
Or the grocer's boy with his apron on
　　And a basket on his shoulder;
It may be the old umbrella-man
　　Giving his queer, cracked call,
Or a lady dressed in rustly silk,
　　With card-case and parasol.
Doorbells are like a magic game,
　　Or the grab-bag at a fair—
You never know when you hear one ring
　　Who may be waiting there!

[1] Used by permission of Arthur S. Pederson.

## "WHO'S THERE?"[1]

### Miriam Clark Potter

*All the stories in* Mrs. Goose of Animaltown *are full of delightful nonsense. This is one of several that are good fun to play.*

Mrs. Goose was just a goose—that's what she was. She lived in Animaltown, over the Faraway Hills.

One morning Mrs. Goose's friends Three-Ducks were down in Blue Pond taking a little early-morning swim. They were kicking their yellow feet in the water and waggling their tails, when along came Mrs. Goose, down Feather Lane and Quack Street.

"She's worried about something," said Three-Ducks to each other. "We can tell tell that, just from the way she puts her big red shoes down. And she's forgotten her hat."

When she came near to them, Mrs. Goose called out; "Hello, Three-Ducks. I am having a great deal of trouble with my closet—the little bedroom closet, where I keep my clothes."

"What's the matter with it?" asked Three-Ducks, turning their heads all together, opening and shutting their bills all together, just like one duck.

Mrs. Goose said, stepping down to the edge of the water; "I think there's something *in* it."

"Of course there's something in your closet," Three-Ducks told her. "A lot of things. Your shoes—your dresses—your old gray wrapper—all your hats—"

"Oh, I don't mean clothes." Mrs. Goose waited a minute, and then she said, in a low voice; "I think there's something else in it—something *alive.*"

Three-Ducks blinked their bright eyes at her, and turned their heads this way and that—three eyes in a row on one side, and then three eyes in a row on the other.

"What makes you think *that?*" they asked, after a while.

"When I opened the door to take out my hat, something in the corner, way back in the dark, where I keep my shoes said, 'Trrrr. Brrrrr.' Like that. Very low."

"What did you do?" asked Three-Ducks.

[1] Reprinted by permission of the publishers, J. B. Lippincott Company, from *Mrs. Goose of Animaltown* by Miriam Clark Potter. Copyright 1937, 1938, 1939, by Miriam Clark Potter.

"I shut the door and locked it, and said, 'Come out of there'."

"But it couldn't come out if the door was locked," said Three-Ducks.

"That's so. I didn't think of that. Well, anyway, I have it all shut up in the closet," said Mrs. Goose. "Tight."

"What are you going to do now?" Three-Ducks asked her.

"I want you to come back to my house and help me chase it out," she told them. "You'd better bring your broom—and your fire poker—and your big feather duster. Because whatever it is may be very big and dangerous."

Three-Ducks came out of the pond, all together, and stood shaking the water off their smooth white backs. Little shining beads of water flew through the air, and some of them hit Mrs. Goose on her worried feather head.

"Oh, do come on," she told Three-Ducks. "Help me! Go on and get your things."

"What are you going to use, yourself, to help chase with?" Three-Ducks asked her.

"Oh, I'll find something. I have an old fish-pole in the corner by the stove."

"Well, all right, we'll come," said Three-Ducks, and they got the broom and the poker and the feather duster.

When Mrs. Squirrel saw them all going by like that, from her little house on Swishtail Avenue, she called across to them: "What's the matter? What's up?"

"We're going to Mrs. Goose's house to help her. She thinks there's something in her closet," Three-Ducks called back.

"What makes her think that?"

"Because when she opened the door to get her hat out, something said 'Trrrrr. Brrrrr.' Very low."

"Maybe it's out now," said Mrs. Squirrel, coming over to them.

"Oh no," Mrs. Goose told her. "I locked it in, just to be sure."

Then along came the Black Cat from Green Street, carrying a shovel. "Hello," he said. "Where are you all going?"

"To Mrs. Goose's house. She's got something alive in her closet. Come and help us chase it out."

"Oh, all right," said Black Cat. "I was going to dig worms—but never mind."

So they all went to Mrs. Goose's house.

She opened her little front door.

"Now see," she said. "There's my closet—locked—and there's something in it."

They all stood and looked and listened, and after a while Black Cat said, "How do you know there's something in it?"

"Because when I opened the door to get out my shoes, something way back in the dark corner, where I keep my hat, said, 'Trrrrr. Brrrrr.' Just like that!"

"Well, there's nothing there now," said Black Cat. "I have very sharp ears; I don't hear anything."

"Maybe it's asleep," said Three-Ducks.

"Open the door, Mrs. Goose." Mrs. Squirrel waved her paw. "Maybe it will wake up and run out."

"No, indeed," said Mrs. Goose, shaking her tail. "Three-Ducks are going to open the door, aren't you, Three-Ducks?"

"No, we are not," Three-Ducks looked very firm. "We think Mrs. Squirrel is going to do that. Didn't you say you were, Mrs. Squirrel?"

"No, I didn't say so. I think you heard Black Cat say *he* was going to open the door."

"No, you didn't hear *me*," said Black Cat, "because I didn't say so. It's not my door. It's not my closet. It's not my something-in-the-dark-corner. All these things are in Mrs. Goose's house, so *she* should open the door."

"Yes, that's so," said all the other animals.

Mrs. Goose blinked. "If I just had something to whack with, like a broom or a poker or a duster or a shovel," she told them. "I'd knock on the door and say, 'Who's there?' But I haven't anything. *You* have!"

"You said you had a fishpole in the corner by the stove," Three-Ducks reminded her. "Go and get that," said the Black Cat from Green Street.

"Oh, all right," said Mrs. Goose. Soon she came slowly plopping back with it. "Good," her friends told her. "Now get to work."

So Mrs. Goose tapped on the door, with the fishpole. "Who's there?" she asked, very softly.

"Harder," said Three-Ducks. "Knock with it. Don't just *tap*."

So Mrs. Goose gave a tremendous whack, and there was a muffled noise, way in the back of the closet.

Three-Ducks and Black Cat and Mrs. Squirrel all got up on the bed.

"Whatever it is has eaten your dresses," said Black Cat. *"That* voice sounded all full of cloth."

"Now open the door, Mrs. Goose," Three-Ducks told her. "That's the thing to do."

But Mrs. Goose just stood there, holding the fishpole.

"Well, we can't stay *here* all day," said Black Cat. "I've got to go and dig worms. What time is it?"

They all looked around for the clock, but there wasn't any.

"That's funny," said Mrs. Goose, stretching her long neck this way and that. "I always keep my little clock on the bureau—but today it's gone."

They all looked at each other.

"Whatever it is in there has stolen it," said Three-Ducks.

But Mrs. Goose was too excited to say anything. She just gulped.

"Hurry up and get it over," said Mrs. Squirrel. "Open the door."

Then Mrs. Goose went to the closet. She shut her eyes and put her feet down hard, and very softly she unlocked the door, very slowly she opened it.

But nothing came out.

"Well, one of us has got to find out what's in there," said Black Cat. "We certainly heard a funny noise, didn't we?"

"You have the longest neck, Mrs. Goose," said Mrs. Squirrel. "You are the one to look inside."

"If you'll get a candle and stand near me," said Mrs. Goose. "I don't know what to expect."

Black Cat lit the candle, and held it up. Mrs. Goose put her head inside the closet, and called, "Who's there?"

Queer shadows danced around the candle flame. There was nothing in the front of the closet—nothing at the sides—but way back among the shoes, there was a rolled-up ball of cloth.

"My old gray wrapper," said Mrs. Goose.

"I'll poke at it with my shovel," said Black Cat.

As soon as he did that there was a funny little sound of wrapped-up bells—a little noise like "Trrrrr. Brrrrr."

They all jumped on the bed.

"Oh, *now* I know what it is!" said Mrs. Goose.

"What?" asked Three-Ducks.

"It's my little old clock," said Mrs. Goose looking very pleased. "I set the alarm, so I could get up very early and make peach jam. Then I decided *not* to make peach jam. So I wrapped up the clock and put it in the back of the closet, where my shoes are, so I wouldn't hear it."

"And it didn't go off," said Three-Ducks. "But when you threw your door open, with quite a jerk, it was all wound up, and it made a little whirring noise."

"And when you knocked on the door it did, and when we poked it," said Black Cat.

"Well, it's all explained now," sighed Mrs. Squirrel. "I must hurry back to my baking."

"And we must finish our swim," said Three-Ducks.

"And I must go and dig worms," said Black Cat.

"Thank you all," said Mrs. Goose, putting her fishpole in the corner, and her clock on the bureau. "I wish I *had* made peach jam, so I could give you some.

"Never mind," said her friends, as they trooped off. "We were glad to help you." And as they went down Feather Lane they said to each other; "Mrs. Goose is just a goose, that's what she is—but she is our good friend, too."

And back in her little home Mrs. Goose took her hat out of the closet and put it on her head; but by that time she had forgotten where she had wanted to go, anyway, so she took it off again.

## THE ELF SINGING

### William Allingham

*A delightful poem for choric speaking combined with pantomime. While most of the children say the poem—some of it "line-a-child"— others pantomime the exciting action of the Elf, the Wizard, and the Mole!*

An Elf sat on a twig,
He was not very big,
He sang a little song,
He did not think it wrong;
But he was on a Wizard's ground,
Who hated all sweet sound.

Elf, Elf,
Take care of yourself,
He's coming behind you,
To seize you and bind you
And stifle your song.
The Wizard! the Wizard!
He changes his shape
In crawling along.
An ugly old ape,
A poisonous lizard,
A spotted spider,
A wormy glider,
The Wizard! the Wizard!
He's up on the bough,
He'll bite through your gizzard,
He's close to you now!

The Elf went on with his song
It grew more clear and strong,
It lifted him into air,
He floated singing away
With rainbows in his hair,
While the Wizard-worm from his creep
Made a sudden leap,
Fell down into a hole,
And, ere his magic word he could say,
Was eaten up by a Mole.

## ROADS[1]

### Rachel Field

*Imagination is stirred by this poem! What kind of a road shall
we plan? Where does it start? Where does it go? Is it straight or
uphill and downhill? Can we picture the witch's house? Miss Pim's
shop? The great, dark cave? What shall we have happen? Who
is going along this road?*

[1] Reprinted from *Pointed People* by Rachel Field. Copyright 1924 by
Yale University Press. Permission from Arthur S. Pederson.

A road might lead to anywhere—
  To harbor towns and quays,
Or to a witch's pointed house
  Hidden by bristly trees.
It might lead past the tailor's door,
  Where he sews with needle and thread,
Or by Miss Pim the milliner's
  With her hats for every head.
It might be a road to a great, dark cave
  With treasure and gold piled high,
Or a road with a mountain tied to its end,
  Blue-humped against the sky.
Oh, a road might lead you anywhere—
  To Mexico or Maine.
But then, it might just fool you, and—
  Lead you back home again!

## GENERAL STORE[1]

### Rachel Field

*What kind of a store is this? How is it different from modern
stores? What kinds of people shall we have as customers?*

Some day I'm going to have a store
With a tinkly bell hung over the door,
With real glass cases and counters wide
And drawers all spilly with things inside.
There'll be a little of everything:
Bolts of calico; balls of string;
Jars of peppermint; tins of tea;
Pots and kettles and crockery;
Seeds in packets; scissors bright;
Kegs of sugar, brown and white;
Sarsaparilla for picnic lunches,
Bananas and rubber boots in bunches.
I'll fix the window and dust each shelf,
And take the money in all myself.
It will be my store and I will say:
"What can I do for you today?"

[1] From *Taxis and Toadstools* by Rachel Field. Copyright 1926 by Double-
.y & Company. Permission from Arthur S. Pederson.

# THE HILLMAN AND THE HOUSEWIFE

## Juliana H. Ewing

It is well known that the Good People cannot abide meanness. They like to be liberally dealt with when they beg or borrow of the human race; and, on the other hand, to those who come to them in need, they are invariably generous.

Now there once lived a certain Housewife who had a sharp eye to her own interests in temporal matters, and gave alms of what she had no use for, for the good of her soul. One day a Hillman knocked at her door.

"Can you lend us a saucepan, good Mother?" said he. "There's a wedding in the hill, and all pots are in use."

"Is he to have one?" asked the servant lass who had opened the door.

"Aye, to be sure," answered the Housewife. "One must be neighborly."

But when the maid was taking a saucepan from the shelf, she pinched her arm, and whispered sharply—"Not that, you slut! Get the old one out of the cupboard. It leaks, and the Hillmen are so neat, and such nimble workers, that they are sure to mend it before they send it home. So one obliges the Good People, and saves sixpence in tinkering. But you'll never learn to be notable whilst your head is on your shoulders."

Thus reproached, the maid fetched the saucepan, which had been laid by till the tinker's next visit, and gave it to the dwarf, who thanked her and went away.

In due time the saucepan was returned, and, as the Housewife had foreseen, it was neatly mended and ready for use.

At supper-time the maid filled the pan with milk, and set it on the fire for the children's supper. But in a few minutes the milk was so burnt and smoked that no one could touch it, and even the pigs refused the wash into which it was thrown.

"Ah, good-for-nothing hussy!" cried the Housewife, as she refilled the pan herself, "you would ruin the richest with your carelessness. There's a whole quart of good milk wasted at once!"

"*And that's twopence,*" cried a voice which seemed to come from the chimney, in a whining tone, like some nattering, discontented old body going over her grievances.

The Housewife had not left the saucepan for two minutes, when the milk boiled over, and it was all burnt and smoked as before.

"The pan must be dirty," muttered the good woman in great vexation; "and there are two full quarts of milk as good as thrown to the dogs."

"*And that's fourpence,*" added the voice in the chimney.

After a thorough cleaning, the saucepan was once more filled and set on the fire, but with no better success. The milk was hopelessly spoilt, and the Housewife shed tears of vexation at the waste, crying, "Never before did such a thing befall me since I kept house! Three quarts of new milk burnt for one meal!"

"*And that's sixpence,*" cried the voice from the chimney. "*You didn't save the tinkering after all, Mother!*"

With which the Hillman himself came tumbling down the chimney and went off laughing through the door

But thenceforward the saucepan was as good as any other.


## THE TOWN MOUSE AND THE COUNTRY MOUSE

### Aesop

*One of the many stories teaching appreciation of what one has. More characters can be introduced.*

Now you must know that a Town Mouse once upon a time went on a visit to his cousin in the country. He was rough and ready, this cousin, but he loved his town friend and made him heartily welcome. Beans and bacon, cheese and bread, were all he had to offer, but he offered them freely.

The Town Mouse rather turned up his long nose at this country fare, and said: "I cannot understand, cousin, how you can put up with such poor food as this, but of course you cannot expect anything better in the country; come with me and I will show you how to live. When you have been in town a week you will wonder how you could ever have stood a country life."

No sooner said than done. The two mice set off for the town and arrived at the Town Mouse's residence late at night.

"You will want some refreshment after our long journey," said the polite Town Mouse, and took his friend into the grand dining room.

There they found the remains of a fine feast, and soon the two mice were eating up jellies and cake and all that was nice.

Suddenly they heard growling and barking. "What is that?" said the Country Mouse.

"It is only the dogs of the house," answered the other.

"Only!" said the Country Mouse. "I do not like that music at my dinner."

Just at that moment the door flew open, in came two huge mastiffs, and the two mice had to scamper down and run off.

"Good-by, my cousin," said the Country Mouse.

"What! going so soon?" said the other.

"Yes," he replied, "better beans and bacon in peace than cakes and ale in fear."

## THE OLD MARKET WOMAN

*Though this is a Mother Goose rhyme, its humor is not appreciated until children are eight or nine. In playing the market scene, and the highway with people passing, they can think of all types of village folk to characterize.*

There was an old woman, as I've heard tell,
She went to market her eggs for to sell;
She went to market all on a market day,
And she fell asleep on the king's highway.

There came a peddler whose name was Stout,
He cut her petticoats all round about;
He cut her petticoats up to the knees,
Which made the old woman shiver and freeze.

When this little old woman first did wake,
She began to shiver and she began to shake;
She began to wonder and she began to cry,
"O! deary, deary me, this is none of I!"

"But if it be I as I hope it be,
I've a little dog at home, and he'll know me;
If it be I, he'll wag his little tail,
And if it be not I, he'll loudly bark and wail!"

Home went the little woman all in the dark,
Up got the little dog, and he began to bark;
He began to bark; so she began to cry,
"O! deary, deary me, this is none of I!"

# TAPER TOM[1]

## Retold by Gudrun Thorne-Thomsen

*A good version of a favorite old folktale. All children can understand the simple characters and enjoy the fun of the action that accompanies Tom's remark, "If you want to come along, hang on!"*

Once on a time there was a King who had a daughter, and she was so lovely that her good looks were well known far and near. But she was so sad and serious she could never be got to laugh, and besides, she was so high and mighty that she said "No" to all who came to woo her. She would have none of them, were they ever so grand—lords or princes,—it was all the same.

The King had long ago become tired of this, for he thought she might just as well marry; she, too, like all other people. There was no use in waiting; she was quite old enough, nor would she be any richer, for she was to have half the kingdom,—that came to her as her mother's heir.

So he had word sent throughout the kingdom, that anyone who could get his daughter to laugh should have her for his wife and half the kingdom besides. But, if there was anyone who tried and could not, he was to have a sound thrashing. And sure it was that there were many sore backs in that kingdom, for lovers and wooers came from north and south, and east and west, thinking it nothing at all to make a King's daughter laugh. And gay fellows they were, some of them too, but for all their tricks and capers there sat the Princess, just as sad and serious as she had been before.

Now, not far from the palace lived a man who had three sons, and they, too, had heard how the King had given it out that the man who could make the Princess laugh was to have her to wife and half the kingdom.

The eldest was for setting off first. So he strode off, and when he came to the King's grange, he told the King he would be glad to try to make the Princess laugh.

"All very well, my man," said the King, "but it's sure to be of no use, for so many have been here and tried. My daughter is so sorrowful it's no use trying, and it's not my wish that anyone should come to grief."

[1] From Gudrun Thorne-Thomsen's *East o' the Sun and West o' the Moon*. Reproduced by special permission of the publisher, Row, Peterson & Co.

But the lad thought he would like to try. It couldn't be such a very hard thing for him to get the Princess to laugh, for so many had laughed at him, both gentle and simple, when he enlisted for a soldier and was drilled by Corporal Jack.

So he went off to the courtyard, under the Princess's window, and began to go through his drill as Corporal Jack had taught him. But it was no good, the Princess was just as sad and serious and did not so much as smile at him once. So they took him and thrashed him well, and sent him home again.

Well, he had hardly got home before his second brother wanted to set off. He was a schoolmaster, and the funniest figure one ever laid eyes upon; he was lopsided, for he had one leg shorter than the other, and one moment he was as little as a boy, and in another, when he stood on his long leg, he was as tall and long as a Troll. Besides this he was a powerful preacher.

So when he came to the king's palace, and said he wished to make the Princess laugh, the King thought it might not be so unlikely after all. "But mercy on you," he said, "if you don't make her laugh. We are for laying it on harder and harder for every one that fails."

Then the schoolmaster strode off to the courtyard, and put himself before the Princess's window, and read and preached like seven parsons, and sang and chanted like seven clerks, as loud as all the parsons and clerks in the country round.

The King laughed loud at him, and the Princess almost smiled a little, but then became as sad and serious as ever, and so it fared no better with Paul, the schoolmaster, than with Peter the soldier—for you must know one was called Peter and the other Paul. So they took him and flogged him well, and then they sent him home again.

Then the youngest, whose name was Taper Tom, was all for setting out. But his brothers laughed and jeered at him, and showed him their sore backs, and his father said it was no use for him to go for he had no sense. Was it not true that he neither knew anything nor could do anything? There he sat in the hearth, like a cat, and grubbed in the ashes and split tapers. That was why they called him "Taper Tom." But Taper Tom would not give in, and so they got tired of his growling; and at last he, too, got leave to go to the king's palace to try his luck.

When he got there he did not say that he wished to try to make the Princess laugh, but asked if he could get work there. No, they had no place for him, but for all that Taper Tom would not give up. In such a big palace they must want someone to carry wood and water for the kitchen maid,—that was what he said. And the king thought it might very well be, for he, too, got tired of his teasing. In the end Taper Tom stayed there to carry wood and water for the kitchen maid.

So one day, when he was going to fetch water from the brook, he set eyes upon a big fish which lay under an old fir stump, where the water had eaten into the bank, and he put his bucket softly under the fish and caught it. But as he was going home to the grange he met an old woman who led a golden goose by a string.

"Good-day, godmother," said Taper Tom, "that's a pretty bird you have, and what fine feathers! If one only had such feathers one might leave off splitting fir tapers."

The goody was just as pleased with the fish Tom had in his bucket and said, if he would give her the fish, he might have the golden goose. And it was such a curious goose. When any one touched it he stuck fast to it, if Tom only said, "If you want to come along, hang on." Of course, Taper Tom was willing enough to make the exchange. "A bird is as good as a fish any day," he said to himself, "and, if it's such a bird as you say, I can use it as a fish hook." That was what he said to the goody, and he was much pleased with the goose.

Now, he had not gone far before he met another old woman. As soon as she saw the lovely golden goose she spoke prettily, and coaxed and begged Tom to give her leave to stroke his lovely golden goose.

"With all my heart," said Taper Tom, and just as she stroked the goose he said, "If you want to come along, hang on."

The goody pulled and tore, but she was forced to hang on whether she would or not, and Taper Tom went on as though he alone were with the golden goose.

When he had gone a bit farther, he met a man who had had a quarrel with the old woman for a trick she had played him. So, when he saw how hard she struggled and strove to get free, and how fast she stuck, he thought he would just pay her off the old grudge, and so he gave her a kick with his foot.

"If you want to come along, hang on!" called out Tom, and then the old man had to hop along on one leg, whether he would or not. When he tore and tugged and tried to get loose—it was still worse for him, for he all but fell flat on his back every step he took.

In this way they went on a good bit till they had nearly reached the King's palace.

There they met the King's smith, who was going to the smithy, and had a great pair of tongs in his hand. Now you must know this smith was a merry fellow, full of both tricks and pranks, and when he saw this string come hobbling and limping along, he laughed so that he was almost bent double. Then he bawled out, "Surely this is a new flock of geese the Princess is going to have—Ah, here is the gander that toddles in front. Goosey! goosey! goosey!" he called, and with that he threw his hands about as though he were scattering corn for the geese.

But the flock never stopped—on it went and all that the goody and the man did was to look daggers at the smith for making fun of them. Then the smith went on:

"It would be fine fun to see if I could hold the whole flock, so many as they are," for he was a stout strong fellow. So he took hold with his big tongs by the old man's coat tail, and the man all the while screeched and wriggled. But Taper Tom only said:

"If you want to come along, hang on!" So the smith had to go along too. He bent his back and stuck his heels into the ground and tried to get loose, but it was all no good. He stuck fast, as though he had been screwed tight with his own vise, and whether he would or not, he had to dance along with the rest.

So, when they came near to the King's palace, the dog ran out and began to bark as though they were wolves and beggars. And when the Princess, looking out of the window to see what was the matter, set eyes on this strange pack, she laughed softly to herself. But Taper Tom was not content with that:

"Bide a bit," he said, "she will soon have to make a noise." And as he said that he turned off with his band to the back of the palace.

When they passed by the kitchen the door stood open, and the cook was just stirring the porridge. But when she saw Taper Tom and his pack she came running out at the door, with her broom in one hand and a ladle full of smoking porridge in the other, and she laughed as though her sides would split. And when she saw the smith there too, she bent double and went off again in a loud peal of laughter. But when she had had her laugh out, she too thought the golden goose so lovely she must just stroke it.

"Taper Tom! Taper Tom!" she called out, and came running out with the ladle of porridge in her fist, "Give me leave to pet that pretty bird of yours?"

"Better come and pet me," said the smith. But when the cook heard that she got angry.

"What is that you say?" she cried and gave the smith a box on his ears with the ladle.

"If you want to come along, hang on," said Taper Tom. So she stuck fast too, and for all her tricks and plunges, and all her scolding and screaming, and all her riving and striving, she too had to limp along with them.

Soon the whole company came under the Princess's window. There she stood waiting for them. And when she saw they had taken the cook too, with her ladle and broom, she opened her mouth wide, and laughed so loud that the King had to hold her upright.

So Taper Tom got the Princess and half the kingdom, and they say he kept her in high spirits with his tricks and pranks till the end of her days.


## THE THREE WISHES[1]

### Retold by Olive Beaupre Miller

*A good version of this old story which has long been a favorite for dramatization. If desirable to add characters, what part might they play in the story?*

One winter's night many years ago, an old man, named Pedro, and his wife, Joanna, sat by their cozy fire, talking to one another, in a little old village in Spain. Now Pedro was comfortably well off in the goods of this world, but instead of giving thanks to God for the benefits they enjoyed, he and his wife spent all their time in wishing for the good things possessed by their neighbors.

"Bah!" cried Pedro. "This wretched little hut of ours is only fit to house a donkey! Would that we owned the fine house and farm of our neighbor, Diego!"

"Aye! Diego's house and farm are well enough and better than ours by far," answered Joanna. "Still I could wish to have such a mansion as the grandees possess—such a one as that of Don Juan de la Rosa."

[1] From *My Book House.* Used by permission of the author, Olive Beaupré Miller, and the publishers, *The Book House for Children,* Chicago, Illinois.

"Then there's that old donkey of ours," went on Pedro sullenly. "Good for nothing—nothing at all. He cannot carry so much as an empty sack. How I should like to have for my own Diego's strong Andalusian mule!"

"O aye! Diego's mule is better than our donkey," said Joanna. "Yet, for me, I should like a fine white horse with trappings of scarlet and gold, like the one that bears Donna Isabella. It is strange how some people have only to wish for a thing in order to get it. I have never been in such luck. Would that we had only to speak to have our wishes come true!"

Scarcely were the words out of Joanna's mouth when lo! on the hearth before the old couple appeared a beautiful little lady. She was not more than eighteen inches high and her garments, that drifted lightly back and forth, were white and filmy and full of opal tints as though made of smoke, while a veil of the same airy stuff floated down from a crown of glowing sparks on her head. In her hand she bore a little gold wand, on the end of which was a single spark that glowed like a ruby.

"I am the Fairy Fortunata," said she from the midst of the rosy flames. "I have heard your complaints and am come to give you what you desire. Three wishes you shall have,—one for you, Joanna, —one for you, Pedro,—and the third you shall agree upon between you and I will grant it in person when I return at this time to-morrow."

So saying, the Fairy Fortunata sprang through the flames and disappeared in a cloud of smoke. Ah! but the old couple were delighted. Three wishes! Three wishes to come true! They began to think at once of what they most desired in all the world. Wishes came swarming to them as thick as bees to a hive. The old man would be content with such prosperity as his neighbor, the farmer Diego, enjoyed, but the old woman—ah! her desires flew high—a palace with domes and spires and cupolas, and floors tiled with sapphire, and walls and ceilings done with arabesques of crimson, blue and gold; colonnaded courtyards with fountains playing in the centre, and gardens and servants and what not besides! Well, so many were the desires that came crowding to the old couple, that they could not agree off-hand on just which three to wish for. So they determined to put off their decision until the next day and began talking of different things altogether. In a little while their conversation began to drift, as usual, to their wealthier neighbors whom they were forever envying.

"I dropped in at Diego's house this morning," said Pedro, "and they were making black puddings there in the kitchen. Um! but they smelled good—those puddings! Diego can buy the best of raisins and everything else. He does not have to put up with such poor stuff as we have to eat!"

"True! True!" said Joanna. "I wish I had one of Diego's puddings here this minute to roast on the ashes for supper!"

The words were not out of Joanna's mouth when there appeared on the ashes before her the most delicious black pudding that could possibly be imagined! The woman's eyes nearly started out of her head! But Pedro jumped up in a rage.

"You greedy creature!" he cried. "Through your gluttony you have used up one of our precious wishes! Good heavens, to wish for nothing more than a poor little pudding! It makes me wild! You're more stupid than a goose, and I wish the pudding were stuck fast to your nose!"

At that—whisk! there flew the black pudding and hung from the very place he had indicated. Then was the old man struck with horror, for shake her head as she might, Joanna could no more shake off the pudding than she could shake off her nose!

"See what you have done, evil tongue!" she wailed. "If I employed my wish badly, at least it injured no one but myself, but you—you—see how you have made use of your wish!"

Thereupon, the dog and cat, having sniffed the savory pudding, came leaping up and began springing and pawing, in hopes to get one little lick of that luscious morsel that was now become Dame Joanna's nose!

"Down! Down!" shrieked Joanna, as she wildly defended the part attacked. "I shall agree to nothing else for our third wish than that this miserable pudding be taken off my nose!"

"Wife, for heaven's sake!" cried Pedro, "don't ask that! What of the new farm I wanted?"

"I will never agree to wish for it!"

"But listen to reason! Think of the palace you desired, with domes and spires and cupolas, and floors tiled with sapphire, and walls and ceilings in arabesques of crimson, blue and gold!"

"It does not matter!"

"O my dear! let us wish at least for a fortune, and then you shall have a golden case set with all the jewels you please, to cover the pudding on your nose!"

"I will not hear of it!"

"Then, alas and alack, we shall be left just as we were before!"

"That is all I desire! I see now we were well enough off as we were!"

And for all that the man could say, nothing could alter his wife's determination. So at last they agreed, and when on the following night the Fairy rose from the flames and bade them tell her their third wish, they made answer:

"We wish only to be as we were before."

So that was the wish she granted.

## A LEGEND OF SPRING

### An old Indian tale retold by Geraldine Brain Siks

*The plan followed by the author in guiding children to drama-tize this story is given at the end of the tale.*

Blue Thunder was chief of an Indian tribe. He was deeply troubled. For many, many moons his tribe had seen no deer. No bear roamed the forest. Buffalo and antelope were nowhere to be found. Streams were frozen and fish were scarce. It was bitterly cold, and deep snow covered the ground. At last, with the beat of his drums, Blue Thunder called his tribe into council. (*An Indian drum is played.*)

Old Indians and braves and squaws left their wigwams. They gathered in a great circle around the council fire.

Blue Thunder spoke. "For many moons winter has been with us. We must call to Great Spirit Father to look upon our valley. We must call for sun to bring life to our hunting-grounds. We must call for winds and rains. Come, my brothers, we call to Great Spirit Father to help us." (*Drums.*)

Blue Thunder beat upon his drums. All of the Indians joined in a sun dance. Then they called for strong winds. Then they called for warm rains. When the drums were silent, the Indians sat in the council circle. They looked upward to the sky. Only dark clouds could be seen. They listened for the sound of winds. The valley was quiet and still.

The old chief studied his tribe. He knew that the Indians would not want to move their village, but he knew that their food was nearly gone. All of the Indians watched Blue Thunder closely

112

At last he sounded the hunting call. The braves knew that it was too cold for forest animals. They wondered why Blue Thunder was asking them to hunt in deep snows. Each young brave sat silently as he wondered what his brothers would do. Silently White Cloud, youngest of the braves, rose to his feet. He was strong and brave, and a good hunter. He moved to the old chief.

"Chief Blue Thunder," he said, "my bow is strong. My arrows are sharp. My moccasins are warm. I will hunt for food for my brothers. I will run swiftly through the snowy forests."

Blue Thunder raised his hands upward. "You are brave, White Cloud. Great Spirit Father will watch over you."

The other braves looked at one another. One by one they joined White Cloud. Soon many braves were ready to search for food for the tribe. Then once again Blue Thunder sounded the hunting call. White Cloud and the other braves ran swiftly into the forest while the rest of the tribe danced to the Great Spirit Father. They called for bear. They called for deer. They called for mighty buffalo. (Drum)

While the Indians were dancing, a large Golden Bird flew into the clearing. Blue Thunder silenced the drums. The old braves drew their bows and aimed at the bird. The Golden Bird darted higher and higher into the air.

Suddenly a loud shout sounded through the valley. It was the voice of White Cloud. He called to the Indians. "Kill not the Golden Bird," he cried. The old braves lowered their bows. Once more the Golden Bird flew near. White Cloud and the young braves ran swiftly to the council circle. White Cloud spoke: "Golden Bird comes from Great Spirit Father. Golden Bird flew from dark cave. Hark, Golden Bird brings message."

As soon as White Cloud had spoken, the beautiful, graceful bird flew around the council circle. When she saw that the Indians meant no harm, she flew down to the council fire. As her feet touched the snow, she instantly became a beautiful Indian maiden, dressed in a long golden robe. In her hands she carried a golden arrow.

The Indians were filled with great wonder as they watched the lovely maiden. The old chief raised his hand in welcome. "Golden Bird Maiden, welcome to our tribe. Welcome to our valley. We have little food in our wigwams. We will share it with Golden Bird Maiden."

"You are kind, Great Chief," the maiden said. "I come from Great Spirit Father. I bring a golden arrow. One of your braves will be chosen to shoot the golden arrow through dark clouds yonder. If he succeeds, spring will again come to your valley. If he fails, winter will be with you for many moons."

The Indians looked upward. The clouds were very high in the sky. Blue Thunder spoke. "Golden Maiden, we ask you to choose the young brave to shoot the golden arrow."

Silently the Golden Maiden moved around the circle. She looked closely at each brave. After she had circled the council fire, she went straight to White Cloud. She placed the golden arrow in his hands. "Shoot the arrow into dark clouds," she said clearly. "There is only one arrow, White Cloud."

White Cloud nodded slowly as he studied the golden arrow. He placed it carefully in his bow. Then he drew his bow with great force. Everyone watched in silence. White Cloud let the arrow fly. It rose so high into the clouds that it disappeared from sight. Some of the old braves grew fearful, but Golden Maiden, White Cloud, and Blue Thunder looked straight at the sky. Suddenly the golden sun burst through the black clouds, and bright sunlight shone over the valley.

Blue Thunder sounded the song of rejoicing. All of the Indians joined in a dance of Thanksgiving, for at last Spring had come to their valley.

*Before dramatizing this story, a general feeling for Indians was aroused by taking the children to a fine museum exhibit of Indian treasures. Afterward, they were encouraged to try sign language (pantomime) to convey meanings to others: signs of welcome; signs meaning I am hungry; I saw buffalo; I am going hunting, fishing; I am building a fire; I have a little papoose sister; white man comes; white man takes hunting grounds, etc.*

*Then the Indian drum was introduced. It was explained that the drum could speak to the Indians. It could mean raindrops, galloping horses, and many other things.*

*At this point the legend was introduced, as one that had been told to Indian boys and girls as they sat around the campfire at night; and as the story was told the drum was used at intervals to heighten its effect.*

*The children planned to have the wigwams in five different areas of the room. Before they played the story, they discussed and*

114

*then pantomimed the effect of the sun: flowers growing up from the ground, shady trees moving in the breeze, sunbeams shining from the sky.*

*The wind dance and the rain dance were motivated in a similar way. The Indians called in an eerie minor chant for the wind. They gave a feeling of gentle breezes, then a stronger wind as the old chief sounded his drum with more force. All of the braves joined the chief and beat upon make-believe drums (the floor) as the girls danced the graceful rain dance alone.*

## BEHIND THE WATERFALL[1]

### Winifred Welles

*Who is this little old woman? What do they find behind the door? Is the crystal city Fairyland? Storyland? The Land Where Wishes Come True? It is a poem to stir young imaginations. Soft music may intensify its mood and help the children to create a beautiful pantomime.*

A little old woman
In a thin white shawl,
Stept straight through the column
Of the silver waterfall,
As if the fall of water
Were not anything at all.
I saw her crook her finger,
I heard her sweetly call;
Over stones all green and glossy
I fled and did not fall;
I ran along the river
And through the waterfall,
And that heavy curve of water
Never hindered me at all.
The little old woman
In the thin white shawl
Took my hand and laughed and led me
Down a cool, still hall,

From *Skipping Along Alone*, by Winifred Welles. Permission from the ~st Stamford Bank and Trust Company.

Between two rows of pillars
That were glistening and tall.
At her finger's tap swung open
A wide door in the wall,
And I saw the crystal city
Behind the waterfall.


## PHARAOH'S DAUGHTER FINDS LITTLE MOSES

### Retold from Exodus II. 1-10

*The story of the saving of a babe who was to become one of the world's great leaders is especially effective when played out of doors, near a lake or river. It has sometimes been used on a Sunday afternoon program at girls' camps.*

*One mixed group of children[1] added interesting details by introducing Egyptian soldiers searching the river bank after the babe was set adrift there. There was strong suspense as they were ordered to search and began to do so. However, discovering a dead snake one of them had killed the day before, they proved that they had so recently been here that there was no reason to search again.*

*The same group had Pharaoh's daughter and maidens listening to an exciting story when the baby's cries were heard. And later, the Princess, having laid aside her royal head-dress and veil, was not recognized by some officers who came by (while Miriam had gone for her mother) and demanded that the Hebrew baby be given up. The scene in which Pharaoh's daughter scornfully put the officer in his place was both dramatic and amusing.*

Do you remember the story of Joseph? How his brothers, jealous because he was his father's favorite, sold him to Egyptian slave-dealers? How Joseph became the favorite of the Pharaoh; and when there was a famine in Israel, Joseph returned good for evil by bringing his father and brothers to live in Egypt?

The story of Moses came many, many years later, when the Israelites had increased greatly in numbers and were held as slaves by the Egyptians. Because they had grown so strong and numerous, there was danger, Pharaoh thought, that they might rise up and become masters instead of slaves. Therefore, the Egyptians

[1] In *Directed Drama*, by David C. Pethybridge. University of London Press.

116

took counsel and made a proclamation that all boy babies born to Israelites should be put to death.

Now at that time there was born to a certain Israelite family a fine baby boy. The parents were so determined that the Egyptian soldiers should not find him that the mother kept him hidden for three months. But she knew that there was great danger whenever the soldiers came to search, and that sooner or later the baby's cries would be heard.

Finally she thought of a plan. It was a dangerous plan, but there was a chance that it might work out. Taking a small basket of reeds, she made it waterproof by covering it with pitch. Then she placed the baby inside and called her twelve-year-old daughter Miriam.

"We must take the basket to the river," she said. "I will put these clothes on top so that if anyone sees us, he will think it is our washing."

"But mother," Miriam protested, "the soldiers search even along the river bank. How do you know that they will not find him?"

"They came through the town only yesterday," the mother replied, "so that they are not likely to come again today. That is why I determined to put the baby in the water this morning. Help me with the basket, Miriam."

Fearfully and quickly, the mother and daughter walked through the streets with basket and clothes. When they came to the river bank where a number of women were washing, the mother said, "Not here, Miriam. Farther up the river."

A few minutes later she paused and set down the basket near a beautiful little pool surrounded by rushes. "Now listen carefully, Miriam," she said. "This is the place where the daughter of Pharaoh and her ladies come to bathe. You know—we have often seen them pass."

"Yes, I know, mother, but won't it be dangerous to leave him here? Even if the Princess finds him, she might give him to the soldiers."

"It is a terrible risk, I know," the mother answered, "but I have to do it. I shall pray that they will not fail to come today, and that they will find my baby and save him."

"Let me hide in the reeds and watch over him, mother," begged the little girl.

"That is part of my plan," replied the mother. "Watch every minute, and when something happens, run and tell me."

With that, she opened the basket, kissed her precious baby, and then, closing the lid carefully, gave it to Miriam.

The girl waded out into the water and placed it in the middle of the pool; and then she hid nearby, while the mother walked swiftly toward her home, her heart heavy and fearful.

An hour passed, then another, and still Miriam waited anxiously in the rushes. Then at last she heard laughter and talking and her heart beat fast. The daughter of Pharaoh and her maidens were coming to the pool!

All this time there had been no sound from the baby. He had been sleeping peacefully while his basket drifted about in the pool. As the royal party made ready to enter the water, however, one of the maidens heard a faint sound of crying.

"Your Highness," she exclaimed, "I thought I heard a child crying!" The talk stopped suddenly, and again the cry came.

"It *is* a baby cry," said the Princess. "It comes from over there near the water's edge. Can you see anything?"

"There it is, just a little way from the edge!" called one of the maidens. It is in a basket. I will wade into the water and get it.'

There was much excitement as the basket was brought to the Princess and opened, disclosing a pretty baby, no longer crying but holding out his arms as if he wanted to be lifted from his little boat.

"What a dear baby," exclaimed the Princess, taking him in her arms. "Why should anyone have put him in the water?" Then the thought came to her, as it came to all, that this must be an Israelite baby, hidden here to save his life. He was so tiny and so sweet that once the thought of taking him home to the palace had been suggested, the Princess could not bear to do anything else.

It was then that Miriam came out of her hiding-place and offered to find a nurse for the baby. This was all that the Princess needed to help her decide, and she said quickly, "Run, child, and bring her!" And she added, "I shall call his name Moses because he was drawn out of the water."

Miriam's feet flew over the ground. "Mother! Mother!" she cried as she entered the house. "Pharaoh's daughter came and she found our baby and loved him! And I thought of a plan, and asked her if she wanted a Hebrew woman to be a nurse for him, and she said, 'Yes, go find a nurse.' So I've come for you!"

The mother took the little girl in her arms and cried gently. Her plan had succeeded even better than she had hoped, for she knew that not only was her little son safe, but she herself could care for him!

With a prayer of thanks, she took Miriam's hand, and together they hastened back to the Princess.

## THE SHEPHERD BOY AND THE WOLF

### Aesop

*This fable may be built up into an interesting play by developing many definite characterizations for the villagers.*

There was once a young Shepherd Boy who tended his sheep at the foot of a mountain near a dark forest. It was rather lonely for him all day, so he thought upon a plan by which he could get a little company and some excitement. He rushed down towards the village calling out "Wolf! Wolf!" and the villagers came out to meet him, and some of them stopped with him for a considerable time. This pleased the boy so much that a few days afterwards he tried the same trick, and again the villagers came to help. But shortly after this a Wolf actually did come out from the forest, and began to worry the sheep, and the boy of course cried out "Wolf! Wolf!" still lounder than before. But this time the villagers, who had been fooled twice before, thought the boy was again deceiving them, and nobody stirred to come to his help. So the Wolf made a good meal off the boy's flock, and when the boy complained, the wise man of the village said:

"A liar will not be believed, even when he speaks the truth."

## THE MAID WHO DEFIED MINERVA[1]

### Flora J. Cooke

*When children are reading Greek myths in the fourth or fifth grade, they often like to dramatize one of them. This story of the spinner Arachne is simple and very dramatic to play.*

Arachne was a beautiful maiden who had wonderful skill in weaving and embroidery. The nymphs left their groves and foun-

[1] From *Nature Myths and Stories*, by Flora J. Cooke. Published by A. Flanagan. Permission from author.

tains to gather round her loom. The naiads came from the rivers and the dryads from the trees, and were never tired of watching her.

She took the wool as it came from the backs of the newly-washed sheep and formed it into rolls; she separated it with her deft fingers, and carded it until it looked as light and soft as a cloud. She twirled the spindle in her skillful hands and wove the web. Often she embroidered it with her needle in beautiful, soft colors.

Arachne's father was famed throughout the land for his skill in coloring. He dyed her wool in all the hues of the rainbow.

Her work was so wonderful that people said, "Surely Athene must have taught this maiden." But Arachne proudly denied this. She could not bear to be thought a pupil even of the goddess of the loom.

"If Athene thinks she can weave better than I, let her try her skill with mine," said she boastfully. "If I fail, I will pay the penalty."

In vain her father told her that perhaps Athene, unseen, guided her hands. Arachne would not listen, and would thank no one for her gift, for vanity had turned her head. She said again, "Let Athene try her skill with mine if she dares."

One day as she was boasting to the nymphs of the beauty of her work, an old woman appeared before her and advised her to accept her rare gift humbly. Arachne looked at the old woman angrily and said, "Keep your advice for others, old dame. I do not need it." But the old woman said, "Listen to me. I have great age and much experience, and I have come to warn you. Hitherto Athene has aided you, asking for no gratitude, but she can help you no more until you grow less selfish and vain. Above all, I advise you to ask forgiveness of Athene. Perhaps she may yet pardon your selfish pride. Challenge your fellow mortals, if you will, but do not, I beg of you, seek to compete with the goddess."

But Arachne said, "Begone. I fear not Athene, no, nor any one else. Nothing would please me so much as to weave with Athene, but she is afraid to weave with me."

Then suddenly the old woman threw aside her cloak, and there before Arachne's very eyes stool a tall, majestic, grey-eyed goddess, crowned with a golden helmet.

"Athene is here," she said. Then the nymphs bent low in homage; but Arachne stool erect. She grew pale but gave no other sign of fear.

"Come, foolish girl, since you wish to try your skill with me," said Athene, "let the contest begin."

Both went quickly to work, and for hours their shuttles flew swiftly in and out. Athene used the sky for her loom, and in it she wove a picture too beautiful to describe. If you wish to know more about it, look at the western sky when the sun is setting.

She was still merciful, and at length she began a smaller web nearer to Arachne's loom. In this she wove a warning, showing how other boastful mortals had failed when they dared to compete with the gods. She hoped that the girl would even yet repent her rashness. But Arachne refused this last chance to save herself. She would not lift her eyes from her own work.

Her weaving was so fine and beautiful that even Athene was forced to admire it. The figures upon it seemed ready to speak and to live, but into her web she had woven many of the faults and failings of the gods, and her work was full of spite.

When the task was finished, Arachne lifted her eyes to Athene's work. Instantly she knew that she had failed. Ashamed and miserable, she tried to hang herself in her own web, but Athene cried, "Stay, wretched and perverse girl. You shall not die. You shall live to do the work for which you are best fitted. You and your children shall be among the greatest spinners and weavers upon the earth. You shall be the mother of a great race, which shall be called spiders. Wherever men shall see your web, they shall destroy it even as I destroy yours," and as she spoke, the goddess with her shuttle, tore the maiden's wonderful web from top to bottom.

Then Athene touched Arachne's forehead with her spindle thrice, and she became smaller and smaller, until she was scarcely larger than a fly.

And from that day to this Arachne and her family have been faithfully spinning and weaving, but they do their work so quietly and in such dark places that few people know what marvelous webs they weave. Some early morning you may see their webs gleaming with a dew, spread across the grass or hanging between the branches of a tree.

# THE UNHAPPY ECHO[1]

## Edith Ballinger Price

*A story which is especially popular with Brownies. Some groups like to open their play with a beach scene, and a number of children curious about the sign Silvertoes is making. After she turns it over to show what she has printed, there is a flashback as she starts telling them about her experience.*

Once upon a time there was an Echo that lived at the other end of a lake. At this end of the lake were a lot of summer camps, but at the other end there was nobody at all but the Echo, and it lived all alone in its own little house. It was a round, small Echo, quite soft and fuzzy, and it looked as though it ought to be happy—but it wasn't. It had a nice house, with stepping-stones that led down to the lake, and a chimney, and ever so many bright shiny pots and pans, and a bed stuffed entirely with milkweed seeds, but it wasn't happy. It had a pine-cone fire on cold nights, and a window that looked away among the trees to the sunset, and a cupboard full of little green dishes, and a pet frog on a lily pad under the kitchen window—but still it wasn't happy.

It was sad for lots of reasons. One was that it never could speak until somebody at the other end of the lake said something; but it was used to that. Another was that it could never go far away for fear that it wouldn't be there to answer when somebody shouted. Then all the people would have said, "My goodness! What's become of the Echo?" and professors would have come paddling over in canoes to find out. This would have been terrible. But the Echo was used to staying at home, too. The biggest reason for its being sad was that the people shouted such cross, stupid, selfish, lazy, horrid things at one another, which the poor little Echo had to shout back and it never could get used to that.

It was such a bother, too. Perhaps the Echo might just have put its supper on the table—a nice, hot loaf of acorn bread, and a cup of milkweed milk, and a thimbleberry pie—and be sitting down to eat it, when some little boy at the other end of the lake would yell: "Aw, watcha tryin' to do?" and the poor Echo would have to jump up with its mouth full, and put its head out of the door and shout:

[1] Reprinted by permission of *The American Girl*, a magazine for all girls published by the Girl Scouts of the U. S. A.

"Aw, watcha tryin' to do?" Sometimes it even had to get out of its warm little milkweed bed to answer people who came out in canoes in the moonlight and shrieked and yodeled—just to see if the Echo could do it. Of course it could—it had to—but it would get up rather cross the next morning from having lost so much sleep.

Now at the other end of the lake where the people lived, there was a Brownie. Not a really-truly, sure-enough, fairy Brownie, but a little girl who was trying to be as much like one as ever she could. Her magic name was Silvertoes, and she was a Sixer, at that. Her Pack was scattered, for of course it was summer-time, but she found plenty of magic surprises to do, never fear. Feeding birds and bunnies, and setting the table before anybody was supposed to be awake, and untangling her daddy's fishing-line that he thought would never be the same again, and bailing out the boat before breakfast—and oh, ever so many things!

One afternoon, she was exploring through a little path in the woods, trying to find again a fairy toadstool ring in a wee mossy glade, where she had been the day before. She thought it seemed farther than last time. And then she saw that she was not on the right path at all, and that the sun was getting rather low behind the trees. She had come so far that she was almost at the other end of the lake.

Silvertoes tried to remember that Brownies are never frightened and she ran on through the woods. Branches snapped back and things jumped aside, but she felt sure they were only startled fairies making way for her. All at once she saw a little curl of blue smoke among the trees, and she was certainly Scout enough to know that where there's smoke there's fire and probably somebody who made it.

Then she almost tumbled against a little house—oh much, much smaller than a camp; so small that to go through its door Silvertoes, who was only eight, had to duck her head. But she knocked before she went in, and the door was opened by a little round fuzzy something who looked quite as surprised as she did. It had on an apron and held a frying-pan in its hand. In the frying pan was an oak-apple fritter cooked in honey. In spite of her surprise Silvertoes remembered to be polite, so she said:

"How do you do?"

"How do you do?" said the little thing, who, of course, was our friend, the Echo.

"Who are you?" asked Silvertoes.

"Who are you?" asked the Echo.

"Well," thought the little girl, "I'll tell it first, if it likes. Why, I'm a Brownie."

"A Brownie!" repeated the Echo in some astonishment.

"Trying to be one," explained Silvertoes. "I declare, you sound just like an Echo!"

"An Echo," it assured her, nodding in a pleased way and pointing to its furry little self.

"Well!" said Silvertoes, "How funny! May I come in a minute and sit down?"

"Sit down!" said the Echo cordially, putting down the pan and pulling up a little chair made of hickory shoots with the bark on. Silvertoes fitted into it rather tightly.

"You see," she told her host, "I got lost."

"Lost?" said the Echo sympathetically.

"And I don't know how I'll ever find the way back."

"The way back," the Echo told her, pointing out the door to a clear little path which suddenly seemed to have opened through the woods.

"Why, so it is!" cried the Brownie. "It looks perfectly easy."

"Perfectly easy," agreed the Echo.

"Oh," said Silvertoes, "I do wish I had something to eat!"

She hadn't meant it to sound so very much like a hint.

It was just that she suddenly realized how hungry she was.

But, "Eat!" said the Echo pleasantly, pointing to the table which it had set for supper just before the little girl knocked. Silvertoes ran and helped the little thing put another green cup and plate on the table. The Echo brought in a fat jug of milkweed milk and a pat of yellow butter from a cold pool at the edge of the lake and they sat down.

"Oh, but it looks good!" Silvertoes said hungrily.

"Good," the Echo agreed, smiling, as it picked up the carving knife.

Just as they had begun to eat, there was a sound of loud voices at the other end of the lake, and then somebody shouted crossly, "Oh, shut up!"

The Echo dropped its napkin, jumped up, ran to the door and called "Shut up!" across the lake. Then it came back and sat down, sighing.

"Why, dear me!" said Silvertoes.

"Dear me," said the Echo sadly, shaking its head.

"Do you always have to jump up and answer just like that?" she asked.

"Just like that," the Echo replied sorrowfully.

"What a bother!" Silvertoes pondered.

"A bother!" said the Echo, a little crossly.

"But that's a shame—when the things they say are so horrid!"

"Horrid!" it agreed. And Silvertoes was distressed to see tears in its wistful eyes.

"If they said kind, happy, funny things, wouldn't it be much nicer?" she asked, passing her plate for more nut-bread and oak-apple fritter.

"Much nicer!" cried the Echo, nodding with delight. "Well, anyhow," Silvertoes stated, "I for one am going to do it."

"Do it!" the Echo begged earnestly.

When they had finished supper the Echo closed the front windows, for the air was beginning to grow cool from off the water. It put more pine-cones on the little fire and it and Silvertoes sat warming their fingers.

"I'm so glad I got lost," Silvertoes said. "I do like you!"

"I do like you!" the Echo told her, and patted her shyly.

"Oh, dear!" the little girl cried suddenly, "It's getting dark! I must run fast through your little path. Oh, Echo, thank you!"

"THANK YOU!" it said, at the doorstep.

"Good-bye, dear thing!" and she kissed the top of its fuzzy little head.

"Bye, dear thing . . ." Silvertoes heard its lonely little voice as she started running down the trail.

The Echo was so excited that it could hardly wash the dishes. It lay awake a long time in its milkweed bed, and heard people who had come to look for the little lost Brownie calling, "Silvertoes! Oh, Silvertoes!" So it leaned out of the bedroom window and called, "Silvertoes," too.

Then it heard the same deep voice cry, "Here she is—thank heaven!"

And the Echo said, "Thank heaven!" and turned over and went to sleep.

Silvertoes didn't wait long to tell everybody she could about how unhappy it made the Echo to repeat so many rough, cross things. She told all the big boys and some of them laughed at her. But they felt a little foolish after that when they heard the Echo snapping back at them, and they stopped after awhile. Silvertoes put up a big sign on the wharf, which said, "Please be Kind to the Echo" and every day she went and stood on the end of the wharf herself and shouted the nicest things she could think of. She always started with "Lend a hand!" and she finished with "I'm so happy!" It made her jump up and down with glee to hear how jolly the Echo's voice sounded as it called back to her, "I'm so happy!"

And the little Echo—it put up its shutters when the lake froze over, and piled ever so many pine-cones on the fire. And as it snuggled down in bed each night it whispered, "I'm so happy!"

It couldn't say it aloud, but enough of Silvertoes' shout was left to keep the Echo company all winter with that little whisper.


## RUMPELSTILTSKIN

### The Brothers Grimm

*One can scarcely believe that there could be a father so heartless as to say that his daughter could spin straw into gold. Therefore, we are justified in adapting the story so that it will be more convincing. A suggestion for doing this is given in the chapter on dramatizing a story. In spite of the characters of the miller and the king, the story is a popular one for dramatization.*

Once there was a miller who was poor, but who had a beautiful daughter. Now it happened that he had to go and speak to the King, and in order to make himself appear important he said to him, "I have a daughter who can spin straw into gold."

The King said to the miller, "That is an art which pleases me well. If your daughter is as clever as you say, bring her tomorrow to my palace, and I will try what she can do."

And when the girl was brought to him he took her into a room which was quite full of straw, gave her a spinning-wheel and a reel, and said, "Now set to work, and if by tomorrow morning early you have not spun this straw into gold during the night, you must die." Thereupon he himself locked up the room, and left her in it alone. So there sat the miller's poor daughter, and for her life could not tell what to do. She had no idea how straw could be spun into gold, and she grew more and more miserable, until at last she began to weep.

But all at once the door opened, and in came a little man and said, "Good evening, Mistress Miller; why are you crying so?"

"Alas!" answered the girl, "I have to spin straw into gold, and I do not know how to do it."

"What will you give me," said the manikin, "if I do it for you?"

"My necklace," said the girl. The little man took the necklace, seated himself in front of the wheel, and "whir, whir, whir," three turns, and the reel was full: then he put another on, and "whir, whir, whir," three times round, and the second was full, too. And so it went on until the morning, when all the straw was spun, and all the reels were full of gold. By daybreak the King was already there, and when he saw the gold he was astonished and delighted, but his heart became only more greedy. He had the miller's daughter taken into another room full of straw, which was much larger, and commanded her to spin that also in one night if she valued her life. The girl knew not how to help herself, and was crying, when the door again opened, and the little man appeared and said, "What will you give me if I spin the straw into gold for you?"

"The ring on my finger," answered the girl.

The little man took the ring, again began to turn the wheel, and by morning had spun all the straw into glittering gold.

The King rejoiced beyond measure at the sight, but still he had not gold enough; and he had the miller's daughter taken into a still larger room full of straw. "You must spin this, too, in the course of this night; but if you succeed, you shall be my wife."

When the girl was alone the manikin came again for the third time, and said, "What will you give me if I spin the straw for you this time also?"

"I have nothing left that I could give," answered the girl.

"Then promise me, if you should become Queen, your first child."

"Who knows whether that will ever happen?" thought the miller's daughter; and, not knowing how else to help herself in this strait, she promised the manikin what he wanted, and for that he once more spun the straw into gold.

And when the King came in the morning, and found all as he wished, he took her in marriage, and the miller's pretty daughter became a Queen.

A year after, she had a beautiful child, and she never gave a thought to the manikin. But suddenly he came into her room, and said, "Now give me what you promised."

The Queen was horror-struck, and offered the manikin all the riches of the kingdom if he would leave her the child. But the manikin said, "No, something that is living is dearer to me than all the treasures of the world."

Then the Queen began to weep, so that the manikin pitied her. "I will give you three days' time," said he; "if by that time you find out my name, then shall you keep your child."

So the Queen thought the whole night of all the names that she had ever heard, and she sent a messenger over the country to inquire, far and wide, for any other names that there might be. When the manikin came the next day, she began with Caspar, Melchior, Balthazar, and said all the names she knew, one after another; but to every one the little man said, "That is not my name." On the second day she had inquiries made in the neighborhood as to the names of the people there, and she repeated to the manikin the most uncommon and curious. "Perhaps your name is Shortribs, or Sheepshanks, or Laceleg?" but he always answered, "That is not my name."

On the third day the messenger came back again, and said, "I have not been able to find a single new name, but as I came to a high mountain at the end of the forest, where the fox and the hare bid each other good-night, there I saw a little house, and before the house a fire was burning, and round about the fire quite a ridiculous little man was jumping; he hopped upon one leg, and shouted,

"Merrily the feast I'll make.
Today I'll brew, tomorrow bake;
Merrily I'll dance and sing,
For next day will a stranger bring.
Little does my lady dream
Rumpelstiltskin is my name!"

You may think how glad the Queen was when she heard the name! And when soon afterwards the little man came in, and asked, "Now, Mistress Queen, what is my name?"

At first she said, "Is your name Conrad?"

"No."

"Is your name Harry?"

"No."

"Perhaps your name is Rumpelstiltskin?"

"Who told you that? Who told you that?" cried the dwarf, stamping about in fury. He was so angry that he darted out of the room and ran off to the forest—and no one ever heard of him again. So the young queen kept her baby and lived happily ever after.

## CINDERELLA[1]

### Charles Perrault

*The favorite, without doubt, of all fairy tales, and one that almost every little girl delights in playing. Though this version by Perrault is one of the most charming, every group will surely take for granted that the father has died before Cinderella is sent to live in the attic. For what father would stand by and allow his daughter to be so treated?*

There was once an honest gentleman who took for his second wife the proudest and most disagreeable lady in the whole country. She had two daughters exactly like herself. He himself had one little girl, who resembled her dead mother, the best woman in all the world. Scarcely had the second marriage taken place before the stepmother became jealous of the good qualities of the little girl, who was so great a contrast to her own two daughters. She gave her all the hard work of the house, compelling her to wash the floors and staircases, to dust the bedrooms, and clean the grates. While her sisters occupied carpeted chambers hung with mirrors, where they could see themselves from head to foot, this poor little girl was sent to sleep in an attic, on an old straw mattress, with only one chair and not a looking-glass in the room.

She suffered all in silence, not daring to complain. When her daily work was done she used to sit down in the chimney-corner among the ashes, from which the two sisters gave her the nickname of "Cinderella." But Cinderella, however shabbily clad, was handsomer than they were, with all their fine clothes.

It happened that the King's son gave a series of balls, to which were invited all the rank and fashion of the city, and among the rest the two elder sisters. They were very proud and happy, and occupied their whole time in deciding what they should wear. This was a source of new trouble to Cinderella, whose duty it was to make

[1] From Dinah Maria Mulock Craik, *The Fairy Book.*

129

ready their fine linen and laces, and who never could please them, however much she tried. They talked of nothing but their clothes.

"I," said the elder, "shall wear my velvet gown and my trimmings of English lace."

"And I," added the younger, "will have but my ordinary silk petticoat, but I shall adorn it with an upper skirt of flowered brocade, and shall put on my diamond tiara, which is a great deal finer than anything of yours."

Here the elder sister grew angry, and the dispute began to run so high that Cinderella, who was known to have excellent taste, was called upon to decide between them. She gave them the best advice she could, and gently and submissively offered to dress them herself, and especially to arrange their hair, an accomplishment in which she excelled many a noted coiffeur. The important evening came, and she exercised all her skill in adorning the two young ladies. While she was combing out the elder's hair this ill-natured girl said sharply, "Cinderella, do you not wish you were going to the ball?"

"Ah, madam"—they obliged her always to say madam—"you are only mocking me; it is not my fortune to have any such pleasure."

"You are right; people would only laugh to see a little cinderwench at a ball."

After this any other girl would have dressed her hair all awry, but Cinderella was good, and made it perfectly even and smooth.

The sisters had scarcely eaten for two days, and had broken a dozen stay-laces a day in trying to make themselves slender; but to-night they broke a dozen more, and lost their tempers over and over again before they had completed their toilet. When at last the happy moment arrived Cinderella followed them to the coach, and after it had whirled them away she sat down by the kitchen fire and cried.

Immediately her godmother, who was a fairy, appeared beside her. "What are you crying for, my little maid?"

"Oh, I wish—I wish—" Her sobs stopped her.

"You wish to go to the ball; isn't it so?"

Cinderella nodded.

"Well, then, be a good girl, and you shall go. First run into the garden and fetch me the largest pumpkin you can find."

Cinderella did not understand what this had to do with her going to the ball, but, being obedient and obliging, she went. Her godmother took the pumpkin, and, having scooped out all its inside, struck it with her wand. It then became a splendid gilt coach, lined with rose-coloured satin.

"Now fetch me the mouse-trap out of the pantry, my dear."

Cinderella brought it; it contained six of the fattest, sleekest mice.

The fairy lifted up the wire door, and as each mouse ran out she struck it and changed it into a beautiful black horse.

"But what shall I do for your coachman, Cinderella?"

Cinderella suggested that she had seen a large black rat in the rap-trap, and he might do for want of better.

"You are right. Go and look again for him."

He was found, and the fairy made him into a most respectable coachman, with the finest whiskers imaginable. She afterwards took six lizards from behind the pumpkin and changed them into six footmen, all in splendid livery, who immediately jumped up behind the carriage, as if they had been footmen all their days.

"Well, Cinderella, now you can go to the ball."

"What, in these clothes?" said Cinderella piteously, looking down on her ragged frock.

Her godmother laughed, and touched her also with the wand, at which her wretched, threadbare jacket became stiff with gold and sparkling with jewels, her woolen petticoat lengthened into a gown of sweeping satin, from underneath which peeped out her little feet, covered with silk stockings and the prettiest glass slippers in the world.

"Now, Cinderella, you may go; but remember, if you stay one instant after midnight your carriage will become a pumpkin, your coachman a rat, your horses mice, and your footmen lizards, while you yourself will be the little cinder-wench you were an hour ago."

Cinderella promised without fear, her heart was so full of joy.

Arrived at the palace, the King's son, whom some one, probably the fairy, had told to await the coming of an uninvited princess whom nobody knew, was standing at the entrance, ready to receive her. He offered her his hand, and led her with the utmost courtesy through the assembled guests, who stood aside to let her pass, whispering to one another, "Oh, how beautiful she is!" It might have turned the head of anyone but poor Cinderella who was so used to being despised, but she took it all as if it were something happening in a dream.

Her triumph was complete; even the old King said to the Queen that never since her Majesty's young days had he seen so charming a person. All the Court ladies scanned her eagerly, clothes and all, and determined to have theirs made the next day of exactly the same pattern. The King's son himself led her out to dance, and she danced so gracefully that he admired her more and more. Indeed, at supper, which was fortunately early, his admiration quite took away his appetite. Cinderella herself sought out her sisters, placed herself beside them, and offered them all sorts of civil attentions. These, coming as they supposed from a stranger, and so magnificent a lady, almost overwhelmed them with delight.

While she was talking with them she heard the clock strike a quarter to twelve, and, making a courteous *adieu* to the royal family, she re-entered her carriage, escorted gallantly by the King's son and arrived in safety at her own door. There she found her godmother, who smiled approval, and of whom she begged permission to go to a second ball the following night, to which the Queen had invited her.

While she was talking the two sisters were heard knocking at the gate, and the fairy godmother vanished, leaving Cinderella sitting in the chimney-corner, rubbing her eyes and pretending to be very sleepy.

"Ah," cried the eldest sister spitefully, "it has been the most delightful ball, and there was present the most beautiful princess I ever saw, who was so exceedingly polite to us both."

"Was she?" said Cinderella indifferently. "And who might she be?"

"Nobody knows, though everybody would give their eyes to know, especially the King's son."

"Indeed!" replied Cinderella, a little more interested. "I should like to see her." Then she turned to the elder sister and said, "Miss Javotte, will you not let me go to-morrow, and lend me your yellow gown that you wear on Sundays?"

"What, lend my yellow gown to a cinder-wench! I am not so mad as that!" At which refusal Cinderella did not complain, for if her sister really had lent her the gown she would have been considerably embarrassed.

The next night came, and the two young ladies, richly dressed in different toilettes, went to the ball. Cinderella, more splendidly attired and more beautiful than ever, followed them shortly after. "Now, remember twelve o'clock," was her godmother's parting speech; and she thought she certainly should. But the prince's attentions to her were greater even than on the first evening, and in the delight of listening to his pleasant conversation time slipped by unperceived. While she was sitting beside him in a lovely alcove and looking at the moon from under a bower of orange-blossoms she heard a clock strike the first stroke of twelve. She started up, and fled away as lightly as a deer.

Amazed, the prince followed, but could not catch her. Indeed, he missed his lovely princess altogether, and only saw running out of the palace doors a little dirty lass whom he had never beheld before, and of whom he certainly would never have taken the least notice. Cinderella arrived at home breathless and weary, ragged and cold, without carriage or footmen or coachman; the only remnant of her past magnificence being one of her little glass slippers; the other she had dropped in the ballroom as she ran away.

When the two sisters returned they were full of this strange adventure: how the beautiful lady had appeared at the ball more beautiful than ever, and enchanted every one who looked at her; and how as the clock was striking twelve she had suddenly risen up and fled through the ballroom, disappearing no one knew how or where, and dropping one of her glass slippers behind her in her flight.

The King's son remained inconsolable until he chanced to pick up the little glass slipper, which he carried away in his pocket and was seen to take out continually, and look at affectionately, with the air of a man very much in love; in fact, from his behaviour during the remainder of the evening all the Court and the royal family were sure that he was desperately in love with the wearer of the little glass slipper.

Cinderella listened in silence, turning her face to the kitchen fire, and perhaps it was that which made her look so rosy; but nobody ever noticed or admired her at home, so it did not signify, and next morning she went to her weary work again just as before.

A few days after, the whole city was attracted by the sight of a herald going round with a little glass slipper in his hand, publishing, with a flourish of trumpets that the King's son ordered this to be fitted on the foot of every lady in the kingdom, and that he wished to marry the lady whom it fitted best, or to whom it and the fellow-slipper belonged. Princesses, duchesses, countesses, and simple gentlewomen all tried it on, but, being a fairy slipper, it fitted nobody; and, besides, nobody could produce its fellow-slipper, which lay all the time safely in the pocket of Cinderella's old woolen gown.

At last the herald came to the house of the two sisters, and though they well knew neither of themselves was the beautiful lady, they made every attempt to get their clumsy feet into the glass slipper, but in vain.

"Let me try it on," said Cinderella from the chimney-corner.

"What, you?" cried the others, bursting into shouts of laughter; but Cinderella only smiled and held out her hand.

Her sisters could not prevent her, since the command was that every maiden in the city should try on the slipper, in order that no chance might be left untried, for the prince was nearly breaking his heart; and his father and mother were afraid that, though a prince, he would actually die for love of the beautiful lady.

So the herald bade Cinderella sit down on a three-legged stool in the kitchen, and he himself put the slipper on her pretty little foot. It fitted exactly. She then drew from her pocket the fellow-slipper, which she also put on, and stood up. With the touch of the magic shoes all her dress was changed likewise. No longer was she the poor, despised cinder-wench, but the beautiful lady whom the King's son loved.

Her sisters recognized her at once. Filled with astonishment, mingled with no little alarm, they threw themselves at her feet, begging her pardon for all their former unkindness. She raised and embraced them, telling them she forgave them with all her heart, and only hoped they would love her always. Then she departed with the herald to the King's palace, and told her whole story to his Majesty and the royal family. They were not in the least surprised, for everybody believed in fairies, and everybody longed to have a fairy godmother.

As for the young prince, he found her more lovely and lovable than ever, and insisted upon marrying her immediately. Cinderella never went home again, but she sent for her two sisters to come to the palace, and married them shortly after to two rich gentlemen of the Court.

# THE SLEEPING BEAUTY[1]

## The Brothers Grimm

*Plays, ballets. and children's spontaneous dramatizations give evidence of the magic this tale has held for children for hundreds of years. Its symbolism of winter's sleep and spring's awakening is inconsequential to children, who delight in it simply as a dramatic fairy tale which is charming for a creative play.*

Once upon a time, there lived a king and queen who had no children; and this they lamented very much. When at last the queen had a little girl, the king could not cease looking on her for joy, and determined to hold a great feast. So he invited not only his relations, friends, and neighbors, but also all the fairies, that they might be kind and good to his little daughter.

Now there were thirteen fairies in his kingdom, and he had only twelve golden dishes for them to eat out of, so he was obliged to leave one of the fairies without an invitation. The rest came, and after the feast was over they gave all their best gifts to the little princess: one gave her virtue, another beauty, another riches, and so on till she had all that was excellent in the world. When eleven had done blessing her, the thirteenth, who had not been invited and was very angry on that account, came in and determined to take her revenge. So she cried out, "The king's daughter shall in her fteenth year be wounded by a spindle, and fall down dead."

Then the twelfth, who had not yet given her gift, came forward and said that the bad wish must be fulfilled, but that she could often it, and that the king's daughter should not die, but fall sleep for a hundred years.

But the king hoped to save his dear child from the threatened evil ad ordered that all the spindles in the kingdom should be bought p and destroyed. All the fairies' gifts were in the meantime fulled, for the princess was so beautiful, and well-behaved, and niable, and wise that every one who knew her loved her. Now it ppened that on the very day she was fifteen years old the king d queen were not at home, and she was left alone in the palace. she roved about by herself and looked at all the rooms and ambers till at last she came to an old tower, to which there was narrow staircase ending with a little door. In the door there was

From Edgar Taylor, *Grimm's Popular Stories*.

a golden key, and when she turned it the door sprang open, and there sat an old lady spinning away very busily. "Why, how now, good mother," said the princess, "what are you doing there?"

"Spinning," said the old lady, and nodded her head.

"How prettily that little thing turns round!" said the princess, and took the spindle and began to spin. But scarcely had she touched it before the prophecy was fulfilled, and she fell down lifeless on the ground.

However, she was not dead, but had only fallen into a deep sleep; and the king and the queen, who just then came home, and all their court, fell asleep too; and the horses slept in the stables, and the dogs in the court, the pigeons on the housetop and the flies on the walls. Even the fire on the hearth left off blazing and went to sleep; and the meat that was roasting stood still; and the cook, who was at that moment pulling the kitchenboy by the hair to give him a box on the ear for something he had done amiss, let him go, and both fell asleep; and so everything stood still, and slept soundly.

A large hedge of thorns soon grew round the palace, and every year it became higher and thicker till at last the whole palace was surrounded and hid, so that not even the roof or the chimneys could be seen. But there went a report through all the land of the beautiful sleeping princess; so that from time to time several kings sons came and tried to break through the thicket into the palace. This they could never do, for the thorns and bushes laid hold of them as it were with hands, and there they stuck fast and died miserably.

After many, many years there came a king's son into that land and an old man told him the story of the thicket of thorns, and how a beautiful palace stood behind it, in which was a wondrous princess, asleep with all her court. He told, too, how he had heard from his grandfather that many, many princes had come, and had tried to break through the thicket, but had stuck fast and died. Then the young prince said, "All this shall not frighten me. I will go and see the princess." The old man tried to dissuade him, but he persisted in going.

Now that very day were the hundred years completed; and as the prince came to the thicket, he saw nothing but beautiful flowering shrubs, through which he passed with ease, and they closed after him as firm as ever. Then he came at last to the palace, and there in the court lay the dogs asleep, and the horses in the stables, and on the roof sat the pigeons fast asleep with their heads under their wings; and when he came into the palace, the flies slept on the walls, and the cook in the kitchen was still holding up her hand as if she would beat the boy, and the maid sat with a black fowl in her hand ready to be plucked.

Then he went on still further, and all was so still that he could hear every breath he drew; till at last he came to the old tower and opened the door of the little room in which the princess was; and there she lay fast asleep, and looked so beautiful that he could not take his eyes off her, and he stooped down and gave her a kiss. But the moment he kissed her she opened her eyes and awoke and smiled upon him. Then they went out together, and presently the king and queen also awoke, and all the court, and they gazed on one another with great wonder. And the horses got up and shook themselves, and the dogs jumped about and barked; the pigeons took their heads from under their wings and looked about and flew into the fields; the flies on the walls buzzed away; the fire in the kitchen blazed up and cooked the dinner, and the roast meat turned round again; the cook gave the boy the box on his ear so that he cried out, and the maid went on plucking the fowl. And then was the wedding of the prince and the princess celebrated, and they lived happily together all their lives long.


## SNOW WHITE AND THE SEVEN DWARFS[1]

### The Brothers Grimm

*All the fascination of "once upon a time" is in this great fairy tale. It is elaborate in number of incidents, yet a good play can easily be made from it.*

It was in the middle of winter, when the broad flakes of snow were falling around, that a certain queen sat working at a window, the frame of which was made of fine black ebony; and as she was looking out upon the snow, she pricked her finger, and three drops of blood fell upon it.

Then she gazed thoughtfully upon the red drops which sprinkled the white snow, and said, "Would that my little daughter may be

[1] From Edgar Taylor, *Grimms' Popular Stories.*

white as that snow, as red as the blood, and as black as the ebony window-frame!"

The little girl grew up so. Her skin was as white as snow, her cheeks as rosy as blood, and her hair as black as ebony; and she was called Snow White.

But this queen died; and the king soon married another wife, who was very beautiful, but so proud that she could not bear to think that any one could surpass her. She had a magical looking glass, to which she used to go and gaze upon herself, and say,

> "Mirror, mirror, in my hand,
> Who is fairest in the land?"

The glass answered,

> "Thou, queen, art fairest in the land."

But Snow White grew more and more beautiful; and when she was seven years old, she was as bright as the day, and fairer than the queen herself. Then the glass one day answered the queen, when she went to consult it as usual,

> "Queen, thou art of beauty rare.
> But Snow White is a thousand times more fair."

When the queen heard this she turned pale with rage and envy; and called to one of her servants and said, "Take Snow White away into the wide wood and kill her, that I may never see her more."

The servant led Snow White away; but his heart melted when she begged him to spare her life, and he said, "I will not hurt thee, thou pretty child."

So he left her by herself. Though he thought it most likely that the wild beasts would tear her in pieces, he felt as if a great weight were taken off his heart when he had made up his mind not to kill her, but leave her to her fate.

Poor Snow White wandered along through the wood in great fear, and the wild beasts were about her but none did her any harm. In the evening she came to a little cottage, and went in there to rest herself, for her little feet would carry her no farther.

Everything was spruce and neat in the cottage. On the table was spread a white cloth, and there were seven little plates with seven little loaves, and seven little glasses, and knives and fork laid in order; and by the wall stood seven little beds. Then a she was very hungry, she picked a little piece off each loaf, and drank a little from each glass; and after that she thought she woul lie down and rest. So she tried all the little beds; and one wa too long, and another was too short, till at last the seventh suited her; and there she laid herself down and went to sleep.

Presently in came the masters of the cottage, who were seven little dwarfs that lived among the mountains, and dug and searched about for gold. They lighted up their seven lamps, and saw directly that all was not right.

The first said, "Who has been sitting on my stool?" The second, "Who has been eating from my plate?" The third, "Who has been picking my bread?" The fourth, "Who has been meddling with my spoon?" The fifth, "Who has been handling my fork?" The sixth, "Who has been cutting with my knife?" The seventh, "Who has been drinking from my glass?"

Then the first looked round and said, "Who has been lying on my bed?" And the rest came running to him, and every one cried out that somebody had been upon his bed. But the seventh saw Snow White, and called all his brethren to come and see her.

They cried out with wonder and astonishment, and brought their lamps to look at her, and said, "What a lovely child she is!"

They were delighted to see her, and took care not to wake her. The seventh dwarf slept an hour with each of the other dwarfs in turn, till the night was gone.

In the morning Snow White told them all her story. They pitied her and said if she would keep all things in order, and cook and wash, and knit and spin for them, she might stay where she was, and they would take good care of her.

Then they went out all day long to their work, seeking for gold and silver in the mountains; and Snow White remained at home. They warned her, and said, "The queen will soon find out where you are, so take care and let no one in."

The queen, now that she thought Snow White was dead, believed that she was certainly the handsomest lady in the land; so she went to her glass and said,

> "Mirror, mirror in my hand,
> Who is fairest in the land?"

The glass answered,

> "Thou queen, art the fairest in all this land;
> But over the hills, in the greenwood shade,
> Where the seven dwarfs their dwelling have made,
> There Snow White is hiding her head, and she
> Is lovelier far, O queen, than thee."

139

The queen was very much alarmed; for she knew that the glass always spoke the truth, and was sure that the servant had betrayed her. She could not bear to think that any one lived who was more beautiful than she was; so she disguised herself as an old peddler and went her way over the hills to the place where the dwarfs dwelt.

She knocked at the door, and cried, "Fine wares to sell!"

Snow White looked out at the window, and said, "Good day, good woman; what have you to sell?"

"Good wares, fine wares," said she; "laces and bobbins of all colors."

"I will let the old lady in; she seems to be a very good sort of body," thought Snow White; so she ran down, and unbolted the door.

"Bless me!" said the old woman, "how badly your stays are laced! Let me lace them up with one of my nice new laces."

Snow White did not dream of any mischief so she stood up before the old woman, who set to work so nimbly, and pulled the lace so tight, that Snow White lost her breath, and fell down as if she were dead.

"There's an end of all thy beauty," said the spiteful queen, and went away home.

In the evening the seven dwarfs returned; and I need not say how grieved they were to see their faithful Snow White stretched upon the ground motionless, as if she were quite dead. However, they lifted her up, and when they found what was the matter, they cut the lace; and in a little time she began to breathe, and soon came to life again.

Then they said, "The old woman was the queen herself; take care another time, and let no one in when we are away."

When the queen got home, she went straight to her glass, and spoke to it as usual; but to her great surprise it still said,

> "Thou, queen, art the fairest in all this land;
> But over the hills, in the greenwood shade,
> Where the seven dwarfs their dwelling have made,
> There Snow White is hiding her head, and she
> Is lovelier far, O queen! than thee."

The blood ran cold in her heart with spite and malice to see that Snow White still lived; and she dressed herself up again in a disguise, but very different from the one she wore before, and took with her a poisoned comb.

When she reached the dwarfs' cottage, she knocked at the door, and cried, "Fine wares to sell!"

But Snow White said, "I dare not let any one in."

Then the queen said, "Only look at my beautiful combs;" and gave her the poisoned one.

It looked so pretty that Snow White took it up and put it into her hair to try it. The moment it touched her head the poison was so powerful that she fell down senseless.

"There you may lie," said the queen, and went her way.

By good luck the dwarfs returned very early that evening. When they saw Snow White lying on the ground, they guessed what had happened, and soon found the poisoned comb. When they took it away, she recovered, and told them all that had passed; and they warned her once more not to open the door to any one.

Meantime the queen went home to her glass, and trembled with rage when she received exactly the same answer as before; and she said, "Snow White shall die, if it costs me my life."

So she went secretly into a chamber, and prepared a poisoned apple. The outside looked very rosy and tempting, but whoever tasted it was sure to die. Then she dressed herself up as a peasant's wife, and traveled over the hills to the dwarfs' cottage, and knocked at the door.

Snow White put her head out of the window, and said, "I dare not let any one in, for the dwarfs have told me not."

"Do as you please," said the old woman, "but at any rate take this pretty apple; I will make you a present of it."

"No," said Snow White, "I dare not take it."

"You silly girl!" answered the other, "what are you afraid of? Do you think it is poisoned? Come! You eat one part, and I will eat the other."

Now the apple was so prepared that one side was good, though the other side was poisoned. Snow White was very much tempted to taste, for the apple looked exceedingly nice. When she saw the old woman eat, she could refrain no longer, but she had scarcely put the piece into her mouth, when she fell down dead upon the ground.

"This time nothing will save you," said the queen; and she went home to her glass, and at last it said,

"Thou queen art the fairest of all the fair."

Then her envious heart was glad, and as happy as such an evil heart could be.

When evening came, and the dwarfs returned home, they found Snow White lying on the ground. No breath passed her lips, and they were afraid that she was quite dead. They lifted her up, and combed her hair, and washed her face with water; but all was in vain, for the little girl seemed quite dead.

So they laid her down upon a bier, and all seven watched and bewailed her three whole days. Then they proposed to bury her; but her cheeks were still rosy, and her face looked just as it did while she was alive. So they said, "We will never bury her in the cold ground."

They made a coffin of glass so that they might still look at her, and wrote her name upon it, in golden letters, and that she was a king's daughter. And the coffin was placed upon the hill, and one of the dwarfs always sat by it and watched. And the birds of the air came too, and bemoaned Snow White; first of all came an owl, and then a raven, and at last came a dove.

And thus Snow White lay for a long, long time, and still looked as though she were only asleep; for she was even now as white as snow, and as red as blood, and as black as ebony.

At last a prince came and called at the dwarfs' house; and he saw Snow White, and read what was written in golden letters. Then he offered the dwarfs money, and earnestly prayed them to let him take her away but they said, "We will not part with her for all the gold in the world."

At last, however, they had pity on him, and gave him the coffin. The moment he lifted it up to carry it home with him, the piece of apple fell from between her lips and Snow White awoke, and said, "Where am I?"

The prince answered, "Thou art safe with me." Then he told her all that had happened, and said, "I love you better than all the world. Come with me to my father's palace, and you shall be my wife."

Snow White consented, and went home with the prince. And every thing was prepared with great pomp and splendor for their wedding.

To the feast was invited, among the rest, Snow White's old enemy, the queen. As she was dressing herself in fine rich clothes, she looked in the glass and said,

> "Mirror, Mirror in my hand,
> Who is fairest in the land?"

The glass answered,

> "Thou, lady, art loveliest *here*, I ween;
> But lovelier far is the new-made queen."

When she heard this, she started with rage. But her envy and curiosity were so great, that she could not help setting out to see the bride.

When she arrived, and saw that it was no other than Snow White, who, as she thought, had been dead a long while, she choked with passion, and fell ill and died. But Snow White and the prince lived and reigned happily over that land many, many years.

# CHAPTER VI

# Reality and Imagination

Wonderfully fine material is available for children of ten and eleven years. And there are perhaps no better years for satisfying results than these. The children have a large enough vocabulary to express their ideas reasonably well, and they usually have little fear of doing so. They have a richer background of experience on which their imaginations can draw, so that by the time they reach the sixth grade they often do surprisingly fine things with creative drama.

Ten- and eleven-year-olds are in a definitely realistic period, when tales of pioneers and adventurous heroes have a strong appeal. Physical bravery awakens their admiration, and it is not easy for them to understand moral and spiritual courage. Because they admire the physical prowess of Robin Hood, there is a good chance that they will be impressed also by his finer qualities. Stories that glorify moral courage, yet are red-blooded and adventurous, will be sought by the teacher who wishes to develop emotional maturity in young people.

In addition to stories from literature, the teacher may make use of dramatic situations in the children's social studies: life in pioneer days, the coming of immigrants to this country, studies in prejudice, incidents in the lives of our American heroes.

Problems in their own lives: what would you do if—? along with interesting pantomimes for characterization and for fun, can be used. A lazy boy shovelling heavy snow, a haughty, well-dressed lady who has to sit by a playful child, a timid girl learning to skate—pantomimes such as these can be made still more interesting by putting different types of people into the same situation.

The zest with which most children of this age go into dramatic play and story dramatization, and their sustained interest in developing a long play in which several school subjects are combined, indicate that it is an especially good age for integrated projects.

## TOM SAWYER DISCOVERS A LAW OF HUMAN ACTION[1]

### Mark Twain

*The best episode from what is probably the most popular children's novel ever written. Many children of eleven and twelve will enjoy introducing other village characters in addition to the one mentioned. The first paragraph offers a delightful opportunity for this.*

Saturday morning was come, and all the summer world was bright and fresh, and brimming with life. There was a song in every heart; and if the heart was young the music issued at the lips. There was cheer in every face and a spring in every step. The locust-trees were in bloom and the fragrance of the blossoms filled the air. Cardiff Hill, beyond the village and above it, was green with vegetation, and it lay just far enough away to seem a Delectable Land, dreamy, reposeful, and inviting.

Tom appeared on the sidewalk with a bucket of whitewash and a long-handled brush. He surveyed the fence, and all gladness left him and a deep melancholy settled down upon his spirit. Thirty yards of board fence nine feet high. Life to him seemed hollow, and existence but a burden. Sighing, he dipped his brush and passed it along the topmost plank; repeated the operation; did it again; compared the insignificant whitewashed streak with the far-reaching continent of unwhitewashed fence, and sat down on a tree-box discouraged. Jim came skipping out at the gate with a tin pail, and singing *Buffalo Gals.* Bringing water from the town pump had always been hateful work in Tom's eyes, before, but now it did not strike him so. He remembered that there was company at the pump. White, mulatto, and negro boys and girls were always there waiting their turns, resting, trading playthings, quarrelling, fighting, skylarking. And he remembered that although the pump was only a hundred and fifty yards off, Jim never got

[1] From *The Adventures of Tom Sawyer.* Published by Harper & Brothers.

145

back with a bucket of water under an hour—and even then somebody generally had to go after him. Tom said:

"Say, Jim, I'll fetch the water if you'll whitewash some."

Jim shook his head and said:

"Can't, Mars Tom. Ole missis, she tole me I got to go an' git dis water an' not stop fooling 'roun' wid anybody. She say she spec' Mars Tom gwine to ax me to whitewash, an' so she tole me go 'long an' 'tend to my own business—she 'lowed *she'd* 'tend to de whitewashin'."

"Oh, never you mind what she said, Jim. That's the way she always talks. Gimme the bucket—I won't be gone only a minute. *She* won't ever know."

"Oh, I dasn't, Mars Tom. Ole missis she'd take an' tar de head off'n me. 'Deed she would."

"*She!* She never licks anybody—whacks 'em over the head with her thimble—and who cares for that, I'd like to know. She talks awful, but talk don't hurt—anyways it don't if she don't cry. Jim, I'll give you a marvel. I'll give you a white alley!"

Jim began to waver.

"White alley, Jim! And it's a bully taw."

"My! Dats a mighty gay marvel, I tell you! But Mars Tom I's powerful 'fraid ole missis—"

"And besides, if you will I'll show you my sore toe."

Jim was only human—this attraction was too much for him. He put down his pail, took the white alley, and bent over the toe with absorbing interest while the bandage was being unwound. In another moment he was flying down the street with his pail and a tingling rear, Tom was whitewashing with vigor, and Aunt Polly was retiring from the field with a slipper in her hand and triumph in her eye.

But Tom's energy did not last. He began to think of the fun he had planned for this day, and his sorrows multiplied. Soon the free boys would come tripping along on all sorts of delicious expeditions, and they would make a world of fun of him for having to work—the very thought of it burnt him like fire. He got out his worldly wealth and examined it—bits of toys, marbles, and trash; enough to buy an exchange of work, maybe, but not half enough to buy so much as half an hour of pure freedom. So he returned his straitened means to his pocket, and gave up the idea of trying to buy the boys. At this dark and hopeless moment an inspiration burst upon him! Nothing less than a great, magnificent inspiration.

He took up his brush and went tranquilly to work. Ben Rogers hove in sight presently—the very boy, of all boys, whose ridicule he had been dreading. Ben's gait was hop-skip-and-jump—proof enough that his heart was light and his anticipations high. He was eating an apple, and giving a long, melodious whoop, at intervals, followed by a deep-toned ding-dong-dong, ding-dong-dong, for he was personating a steamboat. As he drew near, he slackened speed, took the middle of the street, leaned far over to starboard and rounded to ponderously and with laborious pomp and circumstance—for he was personating the *Big Missouri*, and considered himself to be drawing nine feet of water. He was boat and captain and engine-bells combined, so he had to imagine himself standing on his own hurricane-deck giving the orders and executing them:

"Stop her, sir! Ting-a-ling-ling!" The headway ran almost out, and he drew up slowly toward the sidewalk.

"Ship up to back! Ting-a-ling-ling!" His arms straightened and stiffened down his sides.

"Set her back on the stabboard! Ting-a-ling-ling! Chow! ch-chow-wow! Chow!" His right hand, meantime, describing stately circles—for it was representing a forty-foot wheel.

"Let her go back on the labboard! Ting-a-ling! Chow-ch-chow-chow!" The left hand began to describe circles.

"Stop the stabboard! Ting-a-ling-ling! Stop the labboard! Come ahead on the stabboard! Stop her! Let your outside turn over slow! Ting-a-ling-ling! Chow-ow-ow! Get out that head-line! *Lively* now! Come—out with your spring-line—what're you about there! Take a turn round that stump with the bight of it! Stand by that stage, now—let her go! Done with the engines, sir! Ting-a-ling-ling! *Sh't! s'ht't! sh't!*" (trying the gauge-cocks).

Tom went on whitewashing—paid no attention to the steamboat. Ben stared a moment and then said:

"Hi-*yi! You're* up a stump, ain't you!"

No answer. Tom surveyed his last touch with the eye of an artist, then he gave his brush another gentle sweep and surveyed the result, as before. Ben ranged up alongside of him. Tom's mouth watered for the apple, but he stuck to his work. Ben said:

"Hello, old chap, you got to work, hey?"

Tom wheeled suddenly and said:

"Why, it's you, Ben! I warn't noticing."

"Say—I'm going in a-swimming, I am. Don't you wish you could? But of course you'd druther *work*—wouldn't you? Course you would!"

Tom contemplated the boy a bit, and said:

"What do you call work?"

"Why, ain't *that* work?"

Tom resumed his whitewashing, and answered carelessly:

"Well, maybe it is, and maybe it ain't. All I know, is, it suits Tom Sawyer."

"Oh come, now, you don't mean to let on that you like it?"

The brush continued to move.

"Like it? Well, I don't see why I oughtn't to like it. Does a boy get a chance to whitewash a fence every day?"

That put the thing in a new light. Ben stopped nibbling his apple. Tom swept his brush daintily back and forth—stepped back to note the effect—added a touch here and there—criticised the effect again—Ben watching every move and getting more and more interested, more and more absorbed. Presently he said:

"Say, Tom, let *me* whitewash a little."

Tom considered, was about to consent; but he altered his mind:

"No—no—I reckon it wouldn't hardly do, Ben. You see, Aunt Polly's awful particular about this fence—right here on the street, you know—but if it was the back fence I wouldn't mind and *she* wouldn't. Yes, she's awful particular about this fence; it's got to be done very careful; I reckon there ain't one boy in a thousand, maybe two thousand, that can do it the way it's got to be done."

"No—is that so? Oh come, now—lemme just try. Only just a little—I'd let *you*, if you was me, Tom."

"Ben, I'd like to, honest injun; but Aunt Polly—well, Jim wanted to do it, but she wouldn't let him; Sid wanted to do it, and she wouldn't let Sid. Now don't you see how I'm fixed? If you was to tackle this fence and anything was to happen to it—"

"Oh, shucks, I'll be just as careful. Now lemme try. Say—I'll give you the core of my apple."

"Well, here—No, Ben, now don't. I'm afeard—"

"I'll give you *all* of it!"

Tom gave up the brush with reluctance in his face, but alacrity in his heart. And while the late steamer *Big Missouri* worked and sweated in the sun, the retired artist sat on a barrel in the shade close by, dangled his legs, munched his apple, and planned the slaughter of more innocents. There was no lack of material; boys happened along every little while; they came to jeer, but remained to whitewash. By the time Ben was fagged out, Tom had traded the next chance to Billy Fisher for a kite, in good repair; and when *he* played out, Johnny Miller bought in for a dead rat and a string to swing it with—and so on, and so on, hour after hour. And when the middle of the afternoon came, from being a poor poverty-stricken boy in the morning, Tom was literally rolling in wealth. He had besides the things before mentioned, twelve marbles, part of a jew's-harp, a piece of blue bottle-glass to look through, a spool cannon, a key that wouldn't unlock anything, a fragment of chalk, a glass stopper of a decanter, a tin soldier, a couple of tadpoles, six fire-crackers, a kitten with only one eye, a brass doorknob, a dog-collar—but no dog—the handle of a knife, four pieces of orange-peel, and a dilapidated old window sash.

He had had a nice, good, idle time all the while—plenty of company—and the fence had three coats of whitewash on it! If he hadn't run out of whitewash he would have bankrupted every boy in the village.

Tom said to himself that it was not such a hollow world, after all. He had discovered a great law of human action, without knowing it—namely, that in order to make a man or a boy covet a thing, it is only necessary to make the thing difficult to attain. If he had been a great and wise philosopher, like the writer of this book, he would now have comprehended that Work consists of whatever a body is *obliged* to do, and that Play consists of whatever a body is not obliged to do. And this would help him to understand why constructing artificial flowers or performing on a tread-mill is work, while rolling ten-pins or climbing Mont Blanc is only amusement. There are wealthy gentlemen in England who drive four-horse passenger-coaches twenty or thirty miles on a daily line, in the summer, because the privilege costs them considerable money; but if they were offered wages for the service, that would turn it into work and then they would resign.

The boy mused awhile over the substantial change which had taken place in his worldly circumstances, and then wended toward headquarters to report.

# THE BAD JOKE THAT ENDED WELL[1]

## Roger Duvoisin

*This humorous story is so simple and direct that it is a good choice for older children who have had little or no experience with creative drama.*

In a certain little town in French Switzerland things were going very badly. The communal forest was fast becoming bare of trees and the communal chest bare of money. The people found the taxes too high, and complained that they got nothing in return. It was a sad state of affairs. The Council scratched their heads over the council table, and finally came to the conclusion that such a desperate situation required a desperate remedy. After much discussion a remedy was hit upon. Perhaps it was a good one, perhaps not, but in any case they actually made a decision.

And what was the decision?

It was this. The next town was as well run as this town was poorly run. Surely the Council in that next town must be made up of very wise men. Undoubtedly it would be a good thing to ask their advice. They might even be induced to part with some of their wisdom. Was not that a good idea? The Council thought so.

The next day they departed: the Mayor carrying an empty bag under his arm, followed by his Councilmen and the Clerk. It was hot, and the grass bordering the side of the winding road was covered with dust, but still, it was a fine day.

Noon had come by the time the Council entered the Town Hall of the next town. The Clerk there bade them be seated.

"Pray, Mr. Mayor and Gentlemen, to what good fortune do we owe the great honor of your visit?"

The Mayor cleared his throat and explained.

"Mr. Clerk, the whole world knows and admires the administration of your town. You must indeed be wise men. And we have come to seek your advice, and beg you to spare us some of your wisdom. We greatly need it. See, I have brought a bag for it." The Mayor here hopefully unfolded the bag.

The Clerk was rather amazed, but he was also quick-witted. The empty bag gave him an idea.

[1] Reprinted from *The Three Sneezes*, by Roger Duvoisin. By permission of Alfred A. Knopf, Inc. Copyright, 1941, by A. A. Knopf, Inc.

"Gentlemen," he said, smiling and rubbing his hands together, "we are proud of your request and shall do our best to help you. If you will give me your bag, it will take but a moment to put the Spirit of Wisdom into it."

The Clerk ran into the garden behind the Town Hall. Making sure that he was not seen, he managed to detach a wasp's nest which hung from the pear tree. He put it in the bag and carefully tied the strings.

"Mr. Mayor," he said as he re-entered, "I think I have what you want. Here is the Spirit of Wisdom, in the bag. Keep it carefully until you reach your town. Do not be disturbed if it seems to move, or make humming, buzzing sounds. That will be a good sign: a sign that the Spirit is very much alive. When you get home go into your Council Room. Close the door and all the shutters. Then shake the bag and open it. I can assure you, gentlemen, that almost at once you will feel the effect."

"Mr. Clerk," said the Mayor, rising from his chair, "we thank you from the bottom of our hearts."

With light feet the Council started home. The Mayor tied the bag to his blue umbrella, and carried it over his shoulder. He was proud to bear this precious and historic burden.

The wasps soon began to stir and buzz inside the bag. It was music to the Council's ears.
"Hear it?" asked the delighted Mayor. "Ah! What a good little Spirit we have here."
"Lively as a kitten," said the President.

It was late when the Council reached their town. Some peasants were already returning from the fields, the men balancing their forks and scythes over their shoulders, and the women, in black bodices and wide sleeves, carrying the lunch baskets.

The Mayor and his Council proceeded importantly to the Town Hall and the bag was deposited upon the council table. The door and shutters were tightly closed. The Council took their seats.

It was a solemn moment. The Council fully felt its importance as they waited in silence for the Mayor to untie the bag, which he did, after shaking it vigorously two or three times.

A low distant murmur, the chant of Wisdom, was heard. It grew and grew until it became a furious buzzing and the Spirit began to inoculate its Wisdom. It was a burning inoculation.

"I've got the Spirit on the nose!" shouted the Mayor. "Ouch! On the lips, on the neck too!"

"I have it on the cheeks!" cried the President.

"It stung me on the forehead!" said the Vice-President. "What a lively Spirit!"

"Ouch!" yelled the Clerk, "it just came in through my chin!"

"And me! Good heavens!" shouted a Councilman. "I have it everywhere!"

Only when the buzzing and the stinging seemed to lessen did the Council, feeling that the Spirit of Wisdom had penetrated deeply enough, open the shutters.

What a sight! They hardly knew each other. Their faces were red and swollen beyond recognition. And all around the Council Room and over the table the Spirit of Wisdom was flying and crawling.

"Wasps!" yelped the Council.

"The rascal! It's a joke!" cried the Mayor.

"We have been cheated," wept the President.

But no. They had not been cheated. The neighboring Clerk would never have believed it, but the Spirit of Wisdom bore its fruit. The Council learned that to have a well-ordered town, they must count on themselves. When they recovered from their pains and swellings (which they hid as best they could), they went to work as they had never done before. Their town became a model of good administration.


### THE STONE IN THE ROAD

#### Adaptation of an Old Tale

*Here is a good story which can be dramatized by children of any age. It is as mature as the group makes it. Simple, universal in interest, full of action and of meaning, rich in the opportunity it offers for varied characters, it can be counted on to appeal to practically every group. Children will think of many kinds of reactions to the stone—numerous ways it can be used in the dramatization.*

There was once a Duke who lived in a fine house on the edge of a little village. He was kind and generous to the village folk, and many a time he helped them when they were in trouble.

If the wind blew the roof off a man's barn, the Duke would send his servants to help him build another. If there was illness and distress in the town, he could be counted on to help unfortunate families. When crops were poor, the villagers could be sure that he would not let them go hungry.

As the years passed, however, the Duke realized that people relied too much on his generosity. They were becoming more and more lazy, and instead of being grateful, they were envious and discontented. He resolved, therefore, to test them to find out whether there were not at least a few villagers who would exert themselves for the good of others. He hoped in this way to make the people see themselves as they really were.

One morning very early he went out to the highway and pushed a large stone into the very middle of the road. He had to tug and pull with all his might, but he would allow no one to help him. Just before he pushed it into place, he took from under his cloak a bag of gold, and, dropping it to the ground, he covered it with the stone. Then he went behind a nearby hedge to watch what might happen.

Before long a farmer came along, driving some sheep to market. He could scarcely believe his eyes when he saw the big stone blocking the way.

"Run ahead, lad," he said to his son, "and see if it is really a stone." For it was only beginning to be light, and he thought it might be something that had fallen out of an ox-cart.

"It *is* a stone, father," said the boy after he had explored. "How ever could it have come there?"

"Well, one thing is sure," replied the farmer. "*We'll* not try to move it. Let the Duke's servants get it out of the way." And with the help of the boy, he drove the sheep around the stone, grumbling all the while about the trouble it caused him.

Before long, two country women came along, carrying baskets of eggs to sell. They were so busy talking about the price they hoped to get for their eggs and wishing that it would be enough to pay for the cloth for a new dress that when they saw the stone they did not at first appear to be surprised. Indeed, one of them sat on it to pull up the heel of her shoe, and, discovering that she was somewhat tired, she decided to sit until she was rested. Only then did it occur to the second woman that she had never seen a stone here before.

"Why, a carriage could never get around this thing," she said. "I wonder that the Duke leaves it here!"

But her companion, resting on its broad surface, was dreaming of the fine clothes she would have if she were rich like the Duke's lady. She could not know that well within her reach was a tidy sum of money that would buy more dresses than she could wear in a lifetime.

Hour after hour a procession of people passed along the busy highway, some scolding about the stone, others enjoying the novelty of it, but none offering to move it out of the road. There were laborers, well-to-do merchants, soldiers; some proud ladies who were turned back because there was not room for their carriage to pass; a scholar, so deep in his reading that he stumbled over the stone; a peddler, a minstrel, a beggar.

The Duke had all but given up hope when, about dusk, he heard a gay whistle in the distance. It came from the miller's son, who was trudging along the road with a heavy sack of meal over his shoulder. Suddenly the whistling stopped.

"A stone in the middle of the road!" he said to himself. "That's a queer place for a stone as big as that! Someone will fall over it!" And in less time than it takes to tell about it, he had put his sack of meal on the ground and shoved the stone off the road. As he went back to get the meal, he saw the bag of gold.

"Somebody has lost this," he thought. But no sooner had he picked it up than the Duke stepped out from his hiding-place.

"Read what is written on the bag, my boy," he said.

"For him who moves the stone," read the astonished lad. "Then—?"

"It is for you," said the Duke kindly. "I am glad to find that there is one person in our village who is willing to go to some trouble out of thoughtfulness for others."

"Oh, thank you, thank you, sir!" cried the boy. "It was a little thing to do! You are very kind!" And off he sped to tell his mother of his wonderful good fortune.


## THE WISE PEOPLE OF GOTHAM[1]

### Adaptation of an Old Tale

*This is one of the merry tales told of the simple folk who once lived in Gotham, an old town in England. It is a lively story, with unusual opportunity for varied and interesting characters and action.*

One day, news was brought to Gotham that the king was coming that way, and that he would pass through the town. This did not

[1] From *Fifty Famous Stories Retold*, by James Baldwin.

please the men of Gotham at all, for they knew that the king was a cruel, bad man. If he came to their town, they would have to find food and lodging for him and his men; and if he saw anything that pleased him, he would be sure to take it for his own. What should they do?

They met together to talk the matter over.

"Let us chop down the big trees in the woods, so that they will block up the highway that leads into town," said one of the wise men.

"Good!" said all the rest.

So they went out with their axes, and soon the highway that led to the town was filled with logs and brush. The king's horsemen would have a hard time of it getting into Gotham.

When the king came, and saw that the road had been blocked, he was very angry.

"Who chopped those trees down in my way?" he asked of two country lads that were passing by.

"The men of Gotham," said the lads.

"Well," said the king, "go and tell the men of Gotham that I shall come with my sheriff into their town and have all their noses cut off."

The two lads ran to the town as fast as they could, and made known what the king had said.

Everybody was in great fright. The men ran from house to house, carrying the news, and asking one another what they should do.

"Our wits have kept the king out of the town," said one; "and so now our wits must save our noses."

"True, true!" said the others. "But what shall we do?"

Then one, whose name was Dobbin, and who was thought to be the wisest of them all, said, "Let me tell you something. Many a man has been punished because he was wise, but I have never heard of any one being harmed because he was a fool. So, when the king's sheriff comes, let us all act like fools."

"Good, good!" cried the others. "We will all act like fools."

It was no easy thing for the king's men to open the road; but after a time they succeeded in doing so. Just before they reached the town, they saw a queer sight. Some old men were rolling big stones up the hill, and all the young men were looking on, and grunting very loudly.

The king stopped the horses, and asked what they were doing.

"We are rolling stones uphill to make the sun rise," said one of the old men.

"You foolish fellow!" said the king. "Don't you know that the sun will rise without any help?"

"Ah, will it?" said the old man. "Well, I never thought of that. How wise you are!"

"And what are *you* doing?" said the sheriff to the young men.

"Oh, we do the grunting while our fathers do the working," they answered.

"I see," said the sheriff. "Well, that is the way the world goes everywhere." And they rode on toward the town.

They soon came to a field where a number of people were building a stone wall.

"What are you doing?" asked the king.

"Why, master," they answered, "there is a cuckoo in this field, and we are building a wall around it so as to keep the bird from straying away."

"You foolish people!" said the king. "Don't you know that the bird will fly over the top of your wall, no matter how high you build it?"

"Why, no," they said. "We never thought of that. How very wise you are!"

They next met a man who was carrying a door on his back.

"What are you doing?" the sheriff asked.

"I have just started on a long journey," said the man.

"But why do you carry that door?" asked the sheriff.

"I left my money at home."

"Then why didn't you leave the door at home too?"

"I was afraid of thieves; and you see, if I have the door with me, they can't break it open and get in."

"You foolish fellow!" said the sheriff. "It would be safer to leave the door at home, and carry the money with you."

"Ah, would it though?" said the man. "Now, I never thought of that. You are the wisest man that I ever saw."

Then the king and the sheriff rode on with the men; but every one that they met was doing some silly thing. Soon the king and his men were all laughing.

"Truly, I believe that the people of Gotham are all fools," said one of the horsemen.

"That is true," said another. "It would be a shame to harm such simple people."

"Let us ride back to London," said the king. "They are too stupid to punish."

So they all rode back to the city and never bothered the people of Gotham again.


## THE CONJURE WIVES[1]

### An Old Tale Retold by Frances G. Wickes

*Fun a-plenty around Hallowe'en will come with the playing of this old southern tale. Both boys and girls enjoy being the "conjure wives," or evil spirits. The howling wind, the periodic knocking, and the weird "who-o?" of the conjure wife owls give a delightfully spooky feeling to the dramatization.*

Once on a time when a Hallowe'en night came on the dark o' the moon, a lot o' old conjure wives was a sittin' by the fire an' a cookin' a big supper for theirselves.

The wind was a-howlin' 'round like it does on Hallowe'en nights, an' the old conjure wives they hitched theirselves up to the fire an' talked about the spells they was a-goin' to weave 'long come midnight.

By an' by there come a-knockin' at the door.

"Who's there?" called an old conjure wife. "Who-o? Who-o?"

"One who is hungry and cold," said a voice.

Then the old conjure wives, they all burst out laughin' an' they called out:

"We's a-cookin' for ourselves.
Who'll cook for you?
Who? Who?"

The voice didn't say nothin', but the knockin' just kept on.

"Who's that a-knockin'?" called out another conjure wife. "Who? Who?"

Then there come a whistlin', wailin' sound:

"Let me in, do-o-o-o!
I'se cold thro-o-o-o an' thro-o-o-o,
An' I'se hungry, too-o-o!"

[1] From *Happy Holidays*, published by Rand McNally & Company. Used by permission of the author.

Then the old conjure wives, they all burst out laughin', an' they commenced to sing out:

> "Git along, do!
> We's a-cookin' for ourselves.
> Who'll cook for you?
> Who? Who?"

The voice didn't say nothin' but the knockin' just kept on.

Then the old conjure wives they went to work a-cookin' of the supper for theirselves, an' the voice didn't say nothin' but the knockin' just kept on.

An' then the old conjure wives they hitched up to the fire an' they ate an' they ate—an' the voice didn't say nothin', but the knockin' just kept on. An' the old conjure wives they called out again:

> "Git along, do!
> We's a-cookin' for ourselves.
> Who'll cook for you?
> Who? Who?"

An' the voice didn't say nothin', but the knockin' just kept on.

Then the old conjure wives began to get scared-like, an' one of 'em says, "Let's give it somethin' an' get it away before it spoils our spells."

An' the voice didn't say nothin', but the knockin' just kept on.

Then the old conjure wives they took the littlest piece of dough, as big as a pea, an' they put it in the fry pan.

An' the voice didn't say nothin', but the knockin' just kept on.

An' when they put the dough in the fry pan it begun to swell an' swell, an' it swelled over the fry pan an' it swelled over the top o' the stove an' it swelled out on the floor.

An' the voice didn't say nothin', but the knockin' just kept on.

Then the old conjure wives got scared an' they ran for the door, an' the *door was shut tight.*

An' the voice didn't say nothin', but the knockin' just kept on.

An' then the dough it swelled an' it swelled all over the floor an' it swelled up into the chairs. An' the old conjure wives they climbed up on the backs of the chairs an' they were scareder an' scareder. An' they called out, "Who's that a-knockin' at the door? Who? Who?"

An' the voice didn't say nothin', but the knockin' just kept on.

An' the dough kept a-swellin' and a-swellin', an' the old conjure wives begun to scrooge up smaller an' smaller, an' their eyes got bigger with scaredness, an' they kept a-callin', "Who's that a-knockin'? Who? Who?"

An' then the knockin' stopped, an' the voice called out,

"Fly out the window, do!
There's no more house for you!"

An' the old conjure wives they spread their wings an' they flew out the windows an' off into the woods, all a-callin', "Who'll cook for you? Who? Who?"

An' now if you go into the woods in the dark o' the moon you'll see the old conjure wife owls an' hear 'em callin', "Who'll cook for you? Who! Who!"

Only, on a Hallowe'en night you don't want to go 'round the old owls, because *then* they turns to old conjure wives a-weavin' their spells.


## THE GOLDEN TOUCH

### Adapted from Nathaniel Hawthorne

*One of the few stories for children in which a hero's enemy is within himself. Some background in Greek myth is needed for the full understanding of the Midas story. How sympathetic is the character of Midas? Is he simply a greedy man, or does he have any fine qualities?*

Once upon a time there lived in Phrygia a very rich king whose name was Midas. He was more fond of gold than of anything else in the world except his little daughter Marygold, and he thought that the finest thing he could do for her was to make her the richest of all princesses.

Whenever Midas gazed at the gold-tinted clouds of sunset, he wished that they were real gold, and that they could be squeezed into his strong box. If little Marygold ran to meet him with a bunch of buttercups, he would say, "Pooh, pooh, child! If these flowers were as golden as they look, they would be worth the plucking."

And yet, in his earlier days, King Midas had shown a great taste for flowers. He had planted a garden in which grew the sweetest, most beautiful roses to be found anywhere, and he used to pass many hours gazing at them and inhaling their perfume. But now, if he looked at them at all, it was only to calculate how much the garden would be worth if each of the roses were made of pure gold. And though he once was fond of music, the only music for Midas now was the clink of one coin against another.

As time went on, Midas spent more and more time in the dark and dreary basement room where he kept his wealth. Here, after carefully locking the door, he would take a bag of gold coin, or a gold cup as big as a washbowl, or a heavy golden bar, and bring them from the obscure corners of the room into the one bright and narrow sunbeam that fell from the dungeon-like window. He valued the sunbeam for no other reason but that his treasure would not shine without its help.

One day, when Midas was enjoying himself in his treasure room, he perceived a shadow fall over the heaps of gold; and looking suddenly up, what should he behold but the figure of a stranger standing in the bright sunbeam. It was a young man with a bright, ruddy face. Whether it was that the imagination of King Midas threw a yellow tinge over everything, or whatsoever the cause might be, he could not help fancying that the smile with which the stranger regarded him had a kind of golden radiance in it. Certainly, although his figure intercepted the sunshine, there was now a brighter gleam upon all the piled-up treasures than before.

As Midas knew that he had carefully turned the key in the lock, and that no mortal strength could possibly break into his treasure room, he, of course, concluded that his visitor must be something more than mortal.

The stranger gazed about the room, looking at all the golden objects, and then turned again to Midas.

"You are a wealthy man, friend Midas," he observed. "I doubt whether any other four walls on earth contain so much gold!"

"I have done pretty well—pretty well," answered Midas. "But, after all, it is only a trifle when you consider that it has taken me my whole life to get it together. If one could live a thousand years he might have time to grow rich."

"What!" exclaimed the stranger. "Then you are not satisfied?"

Midas shook his head.

"And pray what would satisfy you?" asked the stranger.

"I wish," said King Midas with a sigh, "that everything I touch might turn to gold."

"The Golden Touch," said the stranger with a broad smile. "And are you quite sure that would make you happy?"

"How could it fail?" said Midas.

"As you wish," said the stranger. "Tomorrow at sunrise you shall have the Golden Touch."

Then the stranger vanished.

At daybreak Midas was broad awake. He reached out and eagerly touched a chair. Nothing happened. The stranger had failed him. Or had it been just a dream? Midas' spirits sank dismally, until suddenly the first sunbeam shone through the window, and by its light Midas saw that the brocaded coverlet of his bed gleamed like gold. The Golden Touch had come to him with the sunrise!

Midas started up in a kind of joyful frenzy, and ran about touching everything. He turned his bedposts to pillars of gold. He pulled aside a window-curtain, and the tassel grew heavy in his hand. He took up a book from the table and ran his fingers through the leaves. Behold! It was a bundle of thin golden plates on which the words had disappeared. He dressed himself in clothes of magnificent gold cloth—which, he had to admit, was somewhat heavy! He drew out a handkerchief which little Marygold had hemmed for him. That was likewise gold, with the neat stitches running all along the border in gold thread. Somehow or other, this last transformation did not quite please King Midas.

"It is no great matter, nevertheless," said he to himself. "We cannot expect any great good without some small disadvantage." And he went downstairs and out into the garden where hundreds of beautiful roses were blooming. There he went about touching every blossom until the whole garden was a mass of gold. By this time the morning air had given him an excellent appetite and he hastened back to the palace for breakfast.

Marygold had not yet made her appearance when he arrived, and her father ordered her to be called. Soon he heard her coming along the passageway, crying bitterly. This surprised him, for she had the sunniest disposition imaginable. When she opened the door he saw she was holding several of his golden roses.

"Look, father," she sobbed, holding them out to him, "all the beautiful blossoms that smelled so sweet are spoiled. They are hard and ugly and have no fragrance at all. What can have happened to them?"

King Midas was ashamed to think he had caused her this unhappiness, and so he said, "Pooh, my dear, don't cry about it. Sit down and eat your breakfast. It will be easy enough to exchange a golden rose like that, which will last hundreds of years, for an ordinary one which would wither in a day."

Meanwhile, Midas helped himself to the delicious grapes on his plate. But before he could get one to his lips, it changed to hard, heavy gold. Midas was aghast! Quickly he raised his cup to his lips. But before he could drink, the water became molten gold, and the next moment hardened into a lump. He tried the fish and the little cakes, but even though he tried to swallow them in a hurry, it was of no use. The future looked dismal indeed. How many days could he survive on such rich fare?

"Father! What is the matter?" exclaimed Marygold, forgetting her sorrow when she saw the horror on her father's face. And running to him, she threw her arms about his knees.

"Ah, my dear, your love is worth more to me than all the gold in the world," he said, and he reached out to take her in his arms.

"My precious, precious Marygold!" he cried.

But Marygold made no answer. The moment he had touched her, her sweet, rosy face, so full of affection, assumed a glittering yellow color. Her beautiful brown ringlets took the same tint. Her soft little form grew hard. Little Marygold was a human child no longer, but a golden statue!

Midas could only wring his hands in despair and wish to be the poorest man in the world if he could only have his little daughter's love again.

As he sat, sunk in despair, he suddenly saw a stranger standing near the door. It was the same man who had visited him the day before, and he was still smiling.

"Well, friend Midas," said the stranger, how is the Golden Touch?"

"I am miserable," said Midas. "Gold is not everything. I have lost what my heart valued most."

"Ah, so you have made a discovery," said the stranger. "Which would you rather have—the Golden Touch or one cup of cold water?"

"Oh, blessed water!" cried Midas.

"The Golden Touch or a crust of bread?"

"A piece of bread is worth all the gold on earth!"

"The Golden Touch or your little daughter?"

"Oh, my child, my dear child!" cried poor Midas, wringing his hands. "I would not have given that one small dimple in her chin for a world of gold."

162

"You are wiser than you were, King Midas," said the stranger. "Tell me now, do you sincerely wish to rid yourself of this Golden Touch?"

"It is hateful to me! Oh, have you the power to rid me of it?"

"Go and plunge into the river at the bottom of the garden. Take a pitcher of the same water and sprinkle it over anything you wish to change back to its former state."

Quickly Midas snatched up an earthen pitcher—no longer earthen after he had touched it—and ran to the river bank. There he plunged in in his golden robes. When he came out he held his pitcher of water very carefully. It was earthware again, and his robes were of fine silk instead of gold! He hastened back to the palace and sprinkled water by handfuls over the golden figure of his little daughter. At once she began to sneeze and sputter.

"Why father," she exclaimed, "why are you spilling water on my fresh frock?"

Her father did not think it was necessary to tell her how foolish he had been, but he took her into the garden and began to sprinkle water on her precious roses. At once their beautiful color and fragrance returned, and Marygold's happiness knew no bounds.

After that morning only one trace of the Golden Touch remained. There were new golden lights in the little princess's hair. Often King Midas touched these golden ringlets gently and said, "To tell you the truth, I hate the sight of every gold but this."


## ROBIN HOOD'S MERRY ADVENTURE WITH THE MILLER[1]

### Howard Pyle

*A collection of stories to dramatize would be incomplete without at least one Robin Hood tale. For Robin is the child's own hero, and though many adults are a bit squeamish about the roughness and the questionable morality of some of his adventures, it is doubtful if any child's standards are lowered by reading or playing them.*

*Much depends on what the leader stresses in reading the stories. Background information concerning the injustice of the laws which caused many honest people to rebel against them is necessary, as well as some discussion of the fact that today we would not condone robbing the rich even for the purpose of giving money to the poor.*

[1] Published by Charles Scribner's Sons.

*Naturally, Friar Tuck is made jolly and rough but not tipsy in children's dramatizations. And, always, Robin's fine qualities are made important.*

*Because every child should be given the opportunity of enjoying Howard Pyle's matchless style of writing, full of flavor, of humor, of red-blooded strength, these stories should be read rather than told to the group—read with zest and enjoyment.*

*Children of eleven and twelve especially enjoy playing this tale of Midge, the miller, even though the flour and the staff are purely imaginary. It occurs one afternoon when Robin, Little John, Will Scarlet, and Arthur a Bland are returning to Sherwood after a morning full of adventure. They are resting and enjoying a song from Little John after "a good stout meal" in a thicket near the road as Midge approaches.*

"Who may yon fellow be comnig along the road?" said Robin, breaking into the song.

"I know not," quote Little John, in a surly voice. "But this I do know, that it is an ill thing to do to check the flow of a good song."

"Nay, Little John," said Robin, "be not vexed, I prythee; but I have been watching him coming along, bent beneath that great bag over his shoulder, ever since thou didst begin thy song. Look, Little John, I pray, and see if thou knowest him."

Little John looked whither Robin Hood pointed. "Truly," quoth he, after a time, "I think yon fellow is a certain young miller I have seen now and then around the edge of Sherwood; a poor wight methinks, to spoil a good song about."

"Now thou speakest of him," quoth Robin Hood, "methinks myself have seen him now and then. Hath he not a mill over beyond Nottingham Town, nigh to the Salisbury road?"

"Thou art right; that is the man," said Little John.

"A good stout fellow," quoth Robin. "I saw him crack Ned o' Bradford's crown about a fortnight since, and never saw I hai lifted more neatly in all my life before."

By this time the young miller had come so near that they coul see him clearly. His clothes were dusted with flour, and over hi back he carried a great sack of meal, bending so as to bring th whole weight upon his shoulders, and across the sack was a thic quarterstaff. His limbs were stout and strong, and he strode alon the dusty road right sturdily with the heavy sack across his shoulder His cheeks were ruddy as a winter hip, his hair was flaxen in colo and on his chin was a downy growth of flaxen beard.

"A good honest fellow," quoth Robin Hood, "and such an one as is a credit to English yeomanrie. Now let us have a merry jest with him. We will forth as though we were common thieves and pretend to rob him of his honest gains. Then will we take him into the forest and give him a feast such as his stomach never held in all his life before, and send him home with crowns in his purse for every penny he hath. What say ye, lads?"

"Truly, it is a merry thought," said Will Scarlet.

But now the Miller, plodding along the road, had come opposite to where the yeomen lay hidden, whereupon all four of them ran at him and surrounded him.

"Hold, friend!" cried Robin to the Miller whereupon he turned slowly, with the weight of the bag upon his shoulder, and looked at each in turn all bewildered, for though a good stout man his wits did not skip like roasting chestnuts.

"Who bids me stay?" said the Miller in a voice deep and gruff, like the growl of a great dog.

"Marry that do I," quoth Robin; "and let me tell thee, friend, thou hadst best mind my bidding."

"And who art thou, good friend?" said the Miller, throwing the great sack of meal from his shoulder to the ground; "and who are those with thee?"

"We be four good Christian men," quoth Robin, "and would fain help thee by carrying part of thy heavy load for thee."

"I give you all thanks," said the Miller, "but my bag is none that heavy that I cannot carry it e'en by myself."

"Nay, thou dost mistake," quoth Robin, "I meant that thou mightest perhaps have some heavy farthings or pence about thee, not to speak of silver and gold."

"Alas!" cried the Miller; "what would ye do to me? Do me no harm, I pray you, but let me depart in peace. Moreover, let me tell you that ye are upon Robin Hood's ground, and should he find you seeking to rob an honest craftsman, he will clip your ears to your heads and scourge you even to the walls of Nottingham."

"In truth I fear Robin Hood no more than I do myself," quoth jolly Robin. "Thou must this day give up to me every penny thou hast about thee. Nay, if thou dost budge an inch I will rattle this staff about thine ears."

"Nay, smite me not!" cried the Miller, throwing up his elbow as though he feared the blow. "Thou mayest search me if thou wilt, but thou will find nothing upon me, pouch, pocket, or skin."

"Is it so?" quoth Robin Hood, looking keenly upon him. "Now I believe that what thou tellest is no true tale. If I am not much mistaken thou hast somewhat in the bottom of that fat sack of meal. Good Arthur, empty the bag upon the ground; I warrant thou wilt find a shilling or two in the flour."

"Alas!" cried the Miller, falling upon his knees, "spoil not all my good meal! It can better you not, and will ruin me. Spare it, and I will give up the money in the bottom of the bag."

"Ha!" quoth Robin, nudging Will Scarlet, "Is it so? I thought that I smelt gold and silver beneath the barley meal. Bring it forth straight, Miller."

Then slowly the Miller arose to his feet, and slowly and unwillingly he untied the mouth of the bag, and slowly thrust his hands into the meal and began fumbling about with his arms buried to the elbows in the barley flour. The others gathered round him, their heads together, looking and wondering what he would bring forth.

So they stood, all with their heads close together, gazing down into the sack. But while he pretended to be searching for the money, the Miller gathered two great handfuls of meal. "Ha," quoth he, "here they are, the beauties." Then, as the others leaned still more forward to see what he had, he suddenly cast the meal into their faces, filling their eyes and noses and mouths with the flour, blinding and half choking them. Arthur a Blank was worse off than any, for his mouth was open, agape with wonder of what was to come, so that a great cloud of flour flew down his throat, setting him a-coughing till he could scarcely stand.

Then, while all four stumbled about, roaring with the smart of the meal in their eyeballs, and while they rubbed their eyes till the tears made great channels on their faces through the meal, the Miller seized another handful of flour and another and another, throwing it in their faces, so that even had they had a glimmering of light before they were now as blind as ever a beggar in Nottinghamshire, while their hair and beards and clothes were as white as snow.

Then catching up his great crab staff, the Miller began laying about him as though he were clean gone mad. This way and that skipped the four, like peas on a drumhead, but they could neither see to defend themselves nor to run away. Thwack! thwack! went the Miller's cudgel across their backs, and at every blow great white clouds of flour rose in the air from their jackets and went drifting down the breeze.

"Stop!" roared Robin at last. "Give over, good friend; I am Robin Hood!"

"Thou liest, thou knave," cried the Miller, giving him a rap on the ribs that sent up a great cloud of flour like a puff of smoke. "Stout Robin never robbed an honest tradesman. Ha! thou wouldst have my money, wouldst thou?" And he gave him another blow. "Nay, thou art not getting thy share, thou long-legged knave. Share and share alike." And he smote Little John across the shoulders so that he sent him skipping half across the road. "Nay, fear not, it is thy turn now, black beard." And he gave the Tanner a crack that made him roar for all his coughing. "How now, red coat, let me brush the dust from thee!" cried he, smiting Will Scarlet. And so he gave them merry words and blows until they could scarcely stand, and whenever he saw one like to clear his eyes he threw more flour in his face.

At last Robin Hood found his horn, and clapping it to his lips blew three loud blasts upon it.

Now it chanced that Will Stutely and a party of Robin's men were in the glade not far from where this merry sport was going forward. Hearing the hubbub of voices, and blows that sounded like the noise of a flail in the barn in winter time, they stopped, listening, and wondering what was toward. Quoth Will Stutely, "Now if I mistake not there is some stout battle with cudgels going forward not far hence. I would fain see this pretty sight." So saying, he and the whole party turned their steps whence the noise came. When they had come near where all the tumult sounded they heard the three blasts of Robin's bugle horn.

"Quick!" cried young David of Doncaster. "Our master is in sore need!" So, without stopping a moment, they dashed forward with might and main and burst forth from the covert into the high-road.

But what a sight was that which they saw! The road was all white with meal, and five men stood there also white with meal from top to toe, for much of the barley flour had fallen back upon the Miller.

"What is thy need, master?" cried Will Stutely. "And what doth all this mean?"

"Why," quoth Robin in a mighty passion, "yon traitor hath come as nigh slaying me as e'er a man in all the world. Hadst thou not come quickly, good Stutely, thy master had been dead."

Hereupon, whilst he and the three others rubbed the meal from their eyes, and Will Stutely and his men brushed their clothes clean, he told them all; how he had meant to pass a jest upon the Miller, which same had turned so grievously upon them.

"Quick, men, seize the vile Miller!" cried Stutely, who was nigh choking with laughter as were the rest; whereupon several ran upon the stout fellow, and seizing him bound his arms behind his back with bowstrings.

"Ha!" cried Robin, when they brought the trembling Miller to him, "Thou wouldst murder me, wouldst thou? By my faith"— Here he stopped and stood glaring upon the Miller with a grim look. But Robin's anger could not hold, so first his eyes twinkled, and then in spite of all he broke into a laugh.

Now when they saw their master laugh, the yeomen who stood around could contain themselves no longer, and a mighty shout of laughter went up from all. Many could not stand, but rolled upon the ground from pure merriment.

"What is thy name, good fellow?" said Robin at last to the Miller, who stood gaping and as though he were in a maze.

"Alas, sir, I am Midge, the Miller's son," said he in a frightened voice.

"I make my vow," quoth merry Robin, smiting him upon the shoulder, "thou art the mightiest Midge that e'er mine eyes beheld. Now wilt thou leave thy dusty mill and come and join my band? By my faith, thou art too stout a man to spend thy days betwixt the hopper and the till."

"Then truly, if thou dost forgive me for the blows I struck, not knowing who thou wast, I will join thee right merrily," said the Miller.

"Then have I gained this day," quoth Robin, "one of the stoutest yeomen in all Nottinghamshire. We will get us away to the greenwood tree, and there hold a merry feast in honor of our new friend." So saying, he turned and led the way, the rest following, and so they entered the forest once more and were lost to sight.

# THE HURDY-GURDY MAN[1]

## Margery Williams Bianco

*Children of eight, nine, ten, or eleven will have a delightful time dramatizing this charming story. Besides the opportunity it affords for interesting action, characterization, and comedy, it has significance of idea. It needs suitable music.*

It, was on a bright spring morning that the hurdy-gurdy man came to town. The sky was blue; there were little green leaves on the maple trees, and the sun shone down on the roofs and sidewalks, making everything look clean and newly washed. The storekeepers were just taking down their shutters and the housewives shaking rugs, and there was a pleasant early morning smell of wood smoke and coffee, which made the hurdy-gurdy man feel very hungry, for he had walked a long way since daybreak. And the first person he set eyes on, as he strode whistling into the town with his hurdy-gurdy strapped to his back, was the fat woman in the Delicatessen Store, just sweeping off her doorstep for the day.

"Good morning! Can I get a cup of coffee here?" asked the hurdy-gurdy man.

The fat woman looked him up and down, for he was very shabby. Still, a customer was a customer, and she was just about to say "yes," when she caught sight of a queer little wrinkled face staring at her over his shoulder. It belonged to the hurdy-gurdy man's monkey, who was perched up there atop of the organ, making no sound but just gazing at her out of his dark solemn eyes.

"You may buy a cup of coffee," she said, "but you can't bring that nasty grinning monkey into my shop, for monkeys I can't and won't abide!"

"Then, in that case," said the hurdy-gurdy man politely, "we will do without the coffee!"

And off he strolled up the street with his monkey on his shoulder.

Presently he came to the Bakery, and there was the Baker in his shirt-sleeves, setting out his fresh loaves on the counter.

"Good morning! Can I get a cup of coffee here and a loaf of bread?" asked the hurdy-gurdy man.

But the Baker too had caught sight of the monkey, staring at him with unwinking eyes.

"I can sell you bread," he answered, "but you'll get your coffee somewhere else, for I won't have that foreign-looking beast sitting at my table and scaring my customers."

"Then we won't have the bread either," said the hurdy-gurdy man, and he went on his way.

Now it so happened that the hurdy-gurdy man had come to the worst little town he could possibly have found. It was a neat and prosperous little town, but all the people who lived in it were so busy being neat and prosperous that they had no time for anything else. Everyone went about his or her business all day long just as serious as ants in an ant-hill. The housewives worked from morning till night. Every window-pane was polished till it shone; every hedge was clipped, and on the front lawns there wasn't so much as a single grassblade out of place. And as for such things as tramps or stray dogs or organ-grinders, the little town would have none of them.

As the hurdy-gurdy man strolled on up the street that spring morning he looked about him. He noticed the shiny window-panes and the front curtains all starched and stiff, and the neat lawns, and once in a while he frowned, and once in a while he nodded, and once in a while he reached his hand up to scratch the ear of the little monkey who sat so quietly on his shoulder. And so he went his way, whistling through his teeth, and presently he reached the end of the Green where the tall maple trees stood. And there, a little back from the road, he came upon two small cottages, side by side.

These two little cottages didn't look as if they belonged to the town at all, and that was exactly what the town itself felt about them. They were shabby and tumble-down; their walls needed painting and their front fences were unmended, and their door-yards, instead of being neat and tidy like all the other door-yards round about, were just a tangle of roses and lilacs and snow-berry bushes, growing any way at all that they chose. And in one yard were yellow day-lilies crowding against the palings and overflowing into the street itself, and in the other a great bed of johnny-jump-ups, hollowed out in the middle where a big striped cat lay curled up asleep in the sun.

Most unsightly little cottages, the whole town agreed.

But for all that there was something gay and cheerful about them, if only for the way the lilacs nodded in the breeze, and the sturdy look of the geraniums on the window-sills. And there was something cheerful about the people who lived in them, which was more than could be said for the rest of the townsfolk, and more too than those same townsfolk could understand.

For why should Mrs. Meeks be cheerful, with a seven year old boy called Tommy to cook and wash and buy shoes for, and only an odd day's work to be had now and then at scrubbing or spring-cleaning? While as for Miss Gay, the Dress-maker next door, everyone knew she was as poor as a church mouse, and wouldn't be able to live at all if the neighbors didn't kindly give her a few curtains to hem once in a while, because, after all, she did sew more cheaply than anyone else.

None of these things the hurdy-gurdy man knew, but something about the cottages seemed to please him, for he walked right in through the first gateway—which happened to be Miss Gay's—and up the little path past the johnny-jump-ups and the sleeping cat, and was about to knock at the door, when the door opened, and there stood Miss Gay herself, a little flustered, and peering short-sightedly through her glasses.

Straight past him she peered, and straight at the little brown face staring over his shoulder, and the first thing she said was:

"Why, look at the dear little monkey!"

At that the monkey moved for the first time. He scrambled down from his master's shoulder and ran through the doorway into Miss Gay's kitchen. He climbed into a chair at the table where Miss Gay had been eating her breakfast, and there he sat.

"See that, bless him!" Miss Gay exclaimed. "He must be hungry! And perhaps you'd take a cup of coffee, too," she added, turning to the hurdy-gurdy man. "It's early in the day to be travelling."

"I will indeed, thank you," said the hurdy-gurdy man, and he followed her in and sat down at the table and took the monkey on his knee.

Miss Gay asked him no questions, but she bustled about and fetched coffee and bread and home-made jam, and an apple for the monkey. When everything was on the table she said, "And now, if you'll excuse me, I must go and call Tommy Meeks next door, for he'd never forgive me if he knew I'd had a monkey to breakfast, and he wasn't here to see him."

And she fluttered out at the door calling: "Tommy! Tommy Meeks! Come and see who's here!"

Tommy was tanned and brown-haired and freckled, and his toes, as usual, were nearly out of his shoes, but the monkey took to him amazingly, and he to the monkey. And while they were making friends, and the monkey offering Tommy bites of his apple, the hurdy-gurdy man asked Miss Gay what she thought about the town.

"They're nice people," Miss Gay told him. "No one could say they aren't kind. But there—they're just taken up with their own affairs. Now where I was born the folk were all neighborly, and they liked to joke or gossip, and if there was music they'd gather round from miles to hear it! But here they aren't like that. They're folk that like everything quiet. And as for a bit of music, you couldn't get them to listen to it!"

"They'll listen to my music," said the hurdy-gurdy man.

"Goodness knows they need it," Miss Gay nodded. "Though I shouldn't be talking about my neighbors this way. But I always liked to see things cheerful!"

"How many tunes can your organ play?" interrupted Tommy. He wanted to know all about it, and how the stops worked.

"It can play three tunes, but as a rule there are only two of them I ever need to play," said the hurdy-gurdy man. "If I pull out that third stop there, then it plays the third tune."

"And what is that like?" Tommy asked.

"It's a queer sort of a tune," said the hurdy-gurdy man, "and I don't play it so often."

"Oh, I hope you play it today!" Tommy cried.

"That we'll see about," said the hurdy-gurdy man. "And now, thank you very much for the breakfast, and we'll have to be getting along!"

At that the monkey swallowed his last bite of apple, very quickly, and jumped to his master's shoulder, and the man picked up his hurdy-gurdy once more and set out.

Tommy went with him. He was very anxious to hear the music, and he didn't mean to lose sight of his friend the monkey.

When they came to the middle of the Green the hurdy-gurdy man stopped. He unslung the strap from his shoulder and began to play. As he turned the handle the first little tune tinkled out, a funny wheezy old tune, such as all hurdy-gurdies play, with a lot of squeaks and trills and deep rumblings to it.

No one seemed to be listening. Here and there a window blind was whisked aside and then whisked back again, in an annoyed sort of way. But no one paid any real attention.

But by the time he had begun his little tune for the second time, someone had heard him certainly.

The children had heard him.

For it is a queer thing that, whatever the grown people may be like in a town, the children are the same the world over, and all children love a hurdy-gurdy. So out they came trooping, to gather round the hurdy-gurdy and his monkey. Children just escaped from the breakfast table, boys and girls on their way to school, they all came scampering across the grass, shouting one to another and paying no heed at all to their parents, who scolded them from the doorways. All they thought of was to see the monkey and listen to the hurdy-gurdy.

When the hurdy-gurdy man played his second tune it was even better than the first. It went faster and had a gayer lilt to it, so that all the children began to prance and jump, while the monkey pulled his cap off and bobbed and ducked to them till they yelled with joy.

And now the school bell began to ring. "Ding-dong, ding-dong," it went, but no one paid any attention to it. And after it had been ringing for a long time, and still no one obeyed it, the Teacher herself came out on the school-house steps, and began to clap her hands at the children very sternly and angrily.

But no one paid any attention to her, either.

Every child in the town, by now, was gathered round the hurdy-gurdy.

Such a thing had never been heard of before!

The fathers and mothers were furious, the School Teacher was furious. The Town Clerk was the most furious of all for he liked quiet and order, and here, almost under the very Town Hall windows, was such a hullabaloo as he had never heard before. He wanted to fetch the police, but he knew that the Town Policeman (there was only one) was in bed that day with a bad cold in his head, and couldn't be routed out. For when had their quiet orderly town ever expected to *need* a policeman?

Out came the Town Clerk himself, waving his hands and spluttering, his pen behind his ear.

"You must go away," he cried. "This is disgraceful! Street music isn't allowed in this town!"

But the hurdy-gurdy man went right on grinding out his tune.

"Do you hear me?" shouted the Town Clerk. "And as for you," he went on, glaring at the mob of children, "go right into school this minute, every one of you!"

But through the noise of the hurdy-gurdy his words only sounded like "Hoo—hoo—hoo!"

"Hoo—hoo!" the children shouted back at him, for they were feeling too happy and excited by this time to care what anyone said to them, whether they could hear it or not.

"I shall fetch the Mayor!" stormed the Town Clerk.

And fetch the Mayor he did.

The Mayor came, puffing and blowing, with his hat on the back of his head. He had been an auctioneer before he was made Mayor, and still had the auctioneer's manner.

"Now then," boomed the Mayor. "Now then!"

It sounded like: "Step up! Step up!"

And everyone stepped up, for by this time half the townsfolk had gathered round, too.

The Mayor pulled a copy of the town by-laws from his pocket and began to read, very fast.

"Whereas, it is hereby decreed that any person or persons causing an obstruction—"

He had just got to the word "obstruction" when the monkey jumped down from the hurdy-gurdy man's shoulder, took a flying leap onto the Mayor's broad back, snatched the copy of the by-laws out of his hand and scrambled up with it to the top of the village flagstaff, where he sat, tearing the paper into tiny shreds and dropping them down on the heads of the crowd below.

"Arrest that monkey!" shouted the Mayor. "Shoot that monkey!"

"Don't you dare!" piped a thin little voice from the outskirts of the crowd. It belonged to Miss Gay, the Dress-maker.

"Shoot him!" shouted the townsfolk. "Shoot him!"

There was a great confusion and noise and fuss, with everyone yelling at the tops of their voices but, through it all, the hurdy-gurdy kept on its tinkling tune.

Meantime Tommy Meeks, who was far more interested in the hurdy-gurdy than in anything else, tugged suddenly at the organ-man's sleeve.

"Play the third tune!" he said. "I want to hear the third tune!"

The hurdy-gurdy man looked down at Tommy, and he looked around on the crowd.

"Yes." he said, "I think now we'll play the third tune!"

And he pushed in that little stop at the side of the hurdy-gurdy that Tommy had been so anxious about all the time.

All at once the hurdy-gurdy broke out into the very maddest and jiggiest little tune that had ever been heard. It was like all the tunes in the world rolled up into one, and yet it was like none of

174

them. It was the sort of little tune that set your brain whirling and your feet jiggling, whether you wanted or not.

At the first notes the townsfolk forgot all about the monkey and the Mayor and the flagstaff. They just stood there and stared. And then a very queer and surprised look came over all their faces. And their heads began to nod and their feet began to fidget, and before they knew it they were all dancing!

There they all were, the Town Clerk and the Druggist, the Grocer and the cross Baker, the fat woman from the Delicatessen Shop, the housewives and all the rest of them, dancing away to the music of the hurdy-gurdy; cheery Mrs. Meeks having the time of her life for once, and little Miss Gay holding up her skirts and skipping with the best of them!

"Stop it!" gasped the Mayor. "Stop it, stop it!" begged the School Teacher, her head bobbing up and her spectacles bouncing on her nose. But no one could stop it, and soon they were too much out of breath even to gasp.

Round and round the Green they went, children and grown folk all together, dancing away like mad, while the hurdy-gurdy wheezed out its strange jiggety tune, and the monkey, who by now had slid down the flagstaff again and was perched on his master's shoulder, waved his little red cap and cheered them on.

And then, suddenly, the music stopped.

Down everyone tumbled, one on top of another, too dizzy to stand on their feet another second. The Town Clerk went sprawling on the grass; the Delicatessen lady clutched the Baker and over they went in a heap, and the School Teacher sat down plump on the Mayor's lap. Red-faced, panting and out of breath, there they sat and stared at one another.

And very silly they all felt!

There was only one thing to do about it. Everyone began to laugh. The others all looked so foolish that they couldn't help it. They laughed and they choked, and they held their sides and laughed again.

The Mayor was the first who could get his breath to speak. And what he said was the strangest thing of all. He said:

"Let's have a picnic!"

For that's what the music had done to *him!*

"A picnic, a picnic!" shouted all the children. "A picnic!" shouted everyone else.

The Delicatessen lady billowed to her feet.

"I'll bring the hot dogs and sandwiches!" she cried.

"I'll bring the buns!" cried the Baker.

"I'll fetch the ice cream and the soda!" shouted the Druggist.

And away they went.

It was the best picnic the town had ever had. In fact it was the very first picnic that the town had ever had. No one worried about anything. No one had time to run home and brush their hair or put on their best clothes. They just sat round on the grass in a big circle, with the Mayor in the middle, and ate and drank and enjoyed themselves.

And it was not until Tommy Meeks was munching his seventh doughnut and scraping his third plate of ice cream, that he looked around and cried out suddenly: "Why, where is the hurdy-gurdy man?"

Where, indeed?

The hurdy-gurdy man had vanished. No one had seen him go. He had just disappeared.

Somewhere undoubtedly, at that moment, he was walking the road whistling, with his monkey on his shoulder, looking for another little town that might need his music.


## TYLL ULENSPIEGEL[1]

### M. A. Jagendorf

*Many stories are told in Germany about Tyll, a legendary little fellow who was always telling people the truth through jests and pranks. He ridiculed folly and stupidity with a kind of healthy good humor, and often caused the victims of his jokes to laugh at themselves. Here are stories about two of his pranks.*

#### A PORTRAIT WHICH SUITED EVERYONE AND PLEASED NO ONE

One day when Tyll was riding his donkey, the beast stopped suddenly and refused to go on. No matter how hard he tugged at the reins, the donkey would not move. So he got down, tore off a handful of thistles, and mounted Master Grayback again. Then he stretched the hand in which he held the thistles before the animal's

[1] Reprinted by permission from *Tyll Ulenspiegel's Merry Pranks* by M. A. Jagendorf. Copyright 1938 by Vanguard Press, Inc.

mouth, and the donkey, seeing the food so close, began following it. In this way Tyll led the beast until they came to the palace of the Landgrave.

The nobleman saw him coming in this strange way and thought it great sport. Said he to Tyll:

"Fellow with the merry face and strange ways, what is your profession?"

"Worthy lord, I am a painter on my way from the land of Flanders, which is famous for its good food and fine painters."

"Let me see your work."

"Here is a sample of it," and Tyll drew from under the saddle a painting on canvas of the Resurrection, in such beautiful colors that is was a joy to look at.

"Would you like to be my court painter?" asked the nobleman.

"Gladly, your worship, but to fit into your court, I must be as well fed and as well dressed as the courtiers around you."

"That is fair enough."

Soon Tyll sat dressed in a rich gown, at a table laden with food and with drink. Spoke the Landgrave to him:

"How would you like to paint a large painting of the forefathers of my wife, the Landgravine; you could show how these nobles brought me the friendship of the King of Hungary and other great lords. I would like to see such a painting on the big wall of my chamber, done in the very best style you know."

"Worthy Landgrave, your desire is my command. I would add something to that which will show you how much I love your lordship. Around this history I should like to paint your noble mistress, the Landgravine, her maids of honor, your fearless captains, your officers, and, in their midst, shining like a sun among the stars, your noble self. And all this will cost only two hundred guilders."

"It's a good idea and a good price, master painter. Here are a hundred guilders as an advance guard and the rest of the golden soldiers will come when the work is done."

"Your lordship pours a warm spring rain on the seeds of my ambition and there will be a beautiful growth in your honor."

## II

The next day Tyll asked that those living nobles whom he was to paint should pass before him.

First came a fat duke, who walked right up to Tyll and whispered to him:

"If you don't paint me without my fat and as I looked when I was young, I'll have my followers hang you from a high tree."

An elderly lady in waiting, narrow and thin, came by and whispered:

"Master painter," she said, "if your painting of me is not beautiful, you'll find yourself in a deep prison."

Came up a young lady in waiting: she had brown hair and was fresh and rosy, but the two front teeth under her upper lip were gone.

"Master," she said, "if I am not painted smiling, showing every tooth in my mouth, my sweetheart will make mincemeat out of you."

Each and every one who passed threatened Tyll in a different way. At the end of the procession came his master, the Landgrave, who said:

"Tyll, I am paying you a good price for your painting; see to it that each face is a perfect likeness; otherwise you'll pay heavily for it." Then he left. Tyll thought hard.

Surely no man was ever given such a difficult task. I must paint each one according to order and yet in perfect likeness, otherwise I'll be hung, drawn, quartered, and imprisoned. And I thought the life of a painter was a merry one. Ha, my fine ladies and gentlemen, I'll treat you to such portraits as were never painted in Christendom. And they surely will do justice to each and every one of you.

He asked the Landgrave for a big chamber with large empty walls. He also demanded long hangings over the walls, for fear the flies and dust would harm the fresh paint. And finally he requested three young painters to help in the work.

They gave him the room, the hangings, and sent to him three lusty young fellows well fit for what Tyll had in mind. The four locked themselves in the chamber and refused to see anyone while hard at the masterpiece.

### III

For thirty days Tyll and his fellows ate the finest foods and drank the best wines, which the Landgrave had brought to them. On the thirty-first day the Landgrave stuck his nose into the door and said:

"Ho, there, Tyll, how is the painting getting along?"

"Fine, noble Lord," he replied.

"May I see it?"

"Not yet, your worship," said Tyll.

On the fortieth day the Landgrave peeped in again.

"Ho, there, Tyll," he shouted.

"Master Landgrave, the painting is almost finished," said Tyll, "but no one may enter yet."

On the fiftieth day the Landgrave grew angry. He walked right in and found the curtains drawn over the walls. Said he:

"Show me the painting this very instant."

"Certainly, your lordship," Tyll replied. "But first you must call together all the noble ladies and gentlemen of your court whom I have painted here."

The Landgrave did so, and they all gathered before the curtain. Said Tyll to them:

"Most noble and generous Master Landgrave and Landgravine, you are about to see a marvelous masterpiece. Here are perfect likenesses painted in magic colors the like of which have never been seen in this land. I learned the great secret of these colors from a famous alchemist. They have the magic property of being invisible to those who are not of noble birth. It will be a simple matter for you all to recognize your faces and those of your ancestors if you are of noble blood, but if there are any among you who are descendants of common people, you will see only a blank wall. Such is the mystic quality of my paints."

Then he drew the curtain apart and all opened their eyes wide to look at—a white, empty wall. But no one dared to say a word.

Tyll pointed out to them various people—on the blank wall—describing their countenances and clothes, and everyone agreed to what he said. For each and all were afraid to say that they saw—nothing—lest they be branded as descendants of common people.

Suddenly the court jester who was present leaped three feet into the air, shook his bells and cried:

"You can call me a descendant from the lowest of the lowest in the land, and I don't mind it a bit. For we all came from the same forefathers; but I'll cry with bells and cymbals that I see only a white unpainted wall there."

Said Tyll:

"When fools tell the truth, it's time for wise men to listen. This time I'll go." But the Landgrave held him back and said:

"Tyll, you are a clever rogue and a wise one. Each one in this court told you how to paint his portrait and you showed us all our folly. Take care, sometimes men are hanged for telling the truth."

"It is best not to hang, Master Landgrave, but if I am to be hanged I'd rather hang for the truth than for robbery and tyranny.

This was the only way I could do a painting that would suit everyone's taste. Pay me for the painting and pay me for the lesson."

"Don't run so fast, Tyll. Here are fifty guilders, and away quickly, lest one of the less kindhearted nobles here pays you with cold steel instead."

Tyll left quickly without even looking once into the dark countenances of the nobles around him.

When he was a good distance from the castle he said to his donkey:

"Friend donkey, listen and learn. The secret of life is laughter. Fifty were ready to kill me, and I laughed them out of it. It makes life easy and gay."

The donkey raised his ears and brayed in agreement, while Tyll held his head high and sang a merry song.

### THE SMELL OF A ROAST IS AS GOOD AS THE CLINK OF A COIN

People say that a hungry man is as good, or as bad, as a hungry wolf, and Tyll was in that way no better than other men.

One time he was sitting in an inn in Cologne, waiting for his dinner, and it was a very, very long waiting. The longer he sat, the louder his stomach growled in anger, and the growling was so strong that Tyll began growling with his voice as well. The innkeeper, a man of quick temper, became annoyed at this, and told Tyll that if he did not like to wait he could eat what he had. Thereupon Tyll lost all patience and ate a small loaf of dry bread. This, with the smell of the meat from the fire, satisfied his appetite for the time.

The roast was done soon after and the hosts and guests sat down to eat, but Tyll did not join them.

"How, Tyll," said the innkeeper, "won't you eat the food with us?"

"I am not hungry any more. The smell of the roast satisfied my appetite."

The host did not like this, for he lost the money Tyll would have paid for the meal. When they were through, the host passed the wooden board for the guests to put down their money for the meal, and when he came to Tyll he asked him also for two Cologne pence, as he had done with the rest.

"Why should I pay when I did not eat?" asked Tyll.

"You satisfied your hunger here in my inn and that is what people pay for. If the smell of the roast did this, you have to pay for it as if you had eaten the roast."

Tyll took out two coins, threw them down on the board and picked them up quickly again.

"Host," said he, "did you hear the clinking of the coins?"

"Why, yes, I heard the clinking of the coins," he replied.

"Well, that is as much as you will get. For since you believe that the smell of a roast satisfies hunger, you must also believe that the clinking of coins satisfies the purse."

Everyone present laughed heartily, and the story spread so far that it is remembered even here.

## THE LANTERN AND THE FAN[1]

### Florence Holbrook

*A charming little nature myth from Japan. Wtih a bit of imagination, the story can be developed into an interesting play.*

In a Japanese village there once lived a man who had two sons. When the sons were grown up, each brought home a wife from another village a long distance away. The father was greatly pleased with his two daughters-in-law, and for many months they all lived very happily together.

At last the two young wives asked to go home to visit their friends. Among the Japanese the sons and the sons' wives must always obey the father, so the two wives said, "Father-in-law, it is a long, long time since we have seen our friends. May we go to our old home and visit them?" The father-in-law answered, "No." After many months they asked again, and again he answered, "No." Once more they asked. The father-in-law thought, "They care nothing for me, or they would not wish to leave me, but I have a plan, and I can soon know whether they love their father-in-law or not." Then he said to the older of the two wives, "You may go if you wish, but you must never come back unless you bring me fire wrapped in paper." To the younger he said, "You may

[1] From *Nature Myths and Stories*, by Florence Holbrook. Reprinted by permission of and agreement with Houghton Mifflin Company, the authorized publishers.

go if you wish, but you must never come back unless you bring me wind wrapped in paper." The father-in-law thought, "Now I shall find out. If they care for me, they will search the country through till they find paper that will hold fire and wind."

The two young wives were so glad to visit their old friends that for almost a month they forgot all about the gifts that they were to carry to their father-in-law. At last, when it was time to go home, they were greatly troubled about what they must carry with them, and they asked a wise man where to find the strange things. "Paper that will hold fire and wind!" he cried. "There is no such paper in Japan." The two women asked one wise man after another, and every one declared, "There is no such paper in Japan." What should they do? They feared they would never see their home again. They were so sad that they left their friends and wandered a long distance into the forest. Great tears fell from their eyes.

"I do not let people cry in my woods," said a voice. "My trees do not grow well in salt water."

The poor wives were so sorrowful that they forgot to be afraid, and the older one said, "Can we help crying? Unless I can carry to my father-in-law fire wrapped in paper, I can never go home." "And I," wailed the younger, "unless I can carry wind wrapped in paper, I can never go home. None of the wise men ever heard of such things. What shall we do?"

"It is easy enough to wrap fire in paper," answered the voice. "Here is a piece of paper. Now watch." They watched, and the strangest thing in all the world happened right before their eyes. There was no one to be seen, but a piece of paper appeared on the ground and folded itself into a Japanese lantern. "Now put a candle inside," said the voice, "and you have paper holding fire. What more could you ask?"

Then the older woman was happy, but the younger was still sad. She saw now that fire could be carried in paper, but surely no one could carry wind. "O dear voice," she cried, "can any one carry wind in paper?"

"That is much easier than to carry fire," replied the voice, "for wind does not burn holes. Watch."

They watched eagerly. Another piece of paper came all by itself and lay on the ground between them. There was a picture on it of a tree covered with white blossoms. Two women stood under the tree, gathering the blossoms.

"The two women are yourselves," said the voice, "and the blossoms are the gifts that the father-in-law will give you when you go home."

"But I cannot go home," the younger wailed, "for I cannot carry wind wrapped in paper."

"Here is the paper, and there is always plenty of wind. Why not take them?"

"Indeed, I do not know how," the younger woman answered sorrowfully.

"This way, of course," said the voice. Some long, light twigs flew to the paper. It folded itself, over, under, together. It opened and closed, and it waved itself before the tearful face of the younger woman. "Does not the wind come to your face?" asked the voice, "and is it not the fan that has brought it? The lantern carries fire wrapped in paper, and the fan carries wind wrapped in paper."

Then, indeed, the two young women were happy, and when they came to the home of their father-in-law, he was as glad as they. He gave them beautiful gifts of gold and silver, and he said, "No one ever had such marvels before as the lantern and the fan, but in my home there are two more precious things than these, and they are my two dear daughters."

## BHIMSA, THE DANCING BEAR[1]

### Christine Weston

*India becomes very real in this little book, which is written with beauty and distinction. An absorbingly interesting tale of two boys, David and Gopala, and their journey from the plains to the mountains, accompanied by Bhimsa, a very unusual bear who can do almost anything. One should read the entire book.*

*Gopala has just been entertaining a crowd of people with Bhimsa's dancing, for which he has played an accompaniment with cymbals and drums. After the dancing is over, a man dressed in yellow and silver comes up to the boys and says: "My master the Prince sends you his greetings, and requests that you accept his hospitality for the night, and that your bear dance for him after supper."*

[1] Reprinted from *Bhimsa, the Dancing Bear*, by Christine Weston; copyright 1945 by Christine Weston; used by permission of the publishers Charles Scribner's Sons.

*The boys were rather frightened, but they enjoyed the delicious*
*food that was served them, and by the time the head servant came*
*to fetch them from the guest house, they felt much more cheerful*
*about everything.*

The boys picked up the drum and cymbals, and with Bhimsa at
their heels they followed the servant across the garden, round a
corner, and through another gate into the royal courtyard. Here
the floor was made of flat bits of colored glass set close together;
there were beds of sweet-smelling flowers, and a great fountain
which, as it spouted upwards, sent forth shoals of tiny gold and
silver fish which fell back into the pool, on which floated several
kinds of water-lilies. Lights were strung among the trees, along
the walls and the verandahs of the palace, and for a few seconds
the boys were quite dazzled by the brillance. Then they heard the
servant whisper behind them: "Go on, go on! The Prince is waiting for you at the top of those stairs. Go forward and pay your
respects."

Followed by Bhimsa, they went forward, until they found themselves facing a flight of steps at the head of which stood a large
company of people, all richly dressed, surrounded by servants and
soldiers in brilliant uniforms. There were young men and old
men and middle-aged men, old ladies and middle-aged ladies and
young ladies dressed in glinting silks and flashing jewels. Both boys
looked eagerly for the figure of the Prince, David for an old man
with a white beard down to his waist, Gopala for a short dark
man with a beard as black as ink and one eye. Imagine their
astonishment when they saw, standing a little by himself in the
center of this grand company, a boy scarcely older than themselves
who addressed them in a clear, cold voice "I am the Prince. My
people tell me you have a dancing bear, and I wish to see him
dance."

The boys stared at the young Prince in wonder. He was dressed
in the same fashion as the others, but in even greater splendor.
Jewels glittered on the breast of his yellow satin jacket and in the
folds of his silver turban. He wore a short gold sword in his belt
and his shoes were of scarlet leather worked in gold and silver
thread. David and Gopala, who had expected to see a grown man,
just stood at the bottom of the staircase, eyes and mouths open,
quite forgetful of their manners.

"What's the matter with you?" demanded the Prince in an arrogant voice, though he did look rather pleased by the effect he had made upon them.

The boys heard the Prince's servant behind them whispering angrily: "Little fools! Speak up! Bow to His Highness."

Neither David nor Gopala were in the habit of bowing and scraping, but somehow they managed to make the proper gestures, and the Prince smiled at their embarrassment. "Tell me," he said, "is it true that this bear of yours is the cleverest dancing bear in India?"

"It is true, your Highness," Gopala answered proudly.

"Well," said the Prince, "make him dance for us, so I can judge for myself."

David and Gopala led Bhimsa into the middle of the courtyard beside the fountain, and Gopala played the drum and David the cymbals, and the bear began to dance for the Prince and his guests. Perhaps Bhimsa understood the importance of the occasion, for he exerted himself even more than usual, and performed some exceedingly graceful and difficult steps which charmed the audience and set them clapping and applauding with great enthusiasm. "More, more!" cried the Prince, forgetting, for a moment, that he was a prince, and behaving like an ordinary boy. "Let's have another dance! Another, another!"

Bhimsa danced on and on, sometimes using old steps and sometimes inventing new ones, and when at last he was forced to stop through sheer weariness, the Prince and his guests cheered and shouted: "Bravo! Well done! That was marvelous. There never was such a dancing bear   Hurray!"

The Prince walked down the steps into the courtyard and said to the boys: "I am very pleased with you both and with your bear. So pleased, in fact, that I want you to become members of my household. You shall live in my guest house, and it will be your duty to entertain me whenever I am in the mood."

Now David and Gopala were terribly embarrassed, because they could think of nothing they wanted less than to become servants to his young Highness. They thought him queer and masterful, unlike other boys. The truth was, he had always lived among mean and selfish people who gave in to him because he was a prince, and so he had learned to despise every one and to believe that he could get whatever he wanted by a mere stamp of his foot. Although David and Gopala did not know this at the time, they did know that they could not be friends with him, so after a slight pause Gopala said: "You are very kind, but it is not possible for us to stay."

The Prince was so surprised by this refusal that he flushed and a look of anger came over his face. "You mean you don't want to stay here with me?" he demanded in a haughty voice.

"You see," explained Gopala, "we are really trying to find our way home. We have been gone a long time, and now we wish to return to our own people."

"Where are your people?" asked the Prince, looking more and more angry.

"They live very far from here, in the mountains."

"M'm," said the Prince contemptuously. "So you prefer to return to your ragged old relations rather than to stay in my palace! Do you know that I have ponies that you could ride, a white camel, a carriage drawn by four Arabian horses, and an automobile especially made for me in America?"

"You are very lucky," answered Gopala, looking him bravely in the eye. "But just the same my friend here and Bhimsa and I would prefer to go our own way, if you don't mind."

When the Prince's company heard this a murmur rose and they all stared as if they couldn't believe their ears. "What, refuse the Prince's hospitality? They must be mad!"

The Prince stared from Gopala to David, then he said: "What do I care if a pair of dirty beggars show so little sense? Go, if you want. But I have taken a fancy to your bear and I shall buy him from you. How much do you want for him?"

Gopala laid his hand on Bhimsa's neck. "I am sorry," he answered, "my bear is not for sale."

Now the Prince was really furious. This was the first time he'd been told that there was something he couldn't have, and for several moments he could think of nothing to say. At last he burst out: "I can take the bear if I wish!"

"Oh, no, you can't," replied Gopala, standing his ground. "He's not yours to take."

"Everything in this palace is *mine!*" shouted the Prince.

The murmur grew louder, some of the Prince's soldiers, carrying spears, moved forward, and David thought: "I wonder what they will do to us." He was frightened, and so was Gopala, but they managed to hide their fear and stood up to their enemies.

The Prince said: "I shall order my servants to throw you out of town and to lock your bear in a cage. What would you say to that?"

"Why," gasped David. "Call yourself a prince? You're nothing but a common thief!"

Now a great uproar broke out. "He called our Prince a thief! A *common* thief! "

"Kill him! Beat him! Beat them both!"

The Prince stuck his knuckles in his eyes and began to whimper: "The bear! I want the bear! Give me the bear! I want it, I want it, I want it!"

At this moment one of the ladies happened to glance at David's feet, and, noticing that he wore shoes, she let out a piercing scream: "Look, look! The hateful beggar-boy is wearing shoes! Can you believe it? Against the laws of our princely council a beggar wears shoes in our presence! Under our very noses!"

"Shoes, shoes!" shouted every one at once. "He's wearing shoes!"

"The bear!" howled the Prince, jumping up and down in a tantrum. "I want the bear, the bear, the bear!"

"Shoes!"

"Bear!"

"Shoes!"

"My goodness!" said David to Gopala. "Have they all gone mad?"

The Prince's soldiers had been forming in a group, and now, brandishing their spears and flashing their swords, they made a rush towards the boys. But they had reckoned without Bhimsa. The bear saw them coming, and with a mighty roar he rose on his hind legs, and swinging right and left with his great paws he sent one soldier crashing against the Prince and another headfirst into the fountain. His usually gentle eyes were filled with a ferocious light; horrible roars came from him, and at the sight of his curved claws and long, pointed teeth the Prince and his companions fell back and began to run towards the palace steps, shouting:

"The bear will kill us! He'll eat us up! Run for your lives, run, run!"

"Now is our chance," whispered Gopala. "Quick, let's escape through that little gate!"

So while the crowd was scattering in wild confusion the two boys and Bhimsa darted across the courtyard and through the gate into the darkness beyond.

# THE ENCHANTED SHIRT[1]

## John Hay

*A "fable in foolscap" which can be played in entire seriousness or with a good deal of fun. A nice study in characterization.*

The King was sick. His cheek was red
    And his eye was clear and bright;
He ate and drank with a kingly zest,
    And peacefully snored at night.

But he said he was sick, and a king should know,
    And doctors came by the score.
They did not cure him. He cut off their heads
    And sent to the schools for more.

At last two famous doctors came,
    And one was as poor as a rat,—
He had passed his life in studious toil
    And never found time to grow fat.

The other had never looked in a book;
    His patients gave him no trouble,
If they recovered they paid him well,
    If they died their heirs paid double.

Together they looked at the royal tongue,
    As the King on his couch reclined;
In succession they thumped his august chest,
    But no trace of disease could find.

The old sage said, "You're as sound as a nut."
    "Hang him up!" roared the King in a gale,
In a ten-knot gale of royal rage;
    The other leech grew a shade pale;

But he pensively rubbed his sagacious nose,
    And thus his prescription ran,—
The King will be well if he sleeps one night
    In the shirt of a Happy Man.

[1] By permission of Houghton Mifflin Company.

Wide o'er the realm the couriers rode,
  And fast their horses ran,
And many they saw, and to many they spoke,
  But they found no Happy Man.

They found poor men who fain would be rich,
  And rich who thought they were poor;
And men who twisted their waist in stays,
  And women that short hose wore.

They saw two men by the roadside sit,
  And both bemoaned their lot;
For one had buried his wife, he said,
  And the other one had not.

At last as they came to a village gate,
  A beggar lay whistling there;
He whistled and sang and laughed and rolled
  On the grass in the soft June air.

The weary couriers paused and looked
  At the scamp so blithe and gay;
And one of them said, "Heaven save you, friend!
  You seem to be happy today."

"Oh, yes, fair sirs," the rascal laughed,
  And his voice rang free and glad,
"An idle man has so much to do
  That he never has time to be sad."

"This is our man," the courier said;
  "Our luck has led us aright.
I will give you a hundred ducats, friend,
  For the loan of your shirt tonight."

The merry blackguard lay back on the grass,
  And laughed till his face was black;
"I would do it, God wot," and he roared with fun,
  "But I haven't a shirt to my back."

Each day to the King the reports came in
  Of his unsuccessful spies,
And the sad panorama of human woes
  Passed daily under his eyes.

And he grew ashamed of his useless life,
  And his maladies hatched in gloom;
He opened his windows and let the air
  Of the free heaven into his room.

And out he went in the world and toiled
  In his own appointed way;
And the people blessed him, the land was glad,
  And the King was well and gay.


## MRS. PETERKIN PUTS SALT IN HER COFFEE

### Lucretia Hale

*The St. Nicholas magazine brought chuckles to thousands of readers years ago by stories of the absurd doings of* THE PETERKINS. *Here is one of them which children have great fun playing.*

This was Mrs. Peterkin. It was a mistake. She had poured out a delicious cup of coffee, and, just as she was helping herself to cream, she found she had put in salt instead of sugar! It tasted bad. What should she do? Of course she couldn't drink the coffee; so she called in the family, for she was sitting at a late breakfast all alone. The family came in; they all tasted, and looked, and wondered what should be done, and all sat down to think.

At last Agamemnon, who had been to college, said, "Why don't we go over and ask the advice of the chemist?" (For the chemist lived over the way, and was a very wise man.)

Mrs. Peterkin said, "Yes," and Mr. Peterkin said, "Very well," and all the children said they would go too. So the little boys put on their india-rubber boots, and over they went.

Now the chemist was just trying to find out something which should turn everything it touched into gold; and he had a large glass bottle into which he put all kinds of gold and silver, and many other valuable things, and melted them all up over the fire, till he had almost found what he wanted. He could turn things into almost gold. But just now he had used up all the gold that he had round the house, and gold was high. He had used up his wife's gold thimble and his great-grandfather's gold-bowed spectacles; and he had melted up the gold head of his great-great-grandfather's cane; and, just as the Peterkin family came in, he was down on his knees before his wife, asking her to let him have her wedding-ring to melt up with all the rest, because this time he knew he should succeed, and should be able to turn everything into gold; and then she could have a new wedding-ring of diamonds, all set in emeralds and rubies and topazes, and all the furniture could be turned into the finest of gold.

Now his wife was just consenting when the Peterkin family burst in. You can imagine how mad the chemist was! He came near throwing his crucible—that was the name of his melting-pot— at their heads. But he didn't. He listened as calmly as he could to the story of how Mrs. Peterkin had put salt in her coffee.

At first he said he couldn't do anything about it; but when Agamemnon said they would pay in gold if he would only go, he packed up his bottles in a leather case, and went back with them all.

First he looked at the coffee, and then stirred it. Then he put in a little chlorate of potassium, and the family tried it all around; but it tasted no better. Then he stirred in a little bichlorate of magnesia. But Mrs. Peterkin didn't like that. Then he added some tartaric acid and some hypersulphate of lime. But no; it was no better. "I have it!" exclaimed the chemist,—"a little ammonia is just the thing!" No, it wasn't the thing at all.

Then he tried, each in turn, some oxalic, cyanic, acetic, phosphoric, chloric, hyperchloric, sulphuric, boracic, silicic, nitric, formic, nitrous nitric, and carbonic acids. Mrs. Peterkin tasted each, and said the flavor was pleasant, but not precisely that of coffee. So then he tried a little calcium, aluminum, barium, and strontium, a little clear bitumen, and a half of a third of a sixteenth of a grain of arsenic. This gave rather a pretty color; but still Mrs. Peterkin ungratefully said it tasted of anything but coffee. The chemist was not discouraged. He put in a little belladonna and atropine, some granulated hydrogen, some potash, and a very little antimony, finishing off with a little pure carbon. But still Mrs. Peterkin was not satisfied.

The chemist said that all he had done ought to have taken out the salt. The theory remained the same, although the experiment had failed. Perhaps a little starch would have some effect. If not, that was all the time he could give. He should like to be paid, and go. They were all much obliged to him, and willing to give him $1.37-1/2 in gold. Gold was now 2.69-3/4, so Mr. Peterkin found in the newspaper. This gave Agamemnon a pretty little sum. He sat himself down to do it. But there was the coffee! All sat and thought awhile, till Elizabeth Eliza said, "Why don't we go to the herb-woman?" Elizabeth Eliza was the only daughter. She was named after her two aunts,—Elizabeth, from the sister of her father; Eliza, from her mother's sister. Now, the herb-woman was an old woman who came round to sell herbs, and knew a great deal. They shouted with joy at the idea of asking her, and Solomon John and the younger children agreed to go and find her too. The herb-woman lived down at the very end of the street; so the boys put on their india-rubber boots again, and they set off. It was a long walk through the village, but they came at last to the herb-woman's house, at the foot of a high hill. They went through her little garden. Here she had marigolds and hollyhocks, and old maids and tall sunflowers, and all kinds of sweet-smelling herbs, so that the air was full of tansy-tea and elder-blow. Over the porch grew a hop-vine, and a brandy-cherry tree shaded the door, and a luxuriant cranberry-vine flung its delicious fruit across the window. They went into a small parlor, which smelt very spicy. All around hung little bags full of catnip, and peppermint, and all kinds of herbs; and dried stalks hung from the ceiling; and on the shelves were jars of rhubarb, senna, manna, and the like.

But there was not the little old woman. She had gone up into the woods to get some more wild herbs, so they all thought they would follow her,—Elizabeth Eliza, Solomon John, and the little boys. They had to climb up over high rocks and in among huckleberry-bushes and blackberry-bushes. But the little boys had their india-rubber boots. At last they discovered the little old woman. They knew her by her hat. It was steeple-crowned, without any vane. They saw her digging with her trowel round a sassafras bush. They told her their story,—how their mother had put salt in her coffee, and how the chemist had made it worse instead of better, and how their mother couldn't drink it, and wouldn't she come and see what she could do. And she said she would, and took up her little old apron, with pockets all round, all filled with everlasting and pennyroyal, and went back to her house.

There she stopped, and stuffed her huge pockets with some of all the kinds of herbs. She took some tansy and peppermint, and caraway-seed and dill, spearmint and cloves, pennyroyal and sweet marjoram, basil and rosemary, wild thyme and some of the other time,—such as you have in clocks,—sappermint and oppermint, catnip, valerian, and hop; indeed, there isn't a kind of herb you can think of that the little old woman didn't have done up in her little paper bags, that had all been dried in her little Dutch-oven. She packed these all up, and then went back with the children, taking her stick.

Meanwhile Mrs. Peterkin was getting quite impatient for her coffee.

As soon as the little old woman came she had it set over the fire, and began to stir in the different herbs. First she put in a little hop for the bitter. Mrs. Peterkin said it tasted like hop-tea, and not at all like coffee. Then she tried a little flagroot and snakeroot, then some spruce gum, and some caraway and some dill, some rue and rosemary, some sweet marjoram and sour, some oppermint and sappermint, a little spearmint and peppermint, some wild thyme, and some of the other time, some tansy and basil, and catnip and valerion, and sassafras, ginger, and pennyroyal. The children tasted after each mixture, but made up dreadful faces. Mrs. Peterkin tasted, and did the same. The more the old woman stirred, and the more she put in, the worse it all seemed to taste.

So the old woman shook her head, and muttered a few words, and said she must go. She believed the coffee was bewitched. She bundled up her packets of herbs, and took her trowel, and her basket, and her stick, and went back to her root of sassafras, that she had left half in the air and half out. All she would take for pay was five cents in currency.

Then the family were in despair, and all sat and thought a great while. It was growing late in the day, and Mrs. Peterkin hadn't had her cup of coffee. At last Elizabeth Eliza said, "They say that the lady from Philadelphia, who is staying in town, is very wise. Suppose I go and ask her what is best to be done." To this they all agreed it was a great thought, and off Elizabeth Eliza went.

She told the lady from Philadelphia the whole story,—how her mother had put salt in the coffee; how the chemist had been called in; how he tried everything but could make it no better; and how they went for the little old herb-woman, and how she had tried in vain, for her mother couldn't drink the coffee. The lady from

Philadelphia listened very attentively, and then said, "Why doesn't your mother make a fresh cup of coffee?" Elizabeth Eliza started with surprise. Solomon John shouted with joy; so did Agamemnon, who had just finished his sum, so did the little boys, who had followed on. "Why didn't we think of that?" said Elizabeth Eliza; and they all went back to their mother, and she had her cup of coffee.

## MR. TOAD'S DISGUISE[1]

### Kenneth Grahame

*Children who are fortunate enough to have had Kenneth Grahame's incomparable tale of* The Wind in the Willows *read to them will love dramatizing episodes concerning Water Rat, Mole, Badger, and rich, conceited Toad. This adventure follows Toad's arrest for stealing a motor-car after he has smashed seven of his own and has been prevented by his friends from buying an eighth!*

When Toad found himself immured in a dank and noisome dungeon, and knew that all the grim darkness of a medieval fortress lay between him and the outer world of sunshine and well-metalled high roads where he had lately been so happy, disporting himself as if he had bought up every road in England, he flung himself at full length on the floor, and shed bitter tears, and abandoned himself to dark despair. "This is the end of everything" (he said), "at least it is the end of the career of Toad, which is the same thing; the popular and handsome Toad, the rich and hospitable Toad, the Toad so free and careless and debonair! How can I hope to be ever set at large again" (he said), "who have been imprisoned so justly for stealing so handsome a motor-car in such an audacious manner, and for such lurid and imaginative cheek, bestowed upon such a number of fat, red-faced policemen!" (Here his sobs choked him.) "Stupid animal that I was" (he said), "now I must languish in this dungeon, till people who were proud to say they knew me, have forgotten the very name of Toad! O wise old Badger!" (he said), "O clever, intelligent Rat and sensible Mole! What sound judgments, what a knowledge of men and matters you possess! O

194

unhappy and forsaken Toad!" With lamentations such as these he passed his days and nights for several weeks, refusing his meals or intermediate light refreshments, though the grim and ancient gaoler, knowing that Toad's pockets were well lined, frequently pointed out that many comforts, and indeed luxuries, could by arrangement be sent in—at a price—from outside.

Now the gaoler had a daughter, a pleasant wench and good-hearted, who assisted her father in the lighter duties of his post. She was particularly fond of animals, and, besides her canary, whose cage hung on a nail in the massive wall of the keep by day, to the great annoyance of prisoners who relished an after-dinner nap, and was shrouded in an antimacassar on the parlour table at night, she kept several piebald mice and a restless revolving squirrel. This kind-hearted girl, pitying the misery of Toad, said to her father one day, "Father! I can't bear to see that poor beast so unhappy, and getting so thin! You let me have the managing of him. You know how fond of animals I am. I'll make him eat from my hand, and sit up, and do all sorts of things."

Her father replied that she could do what she liked with him. He was tired of Toad, and his sulks and his airs and his meanness. So that day she went on her errand of mercy, and knocked at the door of Toad's cell.

"Now, cheer up, Toad," she said coaxingly, on entering, "and sit up and dry your eyes and be a sensible animal. And do try and eat a bit of dinner. See, I've brought you some of mine, hot from the oven!"

It was bubble-and-squeak, between two plates, and its fragrance filled the narrow cell. The penetrating smell of cabbage reached the nose of Toad as he lay prostrate in his misery on the floor, and gave him the idea for a moment that perhaps life was not such a blank and desperate thing as he had imagined. But still he wailed, and kicked with his legs, and refused to be comforted. So the wise girl retired for the time, but, of course, a good deal of the smell of hot cabbage remained behind, as it will do, and Toad, between his sobs, sniffed and reflected, and gradually began to think new and inspiring thoughts: of chivalry, and poetry, and deeds still to be done; of broad meadows, and cattle browsing in them, raked by sun and wind; of kitchen-gardens, and straight herb-borders, and warm snapdragon beset by bees and of the comforting clink of dishes set down on the table at Toad Hall, and the scrape of chair-legs on the floor as every one pulled himself close up to his work. The air of the narrow cell took on a rosy tinge; he began to think of his friends, and how they would surely be able to do something; of lawyers, and how they would have enjoyed his case, and what an ass he had been not to get in a few; and lastly, he thought of his own great cleverness and resource, and all that he was capable of if he only gave his great mind to it; and the cure was almost complete.

When the girl returned, some hours later, she carried a tray, with a cup of fragrant tea steaming on it; and a plate piled up with very hot buttered toast, cut thick, very brown on both sides, with the butter running through the holes in it in great golden drops, like honey from the honeycomb. The smell of that buttered toast simply talked to Toad, and with no uncertain voice; talked of warm kitchens, of breakfasts on bright frosty mornings, of cosy parlour firesides on winter evenings, when one's ramble was over and slippered feet were propped on the fender; of the purring of contented cats, and the twitter of sleepy canaries. Toad sat up on end once more, dried his eyes, sipped his tea and munched his toast, and soon began talking freely about himself, and the house he lived in, and his doings there, and how important he was, and what a lot of friends thought of him.

The gaoler's daughter saw that the topic was doing him as much good as the tea, as indeed it was, and encouraged him to go on.

"Tell me about Toad Hall," said she. "It sounds beautiful."

"Toad Hall," said the Toad proudly, "is an eligible self-contained gentleman's residence, very unique; dating in part from the fourteenth century, but replete with every modern convenience. Up-to-date sanitation. Five minutes from church, post-office, and golf-links. Suitable for——"

"Bless the animal," said the girl, laughing, "I don't want to *take* it. Tell me something *real* about it. But first wait till I fetch you some more tea and toast."

She tripped away, and presently returned with a fresh trayful; and Toad, pitching into the toast with avidity, his spirits quite restored to their usual level, told her about the boat-house, and the fish-pond, and the old walled kitchen-garden; and about the pig-styes, and the stables, and the pigeon-house, and the hen-house; and about the dairy, and the wash-house, and the china-cupboards, and the linen-presses (she liked that bit especially); and about the banqueting-hall, and the fun they had there when the other animals were gathered round the table and Toad was at his best, singing songs, telling stories, carrying on generally. Then she wanted to know about his animal-friends, and was very interested in all he had to tell her about them and how they lived, and what they did to pass their time. Of course, she did not say she was fond of animals as *pets*, because she had the sense to see that Toad would be extremely offended. When she said good night, having filled his water-jug and shaken up his straw for him, Toad was very much the same sanguine, self-satisfied animal that he had been of old. He sang a little song or two, of the sort he used to sing at his dinner-parties, curled himself up in the straw, and had an excellent night's rest and the pleasantest of dreams.

They had many interesting talks together, after that, as the dreary days went on; and the gaoler's daughter grew very sorry for Toad, and thought it a great shame that a poor little animal should be locked up in prison for what seemed to her a very trivial offense. Toad, of course, in his vanity, thought that her interest in him proceeded from a growing tenderness; and he could not help half regretting that the social gulf between them was so very wide, for she was a comely lass, and evidently admired him very much.

One morning the girl was very thoughtful and answered at random, and did not seem to Toad to be paying proper attention to his witty sayings and sparkling comments.

"Toad," she said presently, "just listen, please. I have an aunt who is a washerwoman."

"There, there," said Toad graciously and affably, "never mind; think no more about it. I have several aunts who *ought* to be washerwomen."

"Do be quiet a minute, Toad," said the girl. "You talk too much, that's your chief fault, and I'm trying to think, and you hurt my head. As I said, I have an aunt who is a washerwoman; she does the washing for all the prisoners in this castle—we try to keep any paying business of that sort in the family, you understand. She takes out the washing on Monday morning, and brings it in on Friday evening. This is a Thursday. Now, this is what occurs to me: you're very rich—at least you're always telling me so—and she's very poor. A few pounds wouldn't make any difference to you, and it would mean a lot to her. Now, I think if she were properly approached—squared, I believe is the word you animals use—you could come to some arrangement by which she would let you have her dress and bonnet and so on, and you could escape from the castle as the official washerwoman. You're very alike in many respects—particularly about the figure."

"We're *not*," said the Toad in a huff. "I have a very elegant figure—for what I am."

"So has my aunt," replied the girl, "for what *she* is. But have it your own way. You horrid, proud, ungrateful animal, when I'm sorry for you, and trying to help you!"

"Yes, yes, that's all right; thank you very much indeed," said the Toad hurriedly. "But look here! you wouldn't surely have Mr. Toad, of Toad Hall, going about the country disguised as a washerwoman!"

"Then you can stop here as a Toad," replied the girl with much spirit. "I suppose you want to go off in a coach-and-four!"

Honest Toad was always ready to admit himself in the wrong. "You are a good, kind, clever girl," he said, "and I am indeed a proud and a stupid toad. Introduce me to your worthy aunt, if you will be so kind, and I have no doubt that the excellent lady and I will be able to arrange terms satisfactory to both parties."

Next evening the girl ushered her aunt into Toad's cell, bearing his week's washing pinned up in a towel. The old lady had been prepared beforehand for the interview, and the sight of certain golden sovereigns that Toad had thoughtfully placed on the table in full view practically completed the matter and left little further to discuss. In return for his cash, Toad received a cotton print gown, an apron, a shawl, and a rusty black bonnet; the only stipulation the old lady made being that she should be gagged and bound and dumped down in a corner. By this not very convincing artifice, she explained, aided by picturesque fiction which she could supply herself, she hoped to retain her situation, in spite of the suspicious appearance of things.

Toad was delighted with the suggestion. It would enable him to leave the prison in some style, and with his reputation for being a desperate and dangerous fellow untarnished; and he readily helped the gaoler's daughter to make her aunt appear as much as possible the victim of circumstances over which she had no control.

"Now it's your turn, Toad," said the girl. "Take off that coat and waistcoat of yours; you're fat enough as it is."

Shaking with laughter, she proceeded to "hook-and-eye" him into the cotton print gown, arranged the shawl with a professional fold, and tied the strings of the rusty bonnet under his chin.

"You're the very image of her," she giggled, "only I'm sure you never looked half so respectable in all your life before. Now, good-bye, Toad, and good luck. Go straight down the way you came up;

and if any one says anything to you, as they probably will, being but men, you can chaff back a bit, of course, but remember you're a widow woman, quite alone in the world, with a character to lose."

With a quaking heart, but as firm a footstep as he could command, Toad set forth cautiously on what seemed to be a most hare-brained and hazardous undertaking; but he was soon agreeably surprised to find how easy everything was made for him, and a little humbled at the thought that both his popularity, and the sex that seemed to inspire it, were really another's. The washerwoman's squat figure in its familiar cotton print seemed a passport for every barred door and grim gateway; even when he hesitated, uncertain as to the right turning to take, he found himself helped out of his difficulty by the warder at the next gate, anxious to be off to his tea, summoning him to come along sharp and not keep him waiting there all night. The chaff and the humorous sallies to which he was subjected, and to which, of course, he had to provide prompt and effective reply, formed, indeed, his chief danger; for Toad was an animal with a strong sense of his own dignity, and the chaff was mostly (he thought) poor and clumsy, and the humour of the sallies entirely lacking. However, he kept his temper, though with great difficulty, suited his retorts to his company and his supposed character, and did his best not to overstep the limits of good taste.

It seemed hours before he crossed the last courtyard, rejected the pressing invitations from the last guardroom, and dodged the outspread arms of the last warder, pleading with simulated passion for just one farewell embrace. But at last he heard the wicket-gate in the great outer door click behind him, felt fresh air of the outer world upon his anxious brow, and knew that he was free!

## THE STORY OF WILLIAM TELL[1]

James Baldwin

*There is strong appeal in this dramatic incident from the legend of the famous Swiss patriot. Background material can easily be found.*

The people of Switzerland were not always free and happy as they are today. Many years ago a proud tyrant, whose name was

[1] From *Fifty Famous Stories Retold*.

Gessler, ruled over them, and made their lot a bitter one indeed.

One day this tyrant set up a tall pole in the public square, and put his own cap on the top of it; and then he gave orders that every man who came into the town should bow down before it. But there was one man, named William Tell, who would not do this. He stood up straight with folded arms, and laughed at the swinging cap. He would not bow down to Gessler himself.

When Gessler heard of this, he was very angry. He was afraid that other men would disobey, and that soon the whole country would rebel against him. So he made up his mind to punish the bold man.

William Tell's home was among the mountains, and he was a famous hunter. No one in all the land could shoot with bow and arrow so well as he. Gessler knew this, and so he thought of a cruel plan to make the hunter's own skill bring him to grief. He ordered that Tell's little boy should be made to stand up in the public square with an apple on his head; and then he bade Tell shoot the apple with one of his arrows.

Tell begged the tyrant not to have him make this test of his skill. What if the boy should move? What if the bowman's hand should tremble? What if the arrow should not carry true?

"Will you make me kill my boy?" he asked.

"Say no more," said Gessler. "You must hit the apple with your one arrow. If you fail, my soldiers shall kill the boy before your eyes."

Then, without another word, Tell fitted the arrow to his bow. He took aim, and let it fly. The boy stood firm and still. He was not afraid, for he had all faith in his father's skill.

The arrow whistled through the air. It struck the apple fairly in the center, and carried it away. The people who saw it shouted with joy.

As Tell was turning away from the place, an arrow which he had hidden under his coat dropped to the ground.

"Fellow!" cried Gessler, "what mean you with this second arrow?"

"Tyrant!" was Tell's proud answer, "this arrow was for your heart if I had hurt my child."

And there is an old story, that, not long after this, Tell did shoot the tyrant with one of his arrows; and thus he set his country free.

200

# THE SORCERER'S APPRENTICE[1]

## Richard Rostron

*The mood for dramatizing this famous story, which is more than 1800 years old, can be set beautifully by playing the records of the Paul Dukas music, which tell the complete story. This version of the tale follows most closely in spirit the music by Dukas.*

Many years ago, in far-off Switzerland, there lived a sorcerer. That is, this story took place many years ago. For all we know, the sorcerer may be living yet. His name then was Willibald, which is a little odd, but no stranger than he was. He was tall and thin, and his nose was long and pointed to match. He wore long, loose, trailing gowns. What was left of his hair was white. A small black cap sat on the back of his head.

He was not a very ordinary sorcerer. For instance, his fellow sorcerers specialized in disappearing in puffs of smoke. Then they would bob up, at a moment's notice, in places far away from where they had been a second before. But Willibald felt such tricks were beneath his dignity. To him they were a trifle show-offy. He traveled from place to place on a donkey. Of course, this took a good deal more time. But no one knew better than he did that he was no ordinary sorcerer, and that his customers would wait.

However, he did have a weakness for service. It was his habit to command pieces of furniture—chairs, tables, footstools, even brooms —to do his bidding. Of course, once in a while a passerby would be frightened out of his wits to see a table capering along the street with a bucket of water on its top. But this didn't happen often. The sorcerer lived 'way on the edge of town on a street that wasn't at all fashionable. And he was usually very careful not to let anyone see him work his spells. Not even Fritzl, his apprentice, knew how it was done.

Fritzl was a boy who was learning the sorcery business. He wasn't very bright or industrious. He made mistakes, spilled things, and was a general nuisance. In fact, only Willibald's patience saved him from being sent home in disgrace.

Of course, Fritzl was very pleased to have most of the unpleasant chores done for him. He didn't have to dust, or sweep, or scrub, or fetch water for the tank in the sorcerer's cellar workshop. Willibald used a good deal of water in his spells. And all this happened in the days before there were such things as faucets and sinks and city water supplies.

But in spite of all this, Fritzl wasn't satisfied. There were times when the sorcerer would go away and leave him to do all the work himself. Fritzl disliked those days terribly. So he decided to learn the spell his master used on the furniture. One day he crept to the top of the cellar stairs and peeped over. Willibald was busy stirring something in a kettle over the fire.

He stopped stirring to reach for a piece of firewood, and then exclaimed, "Out of wood again! That boy! Fritzl! *Fritzl!*"

Fritzl trembled, but didn't answer. He was afraid his master would guess that he had been spying.

"Fritzl! Where *is* that boy? Never here when you want him." The sorcerer grumbled a bit. Then he stopped stirring, and went over and stood a broom against the wall. He stepped back three paces, and forward two paces, and clapped his hands three times. Then he said, "Lif! Luf! Laf! Broom, fetch firewood!"

The broom immediately appeared to have arms—somewhat thin ones, and rather splintery, but still, arms. It came toward the stairs, hopping and thumping along on its straws. Willibald went back to his stirring, and Fritzl waited till the broom had thumped past his hiding place. Then he quietly crept away. Now he knew the spell, and he felt quite pleased with himself. He wouldn't have to work nearly so hard when old Willibald went off and left him to do everything alone.

There came a day when the sorcerer had to go off on business to the other side of town in a great hurry. In fact, he was almost tempted to travel in a puff of smoke instead of on his donkey. But he remembered in time who he was and soon he and his donkey were clip-clopping down the street. But before he went, he said to Fritzl:

"This place is a mess. While I'm gone you set about clearing it out. And be sure to scrub the cellar floor clean. I dropped a spell I was mixing last night, and it's left quite a large stain. I'm expecting a visitor from the Sorcerers' Society of Silesia in a few days and I don't want him to think I'm in the habit of spilling things. And then don't forget to refill the water tub in the workshop." You see, Willibald was very vain of the reputation he had of being no ordinary sorcerer.

202

When his master had gone, Fritzl went to work with a broom. He swept clouds of dust—both star and earth—in all directions. Then he started on the furniture, wiping and polishing till everything shone. After that he went downstairs to the workshop and scrubbed the floor there. The stain was very large and very dark, and he scrubbed a long time. By the time he had finished, the water tub was empty. It was a warm day and he had worked very hard. The idea of making many trips to the river with the water bucket didn't appeal to him at all.

Then he had an idea: Why not let the broom fetch the water? Of course, if old Willibald found out, he would very likely be terribly angry. But surely the tub would be full by the time the sorcerer returned and no one would ever know. So Fritzl thought, and he wasted no time in thinking any further.

He seized the broom, stood it up against the wall, stepped back three paces, forward two paces, as he had seen Willibald do, then clapped his hands three times and said the magic words: "Lif! Luf! Laf! Broom, fetch water from the river!" He was delighted when the broom's arms appeared and it picked up the water bucket and started—thump-athump-athump!—up the stairs.

Soon it was back, and before Fritzl knew what was happening, it had tilted the bucket and flung the water across the room with a splash. Then it was off again—thump-athump-athump!—before Fritzl could stop it.

The water ran about and got in Fritzl's shoes, which wasn't very comfortable. He thought: "Well, perhaps I didn't think fast enough. When it comes back I'll make it put the water in the tub instead of spilling it out on the floor."

Almost before he knew it, the broom had returned. As soon as it appeared at the top of the stairs with another bucket of water, Fritzl called out: "Don't throw it. Pour it in the tub!" But the broom paid no heed, flung the water as before, and went off—thump-athump-athump!—for more.

Poor Fritzl was frantic. "Something is wrong here," he thought. "Perhaps I'd better do the job myself and not try to get it done by magic." And when the broom returned again, he clapped his hands three times and cried: "Lif! Luf! Laf! Broom, stop fetching water!" But once more the broom paid no heed and flung the water across the room. And again it went off—thump-athump-athump!—for more.

Again and again the broom went back and forth, each time fetching and sloshing out a bucket of water and returning to the river for another. Fritz became desperate. The water rose higher and higher until it reached his knees. Everything—even the big water tub—started floating around the room. And Fritzl's panic grew and grew. At last he seized an ax and next time the broom came with a bucket of water, he swung wildly and split it down the middle. But instead of stopping, the two pieces went merrily on. Each piece grew another arm, and another bucket appeared from nowhere. Off they went—thump-athump-athump!—to the river.

Higher and higher the flood mounted. The two brooms came and went faster and faster. Fritzl wept and pleaded. He repeated snatches of spells he had heard his master use. He tried to get out of the cellar, but the water had floated the wooden steps out of place. The brooms went on and on and the water rose and rose.

Just as it rose to his chin, Fritzl heard the clip-clop of his master's donkey coming along the street. Then he heard the donkey stop and Willibald coming in the front door. "Help! Help!" he cried.

Willibald quickly appeared at the top of the stairs. "What goes on here?" he howled. Just then the brooms came in with more water and sloshed it down the stairs. Willibald was in the way and his gown was drenched. And there is nothing quite so angry as a wet sorcerer.

"Help, Master, quick!" poor Fritzl wailed. "I tried to make the broom fetch water, and then it wouldn't stop. Do something, before I drown!"

"Dumbhead!" roared Willibald. "I ought to let you drown. It's just what you deserve!" As he said this, he jumped hastily aside, for the brooms could be heard thump-athump-athump!-ing into the house. When they appeared, the sorcerer clapped his hand *four* times. Then he gabbled a long string of words. But Fritzl didn't hear them, for just then the water tub bumped against his head. He lost his footing and went under the water with a gurgle.

Next thing he knew, he was lying on the floor coughing and gasping. He looked around him. The water was gone. In fact, there wasn't anything in the cellar that was even wet. The steps were back in their places in the stairs. One broom stood quietly and peacefully in the woodbox, with a bucket beside it. The other broom and bucket had disappeared.

Fritzl looked fearfully up at his master. The sorcerer stood at the top of the stairs, sputtering and fuming with rage. "Get out of my sight, you blockhead! I've reached the end of my patience! Go on, get out! Go back where you came from!" And he clapped his hands quite a bit and stamped his foot—the left one—and a puff of smoke appeared on the floor beside Fritzl.

The puff of smoke grew and grew. As it grew it moved over and covered the apprentice. He shut his eyes in fright. He felt himself being lifted and heard a whistling in his ears like the wind. Then he was dropped with a hard bump. When he opened his eyes, he saw he was in his mother's front yard.

Fritzl lived to be a very old man, but he never saw the sorcerer again. And he didn't want to. In the fine summer evenings he would sit and tell stories to his grandchildren. They liked best the story of old Willibald and the broom. They remembered it and told it to their grandchildren. And *they* told it to *their* grandchildren. And so it has come down to us.

## WINDS A-BLOWING[1]

### May Justus

*Eight interesting characterizations can be developed from this poem. Some groups will be content with that alone. Others will use their imaginations to create a story by weaving them all together. The plan which follows the poem was developed by a group of eleven- and twelve-year-old girls.[2] With music it could grow into a charming dance-drama.*

The North Wind is a beggar
Who shudders at the cold.
The South Wind is a sailor
With pockets full of gold.
The East Wind is a gypsy
With saucy cap and feather.
The West Wind is a wizard
Who conjures wicked weather.

[1] From *Let's Read Together Poems, Fifth Grade,* Published by Row Peterson & Company.

[2] Pupils of Vivian Fridell Solomon, Highland Park, Illinois.

The Winter Wind's a giant
As grumpy as a bear.
The Summer Wind's a lady
With flowers in her hair.
The Autumn Wind's an old man
As touchy as a thistle.
The Spring Wind's a gay lad
Who blows a silver whistle!

*To make it clear that the characters were symbolic of winds, the children decided on a prologue in which some women meet at a village well. They complain about the wind, which has blown the shawl from one woman's head. An old crone, who is a village character, warns them that the winds are like people, and they will be offended at their words. They scoff, but she tells them the poem to show them it is true.*

*The scene then changes to the grounds of a beautiful mansion belonging to the Summer Wind and her husband, the rich sailor (the South Wind). They give instructions to Autumn Wind, a touchy old caretaker, to keep the place in order, for they are going away for a year—no one knows where (for that is the way of winds).*

*After they leave, as Autumn Wind irritably rakes the leaves, the gay, colorful gypsy East Wind swirls in and scatters the leaves all about, trying to steal some of them. A verbal battle ensues, during which the gypsy laughingly blows away, calling out that he will come back.*

*Hardly has he gone when the giant Winter Wind comes in, grumbling that it is time for the old man to get out. He all but evacuates him bodily; but as he goes, Autumn Wind warns the giant that when his mistress, South Wind, returns, she will melt his breath out of his body.*

*A beggar, North Wind, comes, shuddering with the cold, and the giant roughly pushes him away—but his own days are numbered, for soon the wizard, West Wind, comes and makes life so uncomfortable for him with his tricks that he is glad to leave.*

*Then it is that a gay lad with a silver whistle comes dancing in, charming the young shoots in the garden until they burst into bloom. His whistle has a strange effect on the wizard, who soon closes the wizardy book he has been reading, and goes yawning away.*

*"Now I'll get the place ready for the return of my mother and father," is the idea the lad will carry. And when the lady with flowers in her hair returns with her sailor husband, though they greet him with joy, they soon "shoo" him out into the world to play his silver whistle.*

*The epilogue comes back to the well, where the women laugh at the crone's fantastic story—all but one young girl who gazes at her image in the well and goes away to dream of the lad with the silver whistle.*

## JOHNNIE APPLESEED[1]

### Emily Taft Douglas

*As the center of a study of pioneer life, a creative play about Johnnie Appleseed would be an excellent choice. Many interesting episodes can be found about this kindly man who has become such a legend in our history. "For all his strange appearance," writes Emily Taft Douglas in her book,* Appleseed Farm, *"Johnnie Appleseed was a frontier saint. Old settlers kept records of his visits, sayings, and adventures, and I have tried to follow these accounts faithfully."*

*This book is written from the viewpoint of a ten-year-old pioneer girl, the following incident being the most dramatic scene in the story.*

*With a background of material about Johnnie Appleseed, and an understanding of pioneer life with its hardships and dangers, children might well use this book as the basis for a correlated play.*

*The Bartlett's have come to the wilderness of Indiana from Boston. Their first year has been a terrible one, with drought, the loss of their cow, and, finally, the death of their younger son.*

*On Ada Bartlett's tenth birthday she has two exciting adventures: first, her meeting with the man who is known as Johnnie Appleseed because he helps the pioneers to plant apple orchards; and, later, a startling encounter with an unfriendly Indian. The scene of Johnnie's coming—too long to include here—would, of course, be used in a complete play.*

*Johnnie has stayed for dinner with the Bartlett's, and has now gone out to the field to help Mr. Bartlett build a fence. Mrs. Bart-*

[1] From *Appleseed Farm* by Emily Taft Douglas; copyright 1948 by Stone and Pierce and used by permission of Abingdon-Cokesbury Press, Publishers.

*lett is at the spring, Ada's brother, Ned, is off to get some fish, and Ada is left alone at the house.*

She washed the dishes on the bench outside, and carried a load of clean bowls and spoons back into the house and put them away. Then she started out for more. Halfway across the cabin floor she stopped—stopped in her tracks like an animal frozen by fear.

For the second time that day she was face to face with a stranger. And this one was an Indian. His bare legs, red skin, and black hair left no doubt about that. He stood in the doorway, peering at her. In his cold, black eyes there was no look of friendship.

Ada was too scared to scream. She could not move. She could only stare at him.

"You all 'lone?" the Indian asked softly. "White man gone 'way?"

With her eyes fixed on the Indian, Ada suddenly recalled her father's warning. Never show fear. . . . Pretend to be friends.

She took a deep breath, forced a sickly smile, and said in a wobbly voice, "Hello! Please come in and sit down. Maybe I can find you something to eat."

The Indian stared at her, peered farther into the room, and finally nodded. Then he glided over to the table and sat down.

Ada did not wait. She had control over her legs again and, quick as one of the red man's arrows, she shot behind him, out of the house, and toward the field.

"Indians!" she screamed. "Indians!"

She ran with all her might, but in her panic she tripped over a root a few yards from the house and thudded to the ground. Her breath was knocked out of her, and she lay there, helpless, right within reach of the Indian. She was too winded even to call again. All she could do was to wait for the end. Maybe he would scalp her right there! Maybe he would carry her off to his camp! She wondered if her family would ever find out what had happened to her. She wondered if her father had even heard her scream. In the space of a second she wondered a great many things. Then it occurred to her to wonder why she was still lying there unhurt. She lifted her head.

Along the path charged her father, rifle in hand. Her fine, brave father, who would protect her always! But suddenly the picture changed. A man dashed up and knocked her father's rifle to the ground. It was Johnnie Appleseed.

"I'll take care of this," he cried. Then, raising his voice, he shouted to the Indian, "Friends! W'ere friends!"

Ada sat up, facing the cabin. She saw an ugly sight. The Indian filled the doorway, and in his hands he held Tom Bartlett's second rifle. Her father was unarmed because of Johnnie Appleseed, and the savage covered him with his own rifle. For a moment Ada hated Johnnie Appleseed. He was running toward the cabin, shouting strange words at the Indian. The red man grunted. Johnnie Appleseed spoke again. Then slowly the Indian lowered his rifle.

Johnnie Appleseed, talking and gesturing, was almost at the cabin now. When the reached the door, the Indian laid down the rifle and greeted him as a friend.

Tom Bartlett hurried up with a scowl on his face.

"He came on purpose, hunting me," Johnnie Appleseed explained, beaming with relief. "I was with his people last week. He's come to take me back to settle a quarrel with a trader."

Then he talked to the red man in the Indian tongue. He pointed to Tom Bartlett and then out to the field, as though explaining that he must help the settler finish some work.

While they stood there, the sky grew darker and rain began to fall. Ada conquered her panic enough to come back to the cabin. She sidled up to her father and clung to his hand as they all went in out of the rain.

Johnnie Appleseed saw how uneasy Ada and her father were with the red man. He also saw how sullenly the red man looked at the little girl who had run for help and at her father who had come charging at him with a rifle.

"How would you like to give Hawk Eye a drink of water, Ada?" Johnnie Appleseed asked. "And maybe some of your good corn-bread?"

Ada hurried to place food before the Indian.

That was how it happened that Mrs. Bartlett, when she came home a little later, found an Indian sitting at her table, devouring her cornbread. She could not hide her amazement. However, when Johnnie Appleseed asked her to invite Hawk Eye to stay until the weather cleared, she bravely obeyed.

Hawk Eye looked up and gravely shook his head. Rain would not hurt his clothes, and he wanted to hurry home with the message of the Great White Medicine Man, as he called Johnnie Appleseed.

Before the Indian left, Johnnie Appleseed took a hand of each of the men in his. "You are friends now," he told them. "Hawk Eye has eaten Tom Barlett's bread. Hawk Eye and Tom Bartlett are both friends of Johnnie Appleseed. They must be friends of each other."

Tom Bartlett gave his hand to the Indian. They eyed each other sternly, but they promised to be friends. Then Hawk Eye stalked down the path and out of sight.

"That pledge gives me some peace of mind, Johnnie Appleseed," said Tom Bartlett. "Maybe Hawk Eye is a good Indian, as you say, but I'm thankful you were with us when he called. I wouldn't like to bet on how good he would have been if the Great White Medicine man hadn't been here."


## THE EMPEROR'S NEW CLOTHES

### Hans Christian Andersen

*One of the best of all tales for a creative play—rich in comedy, in characterization, in action. It's idea and plot have very wide appeal, but children of ten or eleven have an especially good time with it. It does not spoil the idea if the rogues are made gay young adventurers instead of swindlers, if they befriend the weavers and expose the wicked minister of the emperor's wardrobe, and if they leave the gold and jewels for the weavers, as in Charlotte Chorpenning's play of this name.*[1]

Many years ago there lived an emperor who was so enormously fond of new clothes that he spent all his money for them. He didn't care for his soldiers, didn't care for the theatre, didn't care for driving in the park except for the chance to show off his new clothes. He had a coat for every hour of the day, and just as people say about a king, "He is in council," so here they always said, "The emperor is in his dressing room."

The big city where he lived was a very gay place. Crowds of visitors came every day, and one day two swindlers came. They pretended they were weavers and said they knew how to weave the most gorgeous cloth you could imagine. Not only were they beautiful, but the clothes made of the stuff had the strange property that

[1] Published by Samuel French.

210

they became invisible to any one who was unfit for the office he held, or who was stupider than the law allowed.

"Those would be nice clothes!" thought the emperor. "If I wore them, I could find out what men in my empire are not fit for the places they have; I could tell the clever from the stupid. Yes, that cloth must be woven for me at once!"

And he gave the two swindlers a lot of money in advance to make them begin work.

And they did put up two looms, and pretended to be working; but they had nothing at all on their looms. They kept on demanding the finest silk and the costliest gold; this they put into their own pockets, and worked at the empty looms till late into the night.

"Now I should really like to know how far they have got on with the stuff," thought the emperor. But he actually had a queer sensation in his heart when he thought that whoever was stupid or no good in his office couldn't see it. He believed, indeed, that he had nothing to fear for himself, but he wanted to send some one else first to see how matters stood. All the people in the whole city knew what peculiar power the stuff possessed, and all were anxious to see how bad or how stupid their neighbors were.

"I will send my honest old cabinet minister to the weavers," thought the emperor. "He can tell best what the stuff looks like, because he's a sensible man and nobody is better in his office than he is."

So the decent old minister went into the hall where the two swindlers sat working at the empty looms.

"Mercy on us!" thought the old minister, and he opened his eyes wide. "I can't see anything at all!" But he didn't say that.

Both the swindlers begged him to be kind enough to come nearer, and asked if he didn't think that was a lovely pattern and beautiful colors. Then they pointed to the empty loom, and the poor old minister went on opening his eyes; but he could see nothing, for there was nothing to see.

"Dear me!" he thought, "could it be that I am stupid? I never thought that, and not a soul must know it. Am I not fit for my office? No, it will never do for me to tell that I couldn't see the stuff."

"Well, haven't you anything to say about it?" said one of the weavers.

"Oh, it is charming!" said the old minister, as he peered through his spectacles. "What a fine pattern, and what colors! Yes, I shall tell the emperor that I am very much pleased with it."

"Well, we're very glad," said both the weavers; and then they named the colors, and explained the strange pattern. The old minister listened carefully, so that he could repeat it when he went back to the emperor. And so he did.

Now the swindlers asked for more money, and more silk and gold, which they said they wanted for weaving. They put everything into their own pockets, and not a thread was put on the loom; but they kept on working at the empty frames as before.

The emperor soon sent another official to see how the weaving was going on, and if the stuff would soon be ready. He had no better luck than the first; he looked and looked, but, as there was nothing to be seen but the empty looms, he could see nothing.

"Yes, isn't this a fine piece of cloth?" asked the two swindlers; and they pointed out and explained the handsome pattern which wasn't there at all.

"I know I am not stupid!" thought the man. "It must be my office, for which I am not fit. That's very queer, but I mustn't let anybody notice it." And so he praised the stuff he didn't see, and expressed his pleasure at the beautiful colors and the charming pattern. "Yes, it is beautiful," he said to the emperor.

All the people in the town were talking of the gorgeous stuff. The emperor now wanted to see it himself while it was still on the loom. With a whole crowd of chosen men, among whom were also the old officials who had already been there, he went to the two cunning swindlers, who were now weaving with might and main without fiber or thread.

"Isn't it magnificent?" said both the good officials, who had already been there once. "Will your majesty see what a pattern, what colors?" And then they pointed to the empty loom, for they thought that the others could probably see the stuff.

"What's this?" thought the emperor. "I can see nothing at all! That is terrible. Am I stupid? Am I unfit to be emperor? That would be the most dreadful thing that could happen to me. Oh, it is *very* pretty!" he said aloud. "It has our approval." And he nodded in a contented way, and gazed at the empty loom, for he wouldn't say that he couldn't see anything. His whole retinue looked and looked, and saw nothing, any more than the rest; but, like the emperor, they said, "That *is* pretty!" and counseled him to wear these splendid new clothes for the first time at the great procession soon to take place. "It is magnificent!" went from mouth to mouth, and they were all marvelously pleased. The emperor gave each of the swindlers a cross to hang at his buttonhole and the title of "Knights of the Loom."

The whole night before the morning on which the procession was to take place the swindlers were up, and had more than sixteen candles burning. The people could see that they were hard at work, finishing the emperor's new clothes. They pretended to take the stuff down from the looms; they made cuts in the air with big scissors; they sewed with needles without thread; and at last they said, "Now the clothes are ready!"

The emperor came himself with his noblest cavaliers; and the two swindlers lifted up one arm as if they were holding something, and said, "See, here are the trousers! here is the coat; here is the cloak." And so on. "It is as light as a spider's web; one would think one had nothing on; but that is just the beauty of it."

"Yes," said the cavaliers; but they couldn't see anything, for nothing was there.

"Will your imperial majesty please to condescend to undress?" said the swindlers; "then we shall put the new clothes on you here in front of the large mirror."

The emperor took off his clothes, and the swindlers pretended to put on him each of the new garments, and they took him round the waist, and seemed to fasten on something; that was the train; and the emperor turned round and round before the mirror.

"Oh, how well they look! How wonderfully they fit!" everybody said. "What a pattern! What colors! That *is* splendid!"

"They are standing outside with the canopy which is to be borne above your majesty in the procession!" announced the head master of the ceremonies.

"Well, I'm ready, of course," said the emperor. "Don't they fit me well?" And then he turned around again in front of the mirror because he wanted it to seem as if he were giving his fine clothes a good look.

The chamberlains, who were to carry the train, groped with their hands on the floor, just as if they were picking up the mantle; then they pretended to be holding something up in the air. They didn't dare to let anybody guess that they couldnt see anything.

So the emperor went in procession under the rich canopy, and every one in the streets said, "Look! See how matchless the emperor's new clothes are! What a lovely train his mantle has! What a miraculous fit!" No one would let it be known that he couldn't see anything, for that would have shown that he was not fit for his office, or was very stupid. Not any of the emperor's clothes had ever had such a success as these.

"But he has nothing on!" a little child cried out at last.

"Dear me, listen to what the innocent says," said the father, and people whispered to each other what the child had said.

"He has nothing on; a little child says that he has nothing on!"

"But he has nothing on!" everybody shouted at last. And the emperor shivered, for it seemed to him that they were right; but he thought within himeslf, "I must go through with the procession." And so he carried himself still more proudly, and the chamberlains walked along holding the train that wasn't there at all.

## THE BOY KNIGHT OF REIMS[1]

### Eloise Lownsbery

*A beautiful and dramatic story of Medieval days in France. The book is ideally suited to be the center of an integrated study of guilds and apprentices, pages, squires, and knights. This is one episode.*

*Young Jean d'Orbais is apprenticed to Master Anton, a goldsmith, though his real desire is to be a sculptor like his father. A clay angel he has made even now stands on the shelf near his bench. In the shop is a friendly young man named Colin who, though his apprenticeship is finished, must stay on three years longer with the title of Companion before he can become a Master himself.*

*One day, a short time after Jean comes to Anton's shop, a page in the livery of the house of Dinard comes riding up to the shop, dismounts, and leans across the counter which is directly on the street. While Jean is talking to Colin, the page asks Master Anton about a certain silver drinking cup.*

"Boy!" called the Master. Jean jumped. His tone implied that he had called before. "Bring me the silver drinking-cup with the three handles."

Jean ran to the shelf and brought it—a large silver cup, with beautifully engraved handles, and feet made of an eagle's claws.

[1] Reprinted by permission of and arrangement with Houghton Mifflin Company, the authorized publishers.

"Aye, that's the one!" cried the page. "My Lady saw it the other day, you remember, and can talk of nothing else. She wants one exactly like it in gold to give to my Lord when he comes home from the war next week. Can you make it for her by Saturday?"

Master's eyes narrowed. He seemed in doubt, began scratching his head. The page opened an embroidered purse he wore at his belt and poured out ten ingots of gold. The Master's hand twitched. He kept working his fingers against each other.

"Pure Arabian gold," added the page, "brought from the Orient. You are to melt it up for the cup."

"Very well, then," assented Master. "You may come for it on Saturday."

The horse neighed and whinnied, pawing and stamping impatiently. Jean leaned out to touch the white nose. What a beauty. He watched admiringly as the page mounted and clattered off.

Master Anton gathered up the gold. They turned back into the shop. As Gran'pere said, it is an interesting craft, thought Jean. Great ladies and lords and kings and queens all came to ask humbly the beautiful things one could make with one's two hands. Jean smiled up at his angel. He was happier than ever before since he had come here to live. He was glad he had brought it.

On the previous Saturday, an order of three gold plates for the head Master of the Bakers' Corporation (or guild) had been finished. Jean had expected to be sent to deliver them. He knew how to go, and would have to pass through the busy and interesting marketplace, so he was eager and had counted on it for days. So you can imagine how disappointed he was when Colin was ordered to go instead. Colin himself looked up, surprised. He knew well that his time was too valuable for errands now that Jean had come. But on top of this one, the Master gave him two other commissions to do. Jean blinked hard. He felt it unjust. Besides Colin didn't want to go, and he did. So Colin had to take off his leather apron, wrap the gold plates in a clean linen cloth so they wouldn't rub together, and set off. He turned to make a sort of salute to Jean, exactly the way the knights lifted their lances. Jean drew himself up. What a friend Colin was! He could stand being disappointed because Colin's eyes were so full of laughter and comradeship.

The Master called him. He seemed nervous and irritable. He was grinding wine stone (a bit of broken crock in which old wine had stood) in a mortar. Now he wanted salt. He added a third part and dumped the two into a large clay crucible, added the water in which Jean had milled the gold, and a little quicksilver, and placed all this on the coals, stirring with a wooden stick.

"Stir this, boy." Jean stirred, watching the Master's preparation with one eye.

He brought the silver cup which the Lady of Dinard had so much admired, tore off a bit of linen from a large cloth hanging on a peg, and reached up to Colin's shelf for one of his brushes. He stopped short on seeing Jean's angel.

"Whose is this?" he demanded.

"Mine, sir," said Jean, wondering why his voice, as well as his nose, was so sharp.

The Master grunted, but made no comment. What he was thinking was that the boy would grow more and more useful to him. But he was unusually silent and intent on his work. He first dipped the cloth into the hot preparation and rubbed it carefully all over the cup, inside and outside. Then he warmed the cup over the coals. Then he dipped a brush into the same solution and rubbed hard into all the hollows of the carving of stem and feet and handles, until the whole cup looked whitish and copperish. Then, squeezing all the quicksilver out of the gold Jean had milled, he cut it with a knife and laid it carefully on the cup, smoothing it with a moistened brush.

"Tongs, boy."

Jean flew for the tongs. The Master grasped the cup in them, heating it over the coals, then smoothing it again with his brush. This whole performance he repeated three times, always adding a layer of gold which stuck fast, then moistening it smoothly with his brush, then reheating it.

At every footfall of passer by, he would turn nervously, muttering that he hoped no one would come to buy. It was a ticklish operation. He began rubbing the gold until it grew pale, spreading it evenly with a dry brush.

"Bring me a bowl of water, boy." Jean brought it at once, watching to see the whole cup immersed and washed. Again it was warmed over the coals until it came out a clear even pale yellow gold. From a bag hanging at his belt, he took out one of the gold ingots. The same color exactly. Satisfied, he set to work at polishing it with a brush made from fine brass wires. Soon it was shining and beautiful.

"It looks exactly like a gold cup," said Jean admiringly. He felt friendly, and glad to have been able to help him.

216

"It *is* a gold cup," the Master corrected him sharply.

"Yes, but only sham gold," laughed Jean. He knew all about the differences between gilded silver and real gold, for Gran'père had carefully explained it to him. "I'm glad the Lady of Dinard wants a real one." He had been counting on seeing those gold ingots from Arabia go into the melting-pot, and come out from the Master's hands, or Colin's, a gold cup.

The Master turned purple. He picked up the tongs and stood menacingly over the boy. Jean looked up at his angel and prayed a swift prayer. "I'm not afraid because you are here to protect me."' The Master followed the direction of his eyes. Suddenly he sprang to the shelf, reached up for the angel, threw it with a crash onto the iron anvil, and snapped his teeth to see it broken into a thousand pieces. A fragment flew into his eye, however, and with a howl of pain, he rushed off upstairs to let his wife extract it.

The shop was very still. Jean sat huddled on a bench, staring down at the fragments, scowling. He rubbed his knuckles into his eyes. Some idea, something that hurt even more than the loss of the angel, was struggling inside of him. What was it? He glanced at the shining cup on the work bench. In a flash he knew. Master Anton had never meant to make a gold cup with all those ingots. He was only gilding the silver one with bits of shavings from a dozen other plates and cups. He set his lower lip forward, his face scarlet with shame. He sprang up and reached for his woolen cap on the peg.

The door opened. Colin entered, closed it, and then stood with his back against it. The smile went out of his eyes. He looked first at Jean's face, then at the shining cup, then at the scattered, broken fragments on the floor, then up to the shelf where the angel had stood. Then he nodded.

Jean strode toward him. "Let me pass, Colin; I'm going home."

For a second, Colin's whole face twisted. Then a look came over it that reminded Jean of the prophets on the south side of the cathedral. Colin reached out his arm and drew the boy down beside him on the bench facing the open fire on the forge. He could feel him trembling.

"There's no going back, little brother, once the papers are signed; not unless your father should make a terrible row, take up the thing with the Guardians of the Guild, and we have not proof enough for that."

Jean stared at the coals.

"Besides, he is your grandfather's friend. Think what that would mean to him."

"But Gran'père didn't know. He hates cheating. Do you suppose he, or my father either, would want an Orbais with such a master as this? How am I ever to learn to do work for my cathedral?"

Colin threw his arms across Jean's shoulders. "I too learned the truth when I was young. But you see, I've had to stick. I have my own principles, though, all the more severe they are too, and high; and I mean to keep them always, and so can you."

Jean was silent. He was battling. He felt as if one of the dreaded gargoyles had come alive and was clawing him. No use to ask help of his angel now. Then something inside seemed to be telling him that it was only the clay angel that Master Anton had broken. There were more, all about the cathedral; more than a hundred, perhaps, and whole hosts of them in heaven—real ones. Then they could help him now. They were alive. He could feel them. And now he was no longer afraid of the Master. He knew he would never be afraid of him again. If Master Anton was powerless to hurt the real angels, he was just as powerless to hurt him, for they would protect him. He knew that now, and that he need never again be afraid of a gargolye, either!

"Look here," said Colin, "I'll make a contract with you. I'll teach you all I can—a lot more than you can learn in any other way for several years to come." . . .

"Whenever the Master is angry keep still and say nothing. Sit down quietly and go to work and think to yourself: 'You have no real power over me. I am not afraid of you.'"

"No," Jean answered, "I'm not afraid of him. He can't break me. I can stick here if I have to. But do you know, all the same, I think we should do something for the honor of our craft."

"Aye, I've thought of that too," admitted Colin, "but I am sure they are bound to know, some day. And without our telling, too."

So when the Master came home at dark, all was serene, within and without.

That night Jean was comforted by something the first Master Jean had said:

"If thou desirest to learn, and art humble and dedicate the work of thy hands to God, then in spite of everything, thou shalt surely succeed."

# THE VOYAGE OF THE WEE RED CAP[1]

## Ruth Sawyer

*A wonderful story to dramatize at Christmastime! It has some-times been used as an all-school creative play, with every age-level represented. Those who did not have acting parts furnished the transitional music. A greatly loved Irish version of the Scrooge story.*

It was the Eve of St. Stephen, and Teig sat alone by his fire with naught in his cupboard but a pinch of tea and a bare mixing of meal, and a heart inside of him as soft and warm as the ice on the water-bucket outside the door. The turf was near burnt on the hearth—a handful of golden cinders left, just; and Teig took to counting them greedily on his fingers.

"There's one, two, three, an' four an' five," he laughed. "Faith, there be more bits o'real gold hid undther the loose clay in the corner."

It was the truth; and it was the scraping and scrooching for the last piece that had left Teig's cupboard bare of a Christmas dinner.

"Gold is betther nor eatin' an' dthrinkin'. An' if ye have naught to give, there'll be naught asked of ye." And he laughed again.

He was thinking of the neighbors, and the doles of food and piggins of milk that would pass over their thresholds that night to the vagabonds and paupers who were sure to come begging. And on the heels of that thought followed another: who would be giving old Shawn his dinner? Shawn lived a stone's-throw from Teig, alone, in a wee tumbled-in cabin; and for a score of years past Teig had stood on the door-step every Christmas Eve, and, making a hollow of his two hands, had called across the road:

"Hey, there, Shawn, will ye come over for a sup?"

And Shawn had reached for his crutches, there being but one leg to him, and had come.

"Faith," said Teig, trying another laugh, "Shawn can fast for the once; 'twill be all the same in a month's time." And he fell to thinking of the gold again.

A knock came to the door. Teig pulled himself down in his chair where the shadow would cover him, and held his tongue.

[1] From *This Way to Christmas*, by Ruth Sawyer. Copyright, 1944, by Ruth Sawyer Durand. Used by permission of the author and Harper & Brothers, publishers.

"Teig, Teig!" It was the Widow O'Donnelly's voice. "If ye are there, open your door. I have not got the pay for the spriggin' this month, an' the childther are needin' food."

But Teig put the leash on his tongue, and never stirred till he heard the tramp of her feet going on to the next cabin. Then he saw to it that the door was tight barred. Another knock came, and it was a stranger's voice this time:

"The other cabins are filled; not one but has its hearth crowded. Will ye take us in, the two of us? The wind bites mortal sharp; not a morsel o' food have we tasted this day. Masther, will ye take us in?"

But Teig sat on, a-holding his tongue; and the tramp of the strangers' feet passed down the road. Others took their place—small feet, running. It was the miller's wee Cassie, and she called out as she went by:

"Old Shawn's watchin' for ye. Ye'll not be forgettin' him will ye, Teig?"

And then the child broke into a song, sweet and clear, as she passed down the road:

"Listen all ye, 'tis the Feast o' St. Stephen,
Mind that ye keep it, this holy even.
Open your door and greet ye the stranger,
For ye mind that the wee Lord had naught but a manger.
                                                    Mhuire as truagh!

"Feed ye the hungry and rest ye the weary,
This ye must do for the sake of Our Mary.
'Tis well that ye mind—ye who sit by the fire—
That the Lord He was born in a dark and cold byre.
                                                    Mhuire as truagh!"

Teig put his fingers deep in his ears. "A million murdthering curses on them that won't let me be! Can't a man try to keep what is his without bein' pesthered by them that has only idled and wasted their days?"

And then the strange thing happened: hundreds and hundreds of wee lights began dancing outside the window, making the room bright; the hands of the clock began chasing each other round the dial, and the bolt of the door drew itself out. Slowly, without a creak or a cringe, the door opened, and in there trooped a crowd of the Good People. Their wee green cloaks were folded close about them, and each carried a rush-candle.

Teig was filled with a great wonderment, entirely, when he saw the fairies, but when they saw him they laughed.

"We are takin' the loan o' your cabin this night, Teig," said they. "Ye are the only man hereabouts with an empty hearth, an' we're needin' one."

Without saying more, they bustled about the room making ready. They lengthened out the table and spread and set it; more of the Good People trooped in, bringing stools and food and drink. The pipers came last, and they sat themselves around the chimneypiece a-blowing their chanters and trying the drones. The feasting began and the pipers played, and never had Teig seen such a sight in his life. Suddenly a wee man sang out:

"Clip, clap, clip, clap, I wish I had my wee red cap!"

And out of the air there tumbled the neatest cap Teig had ever laid his two eyes on. The wee man clapped it on his head, crying:

"I wish I was in Spain!" And—whist!—up the chimney he went, and away out of sight!

It happened just as I am telling it. Another wee man called for his cap, and away he went after the first. And then another and another until the room was empty and Teig sat alone again.

"By my soul," said Teig, "I'd like to thravel like that myself! It's a grand savin' of tickets an' baggage; an' ye get to a place before ye've had time to change your mind. Faith, there is no harm done if I thry it."

So he sang the fairies' rhyme and out of the air dropped a wee cap for him. For a moment the wonder had him, but the next he was clapping the cap on his head, crying:

"Spain!"

Then—whist!—up the chimney he went after the fairies, and before he had time to let out his breath he was standing in the middle of Spain, and strangeness all about him.

He was in a great city. The doorways of the houses were hung with flowers and the air was warm and sweet with the smell of them. Torches burned along the streets, sweetmeat-sellers went about crying their wares, and on the steps of a cathedral crouched a crowd of beggars.

"What's the meanin' o' that?" asked Teig of one of the fairies.

"They are waiting for those that are hearing Mass. When they come out they give half of what they have to those that have nothing, so that on this night of all the year there shall be no hunger and no cold."

And then far down the street came the sound of a child's voice, singing:

"Listen all ye, 'tis the Feast o' St. Stephen,
Mind that ye keep it, this holy even."

"Curse it!" said Teig. "Can a song fly afther ye?" And then he heard the fairies cry, "Holland!" and he cried, "Holland!" too.

In one leap he was over France, and another over Belgium, and with the third he was standing by long ditches of water frozen fast, and over them glided hundreds upon hundreds of lads and maids. Outside each door stood a wee wooden shoe, empty. Teig saw scores of them as he looked down the ditch of a street.

"What is the meanin' o' those shoes?" he asked the fairies.

"Ye poor lad!" answered the wee man next to him. "Are ye not knowing anything? This is the Gift Night of the year, when every man gives to his neighbor."

A child came to the window of one of the houses, and in her hand was a lighted candle. She was singing as she put the light down close to the glass, and Teig caught the words:

"Open your door and greet ye the stranger,
For ye mind that the wee Lord had naught but a manger.
Mhuire as truagh!"

"'Tis the de'il's work!" cried Teig, and he set the red cap more firmly on his head. "I'm for another country."

I cannot be telling you half of the adventures Teig had that night, nor half the sights he saw. But he passed by fields that held sheaves of grain for the birds, and door-steps that held bowls of porridge for the wee creatures. He saw lighted trees, sparkling and heavy with gifts; and he stood outside the churches and watched the crowds pass in, bearing gifts to the Holy Mother and Child.

At last the fairies straightened their caps and cried, "Now for the great hall in the King of England's palace!"

Whist!—and away they went, and Teig after them; and the first thing he knew he was in London, not an arm's-length from the King's throne. It was a grander sight than he had seen in any other country. The hall was filled entirely with lords and ladies; and the great doors were open for the poor and the homeless to come in and warm themselves by the King's fire and feast from the King's table. And many a hungry soul did the King serve with his own hands.

Those that had anything to give gave it in return. It might be a bit of music played on a harp or a pipe, or it might be a dance or a song; but more often it was a wish, just, for good luck and safe-keeping.

Teig was so taken up with the watching that he never heard the fairies when they wished themselves off; moreover, he never saw the wee girl that was fed and went laughing away. But he heard a bit of her song as she passed through the door:

"Feed ye the hungry and rest ye the weary,
This ye must do for the sake of Our Mary."

Then the anger had Teig. "I'll stop your pesterin' tongue once an' for all time!" And, catching the cap from his head, he threw it after her.

No sooner was the cap gone than every soul in the hall saw him. The next moment they were about him, catching at his coat and crying:

"Where is he from? What does he here? Bring him before the King!"

And Teig was dragged along by a hundred hands to the throne where the King sat.

"He was stealing food," cried one.

"He was stealing the King's jewels," cried another.

"He looks evil," cried a third. "Kill him!"

And in a moment all the voices took it up and the hall rang with, "Aye, kill him, kill him!"

Teig's legs took to trembling, and fear put the leash on his tongue; but after a long silence he managed to whisper:

"I have done evil to no one, no one!"

"Maybe," said the King. "But have ye done good? Come, tell us, have ye given aught to any one this night? If ye have, we will pardon ye."

Not a word could Teig say; fear tightened the leash, for he was knowing full well there was no good to him that night.

"Then ye must die," said the King. "Will ye try hanging or be-heading?"

"Hanging, please, your Majesty," said Teig.

The guards came rushing up and carried him off. But as he was crossing the threshold of the hall a thought sprang at him and held him.

"Your Majesty," he called after him, "will ye grant me a last request?"

"I will," said the King.

"Thank ye. There's a wee red cap that I'm mortal fond of, and I lost it awhile ago; if I could be hung with it on I would hang a deal more comfortable."

The cap was found and brought to Teig.

"Clip, clap, clip, clap, for my wee red cap. I wish I was home!" he sang.

Up and over the heads of the dumfounded guard he flew, and—whist!—and away out of sight. When he opened his eyes again he was sitting close by his own hearth, with the fire burnt low. The hands of the clock were still, the bolt was fixed firm in the door. The fairies' lights were gone, and the only bright thing was the candle burning in old Shawn's cabin across the road.

A running of feet sounded outside, and then the snatch of a song:

" 'Tis well that ye mind, ye who sit by the fire,
That the Lord He was born in a dark and cold byre.
                                        Mhuire as truagh!"

"Wait ye, whoever ye are!" And Teig was away to the corner, digging fast at the loose clay, as the terrier digs at a bone. He filled his hands full of the shining gold, then hurried to the door, unbarring it.

The miller's wee Cassie stood there peering at him out of the darkness.

"Take those to the Widow O'Donnelly, do ye hear? And take the rest to the store. Ye tell Jamie to bring up all that he has that is eatable an' dhrinkable; an' to the neighbors ye say, 'Teig's keepin' the feast this night.' Hurry now!"

Teig stopped a moment on the threshold until the tramp of her feet had died away; then he made a hollow of his two hands and called across the road:

"Hey, there, Shawn, will ye come over for a sup?"


THE NATIVITY STORY

For many, many years the Jewish people had been looking for a Messiah. Ever since Israel had been conquered by the Romans, and the proud Jewish people had had to bow before the Roman Emperor, they had been hoping that this Messiah, foretold in the Holy Scriptures, would come to drive out the Romans and make Israel the proud and fortunate nation it once had been.

St. Luke I. 26-33.

And in the sixth month the angel Gabriel was sent from God unto a city of Galilee, named Nazareth, to a virgin espoused to a man whose name was Joseph, of the house of David; and the virgin's name was Mary.

And the angel came in unto her, and said, Hail, thou that art highly favored, the Lord is with thee; blessed art thou among women.

And when she saw him, she was troubled at his saying, and cast into her mind what manner of salutation this should be.

And the angel said unto her, Fear not, Mary: for thou hast found favour with God. And behold, thou shalt conceive in thy womb, and bring forth a son, and shalt call his name JESUS.

He shall be great, and shall be called the Son of the Highest: and the Lord God shall give unto him the throne of his father David; and he shall reign over the house of Jacob forever; and of his kingdom there shall be no end.

One day, some months later, there rode into the village of Nazareth a messenger from Rome. He came with a proclamation from the Emperor which told the people that every family must go to a certain place and give their names, in order that Rome might know the number of people to be taxed. Anyone who belonged in another city must go back and give his name there.

Now Joseph came of the family of David, and so must be enrolled in David's city, Bethlehem. He was troubled when he saw the notice tacked to the door of the synagogue, for he did not want to leave Mary.

When he told her what he had to do, Mary wanted to go with him, for a prophet of old had written, "Out of Bethlehem shall come forth He that is to be the Ruler of Israel."

"It may be there that my babe, the Child of God will be born," she thought. And so, seated on a sturdy little donkey, she started off with Joseph.

It was a long, tiresome journey, and Joseph became very anxious before they reached Bethlehem. So many travellers were on the roads that they were crowded and jostled on every hand. Joseph had hoped that his kinsman would take them in, but his house was full as was every other house in Bethlehem.

Up and down the streets they went, but no shelter could they find. When they came to the inn, the innkeeper almost laughed at them. His rooms were already crowded. He could do nothing for them.

Then he looked at Mary, with her lovely eyes weary and fearful. "Come," he said at length, "there is a stable where you can sleep

225

tonight. It will be better than no room at all." And he led the way to a poor shelter where, by the side of the stalls full of oxen and asses, was a space which Joseph filled with fresh, clean straw.

And there that night, in the lowly cattle shed, the Lord of all the World was born.

### St. Luke II. 8-20

And there were in the same country shepherds abiding in the field, keeping watch over their flock by night. And lo, the angel of the Lord came upon them, and the glory of the Lord shone round about them: and they were sore afraid.

And the angel said unto them, Fear not: for behold, I bring you good tidings of great joy, which shall be to all people. For unto you is born this day in the city of David a Saviour which is Christ the Lord.

And this shall be a sign unto you; Ye shall find the babe wrapped in swaddling clothes, lying in a manger.

And suddenly there was with the angel a multitude of the heavenly host praising God, and saying, Glory to God in the highest, and on earth peace, good will toward men.

And it came to pass, as the angels were gone away from them into heaven, the shepherds said one to another, Let us now go even unto Bethlehem, and see this thing which is come to pass, which the Lord hath made known unto us.

And they came with haste, and found Mary, and Joseph, and the babe lying in a manger. And when they had seen it, they made known abroad the saying which was told them concerning this child. And all that heard it wondered at those things which were told them by the shepherds. But Mary kept all these things, and pondered them in her heart.

And the shepherds returned, glorifying and praising God for all the things that they had heard and seen, as it was told unto them.

### St. Matthew II. 1-12.

Now when Jesus was born in Bethlehem of Judea in the days of Herod the king, behold, there came wise men from the east to Jerusalem, saying, Where is he that is born King of the Jews? for we have seen his star in the east, and are come to worship him.

When Herod the king had heard these things, he was troubled, and all Jerusalem with him. And when he had gathered all the chief priests and scribes of the people together, he demanded of them where Christ should be born. And they said unto him, In Bethlehem of Judea: for thus it is written by the prophet. And thou Bethlehem, in the land of Juda, art not the least among the princes of Juda: for out of thee shall come a governor, that shall rule my people Israel.

Then Herod, when he had privily called the wise men, enquired of them diligently what time the star appeared. And he sent them to Bethlehem, and said, Go and search diligently for the young child; and when ye have found him, bring me word again, that I may come and worship him also.

When they had heard the king, they departed; and, lo, the star, which they saw in the east, went before them, till it came and stood over where the young child was. When they saw the star, they rejoiced with exceeding great joy. And when they were come into the house, they saw the young child with Mary his mother, and fell down, and worshipped him: and when they had opened their treasures, they presented unto him gifts: gold, and frankincense and myrrh.

And being warned of God in a dream that they should not return to Herod, they departed into their own country another way.

## A CHRISTMAS PROMISE[1]

### Ruth Sawyer

*A Spanish story of great beauty, suitable for both this age level and the next. It can be used as an all-school creative play, with a narrator or one of the characters to tell of this Christmas custom in Spain.*

When the Christ-child was born in Bethlehem of Judea, long years ago, three kings rode out of the East on their camels, bearing gifts to Him. They followed the star until at last they came to the manger where He lay, a little, newborn baby. Kneeling down, they put their gifts beside him: gold, frankincense, and myrrh; they kissed the hem of the little white mantle that He wore, and blessed Him. Then the kings rode away to the East again, but before ever they went they whispered a promise to the Christ-child.

And the promise? You shall hear it as the kings gave it to the Christ-child long years ago.

[1] From *This Way to Christmas*, by Ruth Sawyer. Copyright 1944 by Ruth Sawyer Durand. Used by permission of the author and Harper & Brothers, publishers.

"As long as there be children on the earth, on every Christmas Eve we three kings shall ride on camels, even as we rode to Thee this night; and even as we bore Thee gifts so shall we bear gifts to every child in memory of Thee—thou holy Babe of Bethlehem!"

In Spain they have remembered what the Christmas kings promised, and when Christmas Eve comes each child puts his sapatico—his little shoe—between the gratings of the window that they may know a child is in that house and leave a gift.

Often the shoe is filled with grass for the camels, and a plate of dates and figs is left beside it, for the children know the kings have far to go and may be hungry.

At day's end bands of children march out of the city gates, going to meet the kings. But it always grows dark before they come. The children are afraid upon the lonely road and hurry back to their homes, where the good madres hear them say one prayer to the Nene Jesu, as they call the Christ-child, and then put them to bed to dream of the Christmas kings.

Long, long ago there lived in Spain, in the crowded part of a great city, an old woman called Doña Josefa. The street in which she lived was little and narrow, so narrow that if you leaned out of the window of Doña Josefa's house you could touch with your finger-tips the house across the way, and when you looked above your head the sky seemed but a string of blue, tying the houses all together. The sun never found its way into this little street.

The people who lived here were very poor, as you may guess; Doña Josefa was poor, likewise. But in one thing she was very rich—she knew more stories than there were feast-days in the year, and that is a great many. Whenever there came a moment free from work, when Doña Josefa had no water to fetch from the public well, nor gold to stitch upon the altar cloth for the Church of Santa Maria del Rosario, then she would run out of her house into the street and call:

"Niños, niños, come quickly! Here is a story waiting for you."

And the children would come flying like the gray palomas when corn is thrown for them in the Plaza. Ah, how many children there were in that little street! There were José and Miguel and the niños of Enrique, the cobbler, Alfredito and Juana and Esperanza; and the little twin sisters of Pancho, the peddler; and Angela, María Teresa, Pedro, Edita, and many more. Last of all there were Manuel and Rosita. They had no father, and their mother was a lavandera who stood all day on the banks of the river outside the city, washing clothes.

When Doña Josefa had called the children from all the doorways and the dark corners she would sit down in the middle of the street and gather them about her. This was safe because the street was far too narrow to allow a horse or wagon to pass through. Sometimes a donkey would slowly pick its way along, or a stupid goat come searching for things to eat, but that was all.

It happened on the day before Christmas that Doña Josefa had finished her work and sat, as usual, with the children about her.

"To-day you shall have a Christmas story," she said, and then she told them of the three kings and the promise they had made the Christ-child.

"And is it so—do the kings bring presents to the children now?" Miguel asked.

Doña Josefa nodded her head.

"Yes."

"Then why have they never left us one? The three kings never pass this street on Christmas Eve. Why is it, Doña?"

"Perhaps it is because we have no shoes to hold their gifts," said Angela.

And this is true. The poor children of Spain go barefooted, and often never have a pair of shoes till they grow up.

Manuel had listened silently to the others, but now he pulled the sleeve of Doña Josefa's gown with coaxing fingers:

"I know why it is the kings bring no gifts to us. See, the street; it is too small; their camels could not pass between the door-steps here. The kings must ride where the streets are broad and smooth and clean, where their long mantles will not be soiled and torn and the camels will not stumble. It is the children in the great streets, the children of the rich, who find presents in their sapaticos on Christmas morning. Is it not so, Doña Josefa?"

And Miguel cried, "Does Manuel speak true—is it only the children of the rich?"

"Ah, chicito mío, it should not be so! When the promise was given to the Nene Jesu there in Bethlehem they said, 'to every child.' Yes, every little child."

"But it is not strange they should forget us here," Manuel insisted. "The little street is hidden in the shadow of the great ones."

Then Rosita spoke, clasping her hands together with great eagerness:

"I know; it is because we have no shoes! That is why they never stop. Perhaps Enrique would lend us the shoes he is mending, just for one night. If we had shoes the kings would surely see that there are little children in the street, and leave a gift for each of us. Come, let us ask Enrique!"

"Madre de Dios, it is a blessed thought!" cried all. And like the flock of gray palomas they swept down the street to the farthest end, where Enrique hammered and stitched away all day on the shoes of the rich children.

Manuel stayed behind with Doña Josefa. When the last pair of little brown feet had disappeared inside the sapateria he said, softly:

"If some one could go out and meet the kings to tell them of this little street, and how the niños here have never had a Christmas gift, do you think they might ride hither to-night?"

Doña Josefa shook her head doubtfully.

"If that were possible—But never have I heard of any one who met the kings on Christmas Eve."

All day in the city people hurried to and fro. In the great streets flags were waving from the housetops, and wreaths of laurel, or garlands of heliotrope and mariposa, hung above the open doorways and in the windows. Sweetmeat-sellers were crying their wares; and the Keeper-of-the-City lighted flaming torches to hang upon the gates and city walls. Everywhere was merrymaking and gladness, for not only was this Christmas Eve, but the King of Spain was coming to keep his holiday within the city. Some whispered that he was riding from the North, and with him rode his cousins, the kings of France and Lombardy, and with them were a great following of nobles, knights, and minstrels. Others said the kings rode all alone—it was their wish.

As the sun was turning the cathedral spires to shafts of gold, bands of children, hand in hand, marched out of the city. They took the road that led toward the setting sun, thinking it was the East, and said among themselves, "See, yonder is the way the kings will ride."

"I have brought a basket of figs," cried one.

"I have dates in a new pañuela," cried another.

"And I," cried a third, "I have brought a sack of sweet limes, they are so cooling."

Thus each in turn showed some small gift that he was bringing for the kings. And while they chatted together one child began to sing the sweet Nativity Hymn. In a moment others joined until the still night air rang with their happy voices.

"Unto us a Child is born,
    Unto us a gift is given.
Hail with holiness the morn,
    Kneel before the Prince of Heaven.
Blessed by this day of birth,
God hath given His Son to earth.
    Jesu, Jesu, Nene Jesu,
        Hallelujah!"

Behind the little hills the sun went down, leaving a million sparks of light upon the road.

"Yonder come the kings!" the children cried. "See the splendor of their shining crowns and how the jewels sparkle on their mantles! They may be angry if they find us out so late; come, let us run home before they see us."

The children turned. Back to the city gates they ran, back to their homes, to the good madres watching for them and their own white beds ready for them.

But one they left behind them on the road: a little, bare-limbed boy whose name was Manuel. He watched until the children had disappeared within the gates, and then he turned again toward the setting sun.

"I have no gift for the kings," he thought, "but there is fresh green grass beside the way that I can gather for the camels."

He stopped, pulled his hands full, and stuffed it in the front of the little blue vestido that he wore. He followed the road for a long way until heavy sleep came to his eyes.

"How still it is upon the road! God has blown out His light and soon it will be dark. I wish I were with the others, safe within the city; for the dark is full of fearsome things when one is all alone . . . Mamita will be coming home soon and bringing supper for Rosita and me. Perhaps to-night there will be an almond dulce or pan de gloria—perhaps. . . . I wonder will Rosita not forget the little prayer I told her to be always saying. My feet hurt with the many stones; the night wind blows cold; I am weary and my feet stumble with me. . . . Oh, Nene Jesu, listen! I also make the prayer: " 'Send the three kings before Manuel is too weary and afraid'!"

A few more steps he took upon the road, and then, as a reed is blown down by the wind, Manuel swayed, unknowingly for a moment, and slowly sank upon the ground, fast asleep.

How long he slept I cannot tell you; but a hand on his shoulder wakened him. Quickly he opened his eyes, wondering, and saw—

yes, he saw the three kings! Tall and splendid they looked in the starlight, their mantles shimmering with myriad gems. One stood above Manuel, asking what he did upon the road at that late hour. Manuel rose to his feet, thrusting his hand inside the shirt for the grass he had gathered.

"It is for the camels, señor; I have no other gift. But you—you ride horses this Christmas Eve!"

"Yes, we ride horses. What is that to you?"

"Pardon, señores, nothing. The three kings can ride horses if they wish; only—we were told you rode on camels from the East."

"What does the child want?" The voice was kind, but it sounded impatient, as though the one who spoke had work waiting to be done and was anxious to be about it.

Manuel heard and felt all this wondering.

"What if there is not time for them to come, or gifts enough!" He laid an eager, pleading hand on one king's mantle.

"I can hold the horses if you will come this once. It is a little street and hard to find, senores; I thought perhaps you would leave a present—just one little present for the children there. You told the Christ-child you would give to every child. Don't you remember? There are many of us who have never had a gift—a Christmas gift."

"Do you know who we are?"

Manuel answered, joyfully: "Oh yes, Excellencias, you are the Three Christmas Kings, riding from Bethlehem. Will you come with me?"

The kings spoke with one accord, "Verily, we will."

One lifted Manuel on his horse; and silently they rode into the city. The Keeper slumbered at the gates; the streets were empty. On, past the houses that were garlanded they went unseen; and on through the great streets until they came to the little street at last. The Kings dismounted. They gave their bridles into Manuel's hand, and then, gathering up their precious mantles of silk and rich brocade, they passed down the little street. With eyes that scarce believed what they saw, Manuel watched them go from house to house, saw them stop and feel for the shoes between the gratings, the shoes loaned by Enrique, the cobbler, and saw them fill each one with shining gold pieces.

In the morning Manuel told the story to the children as they went to spend one golden doblon for toys and candy and sugared cakes. And a gift they brought for Doña Josefa, too; a little figure of the Holy Mother with the Christ-child in her arms.

232

# CHAPTER VII

# Through Wider Gateways

Watch an eighth grade class playing the witches' scenes from *Macbeth,* the artisans' scenes from *A Midsummer Night's Dream,* or any of the episodes from *The Taming of the Shrew,* if you would like to know what children can achieve in story dramatization! With several years of experience in dramatizing stories, and some background in Elizabethan England and the Shakespearean theatre, they often amaze the adult observer when they dramatize the Shakespeare stories from Mary MacLeod, included in this book.

There is a good deal of difference in interests between the seventh and eighth grades. While the twelve-year-olds are still most interested in the realistic, adventurous stories, the thirteen- and fourteen-year-olds are growing into an appreciation of spiritual values, as well. They enjoy romantic glamor along with realism, and the idealistic has a strong appeal to many of them.

At the same time, the eighth graders are usually more inhibited, more afraid of expressing feeling than are the younger children. For this reason, it is especially important to create situations which will give them legitimate outlets for the emotions which too often are unhealthily stored up within them.

Sometimes "role-playing" is used to help solve problems common at this age. A teacher may write on the blackboard, as the children suggest, a list of possibilities, and the class may then choose one to play. Such problems as the parents' interference with home-work, permission to go to a school dance, the frequent need of staying

233

with small brothers and sisters, and such school problems as the way a child may be received when he transfers to a new school, may arouse much interest. It is perhaps better not to play these situa· tions in a child's own character; and it is most desirable for the children to exchange roles after having played once so that they can feel both sides of the question.

Aside from role-playing, studies in characterizations are valuable. If a teacher collects many interesting bits of costumes and properties, gives one to each child, numbers them by fives, perhaps, allowing ten minutes for them to plan a scene, each five may come forth from its corner with a tiny scene in which the characters are people who might use these particular properties and costumes. Or—and this is simpler and in many cases better—each may do an individual pantomime as a character suggested by his costume or property.

Some of the most successful stories for dramatization are those in which boys and girls play roles so far from their own natures that they lose all feeling of self. The broad comedy of "Hungry Hans" or "The Squire's Bride" delights the seventh grade, and the children thoroughly enjoy the longer story of "The Quest of the Hammer." The mystery and adventure of "The Moor's Legacy" never fails to appeal to them, yet they respond to the quieter "Nuremberg Stove;" and "A Christmas Carol," with its fine spirit, is one of the most popular stories of all for dramatization.

Along with this material, enjoyed also by the eighth grade, are the very beautiful "Christmas Apple," "Our Lady's Juggler," "The Good Samaritan;" and the Shakespeare stories, so rich in characterization, so meaty in plot. Omitting some of the unsuitable scenes, enough good material can be found in the Shakespeare stories for an entire year's work. The slightest suggestion of love-making is enough to make children intensely self-conscious, and no teacher ever tries twice a story involving this kind of romance. They often enjoy the humorous wooing in *The Shrew*, but would never feel at ease playing the Hermia-Lysander scenes in *The Dream*.

One may choose from the following stories the ones best suited to the children in each particular group, using material from the preceding list if the class is inexperienced, and attempting such fine and difficult stories as "The Bishop's Candlesticks" and "Our Lady's Juggler" only for skilled and sensitive children.

# GET UP AND BAR THE DOOR

## An Old Ballad

*Children always enjoy the broad farce of this stubborn old couple.
There is good chance for ingenuity in reading between the lines
and adding people and incidents.*

It fell about the Martinmas time,
    And a gay time it was then,
When our goodwife got puddings to make,
    And she's boiled them in the pan.

The wind sae cauld blew south and north,
    And blew into the floor;
Quoth our goodman to our goodwife,
    "Gae up and bar the door."

"My hand is in my hussyfscap,
    Goodman, as ye may see;
An it should nae be barred this hundred year,
    It'll no be barred by me."

They made a paction 'tween them twa,
    They made it firm and sure,
That the first word whaeer should speak,
    Shoud rise and bar the door.

Then by there came two gentlemen,
    At twelve o'clock at night,
And they could neither see house nor hall,
    Nor coal nor candle-light.

"Now whether is this a rich man's house,
    Or whether is it a poor?"
But ne'er a word wad one o' them speak,
    For barring of the door.

And first they ate the white puddings,
    And then they ate the black;
Tho muckle thought the goodwife to hersel',
    Yet ne'er a word she spake.

Then said the one unto the other,
"Here, man, tak ye my knife;
Do ye tak off the auld man's beard,
And I'll kiss the goodwife."

"But there's nae water in the house,
And what shall we do than?"
"What ails ye at the pudding-broo
That boils into the pan?"

O up then started our goodman,
An angry man was he;
"Will ye kiss my wife before my een,
And scad me wi' pudding-bree?"

Then up and started our goodwife,
Gied three skips on the floor;
"Goodman, you've spoken the foremost word,
Get up and bar the door."

## THE LEGEND OF THE MOOR'S LEGACY[1]

### Washington Irving

*This is a favorite story for dramatization with the seventh grade. Because it is too long to include in its entirety, only three episodes are given here. Whether or not the whole story is played, it is suggested that for fuller understanding the complete story be read.*

The Alhambra, the ruins of which may still be seen in Granada, Spain, was the palace-fortress of the Moorish Kings who for many years ruled that country. Washington Irving, in his book, TALES OF THE ALHAMBRA, related a number of stories about the palace and its surroundings, of which this is one of the most fascinating.

The central figure in this legend is an honest, kind-hearted water-carrier named Peregil. His wife, once the village beauty, is something of a slattern, neglecting her house, children, and everything else, to loiter slipshod in the houses of her gossip neighbors.

At a late hour one summer night, when Peregil made a last trip to the well, he found there a solitary stranger in Moorish garb. As he was faint and ill, Peregil put him on the back of his donkey and, though the law forbade any citizen to take a Moor into his home, Peregil was too humane to refuse a night's shelter to a fellow-being

[1] From *Tales of the Alhambra*, by Washington Irving. Adapted.

*in such a plight. So, in spite of his wife's remonstrances, he brought him in and ministered to him.*

*That night the Moor died, after giving Peregil a small box of sandalwood for his kindness. Appalled by what would probably happen when a dead Moor was found in his house, Peregil decided to take the body outside the city and bury it on the banks of the river. This he did, and all would have been well except that a meddlesome barber, Pedrillo Pedrugo, living opposite Peregil, who was said to sleep with but one eye at a time, heard the unaccustomed sounds, and watched all that happened.*

In the morning, taking a basin under his arm, he sallied forth to shave the *alcalde* (or mayor), who had just risen. Pedrugo seated him in a chair, threw a napkin round his neck, put a basin of hot water under his chin, and began to mollify his beard with his fingers.

"Strange doings!" said Pedrugo who played barber and newsmonger at the same time,—"strange doings!—Robbery and murder and burial all in one night!"

"Hey! How! What is that you say?" cried the *alcalde*.

"I say," replied the barber, rubbing a piece of soap over the nose and mouth of the dignitary, for a Spanish barber disdains to employ a brush,—"I say that Peregil has robbed and murdered and buried a Moor this blessed night."

"But how do you know all this?" demanded the *alcalde*.

"Be patient, *Señor*, and you shall hear all about it," replied Pedrugo, taking him by the nose and sliding a razor over his cheek. He then recounted all that he had seen, going through both operations at the same time, shaving his beard, washing his chin, and wiping him dry with a dirty napkin, while he was robbing, murdering, and burying the Moslem.

Now it so happened that this *alcalde* was one of the most overbearing, and at the same time most griping and corrupt curmudgeons in all Granada. It could not be denied, however, that he set a high value upon justice, for he sold it at its weight in gold. He presumed the case in point to be one of murder and robbery; doubtless there must be a rich spoil; how was it to be secured into the legitimate hands of the law? For as to merely entrapping the delinquent—that would be feeding the gallows; but entrapping the booty—that would be enriching the judge, and such, according to his creed, was the great end of justice. So thinking, he summoned to his presence his truest officer—a gaunt, hungry-looking varlet dressed in rusty-black clothes, a broad black beaver turned up at the sides, and a small black cloak dangling from his shoulders. Such was his speed and certainty that in a few minutes he had brought poor Peregil before this dispenser of justice.

The *alcalde* bent upon him one of the most terrific frowns. "Hark ye, culprit!" roared he, in a voice that made Peregil's knees smite together, "there is no need of denying thy guilt; everything is known to me. A gallows is the proper reward for the crime thou hast committed, but I am merciful, and readily listen to reason. The man that has been murdered in thy house was a Moor, an infidel, the enemy of our faith. It was doubtless in a fit of religious zeal that thou hast slain him. I will be indulgent, therefore; render up the property of which thou hast robbed him, and we will hush the matter up."

The poor water-carrier called upon all the Saints to witness his innocence. He related the whole story of the dying Moor with the straightforward simplicity of truth, but it was all in vain. "Wilt thou persist in saying," demanded the judge, "that this Moslem had neither gold nor jewels which were the object of thy cupidity?"

"As I hope to be saved, your worship," replied the water-carrier, "he had nothing but a small box of sandal-wood, which he bequeathed to me in reward for my services."

"A box of sandal-wood! A box of sandal-wood!" exclaimed the *alcalde,* his eyes sparkling at the idea of precious jewels. "And where is this box? Where have you concealed it?"

"An it please your grace," replied the water-carrier, "it is in one of the panniers of my donkey, and heartily at the service of your worship."

He had hardly spoken the words, when the officer darted off, and reappeared in an instant with the mysterious box of sandal-wood. The *alcalde* opened it with an eager and trembling hand; all pressed forward to gaze upon the treasure it was expected to contain; when, to their disappointment, nothing appeared within but a parchment scroll, covered with Arabic characters, and an end of a waxen taper.

When there is nothing to be gained by the conviction of a prisoner, justice, even in Spain, is apt to be impartial. The *alcalde,* having recovered from his disappointment, and found that there was really no booty in the case, now listened dispassionately to the explanation of the water-carrier, which was corroborated by the testimony of his wife. Being convinced, therefore, of his innocence, he discharged him from arrest; nay, more, he permitted him to carry off the Moor's legacy, the box of sandal-wood and its contents, as the well-merited reward of his humanity; but he retained his donkey in payment of costs and charges.

"Dog of an *alcalde!*" said Peregil to himself after he had left; "to rob a poor man of the means of his subsistence, of the best friend he had in the world!"

Though Peregil had little faith that his "legacy" was worth anything, he at length took the scroll to the shop of a Moor who sold trinkets and perfumery in the Zacatin, and asked him to explain its contents.

The Moor read the scroll attentively, then stroked his beard and smiled. "This manuscript," said he, "is a form of incantation for the recovery of hidden treasure that is under the power of enchantment. It is said to have such virtue that the strongest bolts and bars, nay, the adamantine rock itself, will yield before it!"

"Bah!" cried Peregil, "what is all that to me? I am no enchanter, and know nothing of buried treasure." So saying, he started off. But then of a sudden he recalled the tales he had heard of enchanted riches left by the Moors in various parts of the Alhambra. "If, after all, there should be treasure hid beneath that tower," he thought, "and if the scroll should enable me to get at it!" He turned back to the Moor.

"Suppose we go together to the tower, and try the effect of the charm," he said; "if it fails, we are no worse off than before; but if it succeeds, we will share equally all the treasure we may discover."

"Hold," replied the Moslem; "this writing is not sufficient of itself; it must be read at midnight, by the light of a taper singularly compounded and prepared, the ingredients of which are not within my reach. Without such a taper the scroll is of no avail."

"Say no more!" cried Peregil. And he opened the sandal-wood box and handed the taper to the Moor.

The Moor felt it and smelt it. "Here are rare and costly perfumes," said he, "combined with this yellow wax. This is the kind of taper specified in the scroll. While this burns the strongest walls and most secret caverns will remain open. Woe to him, however, who lingers within until it be extinguished. He will remain enchanted with the treasure."

It was now agreed between them to try the charm that very night. At a late hour, therefore, when nothing was stirring but bats and owls, they ascended the woody hill of the Alhambra, and approached that awful tower, shrouded by trees and rendered formidable by so many traditional tales. By the light of a lantern they groped their way through bushes and over fallen stones to the door of a vault beneath the tower. With fear and trembling they descended a flight of steps cut into the rock. It led to an empty chamber, damp and drear, from which another flight of steps led to a deeper vault. In this way they descended three several flights, leading into as many vaults, one below the other; but the floor of the fourth was solid; and though, according to tradition, there remained three vaults still below, it was said to be impossible to penetrate further, the residue being shut up by strong enchantment. The air of this vault was damp and chilly, and had an earthy smell, and the light scarce cast forth any rays. They paused here for a time, in breathless suspense, until they faintly heard the clock of the watch-tower strike midnight; upon this they lit the waxen taper, which diffused an odor of myrrh and frankincense and storax.

The Moor began to read in a hurried voice. He had scarce finished when there was a noise as of subterraneous thunder. The earth shook, and the floor, yawning open, disclosed a flight of steps. Trembling with awe, they descended, and by the light of the lantern found themselves in another vault covered with Arabic inscriptions. In the center stood a great chest, secured with seven bands of steel, at each end of which sat an enchanted Moor in armor, but motionless as a statue, being controlled by the power of the incantation. Before the chest were several jars filled with gold and silver and precious stones. In the largest of these they thrust their arms up to the elbow, and at every dip hauled forth handfuls of broad yellow pieces of Moorish gold, or bracelets and ornaments of the same precious metal, while occasionally a necklace of Oriental pearl would stick to their fingers. Still they trembled and breathed short while cramming their pockets with the spoils; and cast many a fearful glance at the two enchanted Moors, who sat grim and motionless, glaring upon them with unwinking eyes. At length, struck with a sudden panic at some fancied noise, they both rushed up the staircase, tumbled over one another into the upper apartment, overturned and extinguished the waxen taper, and the pavement again closed with a thundering sound.

Filled with dismay, they did not pause until they had groped their way out of the tower, and beheld the stars shining through the trees. Then, seating themselves upon the grass, they divided the spoil, determining to content themselves for the present with this mere skimming of the jars, but to return on some future night and drain them to the bottom. To make sure of each other's good faith, also, they divided the talismans between them, one retaining the scroll and the other the taper; this done, they set off with light hearts and well-lined pockets for Granada.

As they wended their way down the hill, the shrewd Moor whispered a word of counsel in the ear of the simple little water-carrier.

"Friend Peregil," said he, "all this affair must be kept a profound secret until we have secured the treasure, and conveyed it out of harm's way. If a whisper of it gets to the ear of the *alcalde,* we are undone!"

"Certainly," replied Peregil, "nothing can be more true."

"Friend Peregil," said the Moor, "you are a discreet man, and I make no doubt can keep a secret; but you have a wife."

"She shall not know a word of it," replied the little water-carrier, sturdily.

"Enough," said the Moor, "I depend upon thy discretion and thy promise."

Never was promise more positive and sincere; but, alas! what man can keep a secret from his wife? Certainly not such a one as Peregil the water-carrier, who was one of the most loving and tractable of husbands. On his return home, he found his wife moping in a corner. "Mighty well," cried she as he entered, "you've come at last, after rambling about until this hour of the night. I wonder you have not brought home another Moor as a house-mate." Then bursting into tears, she began to wring her hands and smite her breast. "Unhappy woman that I am!" exlaimed she, "what will become of me? My husband a do-no-good, that no longer brings home bread to his family, but goes rambling about day and night, with infidel Moors! O my children! my children! what will become of us? We shall all have to beg in the streets!"

Honest Peregil was so moved by the distress of his spouse that he thrust his hand into his pocket, hauled forth three or four broad gold pieces, and dropped them into her lap. The poor woman stared with astonishment, and could not understand the meaning of this golden shower. Before she could recover her surprise, Peregil drew forth a chain of gold and dangled it before her, capering with exultation.

"Holy Virgin protect us!" exclaimed the wife. "What hast thou been doing, Peregil? surely thou hast not been committing murder and robbery!"

The idea scarce entered the brain of the poor woman, than it became a certainty with her. She saw a prison and a gallows in the distance, and, overcome by the horrors conjured up by imagination, fell into violent hysterics. What could the poor man do? He had no other means of pacifying his wife, and dispelling the phantoms of her fancy, than by relating the whole story of his good fortune. This, however, he did not do until he had exacted from her the most solemn promise to keep it a profound secret from every living being.

To describe her joy would be impossible. She flung her arms round the neck of her husband, and almost strangled him with her caresses. "Now, wife," exclaimed the little man with honest exultation, "what say you now to the Moor's legacy? Henceforth never abuse me for helping a fellow-creature in distress."

For a day and a half Peregil's wife kept her promise with surprising strictness. True, she could not help giving herself a few airs. She apologized to the neighbors for her ragged dress, and talked of ordering a new one trimmed with gold lace. She hinted that her husband intended to leave off his trade of water-carrying soon, and expected to take the family to the mountains for the summer.

At home, however, she entertained herself by loading her fingers with jewels, and sailing back and forth in her rags with an aigrette of diamonds on her head. She could not resist, on one occasion, showing herself at the window to enjoy the effect of her finery on the passers-by.

As the fates would have it, Pedrillo Pedrugo, the meddlesome barber across the way, caught sight of her. In an instant he was off to report to the mayor. Peregil was once more dragged before him, threatened with the gallows, and when he had related all that had happened, was told that he must prove his words by repeating the incantation in the mayor's presence. Then if there really was treasure, they would share it and say nothing further. It was his secret intention, however, to seize all of it for himself.

That night, the *alcalde*, the officer, and the barber, accompanied by Peregil and the Moor, sallied forth to the Alhambra. As before, the earth opened, and since no one could summon courage to descend except Peregil and the Moor, they once more entered the lower vault, and returned with jars of golden coins and precious stones.

Not content to leave until they had secured all the treasure, the *alcalde* ordered the men to go down once more. But enough was enough, they said, and nothing would induce them to descend again. Finding that threats were useless, the *alcalde* and his two henchmen reluctantly started down the steps to get the treasure themselves. But no sooner were they out of sight than the Moor extinguished the taper, the floor of the vault closed with a crash, and the three men below were enchanted until the day when some future adventurer should arrive to break the charm.

As for Peregil and the Moor, they divided the treasure between them, and for the rest of their lives were free to enjoy the legacy left by the old man to the little water-carrier who had befriended him.

## HUNGRY HANS[1]
### *A Comic Tragedy*

### Keller-Untermeyer

*A Swiss tale easy to dramatize and fun to play. Other characters can be added if desired, both real and visionary.*

Close to Seldwyla there lived an apothecary who could always be found hard at work. Early and late, he busied himself with pills and powders and potions and drugs and ointments and salves. He mixed medicines, distilled extracts, registered letters and never gave himself a moment's leisure. He never invited company to his house, never accepted any invitations, refused to go to places of amusement. Year in, year out, he never set foot in a tavern, and he abused anybody who, after his day's work, sat down to a glass of country-wine. His beloved better half attended to the house. She kept no maid, did everything herself: scouring and scrubbing, baking and broiling, mending and knitting—she attended to every detail. Like her husband, she stayed at home; never went to pay visits or attend the dances in Seldwyla. The only time she left the house was on Sunday, when, with her husband, she walked stiffly to church.

Clever though they were in many ways, they had one fault which everyone noticed at once—and which you have already guessed—their stinginess. They were, so ran the gossip, the stingiest couple in Switzerland. But they were not miserly with themselves. Far

---

[1] From *The Fat of the Oat and Other Stories* by Gottfried Keller, adapted and translated by Louis Untermeyer. Copyright 1925, by Harcourt, Brace and Company, Inc.

from it! They enjoyed the best of food. The most delicate dishes came to their table every day, the finest wines trickled down their throats every evening, the most expensive tobacco was crammed into the apothecary's pipe after every meal. But when it came to sharing anything with someone else, they would not part with the tiniest morsel. She cooked the richest meats—and refused to give the ragged beggars an old crust of bread. He finished a whole bottle of rare claret every night—and wouldn't move from his chair to oblige thirsty travellers with a glass of water.

When I tell you that they did not keep a maid, do not think that they did their own work because they believed in hard work for its own sake. No, the reason is much simpler. They kept no maid because no maid would stay with them. And no maid would stay with them because she never got enough to eat. While these two gluttons gorged themselves, all they ever gave the servants (when they had them!) was a plate of wretched soup, a piece of old bread and, once a week, a few greasy scraps of left-over meat. Because of this kind of treatment, the apothecary's whole staff of assistants had been reduced to one apprentice, a lean and starved-looking boy who had twice run away from his master, but who was bound by contract to serve four years and who had been brought back each time. He was over six feet high—for the only way he could grow was up. This poor youngster was made to do the work of half a dozen able-bodied men; he was continually being called from the laboratory to the kitchen, from the kitchen to the store-room, from the attic to the cellar and back again—all in a few minutes. Often his master in the work-room, and his mistress in the pantry, would call for him at once. And then he would be thrashed for not being in both places at the same time!

Hans—for this was the name of the lanky apprentice—was always hungry. Ever since he could remember, he had not had enough to eat. He had been born hungry. He went about his work in a daze, thinking of nothing but food. The only dreams he had were about wonderful feasts; he imagined Heaven as a place where the good souls ate and ate through all eternity. All day long he went sniffing through the rooms, and if there was anything to eat standing around, you can be sure his five fingers were in it. He had been caught and whipped hundreds of times. His back was black and blue from the marks of his master's brown-lacquered cane; his face showed scratches from his mistress's sharp claws. But his hunger was greater than his fear. He dipped into everything; his muscles seemed to move by themselves, without his will. Often he peeked through the keyhole where his greedy employers were devouring some fragrant repast, and his jaws began working up and down of their own accord, even though he had nothing in his mouth except his teeth.

His favorite place was, as you can imagine, the pantry. Here were kept cocoa, sugar, cookies, chocolate, syrups, delicious flavouring extracts, honey, and so forth. And here, whenever he got a chance, Hans would come, tasting, chewing and swallowing, no matter how often the brown-lacquered cane fell on him in the midst of his stolen sweets. Even when his bruises hurt him most, he would come back to this enchanting spot and console himself with the famous goose-liver paste, which was his master's chief pride. The paste was packed in layers in a large case and Hans, by loosening one of the boards at the bottom, would take out a bit now and then to comfort himself. He only allowed himself this delicacy once in a while, and did not indulge himself oftener for a peculiar reason. He was fond enough of it, you may be sure, but he had to overcome a horrible feeling every time he came near the box which contained the dainties. On top of this case stood three wide-necked, carefully sealed, white glass jars which contained (in his opinion) the juiciest, most appetizing preserved fruits he had ever seen. He felt terribly unhappy because he could never taste these lovely morsels—and it was not his conscience that made him keep his hands off. It was something stronger than his appetite that made him tremble whenever he happened to touch these jars. For, pasted on the glass, was a label, and on the label was a grinning skull and two crossed bones next to the one word "Poison"! Hans shook his head every time he saw the word. "What a pity," he would murmur. "What a shame to use such beautiful fruit for such a terrible purpose." And, with a sigh of disappointment, he would go back to his work.

One morning—it was Sunday—as Hans was helping himself to the goose-liver, he heard the harsh voice of his mistress calling him to the kitchen. His bad conscience almost made him feel her out-stretched claws dig into him as he ran down the steps, choking down the last bite of his stolen breakfast. But a great surprise was awaiting him; an entirely different sight than he expected met his astonished eyes. There stood the apothecary in a cinnamon-brown coat trimmed with steel-blue buttons; he had on narrow nankeen trousers, white silk stockings, fancy buckled shoes, and the hated cane swung from his hand. Next to him stood his owl-faced wife in a bright green dress with a large fur collar. Her fingers were not preparing to scratch him as usual, but were busy sorting out the bad coins from her purse so she could put these—which were not worth anything—in the poor-box at church.

"Hans," the apothecary said, "to-day is the birthday of your indulgent mistress, my dear wife, and so, as a special holiday, we are going to church together."

"And here," that generous lady chimed in, "so that you won't be lonely, here is some work for you to keep you busy while we are away." And a poke in his ribs directed him to the hearth where a suckling-pig was beginning to be broiled on the spit. Already a magical fragrance was arising from it and Hans's thirsty nostrils started to drink it in. But—"Don't stand there all day like a ninny!" came the commanding voice of the mistress of the household. "Here is what you have to do: Keep turning the spit so that the meat gets good and brown all over, pour the gravy over it every few seconds so that it stays moist and tender, don't forget to rake the coals so that the fire is the right heat, but if it gets too hot and you burn any part of the meat, I'll box your ears till the blood comes!" This pleasant speech—which was all delivered in one breath—was scarcely out of her mouth before his master continued, "And I'll do my share, you young rascal! If the Sunday dinner is spoiled, I'll broil *you* on the spit instead of the pig that's on it now! Understand?" And with this sweet farewell, the gentle pair left the house and walked to church, where they sang the sacred hymns louder than anyone in the congregation.

After the lock had turned and the backs of his two slave-drivers had disappeared down the street, Hans began to feel better and, coming nearer the hearth, to breathe deeper.

The wonderful, sweet smell—sweeter than heavenly incense—bewitched his senses. His teeth ached for a single bite and his jaws began to work up and down over their painful emptiness. The pigling grew browner and tenderer, and a thousand little fat bubbles, like tiny pearls, leaped and danced and disappeared and sprang up again on the smooth surface of the roast. The meat crisped and crackled and hummed and hissed, as if something alive were talking to him from the spit. And poor Hans sat there, turning and ladling and dipping and poking the fire, while the crust on the grilled meat grew more tempting and Hans's eyes began to have a glassy stare. Finally, when his mouth watered so that he could not sit there any longer, it seemed as if a voice spoke to him from the hissing spit. "Every cook has the right to taste what he is preparing," said the voice in a juicy whisper, "why shouldn't *you*? How can you tell if I'm cooked properly unless you see how I taste? Here is a tiny crust toward the back; nobody will ever miss that. Besides, it's loose and is just about to fall into the fire, so you may as well have it."

"And why shouldn't I?" said Hans to himself. "The place will get smooth and brown in a minute." No sooner said than done— and down went a good-sized crust into Hans's bottomless pit. . . .

It would be hard to describe the effect of the taste of this morsel on Hans. He sat there, licking his lips, his eyes sparkling, while a tiny trickle of fat crept out of the corners of his mouth.

"Whoever says A must say B and C," runs an old saying. So with Hans. Almost beside himself with the taste of that first scrap, he heard the tempting voice again. "Come," it seemed to say in rich, fat tones, "enjoy yourself, you poor fellow. You have nothing else in the world except your watery soup and mouldy bread and a back that's beaten black and blue. You never have an hour of pleasure; never a decent satisfying meal. Therefore, take another little piece from me—the place will get smooth and brown again— nobody will notice it."

And Hans, the poor chap, listened and obeyed. You can imagine he did not need much urging. The second piece tasted better than the first, the third still better, the fourth better still, and soon— ("that's all right, the place will get brown quickly")—the entire crust had disappeared. The taste of this rich food affected him like strong wine, lifting him into another world, far away from the kitchen in Seldwyla. Strange visions came to him: He dreamed of all the great feasts in history. He fancied himself at these great banquets, helped to all the rare sweetmeats of the olden world. He was at Alexander's feast, at the great tables of the Roman Emperors, at all the festivals mentioned in the Bible. He imagined he was one of the guests at the famous Marriage at Cana and had just devoured an entire game-pie of stuffed capon, as the chief-cook, splendid in scarlet, helped by fourteen assistant-cooks, placed a whole roast ox in front of him, upright on the table. . . . And he ate this colossal dish down to the very bones! Again, he dreamed that he was one of the seven lean Egyptian oxen in the story of Joseph and, after eating all of the fat of the cattle, he found himself in an enormous wheat-field, which he devoured until nothing was left standing but a few rocks.

During these fantastic visions, Hans had been helping himself to what was in front of him, and, naturally, by this time, there was very little left of the pig. As Hans searched for more, his eyes suddenly caught sight of the one thing that remained, and its appearance made him tremble all over. It was the stiff, little, brown-toasted tail, which stuck out from the bones exactly like a tiny copy of the brown-lacquered cane of his master. As quick as lightning, he was hurled back to his present surroundings. The lovely dreams were scattered. The game-pie, the roast ox, the great wheat-field went the way of soap-bubbles. And all Hans saw before him was the bare skeleton of the young pig, which grinned at him as though to say, "Now, my friend, *you* will have to take my place here on the spit!"

This was too much for unhappy Hans. He believed that the apothecary would do exactly what he threatened. The beating he would get would be terrible enough. But to be put on the spit—! No, that was too much. If he had to die, rather than suffer such torture, he would kill himself! But how? He had no gun, and, as he hated water, he could not drown himself. But poison—ah, that was an idea! Poison was the easiest way—and what could be better than the poisoned fruit! So Hans fetched the three glass jars, made himself comfortable, and stuffed himself with preserved oranges, apples, pears, plums, peaches and pineapples. "Ah, delicious fruit," he sighed, "too bad that you are poisonous," and sank, tired and filled to the brim, in front of the hearth. There he lay, with closed eyes, awaiting death.

Suddenly, he heard the door slam, and there stood—not Death—but his master, who stared at him with open mouth and eyes popping out of his head. The apothecary thought he must be dreaming, as he looked first at what remained of the Sunday dinner and then at Hans, who, instead of being frightened, merely smiled at the furious man. "You won't have to cut my throat," murmured Hans, in a weak voice, "let me alone. I will die soon enough. Let me alone. I have poisoned myself."

"Poisoned yourself?" cried the astonished apothecary. "How? When? With what?"

"With the poisoned fruit, master. I ate all of it. The three jars are empty. Three jars, master."

"You idiot, you rascal, you outrageous villain!" shrieked the apothecary, whose face had gone purple. "That was not poison! I only pasted the labels on so that people would keep their hands off! Those two jars contained my most delicate desserts! I was keeping them for some great occasion! You thief, you scoundrel, you unspeakable robber!"—and blow after blow of the brown-lacquered cane fell on Hans's back, till his whole body shook.

But Hans's back was shaking with laughter not with sobs. This was more than the outraged apothecary could stand. When he saw that the more he whipped the boy, the louder Hans laughed and that, to make matters worse, his precious cane snapped in two, his rage knew no bounds. "Get out of my sight!" he screamed, "get out of my sight you plunderer, and never let me see you again!"

And you can be sure that Hans did not wait for the order to be repeated. By the time the apothecary had calmed himself, Hans, although he was almost too full to move, was halfway to Goldach.

And there, a prosperous dealer in medicines, you can find him to-day. Any time you are passing through the town, you will see his peculiar sign-board. Above a picture of two enormous jars, one on each side of a roasted pig, is this curious inscription: *"At the Sign of The Poisoned Fruit. Everything in Food and Drugs. Cure Guaranteed."*

## RIP VAN WINKLE[1]

### Washington Irving

*This great American story is excellent material for drama. The fact that Rip is a ne'er-do-well should always be more than balanced by his lovable qualities in the playing of the tale.*

Whoever has made a voyage up the Hudson must remember the Catskill Mountains. When the weather is fair and settled, they are clothed in blue and purple, and print their bold outlines on the clear evening sky; but sometimes, when the rest of the landscape is cloudless, they will gather a hood of gray vapors about their summits, which, in the last rays of the setting sun, will glow and light up like a crown of glory.

At the foot of these fairy mountains in a sadly time-worn and weather-beaten house there lived many years since, while the coun-

[1] Adapted.

try was yet a province of Great Britain, a simple, good-natured fellow of the name of Rip Van Winkle.

Rip was a great favorite among all the good wives of the village. The children too, would shout with joy whenever he approached. He assisted at their sports, made their playthings, taught them to fly kites and shoot marbles, and told them long stories of ghosts, witches, and Indians. Yet his own children were as ragged and wild as if they belonged to nobody. The great error in Rip's composition was an insuperable aversion to all kinds of profitable labor. It could not be from the want of assiduity or perseverance; for he would carry a fowling-piece on his shoulder for hours together, trudging through woods and swamps, and up hill and down dale, to shoot a few squirrels or wild pigeons.

He would never refuse to assist a neighbor even in the roughest toil, and was a foremost man at all country frolics for husking Indian corn or building stone fences. The women of the village, too, used to employ him to run their errands, and to do such little odd jobs as their less obliging husbands would not do for them. In a word, Rip was ready to attend to anybody's business but his own; but as to doing family duty, and keeping his farm in order, he found it impossible.

Rip Van Winkle, however, would have whistled life away in perfect contentment; but his wife kept continually dinning in his ears about his idleness, his carelessness, and the ruin he was bringing on his family.

Morning, noon, and night, her tongue was incessantly going, and everything he said or did was sure to produce a torrent of household eloquence. Rip had but one way of replying to all lectures of the kind, and that, by frequent use, had grown into a habit. He shrugged his shoulders, shook his head, cast up his eyes, but said nothing. This, however, always provoked a fresh volley from his wife; so that he was fain to draw off his forces, and take to the outside of the house—the only side which, in truth, belongs to a hen-pecked husband.

Rip's sole domestic adherent was his dog Wolf, who was as much hen-pecked as his master; for Dame Van Winkle regarded them as companions in idleness, and even looked upon Wolf with an evil eye, as the cause of his master's going so often astray.

Times grew worse and worse with Rip Van Winkle as years of matrimony rolled on. A tart temper never mellows with age, and a sharp tongue is the only edged tool that grows keener with constant use. For a long while he used to console himself, when driven from home, by frequenting a kind of perpetual club of the sages, philosophers, and other idle personages of the village, which held its sessions on a bench before a small inn, designated by a rubicund portrait of his Majesty George III. Here they used to sit in the shade of a long, lazy, summer's day, talking listlessly over village gossip, or telling endless sleepy stories about nothing. But it would have been worth any stateman's money to have heard the profound discussions which sometimes took place, when by chance an old newspaper fell into their hands from some passing traveler. How solemnly they would listen to the contents, as drawled out by Derrick Van Bummel, the schoolmaster—a dapper, learned little man, who was not to be daunted by the most gigantic word in the dictionary! And how sagely they would deliberate upon public events some months after they had taken place!

From even this stronghold the unlucky Rip was at length routed by his termagant wife, who would suddenly break in upon the tranquillity of the assemblage, and call the members all to naught; nor was the patriarch of the village, Nicholas Vedder himself, sacred from the daring tongue of this terrible virago, who charged him outright with encouraging her husband in habits of idleness.

Poor Rip was at last reduced almost to despair; and his only alternative, to escape from the labor of the farm and the clamor of his wife, was to take gun in hand and stroll away into the woods. Here he would sometimes seat himself at the foot of a tree, and share the contents of his wallet with Wolf, with whom he sympathized as a fellow-sufferer in persecution. "Poor Wolf," he would say, "thy mistress leads thee a dog's life of it; but never mind, my lad, whilst I live thou shalt never want a friend to stand by thee!" Wolf would wag his tail, look wistfully in his master's face, and, if dogs can feel pity, I verily believe he reciprocated the sentiment with all his heart.

In a long ramble of the kind on a fine autumnal day, Rip had unconsciously scrambled to one of the highest parts of the Catskill Mountains. He was after his favorite sport of squirrel shooting, and the still solitudes had echoed and re-echoed with the reports of his gun. Panting and fatigued, he threw himself, late in the afternoon, on a green knoll, covered with mountain herbage, that crowned the brow of a precipice. For some time Rip lay musing on the scene below him. Evening was gradually advancing; the mountains began to throw their long, blue shadows over the valleys;

he saw that it would be dark long before he could reach the village, and he heaved a heavy sigh when he thought of encountering the terrors of Dame Van Winkle.

As he was about to descend, he heard a voice from a distance, hallooing, "Rip Van Winkle! Rip Van Winkle!" He looked around, but could see nothing but a crow winging its solitary flight across the mountain. He thought his fancy must have deceived him, and turned again to descend, when he heard the same cry ring through the still evening air, "Rip Van Winkle! Rip Van Winkle!" At the same time Wolf bristled up his back, and giving a low growl, skulked to his master's side, looking fearfully down into the glen.

Rip now felt a vague apprehension stealing over him. He looked anxiously in the same direction, and perceived a strange figure slowly toiling up the rocks, and bending under the weight of something he carried on his back. He was surprised to see any human being in this lonely and unfrequented place, but, supposing it to be some one of the neighborhood in need of his assistance, he hastened down to yield it.

On nearer approach he was still more surprised at the singularity of the stranger's appearance. He was a short, square built old fellow, with thick, bushy hair, and a grizzled beard. His dress was of the antique Dutch fashion—a cloth jerkin strapped round the waist, and several pairs of breeches, the outer one of ample volume, decorated with rows of buttons down the sides, and bunches at the knees. He bore on his shoulders a stout keg and made signs for Rip to approach and assist him with the load.

Though rather shy and distrustful of this new acquaintance, Rip complied with his usual alacrity; and, mutually relieving each other, they clambered up a narrow gully, apparently the dry bed of a mountain torrent. As they ascended, Rip every now and then heard long, rolling peals, like distant thunder, that seemed to issue out of a deep ravine between lofty rocks, toward which their rugged path conducted. He paused for an instant but, supposing it to be the muttering of one of those transient thunder-showers which often take place in mountain heights, he proceeded.

Passing through the ravine, they came to a hollow, like a small amphitheater, surrounded by perpendicular precipices. During the whole time, Rip and his companion had labored on in silence; for, there was something strange and incomprehensible about the unknown that inspired awe and checked familiarity.

On entering the amphitheater, new objects of wonder presented themselves. On a level spot in the center was a company of odd-looking personages playing at nine-pins. They were dressed in a quaint, outlandish fashion. Some wore short doublets, others, jerkins, with long knives in their belts; and most of them had enormous breeches, of similar style with that of the guide's. Their visages, too, were peculiar. One had a large head, broad face, and small piggish eyes. The face of another seemed to consist entirely of nose, and was surmounted by a white sugar-loaf hat, set off with a little red cock's tail. They all had beards of various shapes and colors.

There was one who seemed to be the commander. He was a stout old gentleman, with a weather-beaten countenance. He wore a doublet, broad belt, high-crowned hat and feather, red stockings, and high-heeled shoes with roses in them. The whole group reminded Rip of the figures in an old Flemish painting in the parlor of Dominie Van Schaick, the village parson, which had been brought over from Holland at the time of the settlement.

What seemed particularly odd to Rip was, that, though these folks were evidently amusing themselves, yet they maintained the gravest faces, the most mysterious silence, and were, withal, the most melancholy party of pleasure he had ever witnessed. Nothing interrupted the stillness of the scene but the noise of the balls, which, whenever they were rolled, echoed along the mountains like rumbling peals of thunder.

As Rip and his companion approached them, they suddenly desisted from their play, and stared at him with such fixed, statue-like gaze, and such strange, uncouth, lack-luster countenances, that his heart turned within him, and his knees smote together. His companion now emptied the contents of the keg into large flagons, and made signs to him to wait upon the company. He obeyed with fear and trembling. They quaffed the liquor in profound silence, and then returned to their game.

By degrees Rip's awe and apprehension subsided. He even ventured, when no eye was fixed upon him to taste the beverage, which he found had an excellent flavor. One taste provoked another; and at length his senses were overpowered, his eyes swam in his head, his head gradually declined, and he fell into a deep sleep.

On waking, he found himself on the green knoll whence he had first seen the old man of the glen. He rubbed his eyes. It was a bright, sunny morning. The birds were hopping and twittering among the bushes; and the eagle was wheeling aloft, and breasting the pure mountain breeze. "Surely," thought Rip, "I have not slept here all night."

He looked round for his gun, but in place of the clean, well-oiled fowling-piece, he found an old firelock lying by him, the barrel incrusted with rust, the lock falling off, and the stock worm-eaten. He now suspected that the grave roisterers of the mountain had robbed him of his gun. Wolf, too, had disappeared; but he might have strayed away after a squirrel or partridge. He whistled after him, and shouted his name, but all in vain; the echoes repeated his whistle and shout, but no dog was to be seen.

As he rose to walk, he found himself stiff in the joints, and wanting in his usual activity. "These mountain beds do not agree with me," thought Rip; "and if this frolic should lay me up with a fit of the rheumatism, I shall have a blessed time with Dame Van Winkle."

By this time the morning was passed away, and Rip felt famished for want of his breakfast. He grieved to give up his dog and gun, he dreaded to meet his wife; but it would not do to starve among the mountains. He shook his head, shouldered the rusty firelock, and, with a heart full of trouble and anxiety, turned his steps homeward.

As he approached the village, he met a number of people, but none whom he knew; which somewhat surprised him, for he had thought himself acquainted with every one in the country round. Their dress, too, was of a different fashion from that to which he was accustomed. They all stared at him with equal marks of surprise, and, whenever they cast their eyes upon him, invariably stroked their chins. The constant recurrence of this gesture induced Rip involuntarily to do the same, when, to his astonishment, he found his beard had grown a foot long.

He had now entered the skirts of the village. A troop of strange children ran at his heels, hooting after him and pointing at his gray beard. The dogs, too, not one of which he recognized for an old acquaintance, barked at him as he passed. The very village was altered; it was larger and more populous. There were rows of houses which he had never seen before, and those which had been his familiar haunts had disappeared. Strange names were over the doors, strange faces at the windows—everything was strange.

His mind now misgave him. He began to doubt whether both he and the world around him were not bewitched. Surely this was his native village, which he had left but the day before. There stood the Catskill Mountains; there ran the silver Hudson at a distance; there was every hill and dale precisely as it had always been. Rip was sorely perplexed. "That flagon last night," thought he, "has addled my poor head sadly."

It was with some difficulty that he found the way to his own house, which he approached with silent awe, expecting every moment to hear the shrill voice of Dame Van Winkle. He found the house gone to decay—the roof fallen in, the windows shattered, and the doors off the hinges. A half-starved dog that looked like Wolf was skulking about it. Rip called him by name; but the cur snarled, showed his teeth, and passed on. This was an unkind cut, indeed. "My very dog," sighed poor Rip, "has forgotten me!"

He entered the house, which, to tell the truth, Dame Van Winkle had always kept in neat order. It was empty, forlorn, and apparently abandoned. This desolateness overcame all his connubial fears. He called loudly for his wife and children; the lonely chambers rang for a moment with his voice, and then all again was silence.

He now hurried forth, and hastened to his old resort, the village inn; but it, too, was gone. A large rickety, wooden building stood in its place, with great, gaping windows, some of them broken and mended with old hats, and petticoats; and over the door was painted, "The Union Hotel, by Jonathan Doolittle." Instead of the great tree that used to shelter the quiet little Dutch inn of yore, there now was reared a tall, naked pole, with something on the top that looked like a flag, on which was a singular assemblage of stars and stripes.

All this was strange and incomprehensible. He recognized on the sign, however, the ruby face of King George, under which he had smoked so many a peaceful pipe; but even this was singularly metamorphosed. The red coat was changed for one of blue and buff, a sword was held in the hand instead of a scepter, the head was decorated with a cocked hat, and underneath was painted in large characters, "General Washington."

There was, as usual, a crowd of folk about the door, but none that Rip recollected. The very character of the people seemed changed. There was a busy, bustling, disputatious tone about it, instead of the accustomed phlegm and drowsy tranquillity. He looked in vain for the sage Nicholas Vedder, with his broad face, double chin, and fair long pipe, uttering clouds of tobacco smoke instead of idle speeches; or Van Bummel, the schoolmaster, doling forth the contents of an ancient newspaper. In place of these, a lean, bilious-looking fellow, with his pockets full of handbills, was haranguing vehemently about the rights of citizens, election, members of Congress, liberty, Bunker's Hill, heroes of seventy-six, and other words, that were a perfect Babylonish jargon to the bewildered Van Winkle. The appearance of Rip, with his long, grizzled beard, his rusty fowling-piece, his uncouth dress, and the army of women and children that had gathered at his heels, soon attracted the attention of the tavern politicians. They crowded round him, eyeing him from head to foot with great curiosity. The orator bustled up to him, and, drawing him partly aside, inquired whether he was a Federal or a Democrat. Rip stared in vacant stupidity.

When a knowing, self-important old gentleman in a sharp cocked hat made his way through the crowd, and, planting himself before Van Winkle, with one arm akimbo, the other resting on his cane, demanded in an austere tone what brought him to the election with a gun on his shoulder and a mob at his heels, and whether he meant to breed a riot in the village, Rip cried out, "Alas! gentlemen, I am a poor, quiet man, a native of the place, and a loyal subject to the King, God bless him!"

Here a general shout burst from the bystanders: "A Tory, a Tory! A spy! A refugee! Hustle him! Away with him!" It was with great difficulty that the self-important man in the cocked hat restored order, and, having assumed a tenfold austerity of brow, demanded again of the unknown culprit what he came there for, and whom he was seeking. The poor man humbly assured him that he meant no harm, but merely came there in search of some of his neighbors, who used to keep about the tavern.

"Well, who are they? Name them."

Rip bethought himself a moment, and inquired, "Where's Nicholas Vedder?"

There was a silence for a little while, when an old man replied in a thin, piping voice, "Nicholas Vedder! Why, he is dead and gone these eighteen years! There was a wooden tombstone in the churchyard that used to tell all about him, but that's rotten and gone, too."

"Where's Brom Dutcher?"

"Oh, he went off with the army in the beginning of the war. Some say he was killed at the storming of Stony Point; others say he was drowned in the squall at the foot of Anthony's Nose. I don't know, he never came back again."

"Where's Van Bummel, the schoolmaster?"

"He went off to the wars, too, was a great militia general, and is now in Congress."

Rip's heart died away at hearing of these sad changes in his home and friends, and finding himself thus alone in the world. Every answer puzzled him, too, by treating of such enormous lapses of time, and of matters which he could not understand—war, Congress, Stony Point. He had no courage to ask after any more friends, but cried out in despair, "Does nobody here know Rip Van Winkle?"

"Oh, Rip Van Winkle!" exclaimed two or three. "Oh, to be sure! that's Rip Van Winkle yonder, leaning against the tree."

Rip looked, and beheld a precise counterpart of himself, as he went up the mountain, apparently as lazy, and certainly as ragged. The poor fellow was now completely confounded. He doubted his own identity, and whether he was himself or another man. In the midst of his bewilderment, the man in the cocked hat demanded who he was, and what was his name.

"God knows!" exclaimed he, at his wits' end. "I'm not myself; I'm somebody else. That's me yonder. No, that's somebody else got into my shoes. I was myself last night, but I fell asleep on the mountain, and they've changed my gun; and everything's changed; and I'm changed; and I can't tell what's my name, or who I am!"

The bystanders began now to look at each other, nod, wink significantly, and tap their fingers against their foreheads. There was a whisper, also, about securing the gun, and keeping the old fellow from doing mischief. At this critical moment a fresh, comely woman pressed through the throng to get a peep at the gray-bearded man. She had a chubby child in her arms, which, frightened at his looks, began to cry.

"Hush, Rip!" cried she. "Hush, you little fool! The old man won't hurt you."

The name of the child, the air of the mother, the tone of her voice, all awakened a train of recollections in his mind. "What is your name, my good woman?" asked he.

"Judith Gardenier "

"And your father's name?"

"Ah, poor man, his name was Rip Van Winkle. It's twenty years since he went away from home with his gun, and never has been heard of since. His dog came home without him; but whether he shot himself, or was carried away by the Indians, nobody can tell. I was then but a little girl."

257

Rip had but one question more to ask, but he put it with a faltering voice:

"Where's your mother?"

"Oh, she too died but a short time since. She broke a blood-vessel in a fit of passion at a New England peddler."

There was a drop of comfort, at least, in this intelligence. The honest man could contain himself no longer. He caught his daughter and her child in his arms. "I am your father!" cried he. "Young Rip Van Winkle once, old Rip Van Winkle now! Does nobody know poor Rip Van Winkle?"

All stood amazed, until an old woman, tottering out from among the crowd, put her hand to her brow, and, peering under it in his face for a moment, exclaimed, "Sure enough! It is Rip Van Winkle! It is himself! Welcome home again, old neighbor! Why, where have you been these twenty long years?"

Rip's story was soon told, for the whole twenty years had been to him but as one night. The neighbors stared when they heard it. It was determined, however, to take the opinion of old Peter Vanderdonk, who was seen slowly advancing up the road. He was a descendant of the historian of that name, who wrote one of the earliest accounts of the province. Peter was the most ancient inhabitant of the village, and well versed in all the wonderful events and traditions of the neighborhood. He recollected Rip at once, and corroborated his story in the most satisfactory manner. He assured the company that it was a fact, handed down from his ancestor the historian, that the Catskill Mountains had always been haunted by strange beings; that it was affirmed that the great Hendrick Hudson, the first discoverer of the river and country, kept a kind of vigil there every twenty years, with his crew of the *Half Moon*, being permitted in this way to revisit the scenes of his enterprise, and keep a guardian eye upon the river, and the great city called by his name; that his father had once seen them in their old Dutch dress, playing at ninepins in the hollow of the mountain; and that he himself had heard, one summer afternoon, the sound of their balls, like distant peals of thunder.

To make a long story short, the company broke up, and returned to the more important concerns of the election. Rip's daughter took him home to live with her. She had a snug, well-furnished house, and a stout, cheery farmer for a husband, whom Rip recollected for one of the urchins that used to climb upon his back. As to Rip's son and heir, who was the ditto of himself, seen leaning against the tree, he was employed to work on the farm, but evinced an hereditary disposition to attend to anything else but his business.

Rip now resumed his old walks and habits. He took his place once more on the bench at the inn door, and was reverenced as one of the patriarchs of the village, and a chronicle of the old times "before the war." It was some time before he could be made to comprehend the strange events that had taken place during his torpor—how that there had been a revolutionary war, that the country had thrown off the yoke of old England, and that, instead of being a subject of His Majesty George III, he was now a free citizen of the United States.

Some always pretended to doubt the reality of Rip's story, and insisted that he had been out of his head, and that this was one point on which he always remained flighty. The old Dutch inhabitants, however, almost universally gave it full credit. Even to this day they never hear a thunderstorm of a summer afternoon about the Catskills, but they say Hendrick Hudson and his crew are at their game of ninepins; and it is a common wish of all hen-pecked husbands in the neighborhood, when life hangs heavy on their hands, that they might have a quieting draught out of Rip Van Winkle's flagon.

## TREE OF FREEDOM[1]

### Rebecca Caudill

*An exciting story of pioneers in Kentucky during the French and Indian War. This is one chapter of a well-written book which might be the center of a correlated project.*

*Jonathan and Bertha Venable have brought their children from North Carolina to take up a claim of four hundred acres. Jonathan and the oldest son, Noel, have built a log house and planted a field of corn in the good black earth. They have no neighbors except a strange creature called Lonesome Tilly. Stephanie, thirteen-year-old daughter, from whose point of view the story is written, had brought with her a single apple seed which she planted with the hope that it would grow into a Tree of Freedom. She and her little brother Willie have just replanted it after one of the hens has scratched it up.*

[1] By permission of The Viking Press, Inc., Publishers, from whom authorization must be obtained for any use other than informal, improvised dramatization.

Hardly had they covered the seed with leaf mold once more when out of the woods from the direction of Harrod's Ford came walking a stranger. He was not a buck-skin, she noticed, such as a body might expect to meet up with in the wilderness, if he met anybody at all, nor a redskin, nor queer-looking like Tilly Balance. Nor did he look like a high-born Tidewater gentleman, though he wore the clothes of a gentleman—breeches buckled at the knees, low buckled shoes, long stockings, a long bright blue broadcloth shad-bellied coat, a satin waistcoat, a flowing cravat, and a low-crowned, broad-brimmed hat.

"Howdy!" said the stranger, as he came across the clearing. His voice was raspy, like the sound of a rat-tail file on metal. His dark face was deeply pock-marked, and his small, hard eyes bored straight ahead of him like gimlets.

"Howdy," muttered Stephanie.

"Run and fetch your pappy," ordered the man, jerking his head in the direction of the chopping. "I have business with him."

Stephanie hurried into the woods, Willie at her heels. At her summons, the Venables came traipsing into the clearing, Stephanie crowding close behind her pappy, Rob and Noel following with hatchet and frow, Cassie clinging to her mammy's hand, and Willie hanging on to her skirt.

"You Jonathan Venable?" rasped the stranger, eyeing Jonathan. "My name's Frohawk. Adam Frohawk."

"Howdy," said Jonathan, cold as an icicle. The other Venables strung out in a line beside Jonathan and stared at the outlandish stranger.

"I've got news for you, Venable," said Frohawk. As he spoke, he stuck his thumbs in his satin waistcoat pockets in such a way that a pearl-handled pistol came to light. "News you'll do mighty well to hear without stirring up any more trouble for yourself than you're already in."

"Spit hit out quick then," ordered Jonathan. Then he added, "This is the first time I knowed I was in any trouble."

"I'd say you're in plenty of trouble, noting all these improvements you're making about here, Venable," Frohawk said. "Happens that this land doesn't belong to you. Happens that this land belongs to a certain gentleman in the West Indies. Name of Garret Bedinger. Ever hear of him?"

"No more'n I ever heard of you," spat out Jonathan.

Noel shifted his weight from one foot to the other, and swallowed hard.

"Tell him to let you see his deed, Pappy," he said.

"Yeah, whar's your deed?" asked Jonathan. "Whar's your proof that anybody by the name of Bedinger 'way off at the end of nowhar has got any proper claim to this land? Let's see your proof."

Casually, Frohawk reached inside his big waistcoat pocket and took from it a silk wallet embroidered with threads of gold and silver. Out of the wallet he took a tattered piece of parchment, yellowed with age and much traveling about, and opened it up.

"Don't reckon anybody here can read," he said, "so I'll read it for you."

"By the King's Most Excellent Majesty and the Right Honorable the Lords of his Majesty's Privy Council:

"*Whereas,* Garret Bedinger, agent for his Majesty's Colony of Virginia, does, by his petition this day read at the Board, humbly represent, that he being employed and instructed by the Government of the Country, petitions His Majesty for a confirmation of his privileges and properties under the great Seal of England; now,

"*Therefore,* upon full debate of the whole matter, it is ordered by His Majesty in Council, believing it to be for His Majesty's service that His loyal subjects should be settled on the aforementioned properties as speedily as may be, and anxious to repay such subjects generously for favors received, that the Right Honorable the Lord Chancellor do cause the said grant of 50,000 acres of transmontane lands lying in the neighborhood south of the Falls of the River Ohio, and westwardly to the Salt River, forthwith to pass under the great Seal of England accordingly.

"Signed, Philip Loyd."

"Fifty thousand acres," said Frohawk, hardly catching his breath after reading the parchment, "lying immediately south of the Falls, takes in this here little neckerchief claim of yours, Venable."

Stephanie glanced anxiously at her pappy. It didn't seem any more likely that he would have anything to say to these words inked in fine handwriting ȯn a piece of parchment than he would have to say to the voice of God if it should speak to him out of thunder, or an earthquake, or a brightly burning bush.

Again Noel shifted his weight, and swallowed.

"Ask him, Pappy, has that paper got a date on it," he said.

"Yeah," echoed Jonathan, finding his tongue. "Has that paper got a date on hit?"

261

Adam Frohawk glanced at the parchment. " 'April 19, 1762. At a Court at Whitehall,' " he read.

"For once in my life I'd give my right hand, I reckon, if I could read writin'," sputtered Jonathan. "Then I'd know how much you're lyin'. Here," he added, suddenly pushing Noel forward, though it was as plain as day he grudged doing it, "let this young un see that paper."

"Certainly," agreed Frohawk. He smoothed out the parchment and held it close enough for Noel to read, but he was mighty particular to hold it out of his reach.

" 'By the King's Most Excellent Majesty, and the Right Honorable the Lords of His Majesty's Privy Council'," read Noel.

Noel's voice in the stillness of the clearing was toned like a bell, and every word he read seemed to Stephanie to toll a death, as Bertha said the church bells of Charleston tolled when a body died. In this case, it was the death of this pleasant place overlooking a river where a cabin with a fine puncheon floor and a chimney of river rock was about to be raised, where a Tree of Freedom had been planted, and corn would soon be rustling in the hot summer winds. It was a tolling bell calling them to pack up their pots and pans, their flax hackles and Betty lamps, to load their creels on Job's back, to round up the cow, the sheep, and the pigs, and be on their way again.

"I only wanted to save you trouble, Venable," said Frohawk, as he folded the parchment when Noel finished reading.

"Whar's your pre-emption papers from the Land Commissioners?" asked Jonathan. "Whar's your surveyor's warrant?"

"Bedinger had the land surveyed years ago," Frohawk told him. "And pre-emption papers aren't necessary. Can't His Majesty grant such lands as he wishes to such subjects as he chooses?"

"Not this land," Noel shot at him. "Virginny does the grantin' in these parts now."

"All right. So Virginia does the granting in these parts," said Frohawk. "This deed's dated prior to October 26, 1763, and according to her own law, Virginia's bound to honor it. The Virginia Land Law says so expressly. It says that any person who has paid money into the public treasury under the regal government is entitled to receive vacant land. This upstart Virginia legislature took pains for good reasons to safeguard holders of old treasury rights. Too many Virginia bigwigs claiming Kentucky lands under such rights granted prior to October, 1763, to ignore that little matter."

262

"Whar's your proof this here Bedinger paid any money into the public treasury?" asked Jonathan, ignoring Frohawk's slurs. "Whar's your receipt showin' that?"

Frohawk opened up the parchment again, and read like a slow rain that sinks into the ground as it falls, . . . "and anxious to repay such subjects generously for favors received."

"Favors mought be money paid into the treasury, same as us honest, hard workin' folks pay," said Jonathan, "an' again, they moughtn't. They mought be spyin', or squeezin' taxes out of farmers, or stirrin' up the red men against us settlers. Any one of 'em, I calculate, 'd be a favor to His Majesty right now."

"That's quibbling, Venable," barked Frohawk, flatly.

Stephanie noticed Noel clenching his fists.

"You wait till Virginny gets her throat out of the stranglehold of His Majesty!" he blurted out, his gray eyes burning in his slim face. "Then let this Bedinger try to claim land he's done favors for! That's what Virginny's fightin' this war for now."

"Well! Well!" scoffed Frohawk. "One of the liberty boys!"

He turned back to Jonathan.

"You can move off now, Venable," he said, "and spend your energy on some other clearing you can hold on to, or you can go ahead here and lose everything you put into this patch of land. I take it you know the Land Law entirely. It provides, you know, that a court be held in December of this year when all contesting claims may be heard. Stay here, if you like, till then. Make as many improvements as you can. The more you make, the better it will be for Bedinger. But, if I were you, Venable, I wouldn't try to buck the law. It doesn't pay. Or," he added, looking straight at Noel, as he put the parchment back into his wallet, "His Majesty the King. Good morning, gentlemen. I'll see you again."

He turned on his polished heel and, like a raucous-voiced bird in fine sweeping plumage, he strutted across the clearing and disappeared into the woods in the direction of Harrod's Fort.

The Venables stared, first after Frohawk then solemnly at one another. Jonathan slumped down on a stump and looked listlessly ahead of him, his shoulders wilting like an empty meal sack when folks are facing starvation.

Suddenly, however, he sat bolt upright, his eyes on the woods in the direction of the spring.

Quickly the other Venables turned about to follow his gaze, and stared awestruck as up the hill came Lonesome Tilly. A few steps he padded at a time, his scraggly white hair covering his stooped shoulders, his heifer-like eyes brimming with shy trust as he studied the curious faces before him. In his cupped hands he held a crude basket made of popple leaves pinned together with thorns.

Bertha Venable, after the first shock of seeing such a critter, took a step forward to meet him.

"You're Tilly Balance, ain't you, comin' to see folks?" she said.

It was a caution, thought Stephanie, how her mammy could smooth out a path for a stumbling body.

Shyly, Lonesome Tilly padded up to Bertha and held out to her the basket in which lay, heaped up and spilling over, sweet, red, wild strawberries.

" 'Pon my word!" said Bertha, taking the basket from his outstretched hands. "And just when a body's starvin' for berries and such like! Here, Tilly," she motioned to a stump, "you sit right down here till we get dinner ready. It's 'way past dinner time, I reckon," she said, looking up at the sun which was already past the zenith, "but we got busy doin' other things."

Lonesome Tilly made no move to sit on the stump and wait for his dinner, however. He made no sign that he had understood a word Bertha had said to him. Instead, with a single grateful flash of his eyes toward Bertha, a look of recollection toward Stephanie, and a yearning in his face as he gazed a second at Willie, he slipped away among the trees as slick as a lizard.

"Well, consarn!" muttered Jonathan, ogling the spot where the old man had been standing so short a minute before. "If that don't beat the Tories! 'Quare old buzzard' is right!"

Bertha busied herself passing the basket of berries round for all to help themselves, and bit into the richly red, sweet-smelling meat of one herself.

"Quare or not, a good neighbor, I'd say," she pronounced. "A mighty good neighbor. I've known lots worse."

"Did he put a hex on these berries, Mammy?" whimpered Willie, his mouth watering for a taste of them while fear kept him from reaching for one.

"Put a hex on 'em?" said Bertha. "Whatever put a notion like that in your head, child? Nobody can hex berries, honey."

She stood looking down tenderly at Willie, sensing he was not fully satisfied. "And can't anybody hex you but yourself," she said.

"Why don't he talk?" asked Willie.

"Maybe he was born that way," explained Bertha. "Or maybe
264

it's a sickness come over him out here in the wilderness by his lonesome with nobody to brew herbs for him, and gather slippery elm bark and lin bark and snake root to make him tea. It could have been a sickness that went to his head. Chances are, we'll never know. And I reckon we don't need to ask. We'll just take Lonesome Tilly as he comes."

"Will he come back?" asked Willie fearfully.

"I shouldn't be a bit surprised," said Bertha. "Now, stop frettin', and eat some berries."

She turned to Stephanie. "Whatever could you have been doin', Steffy, all the time I thought you were startin' dinner?" she scolded.

"I—I got busy, too, doin' other things," Stephanie explained. "But I'll have the pigeons broilin' before you can say 'Wire brier,' Mammy. See if I don't. Here, Willie!" she called. "Where are the chips I told you to gather?"


## ABE LINCOLN'S OTHER MOTHER[1]

### Bernadine Bailey

*This book, which is fiction founded on fact, offers much good material for a creative play based on the life of Abraham Lincoln. It should, of course, be supplemented by biographies of Lincoln if a complete play is attempted. But there is a warmth and a reality about this story told from the viewpoint of Sarah Bush Lincoln, Tom Lincoln's second wife, which makes it good for dramatic use even though, like most biographies, one must be satisfied with a series of incidents rather than the sustained dramatic situations which are needed for really effective plays.*

*At the time (1819) that this book begins, Nancy Hanks Lincoln has been dead for about a year. It is a pathetic little household that tries to get along in this Indiana country without a mother: the father, Tom Lincoln, with Abe, his twelve-year-old sister Sally, and their cousin Dennis Hanks.*

*And now Abe's father has been away for two weeks and they have been lonelier than ever, knowing only that he has gone to Kentucky, and having no idea that he is bringing the sweetheart of his youth to be a mother to them.*

[1] From *Abe Lincoln's Other Mother*, by Bernadine Bailey, by permission of the publisher, Julian Messner, Inc. Copyright Dec. 16, 1941, by Bernadine Bailey.

As the boy left the woods and started across the clearing toward the cabin, he was startled by the sudden squeak of a wagon wheel. Expectantly he looked down the deeply rutted road, overlaid here and there with faint patches of frost, but the only sign of life was a rabbit. With eager steps the boy hurried toward the one-room cabin, his arms filled with small birch logs. It was the middle of December, and the nights were growing cold. He must not let the fire go out again. He knew that his sister had lain awake, shivering, for many hours during the night, although she had not complained.

The sound of the squeaking wagon wheels came nearer and nearer. Before the boy reached the cabin, the wagon came into view. It was a large wagon, much larger than any he had seen before, and it was fairly overflowing with furniture: beds and chests and chairs and tables. The four horses toiled painfully, making slow progress in the rutted road.

The boy dropped his load of wood beside the cabin and watched, fascinated, as the wagon slowly came nearer. Without a word his twelve-year-old sister joined him, and the two children stood there, silent and slender as young saplings.

Now they could see that the wagon overflowed with people as well as furniture. It was good to see their father again, after the two weeks of loneliness without him. But who were these other people? Who was this strange woman beside him and who were the three children? He had not told them, when he left for Kentucky, that he would bring anyone back with him. Perhaps these were cousins from Kentucky who had come to make their home in Indiana.

At last the wagon reached the cabin and stopped. The boy's father jumped down nimbly. Carefully he lifted the three children to the ground and then helped the strange woman climb down from her high seat. The boy noticed that her thick blonde curls were neatly held in place by a close-fitting bonnet. Tall and strong she was, with a pink-cheeked kindly face and gray-blue eyes that had a look of steadiness about them.

Who were these children who stood beside the wagon, with their well-made shoes and their clothing that had no patches or torn places? As if to hide his raggedness from them, the boy drew back a step. Wonder filled his mind as he watched the little group.

At last the boy's father spoke. "Here's your new ma, Abe."

His new ma! A sudden mist blurred the boy's eyes as he thought of the mother whom he had lost a little more than a year ago. There

266

had been a strange sort of emptiness in his life since then, an emptiness that neither father nor sister had been able to fill. And now a stranger had come to take that mother's place.

Her first quick glance had shown Sarah Bush Lincoln the poverty, the wretchedness, the loneliness, of her new home. The rough logs of the cabin had been hastily put in place, with no plaster to hold them firm and to keep out the sharp winter wind. Crude, gaping holes took the place of a door and a window. Tom had told her but little about his home in Indiana, and Sarah had pictured a neat, cozy cabin like her own. There was not even a floor in this bleak hovel, and the footprints of the barefoot boy and girl were plain in the soft, moist earth.

With a mother's instinctive concern for her brood, Sarah Lincoln turned to look at her own well-fed, warmly clothed children. They stood in a silent group, eyeing their new home in childish amazement and awkwardly hesitant about greeting the boy and girl who stood in front of the little cabin. As Sarah Lincoln looked at her son and two daughters, whose childish helplessness was even more startling against the desolation of this scene, for a moment she almost gave way to a feeling of utter despair.

Then her eyes were drawn to Thomas Lincoln's son. Unsmiling, and yet not wholly sad, his face expressed a wordless pleading as his deep-set gray eyes sought hers. Sarah Lincoln saw in them his hunger for mother love, and tears filled her eyes. She held out her arms to him, and the boy went to her.

When Sarah Bush Lincoln took this ten-year-old lad in her arms and held him close, she knew that she had made no mistake in leaving her native Kentucky and coming to this home in the wilderness. Her decision had been the right one. She had no regrets. As she felt the boy's arms tighten around her, she sent up a silent prayer to God. "May I be a real mother to this boy," she prayed, closing her eyes for a moment and then kissing the boy on the forehead. Deep in her heart she knew that she had sealed a bond between herself and this boy who needed her.

"Abe, come meet your new sisters and brother," called the boy's father.

With a new, happy look on his face, the boy stepped forward. The emptiness in his heart was beginning to fill with tenderness. The ache was less than it had been before. The magic of mother love had come once more into his life.

Brushing aside the emotion that had clouded her eyes and yet made her heart sing with joy, Sarah Lincoln turned her mind to more practical matters. The furniture must be unloaded and placed in the cabin at once. Already the sun had disappeared behind the woods, and the winter night would soon be close around them. The children were standing beside the wagon, shivering in the chill December air and shyly regarding their new surroundings.

"Tilda, take John inside the cabin and rub his hands. They're blue with cold. Betsy, you can help carry in the bedding." While she was speaking, Sarah Lincoln noticed almost with horror, that the cabin had no door. Nor was there any glass in the window; it was merely a square hole cut through the logs. Surely, though, there would be a warm fire. But no, not even the tiniest wisp of smoke curled up from the chimney of thick logs. How could children possibly be comfortable in a home like this?

The boy Abe had seen her look of dismay, and his mind seemed to follow hers. "I'll fix a fire right away," he offered. With these, his first words to his new mother, Abe Lincoln set the pattern of understanding and devotion that he was to follow the rest of his life. The new mother was quick to notice the boy's response to her unspoken need. It sent through her body a deeper warmth than any fire could ever give. It gave her the feeling that she had really come *home*.

As Tom Lincoln carried the fine walnut bureau into the cabin, Sarah Lincoln noticed, with fresh significance, that the cabin had no floor. How did it happen that Tom, himself a carpenter, was content to live in such a place as this? Her nice furniture would soon be ruined if left on the damp earth. But this could easily be remedied. Tom could build a floor for their home. Sarah Lincoln resolved that she would see to it the next day.

"Where shall I put these pillows and blankets?" asked Betsy, standing in the cabin doorway, her arms full of bedding. Used to a comfortable, well-arranged home, the child was bewildered by the bareness of this crude cabin.

Sarah Lincoln stepped inside. The dirt and disorder she ignored. These were the natural result of a home that had been without a woman's guiding hand for more than a year. The lack of any sort of comfort was quite a different thing. Vague reports of Tom Lincoln's shiftlessness rushed into her mind with startling force. There would be no use in upbraiding him for having misrepresented his home to her. Actually, now that she searched her memory, she realized that he had said but little about his home. It was she who had built up a picture of coziness and comfort, a picture based upon the kind of home she had always known. Even in the wilderness a home could be clean and comfortable—that she knew.

Abe was kneeling in front of the fireplace, blowing on the birch logs and coaxing them to their brightest blaze. As she watched the kneeling boy, a look of determination came into Sarah Lincoln's face. All would yet be well. Pride came to her aid, and she resolved that Tom Lincoln should never know of her first disappointment in this new home. In a short time she would change all the things that were upsetting to her now. She was needed here. That was enough.

"You can put the coverlets and pillows on the bed in the corner, Betsy," Sarah Lincoln finally answered. As the girl dutifully piled the things on the crude bed with its home-made hickory frame, Sarah Lincoln looked at the other furnishings of the home. Why, there was nothing here but a few three-legged stools and a broad slab, held up by four rough legs, that served as a table. The bed itself was no more than a few boards laid on sticks fastened into two sides of the cabin, with upright pieces of wood to support it on the other two sides.

The fire was now roaring away, and little John held out his cold hands to the welcome blaze. Tilda, too, was warming her fingers before the fire. Gradually the cabin lost some of its chill, save when an occasional gust of winter wind blew through the doorway or window.

Tom Lincoln, now with Abe's help, unloaded the rest of the furniture and brought it inside the cabin. The place was already taking on an air of hominess, merely with the addition of Sarah Lincoln's comfortable furniture. Everything was finally unloaded and put in place, at least for the moment. Tomorrow would be soon enough to make changes, the clear-sighted Sarah decided.

By the time the new Mrs. Lincoln had prepared supper, the children of both families had gotten over some of their shyness.

"Where's Dennis?" asked Tom Lincoln after they were all seated at the narrow board table and grace had been said. Up until that moment he had not thought to ask about the young man, his first wife's cousin, who had lived with them for more than a year.

"He's gone on a huntin' trip," explained Abe. "Most likely he's stayin' all night somewhere."

Tom Lincoln did not worry. Dennis Hanks was twenty-one years old and well able to take care of himself wherever he might be.

The first meal seemed to draw the children of the two families together. Maybe it was the wind blowing outside, or the occasional howl of a wolf in the near-by woods, or perhaps it was just that instinctive drawing together for protection that marked the pioneer life in the wilderness. More likely, though, it was the all-encircling love of a mother. Unconsciously they felt themselves to be part of one family, a complete family now, for they had both a father and a mother.

The children ate their corn pone and bacon with enjoyment, for the all-day ride had made them hungry. Little John fell asleep, with his head on the table, before the rest had finished supper. His mother picked him up and tucked him into the large bed in the corner and wrapped her own coverlet warmly around him. Soon Betsy and Tilda were sound asleep beside him. In a little while, Abe and his sister climbed to their beds of straw up in the loft.

For a long time Sarah and Tom Lincoln sat before the fire, which still burned steadily though without the first bright rush of flames.

"It's not much of a home, Sarah," began Tom, half apologetically.

Sarah was silent, her eyes on the fire. Now and then the wind blew in the open doorway and sent the flames upward in swirls of sparks. Sarah shivered and drew her shawl more closely around her shoulders.

At last she spoke. "Your children need a mother, Tom. I'm glad I came. You and I can make a home for them."

Tom looked at his wife. He was not given to the showing of deep emotion. "You will make a good mother, Sarah."

In mutual trust and affection, the foundations of this new home were laid.

## THE OLD WOMAN AND THE TRAMP[1]

### A Swedish Folk Tale

*This old Swedish tale has been used as the basis of a play called "A Pot of Broth" by W. B. Yeats, and, recently as a story, "Stone Soup," by Marcia Brown.*

*It is simple, full of fun, and very usable for a play. But there are only two characters. How can many more people be introduced? Children will have plenty of ideas.*

[1] Reprinted by permission of the publishers, J. B. Lippincott Co. from *Swedish Fairy Tales* trans. by Frederick Marteno. Copyright 1920 by J. B. Lippincott Co.

*Whatever the number of characters, it is most important to keep the dramatization all good-natured fun. The woman is stingy—and simple. Everybody enjoys seeing a joke played on her!*

There was once a tramp who went plodding his way through a forest. The distance between the houses was so great that he had little hope of finding a shelter before the night set in. But all of a sudden he saw some lights between the trees. He then discovered a cottage, where there was a fire burning on the hearth. How nice it would be to roast one's self before that fire, and to get a bite of something, he thought; and so he dragged himself toward the cottage.

Just then an old woman came toward him.

"Good evening, and well met!" said the tramp.

"Good evening," said the woman. "Where do you come from?"

"South of the sun, and east of the moon," said the tramp; "and now I am on the way home again, for I have been all over the world with the exception of this parish," he said.

"You must be a great traveler, then," said the woman. "What may be your business here?"

"Oh, I want a shelter for the night," he said.

"I thought as much," said the woman; "but you may as well get away from here at once, for my husband is not at home, and my place is not an inn," she said.

"My good woman," said the tramp, "you must not be so cross and hard-hearted, for we are both human beings, and should help one another, as it is written."

"Help one another?" said the woman, "help? Did you ever hear such a thing? Who'll help me, do you think? I haven't got a morsel in the house! No, you'll have to look for quarters elsewhere," she said.

But the tramp was like the rest of his kind; he did not consider himself beaten at the first rebuff. Although the old woman grumbled and complained as much as she could, he was just as persistent as ever, and went on begging and praying like a starved dog, until at last she gave in, and he got permission to lie on the floor for the night.

That was very kind, he thought, and thanked her for it.

"Better on the floor without sleep, than suffer cold in the forest deep," he said; for he was a merry fellow, this tramp, and was always ready with a rhyme.

When he came into the room he could see that the woman was not so badly off as she had pretended; but she was a greedy and stingy woman of the worst sort, and was always complaining and grumbling.

He now made himself very agreeable, of course, and asked her in his most insinuating manner for something to eat.

"Where am I to get it from?" said the woman. "I haven't tasted a morsel myself the whole day."

But the tramp was a cunning fellow, he was.

"Poor old granny, you must be starving," he said. "Well, well, I suppose I shall have to ask you to have something with me, then?"

"Have something with you!" said the woman. "You don't look as if you could ask any one to have anything! What have you got to offer one, I should like to know?"

"He who far and wide does roam sees many things not known at home; and he who many things has seen has wits about him and senses keen," said the tramp. "Better dead than lose one's head! Lend me a pot, granny!"

The old woman now became very inquisitive, as you may guess, and so she let him have a pot.

He filled it with water and put it on the fire, and then he blew with all his might till the fire was burning fiercely all around it. Then he took a four-inch nail from his pocket, turned it three times in his hand, and put it into the pot.

The woman stared with all her might.

"What's this going to be?" she asked.

"Nail broth," said the tramp, and began to stir the water with the porridge-stick.

"Nail broth?" asked the woman.

"Yes, nail broth," said the tramp.

The old woman had seen and heard a good deal in her time but that anybody could have made broth with a nail, well, she had never heard the like before.

"That's something for poor people to know," she said, "and I should like to learn how to make it."

"That which is not worth having will always go a-begging," said the tramp, but if she wanted to learn how to make it she had only to watch him, he said, and went on stirring the broth.

The old woman squatted on the ground, her hands clasping her knees, and her eyes following his hand as he stirred the broth.

"This generally makes good broth," he said; "but this time it will very likely be rather thin, for I have been making broth the whole week with the same nail. If one only had a handful of sifted oatmeal to put in, that would make it all right," he said. "But what one has to go without, it's no use thinking more about," and so he stirred the broth again.

"Well, I think I have a scrap of flour somewhere," said the old woman, and went out to fetch some, and it was both good and fine.

The tramp began putting the flour into the broth, and went on stirring, while the woman sat staring now at him and then at the pot until her eyes nearly burst their sockets.

"This broth would be good enough for company," he said, putting in one handful of flour after another. "If I had only a bit of salted beef and a few potatoes to put in, it would be fit for gentlefolks, however particular they might be," he said. "But what one has to go without, it's no use thinking more about."

When the old woman really began to think it over, she thought she had some potatoes, and perhaps a bit of beef as well; and these she gave the tramp, who went on stirring, while she sat and stared as hard as ever.

"This will be grand enough for the best in the land," he said.

"Well, I never!" said the woman; "and just fancy all with a nail!"

He was really a wonderful man, that tramp! He could do more than drink a sup and turn the tankard up, he could.

"If one had only a little barley and a drop of milk, we could ask the king himself to have some of it," he said; "for this is what he has every blessed evening—that I know, for I have been in service under the king's cook," he said.

"Dear me! Ask the king to have some! Well, I never!" exclaimed the woman, slapping her knees. She was quite awestruck at the tramp and his grand connections.

"But what one has to go without, it's no use thinking more about," said the tramp.

And then she remembered she had a little barley; and as for milk, well, she wasn't quite out of that, she said, for her best cow had just calved. And then she went to fetch both the one and the other.

The tramp went on stirring, and the woman sat staring, one moment at him and the next at the pot.

Then all at once the tramp took out the nail.

"Now it's ready, and now we'll have a real good feast," he said. "But to this kind of soup the king and the queen always take a dram or two. and one sandwich at least. And then they always have a cloth on the table when they eat," he said. "But what one has to go without, it's no use thinking more about."

But by this time the old woman herself had begun to feel quite grand and fine, I can tell you; and if that was all that was wanted to make it just as the king had it, she thought it would be nice to have it exactly the same way for once, and play at being king and queen with the tramp. She went straight to a cupboard and brought out the brandy bottle, dram glasses, butter and cheese, smoked beef and veal, until at last the table looked as if it were decked out for company.

Never in her life had the old woman had such a grand feast, and never had she tasted such broth, and just fancy, made only with a nail!

She was in such a good and merry humor at having learned such an economical way of making broth that she did not know how to make enough of the tramp who had taught her such a useful thing.

So they ate and drank, and drank and ate, until they became both tired and sleepy.

The tramp was now going to lie down on the floor. But that would never do, thought the old woman; no, that was impossible. "Such a grand person must have a bed to lie in," she said.

He did not need much pressing. "It's just like the sweet Christmas time," he said, "and a nicer woman I never came across. Ah, well! Happy are they who meet with such good people," said he; and he lay down on the bed and went asleep.

And next morning, when he woke, the first thing he got was coffee and a dram.

When he was going, the old woman gave him a bright dollar piece.

"And thanks, many thanks, for what you have taught me," she said. "Now I shall live in comfort, since I have learned how to make broth with a nail."

"Well, it isn't difficult if one only has something to add to it," said the tramp as he went his way.

The woman stood at the door staring after him.

"Such people don't grow on every bush," she said.

# THE NUREMBERG STOVE[1]

## Louise de la Ramée

*A wonderfully fine story for a creative play, worthy of research and careful study. It has many possibilities for an integrated project on Germany and Austria.*

In the little town of Hall, in Austria, August Strehla lived with his family in a house four centuries old. August was a boy of nine at this time—a round-faced little fellow with big hazel eyes and curly brown hair. His mother was dead, and his father found it very hard to earn enough money to support his family, for there were many mouths to feed.

One cold, snowy night August was returning home with two silver groschen in his pocket, earned by chopping wood for an old man on the other side of the town. He was half-frozen as he ran down the last street, and was glad when Dorothea opened the door for him at once.

It was a large barren room into which he rushed with so much pleasure, and the brick floor was bare and uneven. A walnut press, handsome and very old, a broad deal table, and several stools were the only pieces of furniture in the place—the only pieces, that is, besides a most wonderful stove which dominated the whole room.

It was truly a tower of porcelain, shining with all the hues of a king's peacock and a queen's jewels, and surmounted by armed figures and shields and flowers of heraldry. In each corner was the statue of a king, and on the very top was a great golden crown. The date on it was 1532, and the letters H. R. H. were plain to be seen. This was the mark of the great potter of Nuremberg, Augustin Hirschvogel.

The stove no doubt had stood in palaces and been made for princes, had warmed the crimson stockings of cardinals and the gold-broidered shoes of archduchesses; no one knew what it had seen or done or been fashioned for; but it was a right royal thing. Yet perhaps it had never been more useful than it was now in this poor desolate room, sending down heat and comfort into the troop of children tumbled together on a wolf-skin at its feet, who received frozen August among them with loud shouts of joy.

[1] Adapted.

"Oh, dear Hirschvogel, I am so cold, so cold!" said August, kissing its gilded lion's claws. "Is father not in, Dorothea?"

"No, dear. He is late."

Dorothea was a girl of seventeen, dark-haired and serious. She was the eldest of the Strehla family; and there were ten of them in all. Next to her there came Jan and Karl and Otho, big lads, gaining a little for their own living; and then came August, who went up in the summer to the high Alps with the farmers' cattle, but in winter could do only odd jobs; and then the little ones, who could only open their mouths to be fed like young birds—Albrecht and Hilda, and Waldo and Christof, and last of all little three-year-old Ermengilda, with eyes like forget-me-nots.

The father was a good man, but weak and weary with so many to find food for and so little to do it with. He worked at the salt-furnaces, and by that gained a few florins. Dorothea almost worked miracles with her housekeeping, and the table was seldom without its big pot of soup once a day. She kept the children clean and happy, but her heart ached with shame, for she knew that her father's debts were many.

"Father says we are never to wait for him; we will have supper, now you have come home, dear," said Dorothea.

Supper was a huge bowl of soup, with big slices of brown bread swimming in it and some onions bobbing up and down. The bowl was soon emptied by ten wooden spoons, and then the three eldest boys slipped off to bed, being tired with their rough bodily labor in the snow all day. Dorothea drew her spinning-wheel by the stove and set it whirring, and the little ones got August down upon the old worn wolf-skin and clamored to him for a picture or a story. For August was the artist of the family.

He had a smooth board that his father had given him, and some sticks of charcoal, and he would draw a hundred things he had seen in the day, sweeping each out with his elbow when the children had seen enough of it and sketching another in its stead—faces and dogs' heads, and men in sledges, and old women in their furs, and pine-trees, and cocks and hens, and all sorts of animals, and now and then—very reverently—a Madonna and Child. It was all very rough, for there was no one to teach him anything. But it was all life-like, and kept the whole troop of children shrieking with laughter, or watching breathless, with wide open, wondering, awed eyes.

They were all so happy! What did they care for the snow outside? Even Dorothea, troubled about the bread for the morrow, laughed as she spun; and August, with all his soul in his work, cried out loud, smiling, as he looked up at the stove that was shedding its heat down on them all:

"Oh, dear Hirschvogel! you are almost as great and good as the sun! No; you are greater and better, I think, because he goes away nobody knows where all these long, dark, cold hours; but you—you are always ready; just a little bit of wood to feed you, and you will make a summer for us all the winter through!"

The grand old stove seemed to smile through all its iridescent surface at the praises of the child. No doubt, though it had known three centuries and more, it had known very little gratitude.

Nothing was known about the stove except that the grandfather Strehla, who had been a master-mason, had dug it up out of some ruins where he was building, and, finding it without a flaw, had taken it home. That was now sixty years past, and ever since then the stove had stood in the big, desolate, empty room, warming three generations of the Strehla family.

All the children loved it, but with August the love of it was a passion; and in his secret heart he often said to himself, "When I am a man I will make just such things, too, and then I will set Hirschvogel in a beautiful room in a house I will build myself."

As August lay now in the warmth of the stove and told the children stories, suddenly a blast of frozen air and a spray of driven snow struck like ice through the room, and reached them even in the warmth of the old wolf-skins and the great stove. It was the door which had opened and let in the cold; it was their father who had come home. The younger children ran joyously to meet him, Dorothea pushed the one wooden arm-chair of the room to the stove, and August flew to fill the long clay pipe; for their father was good to them all, and they had been trained by the mother they had loved to dutifulness and obedience and a watchful affection.

Tonight Karl Strehla responded very wearily to the young ones' welcome, and sat down heavily in the wooden chair, not noticing his pipe.

"Take the children to bed," he said, suddenly, and Dorothea obeyed. August stayed behind, curled before the stove.

When Dorothea came down again, the cuckoo-clock in the corner struck eight; she looked to her father and the untouched pipe, then sat down to her spinning, saying nothing.

There was a long silence; August dropped asleep; Dorothea's wheel hummed like a cat.

Suddenly Karl Strehla struck his hand on the table. "I have sold Hirschvogel," he said; and his voice was husky and ashamed in his throat. The spinning-wheel stopped. August sprang erect out of his sleep.

"Sold Hirschvogel!"

"I have sold Hirschvogel!" said Karl Strehla, in the same husky, dogged voice. "I have sold it to a traveling trader for two hundred florins. What would you?—I owe double that. He saw it this morning when you were all out. He will pack it and take it to Munich tomorrow."

Dorothea gave a low cry: "Oh, father!—the children—in midwinter!" She turned white as the snow without.

August stood, half blind with sleep, staring with dazed eyes.

"It is not true?" he muttered. "You are jesting, father?"

Strehla broke into a dreary laugh.

"It is true. Would you like to know what is true too?—that the bread you eat, and the meat you put in this pot, and the roof you have over your heads, are none of them paid for, have been none of them paid for, for months and months. If it had not been for your grandfather, I should have been in prison all summer and autumn, and he is out of patience and will do no more now. Boy, you stare at me as if I were a mad dog! You have made a god of yon china thing. Well,—it goes; goes tomorrow. Two hundred florins, that is something. It will keep me out of prison for a little, and with the spring things may turn—"

August stood like a creature paralyzed. His eyes were wide open, fastened on his father's with terror and incredulous horror; his face had grown as white as his sister's; his chest heaved with tearless sobs.

"It is not true!" he echoed, stupidly. It seemed to him that the very skies must fall, if they could take away Hirschvogel. They might as soon talk of tearing God's sun out of the heavens.

"You will find it true," said his father, doggedly, and angered because he was in his own soul bitterly ashamed to have bartered away the heirloom and treasure of his race and the comfort of his young children. "The dealer has paid me half the money tonight, and will pay me the other half tomorrow. No doubt it is worth a great deal more—but beggars cannot be choosers. The little black

278

stove in the kitchen will warm you all just as well. Who would keep a gilded, painted thing in a poor house like this, when one can make two hundred florins by it? What is it, when all is said?—a bit of hardware much too grand-looking for such a room as this."

August gave a cry, and threw himself at his father's feet.

"Oh, father!" he cried, his hands closing on Strehla's knees. "Oh, father, dear father, you cannot mean what you say? Send *it* away—our life, our sun, our joy, our comfort? Sell *me* rather. But Hirschvogel! You must be jesting. You could not do such a thing. I will go and try and get work tomorrow! I will ask them to let me cut ice or make the paths through the snow. There must be something I could do, and I will beg the people we owe money to to wait; they are all neighbors, they will be patient. But sell Hirschvogel!—oh, never! never! never! Give the florins back to the man. Oh, father, dear father! do hear me, for pity's sake!"

Strehla was moved by the boy's anguish. He loved his children, and their pain was pain to him. But stronger than emotion, was the anger that August roused in him: he hated and despised himself for the barter of the heirloom of his race, and every word of the child stung him with a stinging sense of shame.

And he spoke in his wrath rather than in his sorrow.

"Get up and go to bed. There is no more to be said. Children like you have nothing to do with such matters. The stove is sold, and goes to Munich tomorrow. What is it to you? Be thankful I can get bread for you. Get on your legs, I say, and go to bed."

Then Strehla took the oil-lamp that stood at his elbow and stumbled off to his own chamber.

August threw himself forward on the stove, covering it with kisses, and sobbing as though his heart would burst.

"August, dear August," whispered Dorothea, piteously. "August, do not lie there. Come to bed. In the morning you will be calmer. It is horrible indeed, but if it be father's will—"

"Let me alone," said August through his teeth, striving to still the storm of sobs that shook him from head to foot. "Let me alone. In the morning!—how can you speak of the morning?"

"Come to bed, dear," sighed his sister. "Oh, August, do not lie and look like that! you frighten me. Do come to bed."

"I shall stay here."

"Here! all night!"

"They might take it in the night. Besides, to leave it *now!*"

"But it is cold! the fire is out."

"It will never be warm any more, nor shall we."

All his childhood had gone out of him; all his careless, sunny temper had gone with it; he spoke sullenly and wearily, choking down the great sobs in his chest. To him it was as if the end of the world had come.

His sister lingered by him, trying to persuade him to go to bed. But it was in vain. "I shall stay here," was all he answered her. And he stayed—all the night long.

The lamps were out; the hours crept on through midnight and past, the cold intensified, and the air of the room grew like ice. Whilst yet it was dark his three elder brothers came down the stairs and let themselves out, each bearing his lantern and going to his work at the salt-works. They did not notice him; they did not know what had happened.

A little later when his sister came down with a light in her hand, she stole up to him and laid her hand on his shoulder timidly.

"Dear August, you must be frozen. August, do look up! do speak! It is morning, only so dark!"

August shuddered all over. "The morning!" he echoed. He slowly rose up to his feet. "I will go to grandfather," he said, very low. "He is always good; perhaps he could save it."

Loud blows with the heavy iron knocker of the house-door drowned his words. A strange voice called aloud through the keyhole: "Let me in! Quick!—there is no time to lose! More snow like this, and the roads will all be blocked. Let me in! Do you hear? I am come to take the great stove."

August sprang erect, his fists doubled, his eyes blazing.

"You shall never touch it!" he shouted. "You will never touch it!"

"Who shall prevent us?" laughed a big man, who was a Bavarian, amused at the fierce little figure fronting him.

"I!" said August. "You shall never have it!"

"Strehla," said the big man, as August's father entered the room, "you have a little mad dog here; muzzle him."

One way and another they did muzzle him. He fought like a little demon, and hit out right and left. But he was soon mastered by four grown men, and his father flung him with no light hand out from the door of the back entrance, and the buyers of the stately and beautiful stove set to work to pack it heedfully and carry it away.

When Dorothea stole out to look for August, he was nowhere in sight. She went back to little 'Gilda, and sobbed, whilst the others stood looking on, dimly understanding that with Hirschvogel was

**going** all the warmth of their bodies, all the light of their hearth. In another moment Hirschvogel was gone—gone forever.

August had stood still for a time, leaning against the back wall of the house. Then an idea came to him. Why not go with it? He ran out of the courtyard and across the street where he could watch.

Presently his heart gave a great leap, for he saw the straw-enwrapped stove brought out and laid with infinite care on the bullock dray. Two of the Bavarian men mounted beside it, and the wagon slowly crept over the snow of the place. Then he crept, unseen by any of his brothers or sisters, and followed in the wake of the dray

Its course lay towards the station of the railway. August heard the Bavarians arguing a great deal, and learned that they meant to go too but that they would go in a passenger train, leaving the stove to be sent by luggage train half an hour later.

As August listened, a desperate resolve made itself up in his mind. Where Hirschvogel went, he would go. He gave one terrible thought to Dorothea—poor, gentle Dorothea!—sitting in the cold at home, then set to work to execute his project. How he managed it he never knew very clearly himself, but certain it is that when the goods-train from the north moved out of Hall, August was hidden inside the stove. He had bought some bread and sausage at the station and this he ate in the darkness.

As the train lumbered on, August found that though his beloved fire-king was not like a bed of down, he could curl up very comfortably. The air came in through the brass fret-work, and he realized that he would be able to remain in it for many hours. So, feeling that God and Hirschvogel would take care of him, August went fast asleep.

Because the train was bearing goods to the King of Bavaria, it was faster than most; but it seemed an endless time before it reached Munich, and August's thirst was almost unbearable by the time the stove was finally set down in a small dark curiosity shop.

"I shall not unpack it till Anton comes," he heard a man's voice say; and then he heard a key grate in a lock, and by the unbroken stillness that ensued he concluded he was alone, and ventured to peep through the straw and hay. What he saw was a small square room filled with pots and pans, pictures, carvings, old blue jugs, old steel armor, shields, daggers, Chinese idols, Vienna china, Turkish rugs and all the rubbish of a *bric-a-brac* dealer's. But, oh! was there one drop of water in it all? That was his single thought. There was not a drop of water, but there was a lattice window grated, and beyond the window was a wide stone ledge covered with snow. August cast one look at the locked door, darted out of his hiding-place, ran and opened the window, crammed the snow into his mouth again and again, and then flew back into the stove, drew the hay and straw over the place he entered by, and shut the brass door down on himself.

Presently the key turned in the lock, he heard heavy footsteps and the voice of the man who had talked to his father. The voice said, "Ay, ay, you have called me a fool many times. Now you shall see what I have gotten for two hundred dirty florins. Never did *you* do such a stroke of work!"

Then they began to strip the stove of its wrappings; that he could tell by the noise they made with the hay and the straw. Soon they had stripped it wholly; that, too, he knew by the exclamations of wonder and surprise and rapture which broke from the man who had not seen it before.

"A right royal thing! A wonderful and never-to-be-rivalled thing. Grander than the great stove of Hohen-Salzburg! Sublime! magnificent! matchless!"

Presently the door opened again sharply. He could hear the two dealers' voices, murmuring unctuous words, in which "honor," "gratitude," and many fine long noble titles played the chief parts. The voice of another person, more clear and refined than theirs, answered then curtly, and then, close by the stove and the boy's ear, ejaculated a single *"Wundershön!"*

The poor little boy, meanwhile, within, was hugged up into nothing, dreading that every moment the stranger would open the stove. And open it truly he did, and examined the brass-work of the door; but inside it was so dark that crouching August passed unnoticed, screwed up into a ball like a hedgehog as he was. After a while they all went away, double-locking the door behind them. He would have to pass the night here, that was certain. So he finally dropped off to sleep.

Midnight was chiming from all the brazen tongues of the city when he awoke, and, all being still, ventured to put his head out the door of the stove to see why such a strange bright light was round him. What he saw was nothing less than all the *bric-a-brac* in motion.

A big jug was solemnly dancing a minuet with a plump Faenza jar; a tall Dutch clock was going through a gavotte with a spindle-legged ancient chair; an old violin of Cremona was playing itself; a queer shrill plaintive music that thought itself merry came from a painted spinet covered with faded roses, and a Japanese bronze was riding along on a griffin. A great number of little Dresden cups and saucers were all skipping and waltzing; the teapots, with their broad round faces, were spinning their own lids like tee-totums; and a little Saxe poodle, with a red ribbon at its throat, was running from one to another. August looked on at these mad freaks and felt no sensation of wonder. He only, as he heard the violin and the spinet playing, felt an irresistible desire to dance too. No doubt his face said what he wished; for a lovely little lady, all in pink and gold and white, with powdered hair, and high-heeled shoes, and all made of the very finest and fairest Meissen china, tripped up to him, and smiled, and gave him her hand, and led him out to a minuet.

"I am the Princess of Saxe-Royale," she said with a smile.

Then he ventured to say to her: "Madame, my Princess, could you tell me kindly why some of the figures dance and speak, and some lie up in a corner like lumber? Is it rude to ask?"

"My dear child," said the powdered lady, "is it possible that you do not know the reason? Why, those silent, dull things are *imitations;* lies, falsehoods, fabrications! They only *pretend* to be what we *are!* They never wake up; how can they? No imitation ever had any soul in it yet."

Then from where the great stove stood there came a solemn voice. All eyes turned upon Hirschvogel, and the heart of its little human comrade gave a great jump of joy. At last he would hear Hirsch-vogel speak.

"My friends," said that clear voice, "we were made in days when men were true creatures, and so we, the work of their hands, were true too. We derive all the value in us from the fact that our makers wrought at us with zeal, with integrity, with faith—not to win fortunes, but to do nobly an honest thing and create for the honor of the Arts and God. I see amidst you a little human thing who loves me and in his childish way loves Art. Now I want him forever to remember that we are what we are, and precious in the eyes of the world, because centuries ago those who were of single mind and of pure hand so created us, scorning sham and haste and counterfeit. Well do I recollect my master, Augustin Hirschvogel. He led a wise and blameless life, and wrought in loyalty and love, and made his time beautiful thereby. Where I go now I know not;

283

but since I go from that humble house where they loved me, I shall be sad and alone."

Then the voice sank away in silence, and a strange golden light that had shone on the great stove faded away. A soft pathetic melody stole gently through the room. It came from the old, old spinet that was covered with the faded roses.

Then that sad, sighing music of a bygone day died too; the clocks of the city struck six of the morning; day was dawning. August awoke with a great start, and found himself lying on the bare bricks of the floor of the chamber, and all the *bric-a-brac* was lying quite still all around.

He rose slowly to his feet. Tramp, tramp, came a heavy step up the stair. He had but a moment in which to scramble back into the great stove, when the door opened and the two dealers entered, bringing candles with them to see their way.

August was scarcely conscious of danger more than he was of cold or hunger, now that he had heard Hirschvogel speak. A marvelous sense of courage, of security, of happiness, was about him, like strong and gentle arms enfolding him and lifting him upwards—upwards—upwards! Hirschvogel would defend him.

Again the stove was wrapped and after one last journey by train and boat, he was in the royal castle of Berg, though he did not know it. All he knew was that the air was warm and fragrant and that from somewhere came dreamy, exquisite music.

Presently he heard a fresh step near him, and he heard a low voice say, close behind him, "So!" An exclamation no doubt of admiration and wonder at the beauty of Hirschvogel. Then the same voice said, after a long pause, during which, as August thought, this new-comer was examining all the details of the wondrous fire-tower, "It was well bought; it is exceedingly beautiful! It is undoubtedly the work of Augustin Hirschvogel."

Then the hand of the speaker turned the round handle of the brass door, and the fainting soul of the poor little prisoner within grew sick with fear. The door was slowly drawn open, some one bent down and looked in, and the same voice called aloud, in surprise, "What is this in it? A live child!"

Then August, terrified beyond all self-control, and dominated by one master-passion, sprang out of the body of the stove and fell at the feet of the speaker.

"Oh, let me stay! Pray, meinheer, let me stay!" he sobbed. "I have come all the way with Hirschvogel!"

Some gentlemen's hands seized him, not gently by any means, and their lips angrily muttered in his ear, "Little knave, peace! be quiet! hold your tongue! It is the king!"

They were about to drag him away, but the voice he had heard said kindly, "Poor child! he is very young. Let him go. Let him speak to me."

The word of a king is law to his courtiers; so, sorely against their wish, the angry and astonished chamberlains let August slide out of their grasp, and he stood there in his little rough sheepskin coat and his thick, mud-covered boots, with his curling hair all in a tangle, in the midst of the most beautiful room he had ever dreamed of, and in the presence of a young man with a handsome face, and eyes full of dreams and fire; and the young man said to him,—

"My child, how came you here, hidden in this stove? Be not afraid, tell me the truth. I am the king."

August in an instinct of homage cast his hat down on the floor of the room, and folded his hands in supplication. He was too intensely in earnest to be in any way abashed; he was too lifted out of himself by his love for Hirschvogel to be conscious of any awe before any earthly majesty. He was only so glad—so glad it was the king.

"Oh, dear king!" he said, with trembling entreaty in his voice, "Hirschvogel was ours. We have loved it all our lives; and father sold it. When I saw that it did really go from us, then I said to myself I would go with it; and I have come all the way inside it. I pray you let me live with it. I will go out every morning and cut wood for it and you, if only you will let me stay beside it. No one ever has fed it with fuel but me since I grew big enough, and it loves me—"

And then his breath failed him, and, as he lifted his eager, pale face to the king's, great tears were falling down his cheeks.

Now, the king liked all poetic and uncommon things, and there was that in the child's face which pleased and touched him. He motioned to his gentlemen to leave the little boy alone.

"What is your name?" he asked him.

"I am August Strehla. My father is Karl Strehla. We live in Hall; and Hirschvogel has been ours so long,—so long!"

His lips quivered with a broken sob.

"And have you truly traveled in this stove all the way from Tyrol?"

"Yes," said August, "no one thought to look inside till you did."

The king laughed; then another view of the matter occurred to him. "Who bought the stove of your father?" he inquired.

"Traders of Munich," said August.

"What sum did they pay, do you know?"

"Two hundred florins," said August, with a great sigh of shame. "It was so much money, and he is so poor, and there are so many of us."

The king turned to his gentlemen-in-waiting. "Did these dealers of Munich come with the stove?"

He was answered in the affirmative. He desired them to be sought for and brought before him. As one of his chamberlains hastened on the errand, the monarch looked at August with compassion.

"You are very pale, little fellow: when did you eat last?"

"I had some bread and sausage with me; yesterday afternoon I finished it."

"You would like to eat now?"

"If I might have a little water I would be glad; my throat is very dry."

The king had water brought for him, and cake also; but August, though he drank eagerly, could not swallow anything. His mind was in too great a tumult.

"May I stay with Hirschvogel?" he said, with feverish agitation.

"Wait a little," said the king, and asked, abruptly, "What do you wish to be when you are a man?"

"A painter. I wish to be what Hirschvogel was,—I mean the master that made *my* Hirschvogel!"

"I understand," said the king.

Then the two dealers were brought into their sovereign's presence. They were so terribly alarmed that they were trembling as though they were being led to the slaughter, and they were so utterly astonished too at a child having come all the way from Tyrol in the stove, as a gentleman of the court had just told them this child had done, that they could not tell what to say or where to look, and presented a very foolish aspect indeed.

"Did you buy this stove of this boy's father for two hundred florins?" the king asked; and his voice was no longer soft and kind as it had been when addressing the child, but very stern.

"Yes, your majesty," murmured the trembling traders.

"And how much did the gentleman who purchased it for me give to you?"

"Two thousand ducats, your majesty," muttered the dealers, frightened out of their wits, and telling the truth in their fright.

286

"You will give at once to this boy's father the two thousand gold ducats that you received, less the two hundred Austrian florins that you paid him," said the king. "You are great rogues. Be thankful you are not more greatly punished."

He dismissed them by a sign to his courtiers.

August heard, and felt dazzled yet miserable. Two thousand gold Bavarian ducats for his father! Why, his father would never need to go any more to the salt-baking! And yet, whether for ducats or for florins, Hirschvogel was sold just the same, and would the king let him stay with it?—would he?

"Oh, do! please do!" he implored, kneeling before the young monarch.

He looked down on the child and smiled once more.

"Rise up, my lad," he said in a kind voice; "kneel only to your God. Will I let you stay with your Hirschvogel? Yes, I will; you shall stay at my court, and you shall be taught to be a painter. You must grow up worthily, and win all the laurels at our Schools of Art, and if when you are twenty-one years old you have done well and bravely, then I will give you your Nuremberg stove. And now go away with this gentleman, and be not afraid, and you shall light a fire every morning in Hirschvogel, but you will not need to go out and cut the wood."

Then he smiled and stretched out his hand; the courtiers tried to make August understand that he ought to bow and touch it with his lips, but August could not understand that anyhow; he was too happy. He threw his two arms about the king's knees, and kissed his feet passionately.

August is only a scholar yet, but he is a happy scholar, and promises to be a great man. Sometimes he goes back for a few days to Hall, where the gold ducats have made his father prosperous. In the old house-room there is a large white porcelain stove of Munich, the king's gift to Dorothea and 'Gilda.

And August never goes home without going into the great church and saying his thanks to God, who blessed his strange winter's journey in the Nuremberg stove. As for his dream in the dealers' room that night, he will never admit that he did dream it; he still declares that he saw it all, and heard the voice of Hirschvogel. And who shall say that he did not, for what is the gift of the poet and the artist except to see the sights which others cannot see and hear the sounds that others cannot hear?

# THE GOOD SAMARITAN[1]

## Retold by Fulton Oursler

*Before playing this dramatic story, the leader should see to it that the children know something about the dark, dangerous road between Jerusalem and Jericho; have an understanding of the attitude toward Samaritans; of the meaning of "Levite;" enough acquaintance with the customs of the time so that they can understand why the man ventures alone on the road. Pictures should be clear and concrete if the dramatization is to seem real. And the attack of the thieves must not be allowed to become so important that the point of the story is lost. The following version, from The Greatest Story Ever Told, may be used to give some sidelights on the beautifully told Bible story. (Saint Luke X.)*

"Master, who is my neighbor?"

This question was asked by a lawyer after Jesus had said, "You shall love the Lord your God with your whole heart, and with your whole soul, and with your whole strength; and you shall love your neighbor as yourself."

Surely, he thought, Jesus did not mean that a Gentile could also be a neighbor! Or, infinitely worse, a depraved, despised, unspeakable Samaritan!

From where He sat, Jesus could look through the open door and portico out to the road beyond, the robber-infested highway. It was as if he were describing a drama being enacted there:

"A certain man went down from Jerusalem to Jericho and fell among thieves . . . "

A situation they all recognized and many had feared. Under the story-teller's spell their imagination went to work. They could see that "certain man" packing his bags for the journey, his worried wife helping him and pleading with him to wait until someone else could go with him. No, no—the business was urgent; he must get to Jericho before dawn tomorrow. And then a small, piping voice spoke up—his ten-year-old's voice: listen to the child; he knew

[1] From *The Greatest Story Ever Told*, published by Doubleday & Company, Inc. Permission from the author.

somebody that was going on that road tonight: his chum's father.

And who might his chum's father be? What did you say, my son? Did I hear you say that your chum's father came from Nablus? Wife, explain this! A son of mine playing with Samaritan boys!

And the father became even more angry when his boy wanted to know what was really wrong with a Samaritan. Why, explain to him, wife! Samaritans were all dirty and untrustworthy. Hundreds of years ago they collaborated with the Persian invaders . . .

"But, Father, is my chum to be punished for what happened hundreds of years ago?"

No more Samaritan boys for you; no son of mine may be seen playing with a Samaritan; it might even hurt me in my business. And so, having refused the suggestion of his boy, and given his orders and prayed in the Temple, the father starts out alone on the dark road. There he is overtaken by robbers, who strip him to the skin, leave him naked on the ground in the dark—beaten, wounded, and half dead.

"And it chanced that a certain priest went down the same way; and, seeing him, passed by.

"In like manner also a Levite, when he was near the place and saw him, also passed by.

"But a certain Samaritan, being on his journey, came near him; and, seeing him, was moved with compassion.

"And going up to him, bound up his wounds, pouring in oil and wine; and setting him upon his own beast, brought him to an inn and took care of him.

"And the next day he took out two pence and gave to the host and said: 'Take care of him, and whatsoever you shall spend, over and above, I, on my return, will repay you'."

Here, for a moment, Jesus paused and looked from the bespelled faces of the people straight at the heckling lawyer.

"Which of these, then, in your opinion was neighbor to him that fell among the robbers?"

And looking back into the smiling face of the Master, the lawyer could answer only:

"He that showed mercy to him." Even then he could not bring himself to use the definite but forbidden word "Samaritan." But that was what he meant.

"Go and do you in like manner!"

# THE PRODIGAL SON[1]

## Retold by E. Jerry Walker

*A moving story, well within the understanding of older children. Of course, no leader would want boys and girls to dramatize an adult idea of "riotous living," with drunken companions and women who lead the boy astray. But children will have ideas about many ways in which he might waste his inheritance. Extravagant spending of money for feasts, for fine clothes, for jewels, for servants, and friends who flatter him as long as he has money, will offer plenty of opportunity for interesting and effective scenes.*

*Whether or not the parable in the beautiful prose of the Bible (Luke XV.) is read before the planning begins or after the play has been developed will depend on the general attitude of the group. To many children the story will seem more real, more close to them if it is presented first in some such manner as the following:*

As long as he could remember, the young man had dreamed of going to a far country, of leaving his father's house and being entirely "on his own." Turning to the other young man who toiled beside him in the field, he said, "My brother, why do we strain our backs and sear our faces toiling in our father's fields? I have heard of a city in a distant land where all is mirth and joy, where no one works, and everyone is gay."

He paused to stare with dissatisfaction at the dust that covered his shoes, his clothes, his hands.

"I am tired of breathing dirt!" he said, and flung his implements to the ground. He turned to his older brother and spoke softly, rapidly, as though carried away by what he himself was saying.

We could ask our father for our inheritance. It would be a sizable sum. Yours would be even more than mine for you are older. With our inheritance we could get away from all this and live luxuriously. We could see life—real life. We could meet people—not just tillers of the soil and laborers, but important people. By investing our wealth, we shall make more wealth. In a short time we shall be rich, my brother, rich!"

The two young men stared at each other. Eagerly, expectantly, the younger waited. For a moment it seemed his daring plan would elicit a favorable response. But without a word, merely passing his

[1] From *Five-Minute Stories from the Bible,* by E. Jerry Walker. Published by the Abingdon-Cokesbury Press. Used by permission of the author.

hand across his perspiring brow as if to push aside an impossible dream, the older youth bent himself again to his task.

The younger man, breathing fast, stared at his brother. Then, with the abruptness of sudden resolve, he stalked from the field.

Pausing before his father's room, he eyed the door as though to measure its weight of resistance, then, nails digging the palms of his hands, he entered and stood before his father.

"My son?" his father acknowledged.

"I . . . I have come to request my inheritance," the youth blurted.

"Your inheritance?"

"Yes, I wish to leave your estate, to live my own life."

His face serious, a depth of sorrowful understanding in his eyes, the father nodded. "As you wish it, my son," he said. "As you wish it."

A few days later, eagerness and excitement in his every move, the young man gathered together the wealth of his inheritance. Bidding his father and his father's hired servants goodbye, he set off for the far country of his dreams. He was well on his way before he realized he had not bade his brother good-by.

"Oh, well," he thought. "If he could not come out of the field long enough to speak with me, I needn't care! He had his chance to get away from the work and the toil. Now, let him bury himself in the dust. As for me, I shall be merry!"

And merry he was, until—as recorded in our scriptures—the substance of his inheritance was used up in riotous living. When he had spent his last coin, he became aware of a terrible famine that was wasting the land where he had sought to know the easy life.

Ragged, hungry, he stumbled from shop to shop. He was a foreigner in a strange country, seeking some small task for which he might be paid. But there was nought for him to do. He dragged himself, weary, starving, disillusioned, from shop to shop and house to house. Then, at last, a citizen of that country who owned an estate accepted him as a hired hand.

"Your job," the man said, "will be to care for my swine. My other servants will show you where the husks for their food are stored. If you wish to work for me long, you will do your job well, for I am jealous of my estate!"

"I am hungry, sir," the young man began, only to be interrupted curtly.

"When you have done your job, then you shall eat!"

Completely fatigued, the young man followed the servant under whom he was to work. Mechanically, without feeling, he threw the husk pods to the swine and stared as they grunted and nudged each other for them. In a sudden passion the young man looked at the husks which he still held in his hand. Ferociously, in panic born of starvation, he thrust them into his mouth and ate with the vigor of his new master's swine

In the morning when he came to himself, he looked with disgust upon his new home. It was smaller than his father's estate. It was more run down, with less pride shown by the owner in his buildings and lands. And the young man's own corner, where he had fallen into a fast slumber the night before, was next to the pig pen. He sat up slowly. Cursing the grunting swine that were rooting noisily in the nearby mire, he felt the almost unbearable pangs of hunger.

"How many of my father's hired servants have bread enough and to spare," he mumbled to the animals, "but I perish here with hunger!"

All at once his throat felt large and his eyes welled with tears. "What a fool I've been," he said. "I will arise and go to my father. I will say to him, 'Father, I have sinned against heaven, and before you; I am no longer worthy to be called your son; treat me as one of your hired servants'."

Many days later when the father saw his son approaching, he was filled with a loving compassion. He called a servant. "Quickly," he said. "Kill the fatted calf. Tonight we shall rejoice!" Another he instructed to bring forth his best robe and put it on his son; and he ordered a ring for his hand and shoes for his feet.

That evening, returning from a weary day in the fields, the older brother heard music and laughter. Calling one of the servants, he inquired the cause of jubilation. When he heard, he was angry, and would not enter. Even under his father's entreaties he remained obstinate.

"Lo these many years," he said, "I have served you. I never disobeyed your command. Yet, you never gave me so much as a kid, that I might make merry with my friends. But when this other son of yours—who has squandered everything that was given him— came, you killed for him the fatted calf!"

The father, his eyes moist, laid his hand gently on his son's shoulder. "Son," he said, "you are always with me. All that is mine is yours. It was fitting to make merry and be glad, for this your brother was dead, and is alive; he was lost, and is found!"

# KING JOHN AND THE ABBOT OF CANTERBURY

## An Old Ballad

*Among the old ballads, this is one which children always like to play. It can be done very simply, but by knowing the historical background, and using some imagination in building up the court scenes, the group can make a far more interesting play. Some classes like to begin with a scene at the abbot's home.*

An ancient story I'll tell you anon
Of a notable prince, that was called King John;
And he ruled England with maine and with might,
For he did great wrong and maintain'd little right.

And I'll tell you a story, a story so merrye,
Concerning the Abbot of Canterburye;
How for his house-keeping and high renowne,
They rode post for him to fair London towne.

An hundred men, the king did heare say,
The abbot kept in his house every day;
And fifty golde chaynes, without any doubt,
In velvet coates waited the abbot about.

"How now, father abbot, I heare it of thee,
Thou keepest a farre better house than mee,
And for thy house-keeping and high renowne,
I fear thou work'st treason against my crown."

"My liege," quo' the abbot, "I would it were knowne,
I never spend nothing but what is my owne;
And I trust your grace will do me no deere
For spending of my owne true-gotten geere."

"Yes, yes, father abbot, thy fault it is highe,
And now for the same thou needest must dye;
For except thou canst answer me questions three,
Thy head shall be smitten from thy bodie.

"And first," quo' the king, "when I'm in this stead,
With my crown of golde so faire on my head,
Among all my liege-men so noble of birthe,
Thou must tell me to one penny what I am worthe.

"Secondlye tell me, without any doubt,
How soone I may ride the whole worlde about.
And at the third question thou must not shrinke,
But tell me here truly what I do thinke."

"O, these are hard questions for my shallow witt,
Nor I cannot answer your grace as yet;
But if you will give me but three weekes space,
I'll do my endeavour to answer your grace."

"Now three weekes space to thee will I give,
And that is the longest thou hast to live;
For if thou dost not answer my questions three,
Thy lands and thy living are forfeit to mee."

Away rode the abbot all sad at that word,
And he rode to Cambridge, and Oxenford;
But never a doctor there was so wise,
That could with his learning an answer devise.

Then home rode the abbot of comfort so cold,
And he mett his shephard a-going to fold:
"How now, my lord abbot, you are welcome home;
What newes do you bring us from good King John?"

"Sad newes, sad newes, shephard, I must give;
That I have but three days more to live:
For if I do not answer him questions three,
My head will be smitten from my bodie.

"The first is to tell him there in that stead,
With his crowne of golde so faire on his head,
Among all his liege-men so noble of birthe,
To within one penny of what he is worthe.

"The seconde, to tell him without any doubt,
How soone he may ride this whole worlde about:
And at the third question I must not shrinke,
But tell him there truly what he does thinke."

"Now cheare up, sire abbot, did you never hear yet
That a fool he may learn a wise man witt?
Lend me horse, and serving-men, and your apparel,
And I'll ride to London to answere your quarrel.

"Nay, frowne not, if it hath bin told unto mee,
I am like your lordship, as ever may bee;
And if you will but lend me your gowne,
There is none shall knowe us at fair London towne."

"Now horses and serving-men thou shalt have,
With sumptuous array most gallant and brave;
With crozier, and miter, and rochet, and cope,
Fit to appeare 'fore our fader the pope."

"Now welcome, sire abbot," the king he did say,
" 'Tis well thou'rt come back to keepe thy day:
For and if thou canst answer my questions three,
Thy life and thy living both saved shall bee.

"And first, when thou see'st me here in this stead,
With my crown of golde so fair on my head,
Among all my liege-men so noble of birthe,
Tell me to one penny what I am worthe."

"For thirty pence our Saviour was sold
Among the false Jewes, as I have bin told:
And twenty-nine is the worth of thee,
For I thinke, thou art one penny worser than Hee."

The king he laugh'd, and swore by St. Bittel,
"I did not think I had been worth so littel!
—Now secondly, tell me, without any doubt,
How soone I may ride this whole world about."

"You must rise with the sun, and ride with the same,
Until the next morning he riseth againe;
And then your grace need not make any doubt,
But in twenty-four hours you'll ride it about."

The king he laugh'd, and swore by St. Jone,
"I did not think it could be done so soone!
—Now from the third question you must not shrinke,
But tell me here truly what I do thinke."

"Yes, that shall I do and make your grace merry:
You thinke I'm the Abbot of Canterburye;
But I'm his poor shephard, as plain you may see,
That am come to beg pardon for him and for mee."

The king he laughed, and swore by the masse,
"I'll make thee lord abbot this day in his place!"
"Now nay, my liege, be not in such speede,
For alacke I can neither write, ne reade."

"Four nobles a weeke, then, I will give thee,
For this merry jest thou hast showne unto me;
And tell the old abbot, when thou comest home,
Thou hast brought him a pardon from good King John."


## THE PRINCE AND THE PAUPER[1]

### Mark Twain

*Mark Twain said of his dramatic story of the two boys who
exchanged clothes and places—the one a young prince, the other
a ragged pauper—"it may be history; it may be only a legend. It
may have happened, it may not have happened; but it could have
happened."*

*It is not an easy story for playmaking, even though it is almost
in dramatic form as it stands. It needs a careful introduction into
the life of the time, with some historical background, and a knowl-*

[1] Published by Harper & Brothers.

*edge of the whole novel. But it is so dramatic and so thoroughly worth doing that it repays the most careful study.*

*The chapter entitled "Tom as King" tells of a striking incident which occurred on the pauper's fourth day in the palace. Late in the forenoon he was in a large audience chamber, conversing with the Earl of Hertford and dully awaiting the striking of the hour appointed for a visit of ceremony from a considerable number of great officials and courtiers.*

After a little while, Tom, who had wandered to a window and become interested in the life and movement of the great highway beyond the palace gates, saw the van of a hooting and shouting mob of disorderly men, women, and children of the lowest and poorest degree approaching from up the road.

"I would I knew what 'tis about!" he exclaimed, with all a boy's curiosity in such happenings.

"Thou art the King!" solemnly responded the earl, with a reverence. "Have I your Grace's leave to act?"

"Oh, blithely, yes! Oh, gladly, yes!" exclaimed Tom, excitedly, adding to himself with a lively sense of satisfaction, "in truth, being a king is not all dreariness—it hath its compensations and conveniences."

The earl called a page and sent him to the captain of the guard with the order:

"Let the mob be halted, and inquiry made concerning the occasion of its movement. By the King's command!"

A few seconds later a messenger returned, to report that the crowd was following a man, a woman, and a young girl to execution for crimes committed against the peace and dignity of the realm.

Death—and a violent death—for these poor unfortunates! The thought wrung Tom's heartstrings. The spirit of compassion took control of him, to the exclusion of all other considerations. He never thought of the offended laws or of the grief or loss which these three criminals had inflicted upon their victims; he could think of nothing but the scaffold and the grisly fate hanging over the heads of the condemned. His concern made him even forget, for the moment, that he was but the false shadow of a king, not the substance; and before he knew it he had blurted out the command:

"Bring them here!"

Then he blushed scarlet, and a sort of apology sprang to his lips, but observing that his order had wrought no sort of surprise in the earl or the waiting page, he suppressed the words he was about to utter. The page, in the most matter-of-course way, made a profound obeisance and retired backward out of the room to deliver the command. Tom experienced a glow of pride and a renewed sense of the compensating advantages of the kingly office.

In a little while the culprits entered the presence in charge of an undersheriff and escorted by a detail of the King's guard. The civil officer knelt before Tom, then stood aside. The three doomed persons knelt, also, and remained so; the guard took position behind Tom's chair. Tom scanned the prisoners curiously. Something about the dress or appearance of the man had stirred vague memory in him. "Methinks I have seen this man ere now . . . but the when or the where fail me"—such was Tom's thought. Just then the man glanced quickly up and quickly dropped his face again, not being able to endure the awful port of sovereignty; but the one full glimpse of the face, which Tom got, was sufficient. He said to himself: "Now is the matter clear; this is the stranger that plucked Giles Witt out of the Thames and saved his life, that windy, bitter, first day of the New Year—a brave, good deed—pity he hath been doing baser ones and got himself in this sad case . . . I have not forgot the day, neither the hour; by reason that an hour after, upon the stroke of eleven, I did get a hiding by the hand of Gammer Canty which was of so goodly and admired severity that all that went before or followed after it were but fondlings and caresses by comparison."

Tom now ordered that the woman and the girl be removed from the presence for a little time; then addressed himself to the under-sheriff, saying:

"Good sir, what is this man's offense?"

The officer knelt, and answered:

"So please your Majesty, he hath taken the life of a subject by poison."

Tom's compassion for the prisoner, and admiration of him as the daring rescuer of a drowning boy, experienced a most damaging shock.

"The thing was proved upon him?" he asked.

"Most clearly, sire."

Tom sighed and said:

"Take him away—he hath earned his death. 'Tis a pity, for he was a brave heart—nay—nay, I mean he hath the *look* of it!"

The prisoner clasped his hands together with sudden energy and wrung them despairingly, at the same time appealing imploringly to the "King" in broken and terrified phrases:

"O my Lord the King, an' thou canst pity the lost, have pity upon me! I am innocent—neither hath that wherewith I am charged been more than but lamely proved—yet I speak not of that. The judgment is gone forth against me and may not suffer alteration; yet in mine extremity I beg a boon, for my doom is more than I can bear. A grace, a grace, my Lord the King! In thy royal compassion grant my prayer—give commandment that I be hanged!"

Tom was amazed. This was not the outcome he had looked for.

"Odds my life, a strange *boon!* Was it not the fate intended thee?"

"O good my liege, not so! It is ordered that I be *boiled alive!*"

The hideous surprise of these words almost made Tom spring from his chair. As soon as he could recover his wits, he cried out:

"Have thy wish, poor soul! An' thou had poisoned a hundred men thou shouldst not suffer so miserable a death."

The prisoner bowed his face to the ground and burst into passionate expressions of gratitude, ending with:

"If ever thou shouldst know misfortune—which God forbid!—may thy goodness to me this day be remembered and requited!"

Tom turned to the Earl of Hertford and said:

"My lord, is it believable that there was warrant for this man's ferocious doom?"

"It is the law, your Grace—for poisoners."

"Oh, prithee, my Lord, let order be taken to change this law. Oh, let no more poor creatures be visited with its tortures."

The earl's face showed profound gratification, for he was a man of merciful and generous impulses—a thing not very common with his class in that fierce age. He said:

"These your Grace's noble words have sealed its doom. History will remember it to the honor of your royal house."

The undersheriff was about to remove his prisoner; Tom gave him a sign to wait; then he said:

"Good sir, I would look into this matter further. The man has said his deed was but lamely proved. Tell me what thou knowest."

"If the King's grace please, it did appear upon the trial that the man entered into a house in the hamlet of Islington where one lay sick—three witnesses say it was at ten of the clock in the morning and two say it was some minutes later, the sick man being alone at the time and sleeping—and presently the man came forth again and went his way. The sick man died within the hour, being torn with spasms and retchings."

"Did any see the poison given?  Was poison found?"

"Marry, no, my liege."

"Then how doth one know there was poison given at all?"

"Please your Majesty, the doctors testified that none die with such symptoms but by poison."

Weighty evidence, this, in that simple age.  Tom recognized its formidable nature and said:

"The doctor knoweth his trade—belike they were right.  The matter hath an ill look for this poor man."

"Yet was not this all, your Majesty; there is more and worse. Many testified that a witch, since gone from the village, none know whither, did foretell and speak it privately in their ears, that the sick man *would die by poison*—and more, that a stranger would give it—a stranger with brown hair and clothed in a worn and common garb.  Surely this prisoner doth answer woundily to the bill.  Please, your Majesty, to give the circumstance that solemn weight which is its due, seeing it was *foretold*."

This was an argument of tremendous force, in that superstitious day.  Tom felt that the thing was settled; if evidence was worth anything, this poor fellow's guilt was proved.  Still he offered the prisoner a chance, saying:

"If thou canst say aught in thy behalf, speak."

"Nought that will avail, my King.  I am innocent; yet cannot I make it appear.  I have no friends, else might I show that I was not in Islington that day; so also might I show that at that hour they name I was above a league away, seeing I was at Wapping Old Stairs.  Yea more, my King, for I could show, that whilst they say I was *taking* life, I was *saving* it.  A drowning boy—"

"Peace!  Sheriff, name the day the deed was done!"

"At ten in the morning, or some minutes later, the first day of the new year, most illustrious—"

"Let the prisoner go free—it is the King's will!"

Another blush followed this unregal outburst, and he covered his indecorum as well as he could by adding:

"It enrageth me that a man should be hanged upon such idle, harebrained evidence!"

A low buzz of admiration swept through the assemblage.  It was not admiration of the decree that had been delivered by Tom, for the propriety or expediency of pardoning a convicted poisoner was a thing which few there would have felt justified in either admitting or admiring; no, the admiration was for the intelligence and spirit which Tom had displayed. Some of the low-voiced remarks were to this effect:

"This is no mad King—he hath his wits sound."

"How sanely he put his question—how like his former natural self was this abrupt, imperious disposal of the matter!"

"God be thanked, his infirmity is spent! This is no weakling, but a king. He hath borne himself like to his own father."

The air being filled with applause, Tom's ear necessarily caught a little of it. The effect which this had upon him was to put him greatly at his ease and also to charge his system with very gratifying sensations.

However, his juvenile curiosity soon rose superior to these pleasant thoughts and feelings; he was eager to know what sort of deadly mischief the woman and the little girl could have been about, so, by his command the two terrified and sobbing creatures were brought before him.

"What is it that these have done?" he inquired of the sheriff.

"Please your Majesty, a black crime is charged upon them and clearly proved; wherefore the judges have decreed, according to the law, that they be hanged. They sold themselves to the devil—such is their crime."

Tom shuddered. He had been taught to abhor people who did this wicked thing. Still, he was not going to deny himself the pleasure of feeding his curiosity, for all that, so he asked:

"Where was this done?—and when?"

"On a midnight, in December—in a ruined church, your Majesty."

Tom shuddered again.

"Who was there present?"

"Only these two, your Grace—and *that other.*"

"Have these confessed?"

"Nay, not so, sire—they do deny it."

"Then prithee, how was it known?"

"Certain witnesses did see them wending thither, good your Majesty. This bred the suspicion, and dire effects have since confirmed and justified it. In particular, it is in evidence that through the wicked power so obtained, they did invoke and bring about a storm that wasted all the region round about. Above forty witnesses have proved the storm; and sooth one might have had a thousand, for all had reason to remember it, sith all had suffered by it."

"Certes, this is a serious matter." Tom turned this dark piece of scoundrelism over in his mind a while, then asked:

"Suffered the woman, also, by the storm?"

Several old heads among the assemblage nodded their recognition of the wisdom of this question. The sheriff, however, saw nothing consequential in the inquiry; he answered, with simple directness:

"Indeed, did she, your Majesty, and most righteously, as all aver. Her habitation was swept away, and herself and child left shelterless."

"Methinks the power to do herself so ill a turn was dearly bought. She had been cheated, had she paid but a farthing for it. That she paid her soul and her child's, argueth that she is mad. If she is mad she knoweth not what she doth, therefore sinneth not."

The elderly heads nodded recognition of Tom's wisdom once more, and one individual murmured, "An' the King be mad himself, according to report, then is it a madness of a sort that would improve the sanity of some I wot of, if by the gentle providence of God they could but catch it."

"What age hath the child?" asked Tom.

"Nine years, please your Majesty."

"By the law of England may a child enter into covenant and sell itself, my Lord?" asked Tom, turning to a learned judge.

"The law doth not permit a child to make or meddle in any weighty matter, good my liege, holding that its callow wit unfitteth it to cope with the riper wit and evil schemings of them that are its elders. The *devil* may buy a child, if he so choose, and the child agree thereto, but not an Englishman—in this latter case the contract would be null and void."

"It seemeth a rude, un-Christian thing, and ill contrived, that English law denieth privileges to Englishmen, to waste them on the devil!" cried Tom, with honest heat.

This novel view of the matter excited many smiles, and was stored away in many heads to be repeated about the court as evidence of Tom's originality as well as progress toward mental health.

The elder culprit had ceased from sobbing and was hanging upon Tom's words with an excited interest and a growing hope. Tom noticed this, and it strongly inclined his sympathies toward her in her perilous and unfriended situation. Presently he asked:

"How wrought they, to bring the storm?"

"*By pulling off their stockings, sire.*"

This astonished Tom and also fired his curiosity to fever heat. He said, eagerly:

"It is wonderful! Hath it always this dread effect?"

"Always my liege—at least if the woman desire it and utter the needful words, either in her mind or with her tongue."

Tom turned to the woman, and said with impetuous zeal:

"Exert thy power; I would see a storm!"

There was a sudden paling of cheeks in the superstitious assemblage and a general, though unexpressed, desire to get out of the place—all of which was lost upon Tom, who was dead to everything but the proposed cataclysm. Seeing a puzzled and astonished look in the woman's face, he added, excitedly:

"Never fear—thou shalt be blameless. More, thou shalt go free; none shall touch thee. Exert thy power."

"Oh, my lord the King, I have it not. I have been falsely accused."

"Thy fears stay thee. Be of good heart, thou shalt suffer no harm. Make a storm—it mattereth not how small a one—I require nought great or harmful, but indeed prefer the opposite. Do this and thy life is spared. Thou shalt go out free, with thy child, bearing the King's pardon and safe from hurt or malice from any in the realm."

The woman prostrated herself and protested, with tears, that she had no power to do the miracle, else she would gladly win her child's life alone, and be content to lose her own, if by obedience to the King's command so precious a grace might be acquired.

Tom urged; the woman still adhered to her declarations. Finally he said:

"I think the woman hath said true. An' my mother were in her place and gifted with the devil's functions, she had not stayed a moment to call her storms and lay the whole land in ruins, if the saving of my forfeit life were the price she got! It is argument that other mothers are made in like mold. Thou art free, good wife—thou and thy child—and I do think thee innocent. Now thou'st nought to fear, being pardoned—pull off thy stockings!—an' thou canst make me a storm, thou shalt be rich!"

The redeemed creature was loud in her gratitude and proceeded to obey, while Tom looked on with eager expectancy, a little marred by apprehension; the courtiers at the same time manifesting decided discomfort and uneasiness. The woman stripped her own feet and her little girl's also, and plainly did her best to reward the King's generosity with an earthquake, but it was all a failure and a disappointment. Tom sighed and said:

"There, good soul, trouble thyself no further; thy power is departed out of thee. Go thy way in peace; and if it return to thee at any time, forget me not, but fetch me a storm."

## THE SQUIRE'S BRIDE[1]

### Gudrun Thorne-Thomsen

*This comic story provides rich fun in the playing. Boys' camps and clubs especially enjoy it.*

There was once a very rich squire who owned a large farm, had plenty of silver at the bottom of his chest, and money in the bank besides; but there was something he had not, and that was a wife.

One day a neighbor's daughter was working for him in the hayfield. The squire liked her very much and, as she was a poor man's daughter, he thought that if he only mentioned marriage she would be more than glad to take him at once. So he said to her, "I've been thinking I want to marry."

"Well, one may think of many things," said the lassie, as she stood there and smiled slyly. She really thought the old fellow ought to be thinking of something that behooved him better than getting married at his time of life.

"Now, you see," he said, "I was thinking that you should be my wife!"

"No, thank you," said she, "and much obliged for the honor."

The squire was not used to being gainsaid, and the more she refused him the more he wanted her. But the lassie would not listen to him at all. So the old man sent for her father and told him that, if he could talk his daughter over and arrange the whole matter for him, he would forgive him the money he had lent him, and would give him the piece of land which lay close to his meadow into the bargain.

"Yes, yes, be sure I'll bring the lass to her senses," said the father. "She is only a child and does not know what is best for her."

But all his coaxing, all his threats and all his talking, went for naught. She would not have the old miser, if he sat buried in gold up to his ears, she said.

[1] From Gudrun Thorne-Thomsen's *East o' the Sun and West o' the Moon.* Reproduced by special permission of the publisher, Row, Peterson & Co.

The squire waited and waited, but at last he got angry and told the father that he had to settle the matter at once if he expected him to stand by his bargain, for now he would wait no longer.

The man knew no other way out of it but to let the squire get everything ready for the wedding; then, when the parson and the wedding guests had arrived, the squire would send for the lassie as if she were wanted for some work on the farm. When she got there they would marry her right away, in such a hurry that she would have no time to think it over.

When the guests had arrived the squire called one of his farm lads, told him to run down to his neighbor and ask him to send up immediately what he had promised.

"But if you are not back with her in a twinkling," he said, shaking his fist at him, "I'll—"

He did not finish, for the lad ran off as if he had been shot at.

"My master has sent me to ask for that which you promised him," said the lad, when he got to the neighbor, "but, pray, lose no time, for master is terribly busy to-day."

"Yes, yes! Run down in the meadow and take her with you—there she goes," answered the neighbor.

The lad ran off and when he came to the meadow he found the daughter there raking the hay.

"I am to fetch what your father has promised my master," said he lad.

"Ah, ha!" thought she, "is that what they are up to?" And with a wicked twinkle of the eye, she said, "Oh, yes, it's that little bay mare of ours, I suppose. You had better go and take her. She stands tethered on the outer side of the pea field."

The boy jumped on the back of the bay mare and rode home at full gallop.

"Have you got her with you?" asked the squire.

"She is down at the door," said the lad.

"Take her up to the room my mother had," said the squire.

"But, master, how can I?" said the lad.

"Do as I tell you," said the squire. "And if you can't manage her alone, get the men to help you," for he thought the lassie might be stubborn.

When the lad saw his master's face he knew it would be no use to argue. So he went and got all the farm hands together to help him. Some pulled at the head and the forelegs of the mare and

others pushed from behind, and at last they got her upstairs an●
into the room. There lay all the wedding finery ready.

"Well, that's done, master!" said the lad, while he wiped his w●
brow, "but it was the worst job I have ever done here on the farm

"Never mind, never mind, you shall not have done it for nothing
said his master, and he pulled a bright silver coin out of his pock●
and gave it to the lad. "Now send the women up to dress her."

"But, I say—master!——"

"None of your talk!" cried the squire. "Tell them to hold h●
while they dress her, and mind not to forget either wreath or crown

The lad ran into the kitchen:

"Listen, here, lasses," he called out, "you are to go upstairs ar
dress up the bay mare as a bride—I suppose master wants to pl●
a joke on his guests."

The women laughed and laughed, but ran upstairs and dress●
the bay mare in everything that was there. And then the l●
went and told his master that now she was all ready, with wrea●
and crown and all.

"Very well, bring her down. I will receive her at the door myself
said the squire.

There was a clatter and a thumping on the stairs, for that brid●
you know, had no silken slippers on.

When the door was opened and the squire's bride entered t●
room, you can imagine there was laughing and tittering and gri
ning enough.

And as for the squire, they say he never went courting again.


## THE QUEST OF THE HAMMER[1]

### Abbie Farwell Brown

*This rollicking Norse myth is wonderfully good material for
play. Following the story is a scenario showing the action whi
was planned for a creative play by a group of young people.*

One morning Thor the Thunderer awoke with a yawn, a●
stretching out his knotted arm, felt for his precious hammer, whi
he kept always under his pillow of clouds. But he started up wi

[1] Used by permission of *The Churchman.*

a roar of rage, so that all the palace trembled. The hammer was gone!

Now this was a very serious matter, for Thor was the protector of Asgard, and Miölnir, the magic hammer which the dwarf had made, was his mighty weapon, of which the enemies of the Aesir stood so much in dread that they dared not venture near. But if they should learn that Miölnir was gone, who could tell what danger might not threaten the palaces of heaven? Thor darted his flashing eye into every corner of Cloud Land in search of the hammer. He called his fair wife, Sif of the golden hair, to aid in the search, and his two lovely daughters, Thrude and Lora. They hunted and hunted; they turned Thrudheim upside down, and set the clouds to rolling wonderfully, as they peeped and pried behind and around and under each billowy mass. But Miölnir was not to be found. Certainly, some one had stolen it.

Thor's yellow beard quivered with rage, and his hair bristled on end like the golden rays of a star, while all his household trembled. "It is Loki again!" he cried. "I am sure Loki is at the bottom of this mischief!" For since the time when Thor had captured Loki for the dwarf Brock and had given him over to have his bragging lips sewed up, Loki had looked at him with evil eyes; and Thor knew that the red rascal hated him most of all the gods.

But this time Thor was mistaken. It was not Loki who had stolen the hammer,—he was too great a coward for that. And though he meant, before the end, to be revenged upon Thor, he was waiting until a safe chance should come, when Thor himself might stumble into danger, and Loki need only to help the evil by a malicious word or two; and this chance came later, as you shall hear in another tale.

Meanwhile Loki was on his best behavior, trying to appear very kind and obliging; so when Thor came rumbling and roaring up to him demanding, "What have you done with my hammer, you thief?" Loki looked surprised, but did not lose his temper nor answer rudely.

"Have you indeed missed your hammer, brother Thor?" he said, mumbling, for his mouth was still sore where Brock had sewed the stitches. "That is a pity; for if the giants hear of this, they will be coming to try their might against Asgard."

"Hush!" muttered Thor, grasping him by the shoulder with his iron fingers. "That is what I fear. But look you, Loki; I suspect your hand in the mischief. Come, confess."

Then Loki protested that he had nothing to do with so wicked a deed. "But," he added wheedlingly, "I think I can guess the thief; and because I love you, Thor, I will help you to find him."

"Humph!" growled Thor. "Much love you bear to me! However, you are a wise rascal, the nimblest wit of all the Aesir, and it is better to have you on my side than on the other, when giants are in the game. Tell me, then: who has robbed the Thunder-Lord of his bolt of power?"

Loki drew near and whispered in Thor's ear. "Look, how the storms rage and the winds howl in the world below. Some one is wielding your thunder-hammer all unskillfully. Can you not guess the thief? Who but Thrym, the mighty giant who has ever been your enemy and your imitator, and whose fingers have long itched to grasp the short handle of mighty Miölnir, that the world may name him Thunder-Lord instead of you. But look! What a tempest! The world will be shattered into fragments unless we soon get the hammer back."

Then Thor roared with rage. "I will seek this impudent Thrym!" he cried. "I will crush him into bits, and teach him to meddle with the weapon of the Aesir!"

"Softly, softly," said Loki, smiling maliciously. "He is a shrewd giant, and a mighty. Even you, great Thor, cannot go to him and pluck the hammer from his hand as one would slip the rattle from a baby's pink fist. Nay, you must use craft, Thor; and it is I who will teach you, if you will be patient."

Thor was a brave, blunt fellow, and he hated the ways of Loki, his lies and his deceit. He liked best the way of warriors,—the thundering charge, the flash of weapons, and the heavy blow; but without the hammer he could not fight the giants hand to hand. Loki's advice seemed wise, and he decided to leave the matter to the Red One.

Loki was now all eagerness, for he loved difficulties which would set his wit in play and bring other folk into danger. "Look, now," he said. "We must go to Freia and borrow her falcon dress. But you must ask; for she loves me so little that she would scarce listen to me."

So first they made their way to Folkvang, the house of maidens, where Freia dwelt, the loveliest of all in Asgard. She was fairer than fair, and sweeter than sweet, and the tears from her flower-eyes made the dew which blessed the earth-flowers night and morning. Of her Thor borrowed the magic dress of feathers in which Freia was wont to clothe herself and flit like a great beautiful bird all about the world. She was willing enough to lend it to Thor when he told her that by its aid he hoped to win back the hammer which he had lost; for she well knew the danger threatening herself and all the Aesir until Miölnir should be found.

"Now will I fetch the hammer for you," said Loki. So he put on the falcon plumage, and, spreading his brown wings, flapped away up, up, over the world, down, down, across the great ocean which lies beyond all things that men know. And he came to the dark country where there was no sunshine nor spring, but it was always dreary winter; where mountains were piled up like blocks of ice, and where great caverns yawned hungrily in blackness. And this was Jotunheim, the land of the Frost Giants.

And lo! when Loki came thereto he found Thrym the Giant King sitting outside his palace cave, playing with his dogs and horses. The dogs were as big as elephants, and the horses were as big as houses, but Thrym himself was as huge as a mountain; and Loki trembled, but he tried to seem brave.

"Good-day, Loki," said Thrym, with the terrible voice of which he was so proud, for he fancied it was as loud as Thor's. "How fares it, feathered one, with your little brothers, the Aesir, in Asgard halls? And how dare you venture alone in this guise to Giant Land?"

"It is an ill day in Asgard," sighed Loki, keeping his eye warily upon the giant, "and a stormy one in the world of men. I heard the winds howling and the storms rushing on the earth as I passed by. Some mighty one has stolen the hammer of our Thor. Is it you, Thrym, greatest of all giants,—greater than Thor himself?"

This the crafty one said to flatter Thrym, for Loki well knew the weakness of those who love to be thought greater than they are.

Then Thrym bridled and swelled with pride, and tried to put on the majesty and awe of noble Thor; but he only succeeded in becoming an ugly, puffy monster.

"Well, yes," he admitted. "I have the hammer that belonged to your little Thor; and now how much of a lord is he?"

"Alack!" sighed Loki again, "weak enough he is without his magic weapon. But you, O Thrym,—surely your mightiness needs no such aid. Give me the hammer, that Asgard may no longer be shaken by Thor's grief for his precious toy."

But Thrym was not so easily to be flattered into parting with his stolen treasure. He grinned a dreadful grin, several yards in width, so that his teeth looked like jagged boulders across the entrance of a mountain cavern.

"Miölnir the hammer is mine," he said, "and I am Thunder-Lord, mightiest of the mighty. I have hidden it where Thor can never find it, twelve leagues below the sea-caves, where Queen Ran lives with her daughters, the white-capped Waves. But listen, Loki. Go tell the Aesir that I will give back Thor's hammer. I will give it back upon one condition,—that they send Freia the beautiful to be my wife."

"Freia the beautiful!" Loki had to stifle a laugh. Fancy the Aesir giving their fairest flower to such an ugly fellow as this! But he only said politely, "Ah, yes; you demand our Freia in exchange for the little hammer? It is a costly price, great Thrym. But I will be your friend in Asgard. If I have my way, you shall soon see the fairest bride in all the world knocking at your door. Farewell!"

So Loki whizzed back to Asgard on his falcon wings; and as he went he chuckled to think of the evils which were likely to happen because of his words with Thrym. First he gave the message to Thor,—not sparing of Thrym's insolence, to make Thor angry, and then he went to Freia with the word for her,—not sparing of Thrym's ugliness, to make her shudder. The spiteful fellow!

Now you can imagine the horror that was in Asgard as the Aesir listened to Loki's words. "My hammer!" roared Thor. "The villain confesses that he has stolen my hammer, and boasts that he is Thunder-Lord! Gr-r-r!"

"The ugly giant!" wailed Freia. "Must I be the bride of that hideous old monster, and live in his gloomy mountain prison all my life?"

"Yes; put on your bridal veil, sweet Freia," said Loki maliciously, "and come with me to Jotunheim. Hang your famous starry necklace about your neck, and don your bravest robe; for in eight days there will be a wedding, and Thor's hammer is to pay."

Then Freia fell to weeping. "I cannot go! I will not go!" she cried. "I will not leave the home of gladness and Father Odin's table to dwell in the land of horrors! Thor's hammer is mighty, but mightier the love of the kind Aesir for their little Freia! Good Odin, dear brother Frey, speak for me! You will not make me go?"

The Aesir looked at her and thought how lonely and bare would Asgard be without her loveliness; for she was fairer than fair, and sweeter than sweet.

"She shall not go!" shouted Frey, putting his arms about his sister's neck.

"No, she shall not go!" cried all the Aesir with one voice.

"But my hammer," insisted Thor. "I must have Miölnir back again."

"And my word to Thrym," said Loki, "that must be made good."

"You are too generous with your words," said Father Odin sternly, for he knew his brother well. "Your word is not a gem of great price, for you have made it cheap."

Then spoke Heimdal, the sleepless watchman who sits on guard at the entrance to the rainbow bridge which leads to Asgard; and Heimdal was the wisest of the Aesir, for he could see into the future, and knew how things would come to pass. Through his golden teeth he spoke, for his teeth were all of gold.

"I have a plan," he said. "Let us dress Thor himself like a bride in Freia's robes, and send him to Jotunheim to talk with Thrym and to win back his hammer."

But at this word Thor grew very angry. "What! dress me like a girl!" he roared. "I should never hear the last of it! The Aesir will mock me, and call me 'maiden'! The giants, and even the puny dwarfs, will have a lasting jest upon me! I will not go! I will fight! I will die, if need be! But dressed as a woman I will not go!"

But Loki answered him with sharp words, for this was a scheme after his own heart. "What, Thor!" he said. "Would you lose your hammer and keep Asgard in danger for so small a whim? Look, now: if you go not, Thrym with his giants will come in a mighty army and drive us from Asgard; then he will indeed make Freia his bride, and moreover he will have you for his slave under the power of his hammer. How like you this picture, brother of the thunder? Nay, Heimdal's plan is a good one, and I myself will help to carry it out."

Still Thor hesitated; but Freia came and laid her white hand on his arm, and looked up into his scowling face pleadingly.

"To save me, Thor," she begged. And Thor said he would go.

Then there was great sport among the Aesir, while they dressed Thor like a beautiful maiden. Brunhilde and her sisters, the nine Valkyrie, daughters of Odin, had the task in hand. How they laughed as they brushed and curled his yellow hair, and set upon it the wondrous headdress of silk and pearls! They let out seams, and they let down hems, and set on extra pieces, to make it larger, and so they hid his great limbs and knotted arms under Freia's fairest robe of scarlet; but beneath it all he would wear his shirt of mail and his belt of power that gave him double strength. Freia herself twisted about his neck her famous necklace of starry jewels, and Queen Frigg, his mother, hung at his girdle a jingling bunch of keys, such as was the custom for the bride to wear at Norse weddings. Last of all, that Thrym might not see Thor's fierce eyes and yellow beard, that ill became a maiden, they threw over him a long veil of silver white which covered him to the feet. And there he stood, as stately and tall a bride as even a giant might wish to see; but on his hands he wore his iron gloves, and they ached for but one thing,—to grasp the handle of the stolen hammer.

"Ah, what a lovely maid it is!" chuckled Loki; "and how glad will Thrym be to see this Freia come! Bride Thor, I will go with you as your handmaiden, for I would fain to see the fun."

"Come, then," said Thor sulkily, for he was ill pleased, and wore his maiden robes with no good grace. "It is fitting that you go; for I like not these lies and maskings, and I may spoil the mummery without you at my elbow."

There was loud laughter above the clouds when Thor, all veiled and dainty seeming, drove away from Asgard to his wedding, with maid Loki by his side. Thor cracked his whip and chirruped fiercely to his twin goats with golden hoofs, for he wanted to escape the sounds of mirth that echoed from the rainbow bridge, where all the Aesir stood watching. Loki, sitting with his hands meekly folded like a girl, chuckled as he glanced up at Thor's angry face; but he said nothing, for he knew it was not good to joke too far with Thor, even when Miölnir was hidden twelve leagues below the sea in Ran's kingdom.

So off they dashed to Jotunheim, where Thrym was waiting and longing for his beautiful bride. Thor's goats thundered along the sea and land and people far below looked up wondering as the noise rolled overhead. "Hear how the thunder rumbles!" they said. "Thor is on a long journey to-night." And a long journey it was, as the tired goats found before they reached the end.

Thrym heard the sound of their approach, for his ear was eager. "Hola!" he cried. "Some one is coming from Asgard,—only one of Odin's children could make a din so fearful. Hasten, men, and see if they are bringing Freia to be my wife."

Then the lookout giant stepped down from the top of his mountain, and said that a chariot was bringing two maidens to the door.

"Run, giants, run!" shouted Thrym, in a fever at this news. "My bride is coming! Put silken cushions on the benches for a great banquet, and make the house beautiful for the fairest maid in all space! Bring in all my golden-horned cows and my coal-black oxen, that she may see how rich I am, and heap all my gold and jewels about to dazzle her sweet eyes! She shall find me richest of the rich; and when I have her,—fairest of the fair,—there will be no treasure that I lack,—not one!"

The chariot stopped at the gate, and out stepped the tall bride, hidden from head to foot, and her handmaiden muffled to the chin. "How afraid of catching cold they must be!" whispered the giant ladies, who were peering over one another's shoulders to catch a glimpse of the bride, just as the crowd outside the awning does at a wedding nowadays.

Thrym had sent six splendid servants to escort the maidens: these were the Metal Kings, who served him as lord of them all. There was the Gold King, all in cloth of gold, with fringes of yellow bullion, most glittering to see; and there was the Silver King, almost as gorgeous in a suit of spangled white; and side by side bowed the dark Kings of Iron and Lead, the one mighty in black, the other sullen in blue; and after them were the Copper King, gleaming ruddy and brave, and the Tin King, strutting in his trimmings of gaudy tinsel which looked nearly as well as silver but were more economical. And this fine troop of lackey kings most politely led Thor and Loki into the palace, and gave them of the best, for they never suspected who these seeming maidens really were.

And when evening came there was a wonderful banquet to celebrate the wedding. On a golden throne sat Thrym, uglier than ever in his finery of purple and gold. Beside him was the bride, of whose face no one had yet caught even a glimpse; and at Thrym's other hand stood Loki, the waiting-maid, for he wanted to be near to mend the mistakes which Thor might make.

Now the dishes at the feast were served in a huge way, as befitted the table of giants: great beeves roasted whole, on platters as wide across as a ship's deck; plum-puddings as fat as feather-beds, with plums as big as footballs; and a wedding cake like a snow-capped haymow. The giants ate enormously. But to Thor, because they thought him a dainty maiden, they served small bits of everything on a tiny gold dish. Now Thor's long journey had made him very hungry, and through his veil he whispered to Loki, "I shall starve, Loki! I cannot fare on these nibbles. I must eat a goodly meal as I do at home." And forthwith he helped himself to such morsels as might satisfy his hunger for a little time. You should have seen the giants stare at the meal which the dainty bride devoured!

For first under the silver veil disappeared by pieces a whole roast ox. Then Thor made eight mouthfuls of eight pink salmon, a dish of which he was very fond. And next he looked about and reached for a platter of cakes and sweetmeats that was set aside at one end of the table for the lady guests, and the bride ate them all. You can fancy how the damsels drew down their mouths and looked at one another when they saw their dessert disappear; and they whispered about the table, "Alack! if our future mistress is to sup like this day by day, there will be poor cheer for the rest of us!" And to crown it all, Thor was thirsty, as well he might be; and one after another he raised to his lips and emptied three great barrels of mead, the foamy drink of the giants. Then indeed Thrym was amazed, for Thor's great appetite had beaten that of the giants themselves.

"Never before saw I a bride so hungry," he cried, "and never before one half so thirsty!"

But Loki, the waiting-maid, whispered to him softly, "The truth is, great Thrym, that my dear mistress was almost starved. For eight days Freia has eaten nothing at all, so eager was she for Jotunheim."

Then Thrym was delighted, you may be sure. He forgave his hungry bride, and loved her with all his heart. He leaned forward to give her a kiss, raising a corner of her veil; but his hand dropped suddenly, and he started up in terror, for he had caught the angry flash of Thor's eye, which was glaring at him through the bridal veil. Thor was longing for his hammer.

"Why has Freia so sharp a look?" Thrym cried. "It pierces like lightning and burns like fire."

But once again the sly waiting-maid whispered timidly, "Oh Thrym, be not amazed! The truth is, my poor mistress's eyes are red with wakefulness and bright with longing. For eight nights Freia has not known a wink of sleep, so eager was she for Jotunheim."

Then again Thrym was doubly delighted, and he longed to call her his very own dear wife. "Bring in the wedding gift!" he cried. "Bring in Thor's hammer, Miölnir, and give it to Freia, as I promised; for when I have kept my word she will be mine,—all mine!"

Then Thor's big heart laughed under his woman's dress, and his fierce eyes swept eagerly down the hall to meet the servant who was bringing in the hammer on a velvet cushion. Thor's fingers could hardly wait to clutch the stubby handle which they knew so well; but he sat quite still on the throne beside ugly old Thrym, with his hands meekly folded and his head bowed like a bashful bride.

The giant servant drew nearer, nearer, puffing and blowing, strong though he was, beneath the mighty weight. He was about to lay it at Thor's feet (for he thought it so heavy that no maiden could lift it or hold it in her lap), when suddenly Thor's heart swelled, and he gave a most unmaidenly shout of rage and triumph. With one swoop he grasped the hammer in his iron fingers; with the other arm he tore off the veil that hid his terrible face, and trampled it under foot; then he turned to the frightened king, who cowered beside him on the throne.

"Thief!" he cried. "Freia sends you *this* as a wedding gift!" And he whirled the hammer about his head, then hurled it once, twice, thrice, as it rebounded to his hand; and in the first stroke, as of lightning, Thrym rolled dead from his throne; in the second stroke perished the whole giant household,—these ugly enemies of the Aesir; and in the third stroke the palace itself tumbled together and fell to the ground like a toppling play-house of blocks.

But Loki and Thor stood safely among the ruins, dressed in their tattered maiden robes, a quaint and curious sight; and Loki, full of mischief now as ever, burst out laughing.

"Oh, Thor! if you could see"—he began; but Thor held up his hammer and shook it gently as he said,—

"Look now, Loki: it was an excellent joke, and so far you have done well,—after your crafty fashion, which likes me not. But now I have my hammer again, and the joke is done. From you, nor from another, I brook no laughter at my expense. Henceforth, we will have no mention of this masquerade, nor of these rags which now I throw away. Do you hear, red laughter?"

And Loki heard, with a look of hate, and stifled his laughter as best he could; for it is not good to laugh at him who holds the hammer.

Not once after that was there mention in Asgard of the time Thor dressed him as a girl and won his bridal gift from Thrym the giant.

But Miölnir was safe once more in Asgard, and you and I know how it came there; so some one must have told. I wonder if red Loki whispered the tale to some outsider, after all? Perhaps it may be so, for now he knew how best to make Thor angry; and from that day when Thor forbade his laughing, Loki hated him with the mean little hatred of a mean little soul.

*This story is so full of dramatic action that it is easy to put it into play form. The scenario is included, to show, first: that even in a richly dramatic story one has to read between the lines in order to add many details—believable details; second, that in turning a story into a play, it is often necessary to bring the incidents which happen in several localities into one place in order to achieve more unity; and third, that some scenes that are effective in the reading need to be adapted to be suitable for playing.*

## SCENARIO PLANNED BY ONE GROUP OF YOUNG PEOPLE

### Scene 1

Before the play opens and for several seconds afterward, a faint sound of thunder in distance. Laughter of young girls. Thrude, one of Thor's daughters, runs in laughing, followed by her sister Lora. Thrude says, "I'll race you to the rainbow bridge!" Suddenly they stop, hearing thunder. Lora says it can't be, because father promised not to make a storm today.

Just then loud bellowings are heard off left. It is Thor, shouting, "It's gone, I tell you," et cetera. Sif asks him if he is sure it is not under his pillow. Thor comes stalking in, calling to his daughters to ask if they have seen it. They all look around among the clouds, sometimes thinking they have caught sight of it but finding it is only a shadow.

The girls tell Thor that they heard thunderings down below, and Thor jumps at once to the conclusion that Loki is at the bottom of the mischief—he must have stolen it because he has been looking for a chance to get even with Thor ever since Thor gave him up to Brock to have his bragging lips sewn up.

With this thought, he calls to Heimdal, guardian of the rainbow bridge, to ask if Loki has crossed it. Heimdal says he has not, but hearing what has happened, offers to go in search of Loki.

As he hurries off, louder thunder is heard, and Lora is frightened. Sif tries to comfort her. Just then Thrude sees Freia flying past in her falcon cloak, and calls, asking Freia if she has seen Loki. Freia enters, (appearing to fly in), and asks why they are all so worried.

316

Just then Heimdal returns with Loki in tow, and Thor accuses him of stealing the precious hammer. Loki is surprised, since he knows nothing about it, and protests in his usual smooth manner that he would not do such a thing because he loves Thor. Louder thunder bears out his innocence, and he says, "You see! I haven't your hammer!"

On being questioned further, he suggests that the thief is probably the giant, Thrym, for who else could wield it so powerfully as to stir up the mighty storm that is raging below? Thor at once declares that he will go down and crush Thrym to bits. He will teach him to meddle with the weapons of the gods!

Loki reminds Thor that he must use craft to get it. At which Thor, knowing that Loki has the nimblest wit in all Asgard, tells him that he must go to Thrym and try to outwit him.

Loki suggests that he will go in disguise, and whispers to Thor, asking him to persuade Freia to lend him her precious falcon cloak. This Thor does, and Freia willingly takes it off, asking Loki to be very careful, for if it were lost she could never fly about the world again.

As Loki leaves, he teases them by starting in the wrong direction. Thor calls, "Come back, you rascal! That's not the way to Joten-heim!" And Loki replies impudently, "Jotenheim? Oh, yes, I forgot." As he turns to fly off in the other direction, he calls back, "I'll give Thrym your love!"

### Scene II

The palace cave of Thrym, King of the Giants. Thrym is sprawled in a large chair with a cup in one hand and the hammer in the other, amusing himself by swinging the hammer and listening to the thunder. Sometimes he gives just a little swing, and it thunders only slightly. Again he swings it widely and there is a big clap.

He laughs as he boasts to a servant that he can swing it better than Thor ever could, and he insists on being addressed as "Thun-der-Lord Thrym." He calls for a map of the universe, and tries to choose a spot for the next storm. Not being able to make up his mind, he closes his eyes and starts encircling the map with his finger, saying,

"Round and round I go,
This (putting finger on map) is the spot where I'll thunder and blow."

He is pleased to find that his finger is on Asgard, and he is about to give the hammer a mighty swing when a second servant announces, "Queen Ran." The stately queen hurries in asking why Thrym has sent for her in such haste. Then seeing the hammer, she realizes what must have happened.

In the ensuing conversation, Thrym asks Ran to hide it twelve leagues below the sea caves until the gods no longer suspect him. She agrees, and they laugh at the fright of the puny folk on earth because of the storms Thrym is stirring up.

Just then a terrified servant bursts into the room, telling of a huge bat that is after him. Ran leaves quickly with the hammer and a moment later the bat-like shadow of Loki is seen flying about. Then, where the shadow settles, Loki appears and greets Thrym.

After the first shock of surprise, Thrym is relieved to see that it is only Loki, though he knows why Loki has come. He ridicules Loki's bird costume, and invites him to take it off and make a little visit. Loki refuses, but says he'd like a fire to dry the feathers, since he has been in a terrible storm. This leads him to make known that Thor's hammer has been stolen, and that Loki has come to see if Thrym has it.

Upon Thrym's ready admission that he has it, Loki tries to get him to agree to trade it for "something just as good." Or will he even *lend* it to Thor so that Thor can build a playhouse for the girls?

At that, Thrym jumps up and seizes Loki by the collar, shouting, "I'll teach you to make fun of the mighty Thrym!" Loki cries out to be careful, as this is Freia's falcon cloak! The mention of Freia puts a sudden thought into Thrym's head. With an ugly smile, he tells Loki to go back and tell the gods that he will give back Thor's hammer on condition that they send Freia to be his wife.

This is a staggering thought, even to Loki, but he flies off, promising to do his best, leaving Thrym gloating over his bargain.


Scene III

The same setting as Scene I. Thor, Sif, Thrude, Lora, Freia, and Heimdal, have supposedly been listening to Loki tell of Thrym's demand.

The scene opens with Thor declaring that the idea is preposterous, and Freia, weeping, exclaims that she can never be the bride of any ugly old giant. In the discussion which follows, they all

318

agree that Freia must not go, yet they realize that Asgard will be in danger if Thor does not get his hammer back.

Presently, Heimdal offers his plan. Suppose Thor disguises himself as a bride and goes to Jotenheim in Freia's place! At first, Thor indignantly refuses, but finally they persuade him that it is their only hope. Thereupon, Freia brings her scarlet robe, starry necklace, and silver veil, and Sif goes for sewing things, while Thrude, Lora, and Loki give Thor a lesson on how to walk like a woman.

Then the fun begins! The robe is much too small for Thor, and Sif, Freia, and the two girls have great sport letting out seams and ripping out the hem to make it fit. For Thor insists on wearing his shirt of mail and his belt of power underneath the robe. Last of all they throw over his head Freia's great silver veil, which is an effective disguise, and even Loki has to admit that Thor makes a handsome bride—for a giant!

In fact, Loki cannot resist the temptation to go along with Thor disguised as a handmaiden, so that he can see the fun. Quickly they dress him in a saffron robe of Sif's, and the two are off!

Scene IV

Same setting as Scene II. Now, however, a long table has been spread with food and large dishes of fruits. Three giantesses are putting the finishing touches to the table, and gossiping about the bride who is coming.

It is plain to be seen that they are jealous because Thrym is to marry a goddess instead of a giantess. They think Thrym is foolish to give back Thor's hammer for a scrawny goddess who probably does not even know how to cook.

Then Thrym enters in gorgeous wedding finery of purple and gold, and the talk suddenly stops. Thrym calls for the small dishes he ordered for Freia, the special chair and silken cushions. When a servant announces that a chariot drawn by goats can now be seen, bringing Freia and her handmaiden, he orders that the metal Kings be sent to escort them to the palace, and then calls for his slaves to bring in gold and jewels to dazzle his bride's eyes.

As all the giants take their places to greet Freia, an imposing procession (including four or more Metal Kings) enters with the bride and her handmaiden. Thrym greets "Freia," while the giantesses comment aside to each other on her large size, handsome robe, and thick veil.

From here on, the plan follows the story closely until Thor waves his hammer and destroys both the palace and the giants. This is a problem which the group solved by having Thor banish the giants to a place where they would never trouble the gods again (perhaps the bottom of the sea). Amid the darkness and noise, all of them disappear. This is admittedly less dramatic than having them fall dead, and the palace tumble to ruins, but it does keep the comedy uppermost.

## OUR LADY'S JUGGLER

### Retold from an Old Legend

*For groups with more than ordinary sensitivity, the playing of this legend can be a beautiful experience. The juggling should, of course, be with imaginary balls.*

Long, long ago there lived in France, a little juggler by the name of Jean Barnabas. Jean was known in every village between the Marne and the Loire, for always on fête days he would appear in his silken tunic of yellow and green stripes, with his scarlet cap perched jauntily over one eye, and give his show in the square.

"Look who is coming!" the children would shout in glee. "A juggler! A juggler!"

And the crowd would gather good-naturedly around the gay little fellow, eager to see the tricks and the tumbling and hear the jokes, without which no fête day would be complete.

First Jean would throw down the shabby rug that held his knives and hoops and balls, and sing some clever ditty until he had collected a large crowd around him. Then he would perform tricks and feats of skill until the sous would shower upon him.

But nowadays it was different. Of late it seemed always that the crowd would drift away while he was performing, so that only children and beggars were left when it came time to pass his hat. And more often than not he had to go hungry to bed.

Today it took all his courage to laugh boldly at the crowd and shout, "Hola! Come, all of you, to See Jean, King of the Jugglers!"

In years gone by the festival crowds had more than half believed his bold claim, but this time they only mocked at him.

"He looks like a king, doesn't he, with his rags and tatters! Are your tricks as old as your clothes?"

"I have new ballads to sing, my friends," Jean retorted. "I have dances you have never seen! And as for my tricks—wait and see!"

Jean picked up his six golden balls that were usually kept for the climax of his act. It was the trick of standing on his hands while, with his feet, he kept the six balls in the air at once. He would show them that he had not lost his skill! But though he started out bravely, he had grown so weak from hunger and weariness that he missed the fourth ball, and so spilled them all to the ground.

The crowd jeered openly, and some of them moved away saying, "Jean's getting too old to juggle." "Let's have a younger fellow." "Why, I could do better than that!"

"I'm sorry!" Jean called out. "I'm clumsy today. But I'll show you a new trick with my knives."

"Better not," warned a motherly soul who had not mocked him as the others had done.

"If he is going to throw knives around, it's time we were leaving," said a fat farmer. "I've no mind to have an ear sliced off!" And he moved away, laughing, with several of his cronies.

The little juggler stood motionless for a few seconds, and then burst into a rollicking song. But his voice was thin and weak, and after a few bars it was drowned out by a demand from the crowd to do tricks instead of singing.

He picked up his hoops and twirled them on a stick, but his arms were too weak to go on long, so he threw the hoops down, and gathering all his strength, began to do the funny old dance and song that had never failed to entertain the crowd. But scarcely had he taken a step, when his thin legs gave way, and he fell exhausted in a pathetic little heap on the ground.

In the confusion that followed, the good Brother Anselm, who was among the crowd that fête day, gathered the poor wizened little juggler into his arms.

"I will take him home," he said, "until he is able to be on his way." And he carried him across the square and gave him sanctuary in the abbey of Cluny.

Good food, a bed to sleep on, a warm habit to wear, and the kindly care of the monks, all helped Jean to gain back his strength. As the months passed, he grew to love more and more the peace of the quiet life and his daily tasks in the kitchen; the beauty of the music and of the singing; the tall white candles burning in the Chapel; and most of all, the lovely, compassionate face of the Virgin.

There was only one thing that kept him from being supremely happy. He confided his disturbing thoughts to Brother Anselm one day as they were preparing dinner.

"Everyone but me is making a gift for Our Lady," he said sadly. "One brother is fitting the last pieces into a stained-glass window for the chapel; another brother is making a beautiful illuminated manuscript; the musician-brother has composed a new Gloria. Everybody is preparing a gift for Our Lady's Day. And I, who love her so much, cannot write nor paint nor make music. I can do nothing!"

Brother Anselm laughed at the earnest little juggler. "We cannot all make beautiful things," he said, "but we can all serve in our own way. And I think that in the eyes of Our Lady all service is acceptable, whether it is carving a wonderful statue of Her Son—or making cabbage soup."

Jean pondered long on what the brother had said. What could he do to serve Her, to show Her how much he cared? She seemed so sad! If only he knew how to please Her, how to make Her smile! A thought came to him at times, but he put it aside as unworthy. And yet—"to Our Lady all service is acceptable," Brother Anselm had said.

One night a monk, passing the chapel on his way to the refectory, was startled by unfamiliar sounds which seemed to come from the altar. He looked in, and by the light of the candles, saw a strange sight. Spread out before the Virgin was the juggler's shabby rug, with all his store of knives and balls and hoops upon it. And there, tossing his shining knives in the air, stood Jean in his tattered green and yellow suit, his face alight with joy and consecration.

The horrified monk hurried to the refectory to call the abbot. A few moments later a group of the brothers were standing in the doorway, scarcely able to believe what they saw. For now Jean was doing the finest trick that he knew—standing on his hands and, with his feet, keeping six golden balls in the air at once. So intent was he on making his masterpiece perfect for Our Lady that he was not conscious of the gasps of horror that came from the gathering crowd in the shadow.

"It is desecration!" muttered the abbot. And he raised his hand to call down the wrath of Heaven upon the blasphemy—when something happened.

As the little juggler sprang to his feet and turned eagerly to the Virgin, hoping that his gift was acceptable to Her, the monks in the doorway saw Her bend toward Jean as if in benediction! And as they fell to their knees in silent wonder, they saw Her smile upon him.

## THE BISHOP'S CANDLESTICKS[1]

### Victor Hugo

*Only older groups of more than usual ability and sensitivity should attempt to dramatize this beautiful story from one of the greatest of all novels. But for such a group, with a teacher who has read and appreciated the complete story, it can be an experience which they will never forget.*

*LES MISERABLES tells the story of Jean Valjean, a French peasant who had once stolen a loaf of bread for his sister's starving children. He had been sentenced to the galleys for five years, which time had been increased for repeated attempts to escape until he had served nineteen years.*

*At last he had been set free; and four days later something happened that changed his whole life.*

*The scene is the small house the bishop chose to live in rather than in the bishop's palace, which he had turned over for use as a hospital. The time is 1815.*

As the bishop entered the dining-room Mme. Magloire, the old servant, had just finished setting the table for supper. She was talking with some warmth to Mdlle. Baptistine, the bishop's sister, about the need for a lock for the front door. It seems that while she had been out making provision for supper, she had heard talk about a suspicious vagabond who was lurking somewhere in the town. It was said that some unpleasant adventures might befall those who came home late that night; and that everyone ought to be careful to bolt his door most carefully.

"We are not safe at all," said Mme. Magloire, "for nothing could be more horrible than a door which opens by a latch on the outside. And monseigneur has the habit of always saying: 'Come in,' even at midnight."

At this moment there was a violent knock on the door.

"Come in," said the bishop.

The door opened.

**Adapted from *Les Miserables*.**

A man entered. He was a man of middle height, strong and hardy; he might have been forty-six or forty-seven years old. A slouched leather cap half hid his face, bronzed by the sun and wind. He wore a coarse yellow shirt open at the neck; shabby blue trousers, white on one knee, and with holes in the other; an old ragged gray blouse patched on one side with a piece of green cloth sewed with twine; upon his back was a well-filled knapsack, strongly buckled and quite new. In his hand he carried an enormous knotted stick; his stockingless feet were in hobnailed shoes; his hair was shorn but bristly, for it seemingly had not been cut for some time.

He came in, took one step, and paused, leaving the door open behind him. There was a rough, hard, tired, and fierce look in his eyes, as seen by the firelight. He was hideous.

Mme. Magloire had not even the strength to scream. She stood trembling, with her mouth open.

Mdlle. Baptistine turned, saw the man enter, and started out half alarmed; then slowly turning back again toward the fire, she looked at her brother, and her face resumed its usual calmness and serenity.

The bishop looked upon the man with a tranquil eye.

As he was opening his mouth to speak, doubtless to ask the stranger what he wanted, the man, leaning with both hands upon his club, glanced from one to another in turn, and without waiting for the bishop to speak, said in a loud voice:

"See here! My name is Jean Valjean. I am a convict; I have been nineteen years in the galleys. Four days ago I was set free; today I have walked twelve leagues. When I reached this place this evening I went to an inn, and they sent me away on account of my yellow passport. I went to another inn; they said: 'Get out!' I went to the prison and the turnkey would not let me in. In the square I laid down upon a stone; a good woman showed me your house, and said: 'Knock there!' I have knocked. What is this place? Is it an inn? I have money; my savings, 109 francs and 15 sous, which I have earned in the galleys by my work for nineteen years. I will pay. I am very tired—and I am so hungry. Can I stay?"

"Mme. Magloire," said the bishop, "put on another plate."

The man stepped forward. "Stop," he exclaimed, as if he had not been understood. "I am a galley slave—a convict—I am just from the galleys." He drew from his pocket a large sheet of yellow paper, which he unfolded. "This is my passport, yellow, as you see. That is enough to have me kicked out wherever I go. It says, 'This man is very dangerous.' There you have it. Everybody has thrust me out; will you receive me? Can you give me something to eat? Have you a stable where I can sleep?"

"Mme. Magloire," said the bishop, "put some sheets on the bed in the alcove." Then he turned to the man. "Monsieur, sit down and warm yourself; we are going to take supper presently, and your bed will be made ready while you sup."

At last the man understood; his face, the expression of which till then had been gloomy and hard, now expressed stupefaction, doubt and joy, and became absolutely wonderful. He began to stutter like a madman.

"What? You will keep me? You won't drive me away—a convict? You call me 'monsieur' and don't say, 'Get out, dog!' as everybody else does. I shall have a supper! a bed like other people, with mattress and sheets—a bed! It is nineteen years since I have slept on a bed. I will pay well. I beg your pardon, Mr. Innkeeper, what is your name? You are an innkeeper, ain't you?"

"I am a priest who lives here."

"A priest," said the man. "How stupid I am. I didn't notice your cap."

While speaking he had deposited his knapsack and stick in the corner, replaced his passport in his pocket and sat down.

Mme. brought in a plate and set it on the table.

"Mme. Magloire," said the bishop, "put this plate as near the fire as you can." Then turning toward his guest he added: "The night wind is raw in the Alps; you must be cold, monsieur."

Every time he said the word 'monsieur' with his gently solemn and heartily hospitable voice the man's countenance lighted up. 'Monsieur' to a convict is a glass of water to a man dying of thirst at sea.

"The lamp," said the bishop, "gives a very poor light."

Mme. Magloire understood him, and going to his bedchamber, took from the mantel the two silver candlesticks, lighted the candles and placed them on the table.

"Monsieur, you are good; you don't despise me. You take me into your house; you light your candles for me, and I haven't hid from you where I come from."

The bishop touched his hand gently and said: "You need not tell me who you are. This is not my house; it is the house of Christ.

It does not ask any comer whether he has a name, but whether he has an affliction. You are suffering; you are hungry and thirsty; be welcome. Whatever is here is yours. What need have I to know your name? Besides, before you told me, I knew it."

The man opened his eyes in astonishment. "You knew my name?"

"Yes," answered the bishop, "your name is my brother."

Meantime Mme. Magloire had served up supper. It consisted of soup, a little pork, a scrap of mutton, a few figs, a green cheese, and a large loaf of rye bread. And she had added without asking a bottle of fine old wine.

"To supper!" said the bishop briskly. When they were seated, he asked the blessing and then served the soup. Suddenly he said: "It seems to me something is lacking on the table."

Mme. Magloire understood the remark; without a word she went out, and a moment afterward returned with the three extra silver plates which they always had on the table when there were guests.

The man ate with the voracity of a starving man, paying no attention to anyone. Meanwhile the bishop chatted pleasantly of Pontarlier, to which place Jean Valjean said he must be on his way by daybreak. He told of the many paper-mills, tanneries, and iron foundries there, saying that during the revolution, when his family was ruined, he himself had worked there. Without giving the stranger any advice, he let him know where there was a place that he could stay, and where he was sure to find work. Never once did he bring into the conversation any sermonizing or advice.

Immediately after the dessert, the bishop said: "You must be in great need of sleep." And bidding goodnight to his sister, he took one of the silver candlesticks from the table, handed the other to his guest, and said to him:

"Monsieur, I will show you to your room."

To reach the alcove where Jean Valjean was to sleep, they had to pass through the bishop's sleeping-chamber. As they went through this room, Mme. Magloire was just putting up the silver in the cupboard at the head of the bed. The bishop left his guest in the alcove before a clean, white bed. The man set down the candlestick upon a small table.

"A good night's rest to you," said the bishop. "Tomorrow morning before you go, you shall have a cup of warm milk from our cows."

"Thank you, monsieur," said the man. A moment afterward, so completely exhausted was he that after blowing out the candle, he fell on the bed, dressed as he was, into a sound sleep.

As the cathedral clock struck two, Jean Valjean awoke.

He had slept only four hours, but he could not get to sleep again. Many thoughts came to him, but there was one which continually presented itself, and which drove away all others. He had noticed the six silver plates and the large ladle that Mme. Magloire placed in the cupboard at the head of the bishop's bed. They were solid, and old silver. With that big ladle they would bring at least 200 francs; double what he had got for nineteen years' labor.

His mind wavered a whole hour, in fluctuation and in struggle. The clock struck three. He opened his eyes, got up hastily in bed, and put his feet on the floor. All at once he stooped down and took off his shoes. Then he rose to his feet, hesitated for a moment longer, and listened. He placed his belongings near the window, and with stealthy steps moved toward the door of the bishop's room. On reaching it he found that it was unlatched. He pushed it a little, then more boldly. This time a rusty hinge sent out into the darkness a harsh creak. For a moment he thought he was lost. But minutes passed and he ventured to look into the room. The bishop had not stirred.

A deep calm filled the chamber. As Jean Valjean paused before the bed, suddenly the dark clouds parted, and a ray of moonlight, crossing the window, lighted up the bishop's face. The effect was startling. The expression of content, hope and happiness on his countenance became radiant, and he appeared as if in a halo.

Jean Valjean standing in the shadow, erect, motionless, was terrified. He had never seen anything comparable to it. He did not remove his eyes from the old man. One would have said he was hesitating between two realms—that of the doomed and that of the saved.

In a few moments he raised his left hand slowly to his forehead and took off his cap. He stood for some time looking at the sleeping bishop. Then suddenly he put on his cap, passed quickly to the cupboard, turned the key, opened it, took the basket of silver, passed quickly to the window in the alcove, stepped out, ran across the garden, leaped over the wall like a tiger and fled.

The next day at sunrise, as the bishop was walking in the garden, Mme. Magloire came running, quite beside herself, to tell him that the silver was stolen, the man was gone! The bishop was silent for a moment, then, raising his serious eyes, he said mildly:

"Mme. Magloire; I have for a long time wrongfully withheld this silver; it belonged to the poor. Who was this man? A poor man evidently."

A short time later the bishop and his sister were having breakfast when there was a knock at the door.

"Come in," said the bishop.

The door opened. A strange, fierce group appeared on the threshold. Three men were holding a fourth by the collar. The three were gendarmes; the fourth, Jean Valjean. One of them stepped forward and saluted the bishop.

"Monseigneur," said he.

The bishop rose and approached as quickly as his great age permitted. "Ah, there you are," he said, looking toward Jean Valjean. "I am glad to see you. But I gave you the candlesticks also, which are silver like the rest, and would bring 200 francs. Why did you not take them along with your plates?"

Jean Valjean opened his eyes and looked at the bishop with an expression which no human tongue could describe.

"Monseigneur," said the gendarme, "then what this man said was true? We met him. He was going like a man who was running away and we arrested him in order to see. He had this silver."

"And he told you," interrupted the bishop, with a smile, "that it had been given him by a good old priest with whom he had passed the night. I see it all. And you brought him back here? it is all a mistake."

"If that is so," said the gendarme, "we can let him go."

"Certainly," replied the bishop.

The gendarmes released Jean Valjean, who shrank back. "You can go. Do you not understand?" said one of them.

"My friend," said the bishop, "before you go away here are your candlesticks; take them." He went to the mantelpiece, took the two candlesticks and brought them to Jean Valjean who was trembling in every limb. He received the two candlesticks mechanically.

"Now," said the bishop, "go in peace." To the gendarmes he said: "Messieurs, you can retire." The gendarmes withdrew.

Jean Valjean felt like a man who is about to faint.

The bishop approached him and said in a low voice: "Forget

not, never forget that you have promised me to use this silver to become an honest man."

Jean Valjean, who had no recollection of this promise, stood confused. The bishop had laid much stress upon these words as he uttered them. He continued solemnly:

"Jean Valjean, my brother, you belong no longer to evil, but to good. It is your soul that I am buying for you. I withdraw it from dark thoughts and from the spirit of perdition and I give it to God."

## A CHRISTMAS CAROL[1]

### Charles Dickens

*Charles Dickens' great ghost story of Christmas holds intense interest for boys and girls, and almost every child from ten to fourteen enjoys dramatizing it. If a creative play based on the story is to be given for an audience, the complete plot is, of course, necessary. But for class use the two scenes given here are favorites.*

#### THE COUNTING-HOUSE SCENE

Marley was dead: to begin with. There is no doubt whatever about that. The register of his burial was signed by the clergyman, the clerk, the undertaker, and the chief mourner. Scrooge signed it: and Scrooge's name was good upon 'Change, for anything he chose to put his hand to. Old Marley was as dead as a door-nail. . . .

Scrooge never painted out Old Marley's name. There it stood, years afterwards, above the warehouse door: Scrooge and Marley. The firm was known as Scrooge and Marley. Sometimes people new to the business called Scrooge Scrooge, and sometimes Marley, but he answered to both names: it was all the same to him.

Oh! But he was a tight-fisted hand at the grindstone, Scrooge! a squeezing, wrenching, grasping, scraping, clutching, covetous old sinner! Hard and sharp as flint, from which no steel had ever struck out generous fire; secret, and self-contained, and solitary as an oyster. The cold within him froze his old features, nipped his pointed nose, shrivelled his cheek, stiffened his gait; made his eyes red, his thin lips blue; and spoke out shrewdly in his grating voice. He carried his own low temperature always about with

[1] Abridged.

him; he iced his office in the dogdays; and didn't thaw it one degree at Christmas.

External heat and cold had little influence on Scrooge. No warmth could warm, nor wintry weather chill him. No wind that blew was bitterer than he, no falling snow was more intent upon its purpose, no pelting rain less open to entreaty. Foul weather didn't know where to have him. The heaviest rain, and snow, and hail, and sleet, could boast of the advantage over him in only one respect. They often "came down" handsomely, and Scrooge never did.

Nobody ever stopped him in the street to say, with gladsome looks, "My dear Scrooge, how are you? when will you come to see me?" No beggars implored him to bestow a trifle, no children asked him what it was o'clock, no man or woman ever once in all his life inquired the way to such and such a place, of Scrooge. Even the blindmen's dogs appeared to know him; and when they saw him coming on, would tug their owners into doorways and up courts; and then would wag their tails as though they said, "no eye at all is better than an evil eye, dark master!"

But what did Scrooge care? It was the very thing he liked. To edge his way along the crowded paths of life, warning all human sympathy to keep its distance, was what the knowing ones call "nuts" to Scrooge.

Once upon a time—of all the good days in the year, on Christmas Eve—old Scrooge sat busy in his counting-house. It was cold, bleak, biting weather: foggy withal: and he could hear the people in the court outside go wheezing up and down, beating their hands upon their breasts, and stamping their feet upon the pavement-stones to warm them. The city clocks had only just gone three, but it was quite dark already: it had not been light all day: and candles were flaring in the windows of the neighboring offices, like ruddy smears upon the palpable brown air. The fog came pouring in at every chink and keyhole, and was so dense without, that although the court was of the narrowest, the houses opposite were mere phantoms. To see the dingy cloud come drooping down, obscuring everything, one might have thought that Nature lived hard by, and was brewing on a large scale.

The door of Scrooge's counting-house was open that he might keep his eye upon his clerk, who in a dismal little cell beyond, a sort of tank, was copying letters. Scrooge had a very small fire, but the clerk's fire was so very much smaller that it looked like one coal. But he couldn't replenish it, for Scrooge kept the coal-box in his own room; and so surely as the clerk came in with the shovel, the master predicted that it would be necessary for them to part. Wherefore the clerk put on his white comforter, and tried to warm himself at the candle; in which effort, not being a man of a strong imagination, he failed.

"A merry Christmas, uncle! God save you!" cried a cheerful voice. It was the voice of Scrooge's nephew, who came upon him so quickly that this was the first intimation he had of his approach.

"Bah!" said Scrooge, "Humbug!" . . . .

"Christmas a humbug, uncle!" said Scrooge's nephew. "You don't mean that, I am sure."

"I do," said Scrooge. "Merry Christmas! what right have you to be merry? what reason have you to be merry? You're poor enough."

"Come, then," returned the nephew gaily. "What right have you to be dismal? what reason have you to be morose? You're rich enough."

Scrooge having no better answer ready on the spur of the moment, said, "Bah!" again; and followed it up with "Humbug."

"Don't be cross, uncle," said the nephew.

"What else can I be" returned the uncle, "When I live in such a world of fools as this? Merry Christmas! Out upon merry Christmas! What's Christmas time to you but a time for paying bills without money; a time for finding yourself a year older, and not an hour richer; a time for balancing your books and having every item in 'em through a round dozen of months presented dead against you? If I could work my will," said Scrooge, indignantly, "every idiot who goes about with 'Merry Christmas,' on his lips, should be boiled with his own pudding, and buried with a stake of holly through his heart. He should!"

"Uncle!" pleaded the nephew.

"Nephew!" returned the uncle, sternly, "keep Christmas in your own way, and let me keep it in mine."

"Keep it!" repeated Scrooge's nephew. "But you don't keep it."

"Let me leave it alone, then," said Scrooge. "Much good may it do you! Much good it has ever done you!"

"There are many things from which I might have derived good, by which I have not profited, I dare say," returned the nephew: "Christmas among the rest. But I am sure I have always thought of Christmas time, when it has come round—apart from the veneration due to its sacred name and origin, if anything belonging to it can be apart from that—as a good time: a kind, forgiving, charitable, pleasant time: the only time I know of, in the long calendar of the year, when men and women seem by one consent to open their shut-up hearts freely, and to think of people below them as if they really were fellow-passengers to the grave, and not another race of creatures bound on other journeys. And therefore, uncle, though it has never put a scrap of gold or silver in my pocket, I believe that it has done me good, and will do me good; and I say, God bless it!"

The clerk in the tank involuntarily applauded: becoming immediately sensible of the impropriety, he poked the fire, and extinguished the last frail spark for ever.

"Let me hear another sound from you" said Scrooge, "and you'll keep your Christmas by losing your situation. You're quite a powerful speaker, sir," he added, turning to his nephew. "I wonder you don't go into Parliament."

"Don't be angry, uncle. Come! Dine with us to-morrow."

Scrooge said that he would see him—yes, indeed he did. He went the whole length of the expression, and said that he would see him in that extremity first.

"But why?" cried Scrooge's nephew. "Why?"

"Why did you get married?" said Scrooge.

"Because I fell in love."

"Because you fell in love!" growled Scrooge, as if that were the only one thing in the world more ridiculous than a merry Christmas. "Good afternoon!"

"Nay, uncle, but you never came to see me before that happened. Why give it as a reason for not coming now?"

"Good afternoon," said Scrooge.

"I want nothing from you; I ask nothing of you; why cannot we be friends?"

"Good afternoon," said Scrooge.

"I am sorry, with all my heart, to find you so resolute. We have never had any quarrel, to which I have been a party. But I have made the trial in homage to Chrismas, and I'll keep my Christmas humour to the last. So A Merry Christmas, uncle!"

"Good afternoon!" said Scrooge.

"And A Happy New Year!"

"Good afternoon!" said Scrooge.

His nephew left the room without an angry word, notwithstanding. He stopped at the outer door to bestow the greetings of the season on the clerk, who, cold as he was, was warmer than Scrooge; for he returned them cordially.

"There's another fellow," muttered Scrooge; who overheard him: "my clerk, with fifteen shillings a week, and a wife and family, talking about a merry Christmas. I'll retire to Bedlam."

This lunatic, in letting Scrooge's nephew out, had let two other people in. They were portly gentlemen, pleasant to behold, and now stood, with their hats off, in Scrooge's office. They had books and papers in their hands, and bowed to him.

"Scrooge and Marley's, I believe," said one of the gentlemen, referring to his list. "Have I the pleasure of addressing Mr. Scrooge, or Mr. Marley?"

"Mr. Marley has been dead these seven years," Scrooge replied. "He died seven years ago, this very night."

"We have no doubt his liberality is well represented by his surviving partner," said the gentleman, presenting his credentials.

It certainly was; for they had been two kindred spirits. At the ominous word "liberality," Scrooge frowned, and shook his head, and handed the credentials back.

"At this festive season of the year, Mr. Scrooge," said the gentleman, taking up a pen, "it is more than usually desirable that we should make some slight provision for the poor and destitute, who suffer greatly at the present time. Many thousands are in want of common necessaries; hundreds of thousands are in want of common comforts, sir."

"Are there no prisons?" asked Scrooge.

"Plenty of prisons," returned the gentleman, laying down the pen again.

"And the Union workhouses?" demanded Scrooge. "Are they still in operation?"

"They are. Still," returned the gentleman, "I wish I could say they were not."

"The Treadmill and the Poor Law are in full vigour, then?" said Scrooge.

"Both very busy, sir."

"Oh! I was afraid, from what you said at first, that something had occurred to stop them in their useful course," said Scrooge. "I'm very glad to hear it."

"Under the impression that they scarcely furnish Christian cheer of mind or body to the multitude," returned the gentleman, "a few of us are endeavouring to raise a fund to buy the Poor some meat and drink, and means of warmth. We choose this time, because it is a time, of all others, when Want is keenly felt, and Abundance rejoices. What shall I put you down for?"

"Nothing!" Scrooge replied.

"You wish to be anonymous?"

"I wish to be left alone," said Scrooge. "Since you ask me what I wish, gentleman, that is my answer. I don't make merry myself at Christmas, and I can't afford to make idle people merry. I help to support the establishments I have mentioned: they cost enough: and those who are badly off must go there."

"Many can't go there; and many would rather die."

"If they would rather die," said Scrooge, "they had better do it, and decrease the surplus population. Besides—excuse me—I don't know that."

"But you might know it," observed the gentleman.

"It's not my business," Scrooge returned. "It's enough for a man to understand his own business, and not to interfere with other people's. Mine occupies me constantly. Good afternoon, gentlemen!"

Seeing clearly that it would be useless to pursue their point, the gentlemen withdrew. Scrooge resumed his labours with an improved opinion of himself, and in a more facetious temper than was usual with him. . . .

Just then a boy passing by the office stooped and sang through the keyhole:

"God bless you merry gentlemen!
May nothing you dismay!"

Scrooge seized the ruler with such energy of action, that the singer fled in terror, leaving the keyhole to the fog and even more congenial frost.

At length the hour of shutting up the counting-house arrived. With an ill-will Scrooge dismounted from his stool, and tacitly admitted the fact to the expectant clerk in the Tank, who instantly snuffed his candle out, and put on his hat.

"You'll want all day to-morrow, I suppose?" said Scrooge.

"If quite convenient, Sir."

"It's not convenient," said Scrooge, "and it's not fair. If I was to stop half-a-crown for it, you'd think yourself ill used, I'll be bound?"

The clerk smiled faintly.

"And yet," said Scrooge, "you don't think me ill-used, when I pay a day's wages for no work."

The clerk observed that it was only once a year.

"A poor excuse for picking a man's pocket every twenty-fifth of

December!" said Scrooge, buttoning his great-coat to the chin. "But I suppose you must have the whole day. Be here all the earlier next morning!"

The clerk promised that he would; and Scrooge walked out with a growl. The office was closed in a twinkling, and the clerk, with the long ends of his white comforter dangling below his waist (for he boasted no great-coat), went down a slide on Cornhill, at the end of a lane of boys, twenty times, in honour of its being Christmas-eve, and then ran home to Camden Town as hard as he could pelt, to play at blindman's-buff.

### THE CRATCHIT SCENE

*When the Ghost of Christmas Present conducted Scrooge to Bob Cratchit's home, he stopped on the threshold to bless the humble dwelling with the sprinklings of his torch.*

Then up rose Mrs. Cratchit, Cratchit's wife, dressed out but poorly in a twice-turned gown, but brave in ribbons, which are cheap and make a goodly show for sixpence; and she laid the cloth, assisted by Belinda Cratchit, second of her daughters, also brave in ribbons; while Master Peter Cratchit plunged a fork into the saucepan of potatoes, and getting the corners of his monstrous shirt-collar (Bob's private property, conferred upon his son and heir in honour of the day) into his mouth, rejoiced to find himself so gallantly attired, and yearned to show his linen in the fashionable parks. And now two smaller Cratchits, boy and girl, came tearing in, screaming that outside the baker's they had smelt the goose, and known it for their own; and basking in luxurious thoughts of sage-and-onion, these young Cratchits danced about the table, and exalted Master Peter Cratchit to the skies, while he (not proud, although his collar nearly choked him) blew the fire, until the slow potatoes bubbling up, knocked loudly at the saucepan-lid to be let out and peeled.

"What has ever got your precious father then," said Mrs. Cratchit. "And your brother, Tiny Tim; and Martha warn't as late last Christmas Day by half-an-hour!"

"Here's Martha, mother!" said a girl, appearing as she spoke.

"Here's Martha, mother!" cried the two young Cratchits. "Hurrah! There's *such* a goose, Martha!"

"Why, bless your heart alive, my dear, how late you are!" said

Mrs. Cratchit, kissing her a dozen times, and taking off her shawl and bonnet for her, with officious zeal.

"We'd a deal of work to finish up last night," replied the girl, "and had to clear away this morning, mother!"

"Well! Never mind so long as you are come," said Mrs. Cratchit. "Sit ye down before the fire, my dear, and have a warm, Lord bless ye!"

"No no! There's father coming," cried the two young Cratchits, who were everywhere at once. "Hide Martha, hide!"

So Martha hid herself, and in came little Bob, the father, with at least three feet of comforter exclusive of the fringe, hanging down before him; and his thread-bare clothes darned up and brushed, to look seasonable; and Tiny Tim upon his shoulder. Alas for Tiny Tim, he bore a little crutch, and had his limbs supported by an iron frame!

"Why, where's our Martha?" cried Bob Cratchit looking round

"Not coming," said Mrs. Cratchit.

"Not coming!" said Bob, with a sudden declension in his high spirits; for he had been Tim's blood horse all the way from church, and had come home rampant. "Not coming upon Christmas Day!"

Martha didn't like to see him disappointed, if it were only in a joke; so she came out prematurely from behind the closet door, and ran into his arms, while the two young Cratchits hustled Tiny Tim, and bore him off into the wash-house, that he might hear the pudding singing in the copper.

"And how did little Tim behave?" asked Mrs. Cratchit, when she had rallied Bob on his credulity and Bob had hugged his daughter to his heart's content.

"As good as gold," said Bob, "and better. Somehow he gets thoughtful sitting by himself so much, and thinks the strangest things you ever heard. He told me, coming home, that he hoped the people saw him in the church, because he was a cripple, and it might be pleasant to them to remember upon Christmas Day, who made lame beggars walk and blind men see."

Bob's voice was tremulous when he told them this, and trembled more when he said that Tiny Tim was growing strong and hearty.

His active little crutch was heard upon the floor, and back came Tiny Tim before another word was spoken, escorted by his brother and sister to his stool beside the fire; and while Bob, turning up his cuffs—as if, poor fellow, they were capable of being made more shabby — compounded some hot mixture in a jug with gin and mons, and stirred it round and round and put it on the hob to nmer; Master Peter and the two ubiquitous young Cratchits ent to fetch the goose, with which they soon returned in high ocession.

Such a bustle ensued that you might have thought a goose the rest of all birds; a feathered phenomenon, to which a black swan as a matter of course: and in truth it was something very like it that house. Mrs. Cratchit made the gravy (ready beforehand in little saucepan) hissing hot; Master Peter mashed the potatoes ith incredible vigour; Miss Belinda sweetened up the apple-sauce; artha dusted the hot plates; Bob took Tiny Tim beside him in a ny corner at the table; the two young Cratchits set chairs for erybody, not forgetting themselves, and mounting guard upon eir posts, crammed spoons into their mouths, lest they should riek for goose before their turn came to be helped. At last the shes were set on, and grace was said. It was succeeded by a eathless pause, as Mrs. Cratchit, looking slowly all along the rving-knife, prepared to plunge it in the breast; but when she d, and when the long expected gush of stuffing issued forth, one urmur of delight arose all round the board, and even Tiny Tim, cited by the two young Cratchits, beat on the table with the ndle of his knife and feebly cried Hurrah!

There never was such a goose. Bob said he didn't believe there er was such a goose cooked. Its tenderness and flavour, size and eapness, were the themes of universal admiration. Eked out by e apple-sauce and mashed potatoes, it was a sufficient dinner for e whole family; indeed, as Mrs. Cratchit said with great delight urveying one small atom of a bone upon the dish), they hadn't e it all at last! Yet every one had enough, and the youngest ratchits in particular, were steeped in sage and onion to the eye- ows! But now, the plates being changed by Miss Belinda, Mrs. ratchit left the room alone—too nervous to bear witnesses—to take e pudding up, and bring it in.

Suppose it should not be done enough! Suppose it should break turning out! Suppose somebody should have got over the wall the back-yard, and stolen it, while they were merry with the ose: a supposition at which the two young Cratchits became vid! All sorts of horrors were supposed.

Hallo! A great deal of steam! The pudding was out of the pper. A smell like a washing-day! That was the cloth. A smell ke an eating-house, and a pastry cook's next door to each other, with a laundress's next door to that! That was the pudding. In half a minute Mrs. Cratchit entered: flushed, but smiling proudly: with the pudding, like a speckled cannonball, so hard and firm, blazing in half of half-a-quartern of ignited brandy, and bedight with Christmas holly stuck into the top.

Oh, a wonderful pudding! Bob Cratchit said, and calmly too, that he regarded it as the greatest success achieved by Mrs. Cratchit since their marriage. Mrs. Cratchit said that now the weight was off her mind, she would confess she had had her doubts about the quantity of flour. Everybody had something to say about it, but nobody said or thought it was at all a small pudding for a large family. It would have been flat heresy to do so. Any Cratchit would have blushed to hint at such a thing.

At last the dinner was all done, the cloth was cleared, the hearth swept, and the fire made up. The compound in the jug being tasted and considered perfect, apples and oranges were put upon the table, and a shovel-full of chestnuts on the fire. Then all the Cratchit family drew around the hearth, in what Bob Cratchit called a circle, meaning half a one; and at Bob Cratchit's elbow stood the family display of glass; two tumblers, and a custard-cup without a handle.

These held the hot stuff from the jug, however, as well as golden goblets would have done; and Bob served it out with beaming looks, while the chestnuts on the fire sputtered and crackled noisily. Then Bob proposed:

"A Merry Christmas to us all, my dears. God bless us!"

Which all the family re-echoed.

"God bless us every one!" said Tiny Tim, the last of all.

He sat very close to his father's side, upon his little stool. Bob held his withered little hand in his, as if he loved the child, and wished to keep him by his side, and dreaded that he might be taken from him.

"Spirit," said Scrooge, with an interest he had never felt before "tell me if Tiny Tim will live."

"I see a vacant seat," replied the Ghost, "in the poor chimney corner, and a crutch without an owner, carefully preserved. If these shadows remain unaltered by the Future, the child will die."

"No, no," said Scrooge. "Oh, no, kind Spirit! say he will be spared."

338

"If these shadows remain unaltered by the Future, none other of my race," returned the Ghost, "will find him here. What then? If he be like to die, he had better do it, and decrease the surplus population."

Scrooge hung his head to hear his own words quoted by the Spirit, and was overcome with penitence and grief. . . . . .

But he raised his eyes on hearing his own name.

"Mr. Scrooge!" said Bob; "I'll give you Mr. Scrooge, the Founder of the Feast!"

"The Founder of the Feast indeed!" cried Mrs. Cratchit, reddening. "I wish I had him here. I'd give him a piece of my mind to feast upon, and I hope he'd have a good appetite for it."

"My dear," said Bob, "the children; Christmas Day."

"It should be Christmas Day, I am sure," said she, "on which one drinks the health of such an odious, stingy, hard, unfeeling man as Mr. Scrooge. You know he is, Robert! Nobody knows it better than you do, poor fellow!"

"My dear," was Bob's mild answer, "Christmas Day."

"I'll drink his health for your sake and the Day's," said Mrs. Cratchit, "not for his. Long life to him! A merry Christmas and a happy new year!—he'll be very merry and very happy, I have no doubt!"

The children drank the toast after her. It was the first of their proceedings which had no heartiness in it. Tiny Tim drank it last of all, but he didn't care twopence for it. Scrooge was the Ogre of the family. The mention of his name cast a dark shadow on the party, which was not dispelled for full five minutes.

After it had passed away, they were ten times merrier than before, from the mere relief of Scrooge the Baleful being done with. . . . . .

They were not a handsome family; they were not well dressed; their shoes were far from being waterproof; their clothes were scanty; and Peter might have known, and very likely did, the inside of a pawnbroker's. But they were happy, grateful, pleased with one another, and contented with the time; and when they faded, and looked happier yet in the bright sprinklings of the Spirit's torch at parting, Scrooge had his eye upon them, and especially on Tiny Tim, until the last.

# THE CHRISTMAS APPLE[1]

## Ruth Sawyer

*A deeply stirring story which has still more potentialities than its parallel,* WHY THE CHIMES RANG. *It is a fine experience for any boy to play Hermann Joseph; and the cathedral scene affords a most interesting study for a large group of children.*

Once on a time there lived in Germany a little clock-maker by the name of Hermann Joseph. He lived in one little room with a bench for his work, and a chest for his wood, and his tools, and a cupboard for dishes, and a trundle-bed under the bench. Besides these there was a stool, and that was all—excepting the clocks. There were hundreds of clocks: little and big, carved and plain, some with wooden faces and some with porcelain ones—shelf clocks, cuckoo clocks, clocks with chimes and clocks without; and they all hung on the walls, covering them quite up. In front of his one little window there was a little shelf, and on this Hermann put all his best clocks to show the passers-by. Often they would stop and look and some one would cry:

"See, Hermann Joseph has made a new clock. It is finer than any of the rest!"

Then if it happened that anybody was wanting a clock he would come in and buy it.

I said Hermann was a little clock-maker. That was because his back was bent and his legs were crooked, which made him very short and funny to look at. But there was no kinder face than his in all the city, and the children loved him. Whenever a toy was broken or a doll had lost an arm or a leg or an eye its careless mütterchen would carry it straight to Hermann's little shop.

"The kindlein needs mending," she would say. "Canst thou do it now for me?"

And whatever work Hermann was doing he would always put it aside to mend the broken toy or doll, and never a pfennig would he take for the mending.

"Go spend it for sweetmeats, or, better still, put it by till Christmas-time. 'Twill get thee some happiness then, maybe," he would always say.

[1] From *This Way to Christmas*, by Ruth Sawyer. Copyright 1944 by Ruth Sawyer Durand. Used by permission of the author and Harper & Brothers, publishers.

Now it was the custom in that long ago for those who lived in the city to bring gifts to the great cathedral on Christmas and lay them before the Holy Mother and Child. People saved all through the year that they might have something wonderful to bring on that day; and there was a saying among them that when a gift was brought that pleased the Christ-child more than any other He would reach down from Mary's arms and take it. This was but a saying, of course. The old Herr Graff, the oldest man in the city, could not remember that it had ever really happened, and many there were who laughed at the very idea. But children often talked about it, and the poets made beautiful verses about it; and often when a rich gift was placed beside the altar the watchers would whisper among themselves, "Perhaps now we shall see the miracle."

Those who had no gifts to bring went to the cathedral just the same on Christmas Eve to see the gifts of the others and hear the carols and watch the burning of the waxen tapers. The little clock-maker was one of these. Often he was stopped and some one would ask, "How happens it that you never bring a gift?" Once the bishop himself questioned him: "Poorer than thou have brought offerings to the Child. Where is thy gift?"

Then it was that Hermann had answered:

"Wait; some day you shall see. I, too, shall bring a gift some day."

The truth of it was that the little clock-maker was so busy giving away all the year that there was never anything left at Christmastime. But he had a wonderful idea on which he was working every minute that he could spare time from his clocks. It had taken him years and years; no one knew anything about it but Trude, his neighbor's child, and Trude had grown from a baby into a little housemother, and still the gift was not finished.

It was to be a clock, the most wonderful and beautiful clock ever made; and every part of it had been fashioned with loving care. The case, the works, the weights, the hands, and the face, all had taken years of labor. He had spent years carving the case and hands, years perfecting the works; and now Hermann saw that with a little more haste and time he could finish it for the coming Christmas. He mended the children's toys as before, but he gave up making his regular clocks, so there were fewer to sell, and often his cupboard was empty and he went supperless to bed. But that only made him a little thinner and his face a little kinder; and meantime the gift clock became more and more beautiful. It was fashioned after a rude stable with rafters, stall, and crib. The

Holy Mother knelt beside the manger in which a tiny Christ-child lay, while through the open door the hours came. Three were kings and three were shepherds and three were soldiers and three were angels; and when the hours struck, the figure knelt in adoration before the sleeping Child, while the silver chimes played the "Magnificat."

"Thou seest," said the clock-maker to Trude, "it is not just on Sundays and holidays that we should remember to worship the Krist Kindlein and bring Him gifts—but every day, every hour."

The days went by like clouds scudding before a winter wind and the clock was finished at last. So happy was Hermann with his work that he put the gift clock on the shelf before the little window to show the passers-by. There were crowds looking at it all day long, and many would whisper, "Do you think this can be the gift Hermann has spoken of—his offering on Christmas Eve to the Church?"

The day before Christmas came. Hermann cleaned up his little shop, wound all his clocks, brushed his clothes, and then went over the gift clock again to be sure everything was perfect.

"It will not look meanly beside the other gifts," he thought happily. In fact he was so happy that he gave away all but one pfennig to the blind beggar who passed his door; and then, remembering that he had eaten nothing since breakfast, he spent that last pfennig for a Christmas apple to eat with a crust of bread he had. These he was putting by in the cupboard to eat after he was dressed, when the door opened and Trude was standing there crying softly.

"Kindlein—kindlein, what ails thee?" And he gathered her into his arms.

" 'Tis the father. He is hurt, and all the money that was put by for the tree and sweets and toys has gone to the Herr Doctor. And now, how can I tell the children? Already they have lighted the candle at the window and are waiting for Kriss Kringle to come."

The clock-maker laughed merrily.

"Come, come, little one, all will be well. Hermann will sell a clock for thee. Some house in the city must need a clock; and in a wink we shall have money enough for the tree and the toys. Go home and sing."

He buttoned on his greatcoat and, picking out the best of the old clocks, he went out. He went first to the rich merchants, but their houses were full of clocks; then to the journeymen, but they said his clock was old-fashioned. He even stood on the corners of the streets and in the square, crying, "A clock—a good clock for sale," but no one paid any attention to him. At last he gathered up his courage and went to the Herr Graff himself.

"Will your Excellency buy a clock?" he said, trembling at his own boldness. "I would not ask, but it is Christmas and I am needing to buy happiness for some children."

The Herr Graff smiled.

"Yes, I will buy a clock, but not that one. I will pay a thousand gulden for the clock thou hast had in thy window these four days past."

"But, your Excellency, that is impossible!" And poor Hermann trembled harder than ever.

"Poof! Nothing is impossible. That clock or none. Get thee home and I will send for it in half an hour, and pay thee the gulden."

The little clock-maker stumbled out.

"Anything but that—anything but that!" he kept mumbling over and over to himself on his way home. But as he passed the neighbor's house he saw the children at the window with their lighted candle and he heard Trude singing.

And so it happened that the servant who came from the Herr Graff carried the gift clock away with him; but the clock-maker would take but five of the thousand gulden in payment. And as the servant disappeared up the street the chimes commenced to ring from the great cathedral, and the streets suddenly became noisy with the people going thither, bearing their Christmas offerings.

"I have gone empty-handed before," said the little clock-maker, sadly. "I can go empty-handed once again." And again he buttoned up his greatcoat.

As he turned to shut his cupboard door behind him his eyes fell on the Christmas apple and an odd little smile crept into the corners of his mouth and lighted his eyes.

"It is all I have—my dinner for two days. I will carry that to the Christ-child. It is better, after all, than going empty-handed."

How full of peace and beauty was the great cathedral when Hermann entered it! There were a thousand tapers burning and everywhere the sweet scent of the Christmas greens— and the laden altar before the Holy Mother and Child. There were richer gifts than had been brought for many years: marvelously wrought vessels from the greatest silversmiths; cloth of gold and cloth of silk brought from the East by the merchants; poets had brought their songs illuminated on rolls of heavy parchment; painters had brought their pictures of saints and the Holy Family; even the King himself had brought his crown and scepter to lay before the Child. And after all these offerings came the little clock-maker, walking slowly down the long, dim aisle, holding tight to his Christmas apple.

The people saw him and a murmur rose, hummed a moment indistinctly through the church and then grew clear and articulate:

"Shame! See he is too mean to bring his clock! He hoards it as a miser hoards his gold. See what he brings! Shame!"

The words reached Hermann and he stumbled on blindly, his head dropped forward on his breast, his hands groping the way. The distance seemed interminable. Now he knew he was past the seats: now his feet touched the first step, and there were seven to climb to the altar. Would his feet never reach the top?

"One, two, three," he counted to himself, then tripped and almost fell. "Four, five, six." He was nearly there. There was but one more.

The murmur of shame died away and in its place rose one of wonder and awe. Soon the words became intelligible:

"The miracle! It is the miracle!"

The people knelt in the big cathedral; the bishop raised his hands in prayer. And the little clock-maker, stumbling to the last step, looked up through dim eyes and saw the Child leaning toward him, far down from Mary's arms, with hands outstretched to take his gift.


## A MIDSUMMER NIGHT'S DREAM[1]

### Told by Mary MacLeod

*The artisan and fairy scenes from "A Midsummer Night's Dream" can very well be used without the unsuitable love plot. If children dramatize the episode in which the artisans perform their play for the court, Theseus, Hippolita and the others are, of course, a part of the scene. The following arrangement of the story was worked*

[1] Adapted from *The Shakespeare Story Book* by Mary MacLeod. Permission from the publishers, Wells Gardner, Darton & Co., Ltd.

*out in three scenes by one group, and played continuously after the children were familiar with it. (Before acting any Shakespearean scene, if the players hear it read from the text, they will get the flavor of the dialogue.)*

Theseus, Duke of Athens, was to wed Hippolyta, Queen of the Amazons, and the whole city was given up to merriment in honour of the occasion. Theseus had won his bride by the sword, but he was to wed her in another fashion—with pomp, with triumph, and with revelling. Four days had yet to elapse before the marriage, and during that time the citizens of Athens were to busy themselves with preparations for the great event.

Several of the petty artisans of Athens, anxious to celebrate the wedding in proper style, had decided to perform a little play—or "interlude," as it was called—in the presence of the Duke and Duchess. Quince, the carpenter, was supposed to direct the proceedings of this little band of amateur actors, but the ruling spirit of the company was in reality Bottom, the weaver. Bursting with self-conceit, never able to keep silent a moment, Bottom was ready to instruct everyone else in his duties, and if it had only been possible for him to have played every character in the piece, in addition to his own, he would have been quite content. As each part was mentioned, and Quince began to apportion them out, Bottom's voice was heard again and again, declaring how well *he* could perform each one. The play was to be "The Most Lamentable Comedy and Most Cruel Death of Pyramus and Thisby," and Bottom was selected for Pyramus, the hero.

"What is Pyramus—a lover or a tyrant?" he inquired.

"A lover that kills himself most gallantly for love," answered Quince.

"That will ask some tears in the true performing of it," said Bottom, swelling with self-importance. "If I do it, let the audience look to their eyes."

The next character was Thisby, the heroine, and this was given to Flute, the bellows-mender, a thin, lanky youth with a squeaky voice.

"Nay, faith, let me not play a woman; I have a beard coming," he said piteously.

"That's all one; you shall play it in a mask, and you may speak as small as you will," said Quince.

"If I hide my face, let *me* play Thisby, too," cried Bottom eagerly. "I'll speak in a monstrous little voice. 'Thisne, Thisne!' 'Ah, Pyramus, my lover dear! Thy Thisby dear, and lady dear!' "

"No, no! you must play Pyramus, and, Flute, you Thisby," said Quince.

"Well, proceed," said Bottom.

Quince went on with his list, and presently he called out the name of Snug, the joiner.

"You will play the lion's part, Snug," he said; "and now, I hope, there is the play fitted."

"Have you the lion's part written? Pray you, if it be, give it me, for I am slow of study," said Snug modestly, for he was a very meek and mild little man.

"You may do it extempore, for it is nothing but roaring," said Quince.

"Let *me* play the lion, too," burst in Bottom. "I will roar that it will do any man's heart good to hear me. I will roar that I will make the Duke say: "Let him roar again.""

"If you should do it too terribly, you would frighten the Duchess and the ladies out of their wits, so that they would shriek, and that were enough to hang us all," said Quince.

"That would hang us, every mother's son," agreed the rest of the little band, quaking with terror.

"I grant you, friends, that if you should frighten the ladies out of their wits, they would have no more discretion but to hang us," said Bottom. "But I will aggravate my voice so that I will roar as gently as any sucking dove; I will roar as if it were any nightingale."

"You can play no part but Pyramus," said Quince firmly. So Bottom had reluctantly to give in, and to devote his energies to deciding what coloured beard it would be best to play the important part of Pyramus in. It was really quite a difficult matter, there were so many to choose from,—straw-colour, orange tawny, purple-in-grain, or French-crown, which was perfect yellow. But Quince said any colour would do, or he might play it without a beard.

"Masters, here are your parts," he concluded, "and I am to entreat you, request you, and desire you, to know them by to-morrow night, and meet me in the palace wood, a mile outside the town, by moonlight. There we will rehearse, for if we meet in the city we shall be dogged with company, and our devices known. I pray you, do not fail me."

Now, the wood where Bottom and his fellow-actors were to meet to rehearse their play, was the favourite haunt of fairies, and on this Midsummer Night Oberon, King of the Fairies, was to hold his revels there. Sad to say, for some time past there had been great dissension between Oberon and his Queen, Titania, and because of their quarrels nothing went well in the surrounding country. The cause of their disagreement was a little boy whom Queen Titania had as her attendant; and jealous Oberon wanted the boy for his own page. Titania refused to give him up; he was the child of a dear friend, now dead, and for her sake she had reared up the boy, and for her sake she would not part with him.

Oberon and Titania never met now, in grove or green, by the clear fountain, or in the spangled starlight, without quarrelling so fiercely that their elves crept for fear into acorn-cups, and hid themselves there. They generally tried to keep out of each other's way, but on this night it happened that as King Oberon, with his little sprite Puck and his train, approached from one direction, Queen Titania and her attendant fairies came near from the other. Titania reproached Oberon with all the ill-luck that was happening because of their dissension, and Oberon replied that it only lay with her to amend it.

"Why should Titania cross her Oberon?" he asked. "I do but beg a little changeling boy to be my henchman."

"Set your heart at rest," replied Titania; "the whole of Fairyland will not buy the child of me."

"How long do you intend to stay in this wood?" asked Oberon.

"Perhaps till after Theseus's wedding-day," said Titania. "If you will join patiently in our dance, and see our moonlight revels, go with us. If not, shun me, and I will take care to avoid your haunts."

"Give me that boy, and I will go with you," said Oberon.

"Not for your fairy kingdom!" was the decided answer. "Fairies, away! We shall quarrel in earnest if I stay any longer."

As he could not win the boy by entreaty, Oberon resolved to try another plan to gain his desire. Calling his little sprite Puck to him, he bade him go and fetch a certain magic flower, which maidens call "love-in-idleness." The juice of this flower had a wonderful charm. When laid on the eyelids of a sleeping man or woman it had the power of making that person dote madly on the next living creature that was seen. Oberon determined to squeeze some of the juice of this flower on Titania's eyes while she slept, so that when she woke up she should immediately fall in love with the first creature she saw, whether it were lion, bear, wolf, or bull, meddling monkey or busy ape. He determined also that he would not take off the charm (which he could do with another herb) until she had rendered up the little boy as page to him.

"Fetch me this herb," he said to Puck, "and be thou here again before the leviathan can swim a league."

"I'll put a girdle round about the earth in forty minutes," cried the prompt little messenger, and away he flew.

*While Oberon is awaiting Puck's return, two of Titania's attendants re-enter to soft music. Oberon steps out of sight, saying, "She comes again!" The attendants make ready Titania's bower, and when she has entered with the other attendants, all of whom wait upon her as she prepares to rest, one says, "Hence, away! Now all is well. One aloof stand sentinel." The smallest attendant remains to guard her while the others dance away.*

*For a few moments there is music. Puck re-enters with the herb and Oberon steps out. In pantomime Puck offers to get rid of the attendant. Oberon nods, and Puck appears to charm him off to magic music.*

*Then Oberon steals to Titania's bower and squeezes the magic juice on her eyelids, repeating the charm:*

> "What thou seest when thou dost wake,
> Do it for thy true love take,
> Love and languish for his sake;
> Be it ounce or cat or bear,
> Pard or boar with bristled hair,
> When thou wakest, it is thy dear.
> Wake when some vile thing is near."

Queen Titania, meanwhile, was quietly sleeping, and she did not even waken when Quince and Bottom, with their ambitious little troupe of actors, came and began to rehearse their play close by. Bottom, as usual, took the lead, and made himself very officious in directing all the rest.

*See Act III., Scene 1. The artisans enter the wood to rehearse their play. Nick Bottom seems to take particular pleasure in bringing to the attention of Quince things which he says will never please the audience, such as the fact that Pyramus must draw a sword and kill himself; that a lion must be brought in; that there must be moonlight and a wall. However, he has happy solutions for all the problems, and the rehearsal gets under way.*

Puck, the little imp, was always alert for any mischief, and being much diverted with the strange crew of petty artisans from Athens, he presently played one of his pranks on the conceited Bottom. The latter, having spoken some of his lines, stood aside for a few minutes, while the others went on with their parts, and, unseen by anyone, Puck seized this opportunity to pop an ass's head on Bottom.

Quite unconscious of the strange change that had taken place in his appearance, Bottom calmly advanced when his turn came again, but at the sight of the ass's head all his companions shrieked and fled in terror, calling out that they were bewitched. Bottom could not imagine why they behaved in this queer fashion, and thought it was some trick to frighten him.

"I will not stir from this place, do what they can," he said stolidly. "I will walk up and down here, and I will sing, so that they shall hear I am not afraid."

So he began to pace up and down, singing in a very harsh, discordant manner, more like an ass's bray than a man's voice:

> "The ousel-cock so black of hue,
>     With orange-tawny bill,
> The throstle with his note so true,
>     The wren with little quill—"

"What angel wakes me from my flowery bed?" cried Titania, starting up from slumber.

The charm was beginning to work, and she gazed with rapture on the curious monster.

Bottom sang on:

> "The finch, the sparrow, and the lark,
>     The plain-song cuckoo gray,
> Whose note full many a man doth mark,
>     And dares not answer nay."

"I pray thee, gentle mortal, sing again," entreated Titania. "My ear is charmed as much with your music as my eye is enthralled with your appearance. Thou art as wise as thou art beautiful."

"Not so, neither," said Bottom bluntly; "but if I had wit to get out of this wood I have enough to serve my own turn."

"Do not desire to go out of this wood," pleaded Titania. "Thou shalt remain here, whether thou wish it or not. I am a spirit of no common kind, and I love thee; therefore go with me. I'll give thee fairies to attend on thee, and they shall fetch thee jewels, and sing while thou liest sleeping on a bank of flowers. Peaseblossom! Cobweb! Moth! and Mustard-seed!"

Four little elves came flying at the summons, and the infatuated Queen of the Fairies introduced them and gave this new object of her affections into their special charge. They led him away to the bower of the Queen, and there they decked him with flowers, while Titania lavished caresses on the clownish monster.

The children often end the playing here, but they know that Oberon soon begins to pity his beautiful Queen, and after Titania has given up her page to him, he takes the spell from her eyes and they go off happily together.

## MACBETH[1]

### Told by Mary MacLeod

*The witches' scenes from this great play are enormously popular with eighth grade boys and girls, especially if they have teachers who know and thoroughly like the play.*

*First of all, they need some background for understanding the superstitions of the time which caused even intelligent people to half believe in witchcraft. They need to realize that these strange, unearthly creatures are not at all like the witch in "Hansel and Gretel," with her harsh, cackling voice. Because they seem to come out of the wind and the fog, their voices, the children often decide, should be strange, weird, unearthly. Their postures would be grotesque, reflecting their twisted and evil spirits.*

*After the children hear the story, it is a good thing to let them project themselves into the characters of the witches; to try to feel them in every muscle. A half-darkened room or stage, rumbling of thunder (by piano or drum) and the entire class playing at once will help them get the feel of the characters without self-conscious ness. And once they let go, they find it is so much fun that they*

[1] Adapted from *The Shakespeare Story Book* by Mary MacLeod. Permission from the publishers, Wells Gardner, Darton & Co., Ltd.

*want to play again and again. It is only after they have all had the experience of pantomiming the witches that the class is divided into groups to try the actual episodes.*

The time when the present story occurred was hundreds of years ago, in the year 1039, before William the Conqueror had come to Britain, and when England and Scotland were entirely separate kingdoms.

The throne of Scotland was then occupied by a King called Duncan. The country at all times was much at the mercy of Northern invaders, and just at that period it was suffering from the inroads of the Norwegian hosts, who, secretly aided by the traitor Thane of Cawdor, had obtained a footing in the eastern county of Fife. But their brief victory was changed to defeat by the valour of the Scotch Generals, Macbeth and Banquo.

News was brought to King Duncan of the victory that had been gained by the valour of Macbeth, and, pronouncing the doom of instant death on the traitor Thane of Cawdor, he ordered that his title should be bestowed as a reward on Macbeth.

It was a wild night, on a desolate heath near Forres. The setting sun, low down on the horizon, cast a blood-red glow over the withered bracken and a group of blasted fir-trees. The thunder rolled overhead, the wind howled in long moaning gusts, the lightning flashed in jagged streaks. But to the three strange figures that approached from different quarters, and met in the centre of this lonely heath, it suited well with their grim and sinister mood. The wholesome sunlight and the breath of day made them shrink and cower in secret lurking-places, but when midnight veiled the sky they stole out to their unholy revels, or on the wings of the tempest they rode forth, bringing death or disaster to all who crossed their track.

"Where hast thou been, sister?" asked the first witch.

And the second replied: "Killing swine."

"Sister, where thou?" asked the third witch.

"A sailor's wife had chestnuts in her lap, and munched, and munched, and munched," said the first witch. " 'Give me,' quoth I. 'Aroint thee, witch!' the pampered creature cried. Her husband's to Aleppo gone, master of the *Tiger;* but in a sieve I'll thither sail, and, like a rat without a tail, I'll do, I'll do, and I'll do," ended the witch spitefully.

"I'll give thee a wind," said the second witch.

"Thou art kind."

"And I another," said the third witch.

"I myself have all the other," continued the first witch, gloating over the revenge she intended to take on the husband of the woman who had repulsed her.

"Look what I have!"

"Show me, show me!" cried the second witch eagerly.

> "Here I have a pilot's thumb,
> Wrecked as homeward he did come."

At this moment across the heath came the roll of a drum and the tramp of marching feet.

"A drum, a drum! Macbeth doth come!" cried the third witch.

Then the three fearsome creatures, linking hands, solemnly performed a wild dance, waving their skinny arms in strange gestures, and uttering a discordant wail:

> "The weird sisters, hand in hand,
> Posters of the sea and land,
> Thus do go about, about;
> Thrice to thine, and thrice to mine,
> And thrice again to make up nine.
> Peace! The charm's wound up."

Macbeth and Banquo, marching across the heath on their way home, after the campaign with the Norwegians, were startled at the sight of these three uncanny figures barring their path.

"What are these, so withered and so wild in their attire, that look not like the inhabitants of earth, and yet are on it?" said Banquo. "Are you alive? Or are you anything that man may question?"

"Speak, if you can; what are you?" said Macbeth.

And the three witches answered by saluting him, each in turn:

"All hail, Macbeth! Hail to thee, Thane of Glamis!"

"All hail, Macbeth! Hail to thee, Thane of Cawdor!"

"All hail, Macbeth! Thou shalt be King hereafter."

"Good sir, why do you start, and seem to fear things that do sound so fair?" said Banquo, for Macbeth stood as if rapt in a dream, amazed at what he heard.

Then Banquo asked the witches, if indeed they could look into the future, to say something to him, who neither begged nor feared their favours nor their hate.

The witches thereupon replied:

"Hail!" "Hail!" "Hail!"

"Lesser than Macbeth and greater!"

"Not so happy, yet much happier!"

"Thou shalt beget Kings, though thou be none. So all hail, Macbeth and Banquo!"

"Banquo and Macbeth, all hail!"

Macbeth would fain have questioned these mysterious creatures further, but not a word would they speak. By the death of a relative, he was certainly Thane of Glamis, but, as far as he knew, the Thane of Cawdor lived, an honourable gentleman, for Macbeth had not yet heard of his treachery, and the news that his title was forfeited. And to be King stood not within the prospect of belief, no more than to be Thane of Cawdor. But when Macbeth again charged the witches to speak, they vanished, seeming almost to melt like bubbles into the misty twilight from which they had emerged.

The two victorious generals stood and looked at each other, mute for awhile with awe and wonder. They had fought with armed hosts on the field of battle, but here was a mystery which might amaze the stoutest heart. The poison was already beginning to work. Deeply ambitious at heart, though lacking in resolution to cut his way ruthlessly to the highest goal, the witches' words had found a ready welcome in Macbeth's secret desires. But not yet could he openly avow them.

"Your children shall be Kings," he said to Banquo; and back came the answer which perhaps he was longing to hear:

"You shall be King!"

"And Thane of Cawdor, too, went it not so?" he asked, with a half-assumed air of incredulity.

"To the self-same tune and words," said Banquo.

The mysterious greeting of the witches now received strange confirmation, for messengers arrived from King Duncan, bringing news that the Thane of Cawdor had been condemned to death for treason, and that his title and estate were conferred on Macbeth.

Such an instant proof of the witches' powers of divination could not fail to fill Macbeth's mind with strange imaginings.

"Glamis, and Thane of Cawdor!" he murmured to himself. "The greatest is behind." Then he spoke to Banquo apart: "Do you not hope your children shall be Kings, when those that gave the Thane of Cawdor to me promised no less to them?"

But Banquo's nature was less easily carried away than Macbeth's. He warned him that it was dangerous to put any trust in doers of evil; often to win people to their harm they would tell truth in trifles, in order to betray them in matters of the deepest consequence.

Macbeth scarcely paid any attention to what Banquo said. His thoughts were fixed now on one idea. The witches had foretold truly that he should be Thane of Cawdor when there seemed no likelihood of such an event taking place. Why, then, should they not have spoken equal truth when they foretold a higher honour?

A dreadful idea was already beginning to take shape in Macbeth's mind. At first he shrank from it in horror, but again and again it came back with renewed force. At last he tried resolutely to thrust it from him.

"If chance will have me King, why, chance may crown me, without my stir," he said to himself. Then, with the feeling that he would leave events to work out as fate chose, he added: "Come what come may, time and the hour runs through the roughest day."

But even yet he could not put the matter from him, and determine to think no more about it, as a wise man would have done. He wanted to reflect over what had passed, and discuss it again with Banquo.

"Let us go to the King," he said to Banquo; for the messengers had come to summon him to Duncan, in order to receive his thanks for the victory. "We will think over what has chanced, and later on, having in the meanwhile pondered it, let us speak our hearts freely to each other."

"Very gladly," agreed Banquo.

"Till then, enough," said Macbeth. "Come, friends;" and away he went with Banquo and the other lords to receive his new honours from the King's hands.

The later scene with the witches, in which Macbeth comes to find out more, is quite as good to play as this one.

354

# THE TAMING OF THE SHREW[1]

## Told by Mary MacLeod

Katharine the curst! That is not a pretty title for a maiden, but that was the nickname given to one, renowned all through Padua for her scolding tongue.

Baptista Minola had two daughters, both young and beautiful, but very different in disposition, for while Bianca, the younger, was so sweet and gentle that she was beloved by all, the elder sister Katharine had such a violent and ungovernable temper that everyone feared and disliked her.

Bianca had several suitors, but Baptista, her father, was firmly resolved not to allow his youngest daughter to marry until he had secured a husband for the elder. In the meantime he declared Bianca should stay quietly at home; but as he loved his daughter, and did not want the time to pass heavily with her, he promised to provide schoolmasters, to instruct her in the studies in which she took most delight—music and poetry.

On the very day when Baptista announced his resolve, there arrived in Padua Petruchio, a young man from Verona. Petruchio sought out his friend Hortensio, who was a suitor of Bianca, and told him that his father was dead, and that he had now come abroad to see the world. He had money in his pockets, possessions at home, and possibly he would marry if he could find a wife.

Hortensio's thoughts, of course, at once flew to Katharine, and half in jest he offered to supply Petruchio with a wife, young, beautiful and rich, but with a violent temper.

"But you are too much my friend," he concluded; "I could not wish you to marry her."

Petruchio, however, was a gentleman of valiant disposition and most determined will, and he was not in the least daunted by what he heard of Katharine's terrible temper.

"Do you think a little noise can frighten me?" he said. "Have I not in my time heard lions roar? Have I not heard the seas puffed up with wind, rage like an angry boar? Have I not in a pitched battle heard loud alarums, neighing steeds, and trumpets clang, and do you tell me of a woman's tongue? Tush, tush! Frighten boys with bogies!"

---

[1] Adapted from *The Shakespeare Story Book* by Mary MacLeod. Permission from the publishers, Wells Gardner, Darton & Co., Ltd.

Bianca's suitors were delighted to have found such a match for Katharine, and the lady's father was equally pleased, and promised a handsome dowry, though he was rather doubtful of Petruchio's success in winning his daughter. But it soon turned out Petruchio had not in the least over-rated his powers.

He knew that kindness and soft words would be thrown away in dealing with such a nature as Katharine's; she was accustomed to everyone's giving in to her, and the very gentleness and submission of Bianca had only the effect of irritating her more. Petruchio determined to adopt an entirely different plan, and to fight Katharine, as it were, with her own weapons. He ignored all her insulting speeches with the most perfect good-humour, and his own self-possession and satirical remarks reduced her to a state of hopeless fury. It was useless for Katharine to get into a passion and shower abuse on him. The ruder she became, the more charming he pretended to think her. In short, he told her calmly that her father had given his consent, the dowry was agreed on, and that, willing or unwilling, he intended to marry her on the following Sunday.

"I'll see thee hanged on Sunday first," was Katharine's wrathful rejoinder; but all the same, when Sunday arrived, the bride was ready, dressed, and waiting for her eccentric bridegroom.

Petruchio intended to teach Katharine a severe lesson. She had never shown the slightest consideration for anyone else. It was his aim to humble her pride thoroughly, and to show her how unpleasant it is for others to have to live with a person who is perpetually flying into a passion.

The first humiliation to Katharine was the lateness of the bridegroom's arrival at the wedding, and when he did at last appear, the extraordinary array in which he had chosen to attire himself. At the wedding he behaved in such a mad fashion that the guests were scandalized, and afterwards he insisted on carrying his bride away before the wedding feast.

After a most unpleasant wedding journey, in which Katharine's horse fell in the mud, they arrived at Petruchio's country house. Supper was brought, but Petruchio pretended it was badly cooked, and threw the food all over the place, refusing to let his wife taste a morsel! She was now really hungry, and would gladly have eaten the food he threw away; but Petruchio intended that she should be much more hungry and submissive before he allowed her anything to eat. She was also very tired, but he took care she should get no sleep that night; he tossed about the furniture in the room, finding fault with everything; and all this was done with the pretence that it was out of loving care for her own comfort.

By the following day Katharine felt almost famished. She implored Grumio to go and fetch her something to eat; she did not mind what it was so long as it was wholesome food. The man tantalized her for some time by suggesting one dish after another, any one of which she would gladly have accepted, and finally ended by saying impertinently he could fetch her some mustard without any beef.

At that moment Petruchio entered, bringing some meat which he said he had himself prepared for her.

"I am sure, sweet Kate, this kindness merits thanks. What, not a word? Nay, then, you do not like it, and all my pains are of no use. Here, take away this dish."

"I pray you let it stand," said Katharine.

"The poorest service is repaid with thanks, and so shall mine be before you touch the meat," said Petruchio.

"I thank you, sir," Katharine compelled her proud lips to murmur, for, indeed, she was nearly starving, and could not endure to see the food carried away untouched.

"Now, my honey love," continued Petruchio, who was always most affectionate in his speech, and pretended that everything he did was out of devotion to his wife, "we will return to your father's house, decked out as bravely as the best in gay apparel;" and, scarcely allowing her a moment in which to snatch a morsel of food, he ordered in the tailor and haberdasher, who had been preparing some fine new clothes.

But, as usual, nothing pleased him.

"Here is the cap your worship bespoke," said the haberdasher.

"Why, this was moulded on a porringer, a velvet dish!" exclaimed Petruchio, with an air of disgust. "It's a cockle or a walnut-shell— a toy, a baby's cap! Away with it! Come, let me have a bigger."

"I'll have no bigger," declared Katharine. "This suits the present style, and gentlewomen wear such caps as these."

"When you are gentle, you shall have one too, and not till then," said Petruchio, in rather a meaning voice.

Katharine's old spirit blazed up again at this rebuke, but the only notice Petruchio took of her angry words was to pretend to think she was agreeing with him in his abuse of the cap. Then he ordered the tailor to produce the gown.

"O heavens! what silly style of stuff is here?" he cried in horror. "What's this? A sleeve? It's like a demi-cannon! What, up and down, carved like an apple-tart? Here's snip and nip, and cut, and slish and slash, like a censer in a barber's shop. Why, what in the name of evil, tailor, do you call this?"

"You bade me make it well and properly, according to the fashion and the time," said the tailor.

"Marry, so I did, but, if you remember, I did not bid you mar it to the time. Come, be off; I'll none of it. Hence, make the best of it you can."

"I never saw a better-fashioned gown," said Katharine, "more quaint, more pleasing, nor more praiseworthy. I suppose you mean to make a puppet of me."

"Why, true, he means to make a puppet of you," said Petruchio, wilfully mistaking to whom she spoke.

"She says your worship means to make a puppet of her," explained the tailor.

But Petruchio would listen to no reason or argument, and sent the tailor away in the most peremptory manner, though privately the man was told he would be paid for the gown, and that he was not to be offended at Petruchio's hasty words.

"Well, come, my Kate, we will go to your father's house even in this honest, mean raiment," said Petruchio. "After all, fine clothes are of no importance. Let me see: I think it is now about seven o'clock; we shall easily get there by dinner-time."

Katharine looked at her husband in astonishment; and well she might, for it was already the middle of the day.

"I assure you, sir, it is almost two o'clock; it will be supper-time before we get there."

"It shall be seven o'clock before I get to horse," declared Petruchio. "Look, whatever I speak or do, or think to do, you are always crossing me! I will not go to-day, and before I do, it shall be whatever time I say it is."

Petruchio's determined will at last gained the day, and Katharine learned that it was useless to attempt to battle with him. When in their journey to her father's house he chose to say it was the moon shining in the sky, she had to agree that it was the moon, although everyone could see it was the sun; and then, when he declared immediately that it was the blessed sun, she had also to change her statement and say it was the sun.

"What you will have it named, even that it is," she said, quite tired out by his strange freaks, "and so it shall be so for Katharine." When matters had come to this point with the haughty Katharine, there was not much fear that she would resume her old imperious ways.

The proof of her taming came later at the banquet table. Bianca had married Lucentio, one of her many suitors; and a rejected suitor, Hortensio, had found consolation in a wealthy widow. During the supper there had been jesting as to the amiability of some of the wives present, and after the ladies had left the table the gentlemen continued the discussion.

"Now, in good sadness, son Petruchio," said Baptista, "I think you have the veriest shrew of all."

"Well, I say no," said Petruchio. "So to make sure, let each one of us send to his wife, and he whose wife is most obedient to come at once when he sends for her, shall win the wager which we will propose."

"Content," said Hortensio. "What is the wager?"

"Twenty crowns," suggested Lucentio.

"Twenty crowns!" cried Petruchio. "I'd venture as much on my hawk or my hound, but twenty times as much on my wife."

"A hundred, then," said Lucentio.

"A match! It's done," said Petruchio.

"Who shall begin?" said Hortensio.

"I will," said Lucentio.

So a message was first sent to Bianca. But she sent back word that she was busy and could not come.

"How? She is busy and she cannot come! Is that an answer?" said Petruchio mockingly.

"Ay, and a kind one too," said one of the guests. "Pray heaven, sir, your wife do not send you a worse."

"I hope, better," replied Petruchio.

"Signor Biondello, go and entreat my wife to come to me forthwith," said Hortensio.

"O, ho! entreat her!" laughed Petruchio. "Nay, then, she must needs come."

"I am afraid, sir, do what you can, yours will not be entreated," retorted Hortensio. Then, as the messenger returned, "Now, where's my wife?"

"She says you have some goodly jest in hand; she will not come. She bids you go to her."

"Worse and worse, 'she will not come!' " said Petruchio. "Intolerable, not to be endured! Grumio, go to your mistress: say I command her to come to me."

"I know her answer," said Hortensio.

"What?"

"She will not come."

But the next moment in walked Katharine.

"What is your will, sir, that you send for me?"

"Where is your sister, and Hortensio's wife?" asked Petruchio.

"They are sitting talking by the parlour fire."

"Go, fetch them hither; if they refuse to come, beat them forth to their husbands. Away, I say, and bring them straight here."

"Here is a wonder, if you talk of a wonder," said Lucentio, as Katharine obediently departed.

"And so it is. I wonder what it bodes," said Hortensio.

"Marry, peace it bodes, and love, and quiet life—in short, everything that is sweet and happy," said Petruchio.

"Now, fair befall you, good Petruchio!" said Baptista. "You have won the wager, and I will add to it twenty thousand crowns—another dowry to another daughter, for Katharine is changed as if she had never been."

"Nay," said Petruchio, "I will win my wager better yet, and show more signs of her obedience. See where she comes and brings your froward wives as prisoners to her womanly persuasion." Then, as Katharine entered with Bianca and Hortensio's wife, he continued: "Katharine, that cap of yours does not become you; off with that bauble, throw it underfoot."

Greatly to the disgust of the other two wives, Katharine instantly obeyed.

"Lord, let me never have a cause to sigh till I be brought to such a silly pass," said Hortensio's wife, and even the gentle Bianca exclaimed with equal disdain:

"Fie! what sort of foolish duty do you call this?"

"I wish your duty were as foolish, too," said her husband. "The wisdom of your duty, fair Bianca, has cost me a hundred crowns since supper-time."

"The more fool you for wagering on my duty!" was Bianca's unkind reply.

Then Petruchio bade Katharine tell the other headstrong women what duty they owed their husbands. And this she straightway did, in a speech of such wonderful grace and submission that all

her hearers were amazed.  As for her husband, he was delighted
with the result of his somewhat rough schooling.  "Come, Kate!" he
said.  "Good-night!"  And he retired triumphantly with his now
loving and devoted wife.

*Children of thirteen and fourteen years like to play many epi-
sodes in this story.  Beginning with the scene in which Katharine
torments her sister, they often play the comic incident where
Petruchio orders Grumio to knock at Hortensio's gate; the proposal;
the homecoming (at the beginning of which Grumio relates what
happened at the wedding); the bit where Grumio tantalizes the
hungry Katharine, followed by the meal served by Petruchio and
the tailor-haberdasher scene.  Occasionally they like to act the scene
on the way to Baptista's; and, almost always, the wager scene.  Many
weeks are required to work out all the scenes, but, as a rule the
children enjoy the story so much that they play most of it.  It is,
of course, necessary to read them the text of the scenes they are to
play so that they can get the inimitable flavor of the dialogue.*

CHAPTER VIII

# *Integrated Projects*

As the great ship steamed slowly past the Statue of Liberty in New York harbor, a group of immigrants standing on the deck, looked up at that symbol of freedom with a new light in their eyes. Each one was telling what he hoped for in the new land—and though both the ship and the Statue were entirely imaginary, and the immigrants were children who had known no homeland other than America, they all spoke with deep feeling of what they hoped America would mean to them.

One can never know just how deeply attitudes will be influenced by participation in a creative play like this, but the teacher of these children was impressed with a feeling that something very fine had come to them out of the experience. For the moment spiritual values were lifted up above the material, and they saw their country as our founding fathers wanted it to be. How much better a way to teach love of America than by either facts or precepts!

If a creative play such as this is the center of a study to which a number of other school subjects or activities contribute, it becomes an integrated project. It can best be developed in the classroom with the regular teacher as a guide; or, if there is a dramatic teacher, the two will work together and the play that comes out of the study will usually be a more beautiful one, with far less strain on the always overworked classroom teacher.

Such a project sometimes includes every activity in the school; but almost always it involves the social studies, literature, music, arts, and crafts. It may begin with a study of immigration, as in the above-mentioned play. It sometimes starts with the study of a country or a certain locality within the country; a period in history; a movement; a great man or woman; a fine piece of literature; or one of many other starting-points.

The culmination or climax of such study is the production of a creative play. It is usually presented for an audience because it is likely to be a rather large undertaking, to which a great deal of time and effort has been devoted; and it is right to give the children the opportunity to share it with the school and their parents. The story on which the plot is based may be original, created by the children and their teacher; it may be from history or from a current happening; but it is most often from literature, because working with a fine story gives the children a richer experience and results in a play more worthy of presentation. But whatever its origin, the story should be meaty, significant, worth spending much time in developing. Into it the children should be able to weave much of the material they have learned. In doing so, they will not only enrich the play with interesting details, but they will never forget the information which becomes an integral part of the drama.

Some groups formalize their play by writing it down and memorizing it. The better way is to keep it creative to the last, even though they present it for the whole school and the parents. For even though the language may be less well done than if they had written it, still it remains spontaneous and real rather than recited. The characters must be thinking every minute, and what they say comes from inside. And since the children have worked on it for a long time, it comes out almost as smoothly as if they had learned definite lines.

### RESEARCH

Nothing gives a stronger incentive for research, many teachers say, than a creative drama. If children need Greek designs for screen or costumes; knowledge of architecture for an Egyptian temple; stained glass windows for a medieval chapel, some acquaintance with religious beliefs for background in a Chinese play; Christmas customs of the Mexican people; or occupations and games which will furnish conversation for a manor house family, they see very good reason for careful research.

Excursions to museums, trips to see industries or to visit certain people have much meaning when the children expect to use the information they get. An author or other person who can give them useful facts to use in their play will be listened to eagerly. The motivation is strong for authenticity in the devising of properties and costumes, for the children take great pride in using them or seeing them used on the stage.

363

Though boys and girls often welcome the freshness of a story dramatization which has nothing whatever to do with their other school subjects, an occasional integrated project, with the play as the meeting-place for rich correlated material, is worth all the time, the thought, and the research that goes into it.

Here follows a plan worked out by two sixth grades for

## THE GREEN GINGER JAR[1]
### A Chinatown Mystery

#### Clara Ingram Judson

Chicago's Chinatown is the setting for this interesting and authentic book. There is plenty of excitement in the plot to make it an absorbing story for children, and at the same time it has significance in that it makes real the life and the problems of one of the minority races in this country.

Though the boys and girls who created this play from the story lived less than twenty miles from this part of Chicago, few of them were at all acquainted with it, so that it was necessary to do a good deal of research. They were very fortunate to be able to have the author come and tell them how she went about it to get material for the book, what people helped her, which characters were real, how actual were the places described. She could give them information, too, about customs, attitudes, and points of etiquette, all of which helped them in playing the roles.

Many books on the Chinese were made available to the children, who were divided into committees for research and for building the properties. An excursion by bus to Chinatown was one of the most interesting and helpful parts of their preparation, especially their visits to the handsome building of the On Leong, or Merchants Association, and other places mentioned in the book.

### PLAN FOR THE DEVELOPMENT OF THE PLAY

There are many problems for anyone who undertakes to turn a whole novel into a play. In the first place, there is far more material than can be used for a unified play which is to be not more than an hour and a quarter in length. Furthermore, the scenes of a play cannot jump from one place to another as does a book, and

[1] Published by Houghton Mifflin Company. Used by permission of the author.

364

some scenes which are described cannot be put upon the stage at all if the play is to be done realistically for an audience.

It requires much concentrated thought to choose one dramatic line of action and cut away everything that is not necessary for its development. The children should by all means think this through with the teacher, for it is strongly motivated thinking which is valuable experience in concentration. It would be a great pity for the teacher to do the planning for them, though they need much guidance in the developing of a well-made play. In the case of this book, all incidents except those directly connected with the ginger jar were discarded.

The book, *The Green Ginger Jar*, tells of the kindly, hard-working Chinese Foo Chen, who has a restaurant in Chinatown, and lives in a small house with his wife, his fourteen-year-old son Lu-ping (always called Lu), his twelve-year-old daughter Ai-mei (known as Amy at school), his two small sons Han-lee and Bing, and the old grandmother Lao-po-po, who dominates the family.

The main thread of the story concerns the green ginger jar which came from China years ago with the older members of the family. When Ai-mei, who wants to win the favor of a white girl gives the jar to her, she has no idea that it is her grandmother's most valuable possession. But when she finds that in some strange way it was intended to furnish the means for Lu's education, Ai-mei and Lu begin a feverish search for Joanne, the only name they have for the girl who now has the jar.

A number of exciting events lead the family to hope and then despair in their search: Mrs. Chen actually sees the girl on one occasion; someone inquires about such a jar as their uncle's store; and Ai-mei thinks she has discovered it at the Art Institute. But for a long time nothing comes of their clues, and of course, it is not until the end that Joanne comes to see them and returns it. Along with these lively episodes having to do with the jar are others which, though of real interest, are not necessary to the unravelling of the mystery.

Most interesting of all the characters in the story is Lao-po-po, "The Old One," about whom their family life revolves. She it is who says the final word on every occasion, and it is because of Lao-po-po's refusal to allow her to take on American ways that Ai-mei in a burst of resentment, gives away the ginger jar.

Following are two excerpts from the story and a brief synopsis of the play which the two sixth grades of Willard school[1] developed from the book. Nine scenes would have been too many for one play if several had not been in the nature of interludes played before the curtain while the simple properties on the stage were being changed for the scene to follow.

The following incident is part of the first scene of the play. An accident has occurred near the Chen home, and Lu is outside, binding up the leg of the little dog that was hurt. The girl whose father's car struck the dog comes into the house with the other children to wash her hands. The following scene takes place on her way out.

While the girls were in the kitchen, the sun had moved a little higher. Now a shaft of light came in at the edge of the window shade, crossed the room and illuminated a green jar, standing on a shelf above one of the chests. Joanne noticed it.

"Oh, how beautiful!" she exclaimed, remembering to whisper. (Ai-mei had tiptoed past her grandmother's room.)

"What? *That?*" Ai-mei was amazed.

"It's the loveliest jar I ever saw!" Joanne exclaimed. "That shape! That beautiful tint of green porcelain!"

"That's only an old ginger jar," Ai-mei exclaimed, forgetting in her surprise to keep her voice low. She clapped her hands over her lips—and then felt a hot anger. Always something! A person could not even speak as she pleased.

"A ginger jar? May I see it closely?" Joanne stepped near the chest. "Those lovely sprays of blossoms—are they plum or cherry?"

"Plum," Ai-mei said. "I should know. I dust it every day. My grandmother brought it from China. It's an old thing."

"We saw some porcelains at an exhibit last week—that's how I know about them," Joanne said. "But none was more beautiful than this jar."

Ai-mei hardly heard what she said, being torn with envy and vexation. She, Ai-mei Chen, could never go into a strange house. She couldn't even go to school in peace. She had never been to an exhibit, whatever that was. She was engulfed with self-pity. "My troubles eat into me like a worm," she thought. "I want to be like other people."

Suddenly like the flash of a firecracker, a new idea, a brilliant idea, flared in Ai-mei's mind. Never in her life had she had such

[1] Phyllis Mandler, teacher of dramatics; Gail Beasley and Helen Brink, sixth grade teachers. Evanston, Illinois.

a novel, such a perfect idea! All her own, too. No one suggested it.

In one clever stroke she could please this visiting girl, vex Old Grandmother, and get rid of one of the too-numerous things that must be dusted every day. Moreover, she would be doing what she had always been told was right. (This was the best part of the new idea.) For she had been taught that a polite hostess thinks only of her guest's pleasure and is generous. Indeed, many a time Ai-mei's heart had been heavy because she had had to give away one of her few precious toys merely because a visitor admired it. But *now!* Now she was the one who chose to do the giving.

Ai-mei's face grew radiant. A feeling of power made her strong and sure. She crossed the room and reached above the chest.

"This is really just an old ginger jar," she said casually, remembering to keep her voice quiet for Old Grandmother certainly must not waken now and spoil this. "I am sure you have more beautiful things in your home. But if you will be so good as to accept the old thing, you will give me much pleasure." Old-fashioned phrases such as Uncle Song would use slipped from her tongue as easily as though she spoke them daily.

Joanne stared at her.

"You're giving it to me!" she exclaimed. "Oh, Ai-mei, should you?" She flushed and did not know what to say, in her surprise. "Are you allowed?"

Ai-mei was the poised one now. Joanne's embarrassment was actually a comfort. A Chinese child as young as Bing would know better than to act like that! He would accept a gift graciously and ask no questions.

"This is for you." Ai-mei had the ginger jar down. She put it into Joanne's two hands.

"Isn't it beautiful? Oh, I adore it! Well—if you are sure. I shall love having it."

An automobile honked out in front.

"There's Daddy—tired of waiting for me!" Joanne held the jar tenderly as she turned and hurried from the room. Ai-mei, following her, felt delightfully grown-up and clever.

"I'd be scared to take it if the jar was new, Ai-mei," Joanne said at the steps. "But since you tell me it is an old thing, well, it surely is the perfect color for my room. Thanks, just loads!"

She went down the steps, across the walk, into the waiting car and nodded good-bye. With a rattle of gears the automobile was off—down the block, around the corner. Car, visitor, ginger jar were quickly out of sight.

For a minute Ai-mei's feeling of satisfaction lasted.

"I guess that will surprise the family," she gloated. "I did something smart for once. Got rid of some of the old stuff in that room and had fun doing it."

A cane tapped in the front room. Old Grandmother was awake.

Like a tender blossom blighted by a chill wind, Ai-mei's happiness shriveled and was gone. The chill hit her in the middle. She began to shake.

"What have I done?" she asked herself in a panic. "I don't know whether that jar is valuable or not. I don't really know whose it is. I suppose Old Grandmother's. I don't know Joanne's name nor where she lives. I don't know anything." She clapped her hands over her mouth to hold in a scream of fright. Sickening nausea made her cling to the doorjamb dizzily.

No use now to pretend that the gift was a right and good act. Her own senses gave another answer. But what could she do about it now?

That Saturday is an eventful one from beginning to end. Old Grandmother, having heard unusual sounds, finally gets from Ai-mei the story of the accident and Lu's care of the dog's broken leg, though, of course, no word of the ginger jar!

It pleases her always to hear talk of her favorite grandson, "the smart one," who wants to be a doctor; and today she decides to settle the matter of his education. She sends for Foo Chen and talks with him privately in her room. Then Mrs. Chen, Lu, and Ai-mei, at the supper table, hear him close Old Grandmother's door.

"Hush! Your father comes!" Mrs. Chen cautioned. And the three turned toward the door.

Foo Chen was rubbing his hands together and a smile of satisfaction was on his kindly face.

"All the time we worried and tried to plan," he said to his wife. "And all the time Lao-po-po kept her secret. That one! How fortunate we are to have her!"

The three waited, puzzled. Han-lee ran through to the back steps, hunting the dog, but no one noticed him or spoke.

"I beat my brains. I lie awake nights—me, with my poor wits!" He sat down in the nearest chair. "Make me tea, Ai-mei. I can take my ease for a moment."

Ai-mei warmed a bowl, sprinkled in tea leaves and poured on hot water.

Foo Chen reached for it, chuckling. "For a hundred moons, I ask myself, 'How shall I send my son to high school? To college? How make him a doctor?' And all the while Old Grandmother knows how." He grinned at Lu over the bowl he lifted to his lips.

"*Me!*" Lu exclaimed. "Is the good news about *me?*"

"Who else?" asked Chen, placidly. "Are you not her oldest grandson? Her favorite? Who indeed?"

"But the news, father?" Lu thought he would burst if he must wait longer.

"We make talk about schooling and money," Chen began, "and Old Grandmother says not a word." He grinned, enjoying his mother's strategy. "She waits for a special time. Today she hears about the dog—a mere stray dog——she sends for me and asks, 'Have you made no plans for my grandson's education? He, the smart one? You must educate him to be an *Ih-seng* and send him back to help his people in China.' Doctor, scholar, *Ih-seng* is all the same to her. Then she says, 'Are you so busy making money you cannot think of your son? Or your country?' Old Grandmother is a smart one."

Lu's face had flushed with happiness while his father talked. How wonderful to have the worry about education ended—though just how it would all come about he did not yet see.

Nor did his mother. "How will she do this wonderful kindness to our son?" Mrs. Chen asked while her husband paused for breath. "Where is this magic?—this secret?"

"In our house! In plain sight all the time and we never knew!" Chen leaned back and roared with laughter at their astonishment. "The ginger jar!" he said, his laughter over.

"The ginger jar!" Mrs. Chen exclaimed incredulously.

"The ginger jar! What ginger jar?" Lu asked, groping for understanding. The only ginger jar he recalled was that old thing above the chest in the middle room.

"*The ginger jar!*" Ai-mei whispered in horror, but her voice was so low that no one noticed she had spoken. She put her hand to her throat to stop the choking feeling that threatened to strangle her. But no one noticed that, either.

"Why do you shout at me, 'The ginger jar!' 'The ginger jar!'" Chen demanded angrily. "What ginger jar do we have but that one my mother brought from Canton when she came to America?

Ginger jar, indeed! I shall show you." He turned and stalked into the next room.

### A BRIEF OUTLINE OF THE PLAY PLANNED BY THE CHILDREN

SCENE 1. The kitchen. In the midst of a discussion about the children's education, Old Grandmother, (who comes into the kitchen in place of changing the scene to her room), says that Lu shall be educated for a doctor, but that it is all nonsense for Ai-mei to stay in school. When she leaves there is an outburst from Ai-mei, who resents being brought up as a Chinese girl. Lu goes out to work. Soon the two little boys come running in to tell of a car which has struck a little dog on their corner, and of Lu taking care of it. Ai-mei runs out, and returns with a strange girl who washes her hands, and then, as she leaves, sees the green ginger jar on the shelf. Ai-mei gives it to her, but as soon as she leaves, is overcome by apprehension.

SCENE 2. The kitchen several hours later. It begins with Mrs. Chen and Ai-mei talking of Old Grandmother's mysterious actions in having Ai-mei write a letter for her and then sending for Foo Chen. Lu comes home and they serve his supper. Father enters to tell the family good news about the ginger jar, but they soon discover it is gone (from the shelf in this room). Ai-mei admits giving it away. The father goes back to work, the mother goes to Grandmother, and Lu and Ai-mei try to plan how to recover it.

SCENE 3. In front of the curtain. Ai-mei meets her art teacher and they talk about the art contest for a design for the curtain for the coming school entertainment. The teacher offers to take Ai-mei and several of the other girls to the Art Institute to see a Chinese exhibit which, she thinks, will help them.

SCENE 4. A room in the Art Institute. During the scene there, Ai-mei thinks she has discovered the lost ginger jar, but is assured by the curator that this one has been here for many years. When told the story, she says that doubtless Old Grandmother considered hers so valuable because of the association. It would not be at all likely that a porcelain ginger jar could be worth several thousands of dollars. Ai-mei is downcast as she leaves.

SCENE 5. In front of the curtain. Ai-mei and some friends in Chinese costume are on their way to usher at the school entertainment.

SCENE 6. The school entertainment at which the rhythm band gives a concert. Ai-mei's design has won the prize, and forms the

370

background for the players. Mrs. Chen, who understands little English, thinks she hears talk of their jar, but her sense of propriety is too strong to allow her to turn around and look at the girl who speaks of it.

SCENE 7. Uncle Song's art store near the University of Chicago. Lu makes a trip there to try to find out how he could trace the people in this neighborhood who came to the concert. His uncle laughs at him, but his assistant tells of a lady who came the day before to look for a green ginger jar. Uncle Song promises to watch anyone who so much as whispers "ginger jar!"

SCENE 8. Parade for "Double Ten" day, from back of room. A dragon, music, etc. The Chinese Fourth of July, celebrating the birth of the Chinese Republic.

SCENE 9. Old Grandmother's room. Mother, Lu, and Ai-mei return from the celebration. Grandmother tells them that she has had an American visitor—and that she is coming back. Soon Joanne comes, bringing the jar, saying that she had enjoyed it but felt that she should not keep it. After she goes and the father returns, Grandmother calls for hot water and a hairpin. She opens the bottom of the jar, and discloses a large ruby! It had been sealed into the jar at the family porcelain factory in China by her brother before she left for America. Now it will be sold to pay for Lu's medical education. Thus the story ends.

The play itself was developed over a period of several months, during the two periods a week set aside for dramatics. Because it was a big job to create the play and bring it to production, and because they liked the story very much, the children's interest was sustained throughout. The study of Chinatown and the Chinese was emphasized in the children's social studies, but long before the play, the class had left this subject far behind.

The rhythm band, an important feature of the play, rehearsed during music periods. Properties were designed and made by committees in arts and crafts, though a number of them were made by boys outside of school. For there were many properties: kitchen fixtures, dishes; Chinese hangings, cushions, scrolls, and other oriental objects for Grandmother's room; a dragon backdrop, painted for the concert scene; museum cases (made from the ever-present orange crates!), articles for the Art Institute, and used in different arrangement for Uncle Song's store, and many small articles which were either constructed or brought from home. The Chinese costumes came from the school wardrobe, though most of the costumes were the children's own modern clothes.

The play, which was first presented for the school and then for the parents turned out to be a colorful and dramatic entertainment which gave satisfaction both to children and parents. In no other way, probably, short of actually living among them, could the children have been brought to understand these natives of Chinatown so well, and think of them as people not very different from themselves.

### OTHER PROJECTS

American pioneer life is often used as the subject of integrated or correlated study, and there is much material both for background and for the play. The Laura Ingalls Wilder books, which are favorites with children over a wide age range, are not dramatic enough to furnish good plots for plays, but they make wonderful background material. Johnnie Appleseed stories— and there are a number of good books on this picturesque and lovable figure— will provide play material. So will such a book as *Tree of Freedom*, a chapter of which appears in this book. Pioneers of the Southwest are immortalized in the thrilling *Tree in the Trail*, which sixth or seventh graders can make into a most exciting play. Daniel Boone, Lewis and Clarke, and a host of other pioneers have been so much written about that the teacher's problem is to find the best out of all the books available.

Shelf after shelf of books tell of Abraham Lincoln, some of them old, some by modern authors; and because this great man stands for what we Americans value most in the character of a man, our children should know him as a real person. George Washington, Benjamin Franklin, William Penn, Booker T. Washington, George Washington Carver, and other great leaders need to be real men to our boys and girls.

Though our children always have stories about the American Indian, they seldom know very much about them. It would be a good thing if they were awakened to the injustices which are still being practiced against these people whom we crowded out of their own country. Children love stories of Indians, and they thoroughly enjoy Indian rhythms accompanied by rattles and drums.

Among the fascinating projects are the plays about other countries. A group of children may decide with their teacher that they would like to make a special study of India. After reading and hearing a number of stories set in that country, they might choose

372

the interesting little book, *Bhimsa, the Dancing Bear,* by Christine Weston, because it contains such good material for a play. One group that studied Japan chose to act creatively a play by Eleanor Ellis Perkins called "The Japanese Twins,"[1] which concerned Lucy Fitch Perkins' story of that name except that the twins of the play were older. It tells a dramatic story of the contrast beween the old ideas and the modern in Japan.

"The Nuremberg Stove" is a very fine story for the center of a study on Austria. *Robin Hood* and *The Prince and the Pauper* give opportunity for a study of different periods in English history. *The Boy Knight of Reims* is very rich in possibilities for a French medieval play. *The Singing Tree*[2] is excellent for Hungary. *The Lost Violin*[3] makes a fine play concerning Bohemian immigrants.

Whatever the choice in an integrated project, it is sure to involve a good deal of work. It requires preliminary planning by the teacher before giving the children the choice of several kinds of projects; much extra reading for background material; organization of the group into working units; guidance in the creating of the play; supervision of stage, properties and costumes; and all the arrangements for performances.

But when judged by the interest of the children —usually so much greater than in ordinary school work; the exhilaration which accompanies creative work on the part of both teacher and pupils; and the many kinds of values which result from it, experience in an integrated project with a play as climax at least once a year is worth all it costs and more.

[1] Manuscript from the Association of Junior Leagues, The Waldorf Astoria, New York.
[2] By Kate Seredy. The Viking Press.
[3] By Clara Ingram Judson. Houghton Mifflin Company.

# More Recommended Stories

Many of the following stories are equally as good for dramatization as the stories included in the book. Some of them were not available for reprinting; some were too long; and others, in the editor's judgment, were a little less playable than the stories included. The numbers refer to the Bibliography.

## GROUP I.  CHILDREN OF FIVE, SIX, AND SEVEN YEARS

THE BUTTERBEAN TENT, 3 (b) , 29, 48.

What fun to sit in a butterbean tent and watch the bugs and butterflies go by!  Music adds much to the playing of this poem.

THE CAP THAT MOTHER MADE, 4, 42 (Vol. 2) .

Little Anders will not trade the cap his mother made even for a king's crown.

A FAIRY WENT A-MARKETING, 3 (b) , 7, 31.

Lovely in idea and beautifully expressed.  Each fairy may be different; each stanza may involve a number of other fairy characters.

HAVE YOU WATCHED THE FAIRIES?  57.

Tiny, delicate, imaginative.

THE LARKS IN THE CORNFIELD, 14, 19, 26.

A fable teaching that a thing gets done if one does it himself rather than depending on others.

LITTLE BOY BLUE, 44.

Why is he called Boy Blue?  Does he live in the country?  What does he do when he wakes up?

LITTLE DUCKLING TRIES HIS VOICE, 3 (a) .

After Little Duckling has tried to sound like various other animals, he decides that his own mother sounds best.

THE LITTLE RABBIT THAT WANTED RED WINGS, 4, 5, 42 (Vol. 1).

A discontented little rabbit who found out how to get red wings, and then wished he hadn't!

**Mistress Mary, 44.**

This nonsense rhyme, with its garden of silver bells and cockle shells and pretty maids, is a challenge to the imagination of anyone!

**Mrs. Goose's Rubbers, 46.**

Another story of foolish, lovable Mrs. Goose. This time she loses her rubbers.

**The Pig Brother, 13.**

Cleanliness is its theme—but the story is told with humor, and children like to play it.

**Shhhhh . . . . Bang! 11.**

Everybody whispers in skyscraper town until the little boy comes along and starts some noise.

**The Surprise Party, 46.**

Mrs. Goose decides to have a party and does everything except invite the guests!

**The Weather Factory, 3 (b).**

As soon as summer is gone the little weather folk are all a-flutter with their big job of making frost and snow for winter.


## GROUP II. FOR CHILDREN OF EIGHT AND NINE

**Ameliar Anne And The Green Umbrella, 27.**

Goodies hidden in an umbrella for little brothers and sisters who have colds get Ameliar Anne into trouble at a party. But all ends happily.

**Andy And The Lion, 20.**

Andy reads so many books about lions that he has a fantastic dream in which he is Androcles. Full of humor, and fun for fourth graders to play.

**The Blue Bird For Children, 39.**

Several episodes from this modern fairytale of the two children who seek the blue bird of happiness make excellent material for imaginative children.

**Eeyore's Birthday, 43.**

Eeyore, the pessimistic gray donkey, has a birthday, and Pooh and Piglet bring him rather surprising presents.

**Hansel And Gretel, 17, 26, 29, 42 (Vol. 3).**

Always popular is this tale of the two children who overcame the wicked witch.

THE HILLMAN AND THE HOUSEWIFE, 45.

A scheming housewife finds it of no use to try to deceive one of the Wee Folk.

HOW THE CAMEL GOT HIS HUMP, 34.

Because the camel always replies "humph" when asked to work, he is given a humph—only we call it a hump.

JACK AND THE BEANSTALK, 21.

One of the favorites for dramatization.

THE OLD BOWL, 24.

A story from India which concerns two peddlers, one of whom tries to cheat a poor woman out of a valuable bowl and loses it to an honest peddler who pays what it is worth.

OLD MAN RABBIT'S THANKSGIVING DINNER, 4.

Old Man Rabbit is surprised to find that it is a Thanksgiving dinner he has given to the other animals.

PETER PAN AND WENDY, 6.

The immortal story of the boy who didn't want to grow up offers a number of incidents good to dramatize.

PINOCCHIO, 35.

Any one of many humorous incidents from this book may be used.

THE PLAIN PRINCESS, 41.

After the princess has lived for a time with a poor family, and learned the joy of working and sharing, she is no longer plain.

THE TWELVE DANCING PRINCESSES, 17, 21.

The mystery of the worn-out slippers of the princesses and how it was solved.

TWIG, 32.

A delicate and charming story of the magical happenings in the back yard of a city tenement.

THE WONDERFUL BAKER, 30.

Fat, smiling Poppa, Momma, and the four roly, poly Winklepeck children, sample with glee all the good things Poppa makes for his bake-shop. Finding that they are all getting too fat, Poppa turns to making plain things— and loses his customers. As soon as he begins making rich pies and cakes again, everybody bounces back to happiness!

THE WONDERFUL PEAR TREE, 15.

An old farmer-magician teaches a grasping fruit peddler a lesson in unselfishness.

## GROUP III. FOR CHILDREN OF TEN AND ELEVEN

ADVENTURE IN THE RED LION INN, 22.
The most amusing and exciting episode in *Hans Brinker*.

ALADDIN, 36.
The magic lamp, the genie, and the African magician make this a glamorous and thrilling tale.

ALI BABA AND THE FORTY THIEVES, 36.
Another of the exciting and colorful stories of Scheherazade.

DICK WHITTINGTON, 17, 19, 21, 26, 49.
The story of the boy who went to London to seek his fortune, and found it by selling his cat.

THE DWARF'S GIFTS, 9.
A good version of the story of the making of Thor's hammer.

FRIGGA'S NECKLACE, 52.
Interesting and very usable story in this book of well-told Norse myths.

GABRIEL AND THE HOUR BOOK, 54.
Gabriel is the little color-mixer for a monk who is making an illuminated manuscript. Good material for an integrated project on medieval life.

THE GREAT QUILLOW, 58.
No wonder the giant thought he was losing his wits when no one said anything but "woddly," all the chimneys turned black, and he could see only blue men!

THE HALF-PINT JINNI, 23.
Because he was only a half-pint jinni, he could grant only half of every wish. "But the moral is: half a jinni is better than none!"

HOMER PRICE, 40.
There is both humor and wisdom in the stories about this small-town boy. Children like especially to play the doughnut episode.

HOW ROBIN HOOD BECAME AN OUTLAW, 47.
The beginning of a series of finely told and dramatic stories about the child's own hero. Many others lend themselves to dramatization.

JOSEPH, 25.
The adventurous story of Joseph and his brothers is perhaps the best of all Bible stories for a creative play.

MANY MOONS, 59.
A princess asks for the moon and a jester gets it for her!

**Mary Poppins, 62.**

"Did I understand you to say that I came down from somewhere on the end of a string? Like a monkey or a spinning top? Me?" That was the way Mary Poppins always disclaimed the funny, magical things Jane and Michael were always seeing her do.

**The Miraculous Pitcher, 18, 19, 28.**

Mythological story of Baucis and Philemon who are rewarded for giving the best they have to strangers.

**The Naumburg Children's Festival, 24.**

A story of children who saved their city by going to the general of the enemy troops and asking him to play with them.

**Old Pipes And The Dryad, 19.**

A long but charming story which makes a delightful play.

**Persephone, 18.**

When children are studying Greek myths, they often enjoy making a play from this significant story.

**The Picture On The Kitchen Wall, 24.**

The story behind the picture which many Chinese have on their kitchen wall in memory of Chang Kung who was honored by his Emperor for ruling his family by kindness.

**The Pied Piper Of Hamelin, 12, 13, 26, 29.**

Boys and girls of various ages have enjoyed playing this story of the children who were led away from grasping parents by the piper.

**Princess Nelly And The Seneca Chief, 42 (Vol. 3).**

Charlotte Chorpenning's play "The Indian Captive" (Children's Theatre Press) is based on the same historical facts as is this story.

**Roads, 7, 29.**

It stirs the imagination to plan the places where a road may lead one!

**Stone Soup, 10.**

A good version of the folk tale of "The Old Woman and the Tramp." Three soldiers take the place of the tramp and there are many villagers.

**Why The Chimes Rang, 2.**

How Little Brother's silver piece brings about the miracle of the chimes after a king's crown has failed is a story worth dramatizing.

**Zacchaeus, 37.**

An interesting telling of the story of the little tax collector who climbed into a tree to see Jesus, and whose whole life was changed thereby.

## GROUP IV. FOR YOUNG PEOPLE OF
## TWELVE, THIRTEEN, AND FOURTEEN

ALI COGIA, 36.

Through the sagacity of children, the Caliph finds the thief who stole the gold from the olive jar.

THE BOY WHO FOUND THE KING, 2.

A boy searches for and finds a king who has left his kingdom to live in disguise among his people until he is worthy to be their ruler. A dramatic and interesting story to play.

COUNT HUGO'S SWORD, 54.

An exciting, though rather difficult story about a French boy who, in medieval times, keeps his benefactor from fighting a duel by hiding the sword of his opponent.

IN CLEAN HAY, 33.

A beautiful Christmas story. Some Polish children present a marionette Nativity play, and then give the money to a poor family whose baby has just been born in a stable.

THE INDIANS AND THE QUAKER FAMILY, 28.

A story which tells why the Quakers did not have to fear attacks from the Indians.

KING HENRY AND THE MILLER OF MANSFIELD, 45, 56.

The miller treats the king with so much condescension that when he finds out it is the king, he expects to lose his head. Instead, he is knighted. A humorous ballad.

THE KNIGHTS OF THE SILVER SHIELD, 2, 19, 42.

A fine story which glorifies moral courage above physical bravery.

LITTLE WOMEN, 1.

Christmas at the March's, with the rehearsal and performance of Jo's play, is always popular with the older girls.

MASTER SKYLARK, 8.

A fascinating story of Shakespeare's time, with a basis of fact. Difficult but thoroughly worth doing.

THE PEDDLER OF BALLAGHADEREEN, 49.

A beautiful story of a peddler who had an extraordinary dream— and of a landlord who helped make the dream come true.

THE PRINCESS AND THE VAGABOND, 49.

A most delightful Irish version of *The Taming of the Shrew*.

THE RABBI AND THE DIADEM, 19.

A rabbi, finding a diadem, risks his life by waiting to return it

379

to the Empress until the appointed day is past to show that he does not wish a reward and is not afraid of punishment. He returns it simply because it is right to do so.

THE SINGING TREE, 53.

A very fine story of Hungary during the first World War. It could well be used as the center of an integrated study on Hungary.

SHAKESPEARE'S PLAYS, 38.

Told as stories, episodes from the following plays can be used with great success by eighth grade students with experience: *The Comedy of Errors, Julius Caesar,* the dower scene from *King Lear,* and *Twelfth Night,* in addition to the three most popular stories, included in this book.

TREASURE ISLAND, 55.

This novel is full of dramatic incidents suitable for both informal and formal plays.

WHAT MEN LIVE BY, 61.

The story of the angel who comes to the home of the shoemaker and learns of the three things by which men live.

WHERE LOVE IS, THERE GOD IS ALSO, 60.

The story of Martin, the cobbler, who dreams that the Lord is coming to him on the morrow. The next day he helps three groups of people in need, and at night a vision of each group comes to him saying, "Lo, it is I."

WICKED JOHN AND THE DEVIL, 16.

A folktale of the Southern mountains telling about "the most ornery blacksmith in history and his outwitting of the devil."

# Bibliography

1. Alcott, Louisa M., *Little Women*. Little, Brown, & Company. (Also other publishers.)

2. Alden, Raymond MacDonald, *The Boy Who Found the King, The Knights of the Silver Shield, Why the Chimes Rang*. The Bobbs-Merrill Company.

3. Association for Childhood Education, (a) *Told Under the Magic Umbrella*, (b) *Sung Under the Silver Umbrella*. The Macmillan Company.

4. Bailey, Carolyn S., *For the Story Teller*. Milton Bradley Company.

5. Bailey, Carolyn S., *The Little Rabbit That Wanted Red Wings*. Platt & Munk.

6. Barrie, James M., *Peter Pan and Wendy*. Charles Scribner's Sons.

7. Barrows, Marjorie (ed.), *One Hundred Best Poems for Boys and Girls*. Whitman Publishing Company.

8. Bennett, John, *Master Skylark*. Appleton-Century-Crofts.

9. Brown, Abbie, Farwell, *In the Days of Giants*. Houghton Mifflin Company.

10. Brown, Marcia, *Stone Soup*. Charles Scribner's Sons.

11. Brown, Margaret Wise Brown, *Shhhhh . . . Bang!* Harper & Brothers.

12. Browning, Robert, *Poems*. Frederick Warne & Company.

13. Bryant, Sara Cone, *How to Tell Stories to·Children*. Houghton Mifflin Company.

14. Bryant, Sara Cone, *Stories to Tell to Children*. Houghton Mifflin Company.

15. Carpenter, Frances (ed.), *Tales of a Chinese Grandmother*. Doubleday & Company.

16. Chase, Richard, *Grandfather Tales*. Houghton Mifflin Company.

17. Clark, Barrett H. and Jagendorf, M. (eds.), *A World of Stories for Children*. The Bobbs-Merrill Company.

18. Cooke, Flora J., *Nature Myths and Stories*. A Flanagan Company.
19. Curry, C. M.–Clippinger, E. E., *Children's Literature*. Rand McNally Company.
20. Daugherty, James, *Andy and the Lion*. The Viking Press.
21. De la Mare, Walter, *Told Again*. Alfred A. Knopf.
22. Dodge, Mary Mapes, *Hans Brinker*. Harper & Brothers.
23. Dolbier, Maurice, *The Half-Pint Jinni*. Random House.
24. Fahs, Sophia, *From Long Ago and Many Lands*. The Beacon Press.
25. Genesis, 37-50.
26. Hallowell, Lillian, *A Book of Children's Literature*. Farrar & Rinehart, Inc.
27. Heward, Constance, and Pearse, Susan P., *Ameliar Anne and the Green Umbrella*. Macrae- Smith Company.
28. Hodgkins, Mary D. H. (ed.), *Atlantic Treasury of Childhood Stories*. Atlantic Monthly Press.
29. Huber, Miriam B., *Story and Verse for Children*. The Macmillan Company.
30. Hunt, Mabel Leigh, *The Wonderful Baker*. J. B. Lippincott Company.
31. Johnson, Edna, and Scott, Carrie, *Anthology of Children's Literature*. Houghton Mifflin Company.
32. Jones, Elizabeth Orton, *Twig*. The Macmillan Company.
33. Kelley, Eric, *The Christmas Nightingale*. The Macmillan Company.
34. Kipling, Rudyard, *Just So Stories*, Doubleday & Company.
35. Lorenzini, Carlo, *Pinocchio*. Thomas Nelson & Sons.
36. Lang, Andrew (ed.), *Arabian Nights*. Longmans, Green & Company. (Also other publishers.)
37. Langford, Norman F., *The King Nobody Wanted*. Westminster Press.
38. MacLeod, Mary, *The Shakespeare Story Book*. Wells Gardner, Darton & Company, Ltd.
39. Maeterlinck, Madame Maurice, *The Blue Bird for Children*. Silver Burdett Company.
40. McCloskey, Robert, *Homer Price*. The Viking Press, Inc.
41. McGinley, Phyllis, *The Plain Princess*. J. B. Lippincott Company.
42. Miller, Olive Beaupré, *The Book House*. The Book House for Children.

43. Milne, A. A., *Winnie the Pooh.* E. P. Dutton & Company, Inc.

44. *Mother Goose.* Many publishers.

45. Olcott, Frances J., *Good Stories for Great Holidays. Story Telling Poems.* Houghton Mifflin Company.

46. Potter, Miriam C., *Mrs. Goose and Three Ducks.* J. B. Lippincott Company.

47. Pyle, Howard, *The Merry Adventures of Robin Hood. The Story of King Arthur.* Charles Scribner's Sons.

48. Roberts, Elizabeth Madox, *Under the Tree.* The Viking Press.

49. Sawyer, Ruth, *The Way of the Story Teller.* The Viking Press.

50. Sawyer, Ruth, *This Way to Christmas.* Harper & Brothers.

51. Scudder, Horace E., *The Children's Book.* The Macmillan Company.

52. Sellew, Catherine F., *Adventures With the Giants.* Little, Brown & Company.

53. Seredy, Kate, *The Singing Tree.* The Viking Press.

54. Stein, Evaleen, *Troubadour Tales; Gabriel and the Hour Book.* L. C. Page Company.

55. Stevenson, Robert Louis, *Treasure Island.* Charles Scribner's Sons.

56. Tappan, Eva March, *Old Ballads in Prose.* Houghton Mifflin Company.

57. Thompson, Blanche Jennings, *Silver Pennies.* The Macmillan Company.

58. Thurber, James, *The Great Quillow.* Harcourt, Brace & Company.

59. Thurber, James, *Many Moons.* The Viking Press.

60. Tolstoy, Leo, *Twenty-three Tales.* Oxford University Press.

61. Tolstoy, Leo, *What Men Live By.* Thomas Y. Crowell Company.

62. Travers, Pamela, *Mary Poppins.* Harcourt, Brace & Company.

# *Some Good Books For Integrated Projects*

CHOSEN FOR BACKGROUND, ILLUSTRATIONS, OR STORY

PIONEER DAYS IN THE UNITED STATES

Laura Ingalls Wilder

Who has interpreted the American pioneer home to children "through books they love and reread from the first volume to the last."

*The Little House in the Big Woods* (Wisconsin), *The Little House on the Prairie* (Kansas), *On the Banks of Plum Creek* (Minnesota), *By the Shores of Silver Lake* (Dakota), *Farmer Boy* (New York), *The Long Winter, Little Town on the Prairie* (Dakota), *Those Happy Golden Years.*

Esther Forbes, *Johnny Tremain.* Boston of 1774. Houghton Mifflin Company.

Rebecca Caudill, *Tree of Freedom.* (Kentucky pioneers.) The Viking Press.

Carol Ryrie Brink, *Caddie Woodlawn.* (Wisconsin pioneers.) The Macmillan Company.

Holling C. Holling, *The Tree in the Trail.* (The Santa Fe Trail) Houghton Mifflin Company.

Emily Taft Douglas, *Appleseed Farm.* (Indiana pioneers) Abingdon-Cokesbury Press.

AMERICAN LEADERS

Genevieve Foster, *George Washington's World.* Charles Scribner's Sons.

Clara Ingram Judson, *George Washington, Leader of the People.* Wilcox & Follett.

Augusta Stevenson, *Ben Franklin: Printer's Boy.* The Bobbs-Merrill Company.

Genevieve Foster, *Abraham Lincoln's World.* Charles Scribner's Sons.

384

Augusta Stevenson, *Abe Lincoln: Frontier Boy*. The Bobbs-Merrill Company.

Clara Ingram Judson, *Abraham Lincoln: Friend of the People*. Wilcox & Follett.

Bernadine Bailey, *Abe Lincoln's Other Mother*. Julian Messner.

Carl Sandburg, *Abraham Lincoln: the Prairie Years*. Harcourt, Brace & Company.

Sonia Daugherty, *Ten Brave Men*. (Makers of the American Way.) J. B. Lippincott Company.

Stanley F Horn, *The Boy's Life of Robert E. Lee*. Harper & Brothers.

Helen A. Monsell, *A Boy of Old Virginia: Robert E. Lee*. The Bobbs-Merrill Company.

## THE AMERICAN INDIAN

Lois Lenski, *Indian Captive; the Story of Mary Jemison*. (Senecas) Stokes.

Schultz, James W., *Sinopah, the Indiana Boy*. (Blackfoot Indian) Houghton Mifflin Company.

Grace and Carl Moon, *Chi-Wee*, also *Chi-Wee and Loki*. (Pueblo Indians) Doubleday & Company.

Lyla Hoffine, *Wi Sapa*. (A Sioux Indian Boy) American Book Company.

## THE NEGRO

A. Bontemps, *George Washington Carver*. Row, Peterson and Company.

Joel Chandler Harris, *Uncle Remus*. (Folk tales) Appleton-Century-Crofts.

Elizabeth Yates, *Amos Fortune, Free man*. Aladdin Books.

## MEXICO

Frances Eliot, *Pablo's Pipes*. E. P. Dutton & Company.

Elizabeth K. Tarshis, *The Village That Learned to Read*. Houghton Mifflin Company.

Ann Weil, *The Silver Fawn*. The Bobbs-Merrill Company.

Pachita Crespi, *Gift of the Earth*. Charles Scribner's Sons.

Ruth Sawyer, *The Least One*. The Viking Press.

Thirteenth-century England. Elizabeth Janet Gray, *Adam of the Road*. The Viking Press.

India. Christine Weston, *Bhimsa, the Dancing Bear*. Charles Scribner's Sons.

China. Eleanor F. Lattimore, *Little Pear*. Harcourt, Brace & Company.

China. Elizabeth Lewis, *Young Fu of the Upper Yangtze*. The Winston Company.

Poland. Eric Kelly, *The Trumpeter of Krakow*. The Macmillan Company.

France. Eloise Lownsbery, *The Boy Knight of Reims*. Houghton Mifflin Company.

Denmark. Nora Burglon, *Sticks Across the Chimnay*. Holiday House.

Bohemian Immigrants. Clara Ingram Judson, *The Lost Violin*. Houghton Mifflin Company.

Chicago's Chinatown. Clara Ingram Judson, *The Green Ginger Jar*. Houghton Mifflin Company.

Hungary. Kate Seredy, *The Good Master*. *The Singing Tree*. The Viking Press.

## THE BIBLE

Albert E. Bailey, *Daily Life in Bible Times*. Charles Scribner's Sons.

Ethel L. Smither, *A Picture Book of Palestine*. Abingdon-Cokesbury Press.

Walter de la Mare, *Stories from the Bible*. Cosmopolitan.

Edgar Goodspeed, *The Junior Bible*. The Macmillan Company.

Maud and Miska Petersham, *The Christ Child*. Doubleday. *Stories from the Old Testament*. Winston. *The Story of Jesus*. Macmillan.

Helen Sewell, *A First Bible*. Oxford University Press.

# INDEX